# KENT'S COMMENTARY

ON

# INTERNATIONAL LAW.

Cambridge:
PRINTED BY C. J. CLAY, M.A.
AT THE UNIVERSITY PRESS.

# KENT'S COMMENTARY

ON

# INTERNATIONAL LAW,

*REVISED WITH NOTES AND CASES*

*BROUGHT DOWN TO THE PRESENT TIME.*

EDITED BY

J. T. ABDY, LL.D.,

BARRISTER AT LAW,

REGIUS PROFESSOR OF LAWS IN THE UNIVERSITY OF CAMBRIDGE,

AND LAW LECTURER AT GRESHAM COLLEGE.

CAMBRIDGE:

DEIGHTON, BELL, AND CO.

LONDON: STEVENS AND SONS, BELL YARD.

1866.

# PREFACE.

---

The science of International Law has never lacked able and eloquent exponents from the times of Ayala and Alberic Gentili down to our own. But it must be acknowledged that, among modern authors at all events, there are three whose learning and labour, as judges and writers, have shed glory over the legal literature of the United States, and have earned the singular distinction of being recognized as authorities on International Law throughout Europe. I need scarcely say that I speak of the honoured names of Story, Wheaton, and Kent.

Of these three the expressed views and opinions of the first on public International Law have not been put forth in any regular connected shape, but are to be found in short essays, and in those admirable judgements which have made his name a household word among English lawyers. The second has indeed published an able, a learned, and an impartial treatise, but the notes that now accompany the author's text, laborious and exhaustive as they are, render the work too large and unwieldy for the student, and too discursive and fatiguing to the general reader; in addition to which they are open to the charge of strong prejudice and partial judgement. The third, Mr Chancellor Kent, has given us the result of years of professional labour, and a life spent in study, in a work which, if small so far as International Law is concerned, contains within its pages wisdom, critical skill, and judicial acumen of the highest kind. For my part, I have so often derived pleasure as well as gain from Kent's Commentaries on Law, in every part of that treatise, that I feel a kind of veneration for his name; and I do most cordially assent to the language of praise in which a modern writer speaks of him, "as the greatest jurist whom this age has produced, whose writings may safely be said to be never wrong."

I have therefore selected that portion of his Commentaries which relates to public International Law, and have edited it as a separate volume for two reasons, one because no other writer on International Law is so safe, so impartial, and so recognized a guide and authority, whether in this country, or on the continent of Europe, or across the Atlantic. The other because, in the course of my duties as a teacher of Law, International Law

[1] *Letter on Neutral Trade in Contraband of War*, by Historicus.

having formed a considerable portion of them, I have found the want of a book that shall not be too large, or diffuse, or expensive. I venture to hope I have succeeded in one thing, at all events, that of keeping my subject down to comparatively moderate proportions; and I venture also to hope that I have noticed the principal topics of public International Law. In order to keep within that range, I have adhered, as closely as I could, to the order and arrangement of the work I have edited, adding only one new chapter, that on Foreign Enlistment Acts, which recent events have invested with peculiar importance, and throwing all fresh matter, not into notes, which are often passed over unread, and if read interrupt the thread of the narrative, but into the text itself. I have also aimed at one thing above all, that of not merely preserving the sentiments and opinions of the learned author, but his very language, changing only the style of the original work from the familiar one of lectures, in which the present tense is used, and in which American readers are specially addressed, to a more general and formal one.

All fresh matter coming from my own pen is contained in brackets [ ].

I venture further to hope that the work now given to the public will be useful to the practitioner, as well as to the student. With this view I have added the most recent documents, decisions, and cases on the different topics comprised in it. Let me also add, what perhaps may seem superfluous, that should the book be successful, the praise belongs to him whose treatise I am now presenting to an English public in an English shape; its faults must be mine, its merits his.

One word more, by way of preface, and then I have done. It would be unbecoming in me not to offer my thanks to those from whose kindness I have received assistance in the course of my labours. I therefore now tender my thanks, first and foremost, to Mr Hertslet, the able, the skilful, and the learned Librarian of the Foreign Office. From him I have received valuable suggestions, on his time I have trespassed, and to his kindness I am indebted for documents supplied to me in the course of my work. I therefore seize this opportunity to express my gratitude and my sense of his invaluable kindness towards me, and to say that I am sure that such kindness has been shewn, not to me on personal grounds merely, but as a writer on a subject which he loves, and is thoroughly versed in, public International Law. I have also to thank the learned author of "Letters of Historicus," Mr Vernon Harcourt, Q.C., for valuable suggestions, and for friendly advice; and I also thank most cordially and gratefully the Librarian of the Inner Temple, Mr Martin, for many a kind act in the way of help, and for assistance of the most useful kind in the course of my researches in the Library of the Inner Temple. I have no doubt that Mr Martin's praise will be echoed by many other readers at that comfortable and excellent Library.

It will be seen that a portion of this work was in print during the progress, and before the termination of the late contest in the United States. My only apology for the length of time with which I have been engaged upon it is the interruptions I have received from the various duties I have to discharge.

LAMB BUILDINGS, TEMPLE,
*February*, 1866.

# CONTENTS.

## CHAPTER IV.



## CHAPTER V.



## CHAPTER VI.



## CHAPTER VII.



## CHAPTER VIII.



## CHAPTER IX.

## CHAPTER X.



## CHAPTER XI.

# INDEX OF CASES.

D.



E.



F.



G.

## M.



## N.



## O.



## P.



## R.

W.



Y.

# ERRATA.

Page 8, line 9:

*For* Sir William Stowell *read* Sir William Scott

Page 86, line 28:

*For* 1854 *read* 1858

Page 126, line 18:

*For* our laws *read* the laws of the United States

Page 227:

Add to note (1):—27 and 28 Vict. c. 25, § 45. (See the whole statute in the Appendix.)

Add to note (3), page 276, and to page 289, line 21:—27 and 28 Vict. c. 25.

Page 311, line 24:

*Instead of* "the right possessed by every government of breaking its neutrality" *read* "the right possessed by every government of preventing its subjects from breaking"

# INTERNATIONAL LAW.

---

## CHAPTER I.

### OF THE FOUNDATION AND HISTORY OF THE LAW OF NATIONS.

Introduction.

["THERE can be few nobler objects of contemplation and study," says a modern writer of eminence[1], "than to trace the gradual progress of International Jurisprudence;" and such has been the inspiring influence of this science, that for upwards of three hundred years from the time of Suarez to our own days it has claimed the exclusive attention of a host of writers, with more or less advantage to the progress of that science, and with more or less reputation to themselves. In so large a crowd of authors of different countries, impressed with different feelings, it is not surprising to find some difference of opinion upon the positions of the subject in the body of general Jurisprudence, upon the method of arrangement, and the proper classifications of its parts; but various as are their opinions, and widely as they differ in detail, they are unanimous in the testimony they bear to the influence of International Law upon the well-being and happiness of nations, and in the energy and devotion they shew in stating the principles and explaining the foundation of what some of them, with more zeal than precision, have called the Law

[1] Professor Katchanowsky.

of Nations. For three hundred years and upwards then the study of International Law has been pursued in the great countries of Europe, with such an amount of learning and research, and its doctrines explained with so much vigour and eloquence, "as to raise it from a few simple rules of natural law to the goodly and elaborate fabric it has now become." From the fall of the Roman empire to the Reformation International Law was not directly pursued and illustrated as a separate system of law, but a stimulus of no small nature was given to the study of subjects much akin to it in the publication of those maritime codes, which so remarkably distinguish a period of time when intellectual darkness hung over Europe, and when the science of law lacked that development it had previously received from the genius of Rome. From the era of the Reformation to the peace of Westphalia the stimulus thus given to mercantile law, joined to an increasing fondness for Roman law, was felt in another direction; and the patience of Suarez, the legal acumen of Alberic Gentili, and the vast erudition, the eloquence and the earnest devotion of Grotius, at once drew the attention of the world to the subjects they illustrate so ably. But it is from the peace of Westphalia that International Law, properly so called, dates, that important period in the history of its rise and progress, from which it has grown with the growth and developed with the development of the political system of Europe, has undergone changes that have given it a new character, and by the skill of diplomatists, the discrimination and learning of judges, and the research and eloquence of jurists, has been established among the civilized nations of Europe as their public law. Nor is it in Europe alone that it occupies this prominent position; in the United States[1] it is equally recognised as a part of their public law—recognised and sanctioned from the period when they ceased to be a part of the British empire and assumed the character of an independent nation;] and if during the war

[1] Thirty hogsheads of sugar *v.* Bayle, 9 Cranch, 198.

of the American revolution, Congress, claiming cognizance of all matters arising upon the law of nations, professed obedience to that law[1] "according to the general usages of Europe;" not less does it still profess to acknowledge its influence and be guided by its precepts. [Nor can we wonder at the anxiety displayed on both sides of the Atlantic to preserve the integrity, to uphold the dignity, and to vindicate the majesty of International Law. For when we remember what have ever been professed to be its primary objects, viz. the independence of nations, the inviolability of their several territories, and the maintenance of their honour, it stands to reason that the happiness of states is bound up with the fate and fortunes of this law: "A law whose existence and application," says Daniel Webster, "is as advantageous to states as the existence of private law to the citizens of a country." The faithful observance of this law then is essential to national character and to the happiness of mankind: a necessity not the less urgent, if what Montesquieu says of it be true, "that it is based upon the principle that different nations ought to do each other as much good in peace and as little harm in war as possible, without injury to their true interests[2]." And yet in spite of the advantages which the civilized world has reaped from the cultivation of International Law as a science, it cannot be denied that there are objections of no slight character to it as a system, and no slight difficulties in the way of its study. For whilst on the one hand, the absence of a general tribunal, common judges, and all the means to enforce obedience to its dictates which municipal law commands, lays it too much at the mercy of powerful nations, whose passions often interrupt the peaceful progress of this code, on the other, the want of a clear and precise definition of its precepts, and a recognised authoritative classification of its various parts, are serious lets and hindrances to a proper appreciation of it as a science. The best way to reply to those

[1] Ordinance of the 4th Dec. 1781. *Journals of Congress*, VII. 185.

[2] *Esprit des lois*, Liv. I. ch. 3.

objections, and endeavour to remove these difficulties, is to shew that the legal principles by which nations ought to be bound in their external and international communications are capable of being explained in an orderly and methodical sequence. But some of the difficulties environing the study of International Law meet the student at the very outset of his work; for, if in the progress of his labours he necessarily finds oft-disputed and still unsettled points arising out of the conflict between belligerent and neutral claims, if even in times of peace, he finds nice questions of International Law to which known doctrines do not apply; he finds also to his surprise, that the very sphere and scope, the foundation, the elements, and the evidence of the science are disputed points, and that in these preliminaries the highest authorities differ.

Indeed, these disputes have commenced at the very threshold of the subject[1], and much has been written to establish with accuracy its true title—much that need not here be repeated; for if it be an established fact that the subjects of the law we are now discussing, those who are influenced by and act upon its rules, are sovereign and independent, acknowledging no one superior authority by whom commands can be enforced; if, on the other hand, laws are rules set by a determinate rational being, or a determinate body of rational beings to determinate rational beings owing obedience,—there can be no such thing as a uniform body of rules to govern them, or one that shall come within the term Law of Nations, any more than there can be a uniform body of such law.

Rejecting then the title Law of Nations, and adhering to that of International Law, "as a definite and expressive term," which though not altogether accurate, is convenient and now in common currency, the next step is to note what it means, to describe what International Law is, so as to avoid blending and confounding International Law

[1] See for the whole discussion and the authorities, Wheaton, *Elements*, ed. 1863, Vol. I. pp. 18—20.

as it is with International Law as it ought to be[1]. And here again we find no little variety and no small variation in the definitions given by different writers—a variety that in some cases exhibits vagueness of expression, in others mistaken views as to the proper scope and sphere of International Law.

Various definitions of the term International Law.

To the former class may be relegated Mr Wheaton, who in his valuable and, in its later annotated shape, exhaustive treatise on the elements of International Law, defines it as a collection of rules, deduced by reason as consonant with justice, from the nature of the society existing among independent nations, together with such definitions and modifications as are established by general consent. Thus Klüber[2] calls it "the collection of the reciprocal and perfect rights of nations, and of the law of states in their communications with each other." Gerard de Rayneval[3], calling it "Law of Nations—Code of Nations," defines it as that common rule which natural reason prescribes to nations for their reciprocal preservation. Ortolan[4] describes it as the collection of the rights of nations among themselves, or of the moral necessities of international conduct; while Hautefeuille[5] calls it the reunion of those *rules* which regulate the relations of nations among themselves, and assure the complete exercise of the right, and the complete accomplishment of the duties of each of them. It would be impossible and not very profitable to record them all, "tot homines quot definitiones;" each writer has aimed at describing the science acccording to the peculiarity of his style or the bent of his mind, and the results of such effort, if they produce nothing else, may serve as an illustration of the difficulty as well as the danger attendant upon definitions. To the same class also must be referred Sir R. Phillimore, who in spite of profound learning and abundant diligence has allowed this part

1 Austin, p. 285, (Note), 2nd ed.

2 Tome I. § 1.

3 Tome I. ch. I. §§ 9, 10.

4 *Règles-Inter.* Liv. I. c. 4.

5 *Droit Maritime Intern. Introd.* III.

of his valuable work to be disfigured by vague generalities and unmeaning commonplaces, and who describes International Law as the body of laws which define and govern *certain* rights and obligations necessarily springing from the nature of States; whilst to the second class belongs Mr Manning's definition[1], who, prefixing the term Law of Nations as better known and more completely domesticated in our language, limits it to the rules *controlling* the conduct of independent states in their relations with each other, forgetting that he is about to discuss under this very term rules by which some nations have refused to be controlled, and others which are not of universal application. Nor are the definitions of all, or nearly all, the leading foreign writers on the so-called Law of Nations free from one or other of these faults—their constant straining after generalization leading them into one, their prejudices into the other.

Yet at the risk of incurring that danger we venture to assign a meaning to the term (International Law) viz., that collection of rules, customary, conventional and judicial, which independent states appeal to for the purpose of determining their rights, prescribing their duties and regulating their intercourse, in peace and war, imposed by opinion and based upon the consent of nations.

The definition.

Sources of International Law.

Hence it follows, first, that the sole source of this law, the fountain from which it flows, whether in its customary, conventional, or judicial-customary shape, is the consent of nations. Secondly, this body of rules is utterly deficient in one important element of law proper, namely, a sanction. However sound, however useful, however long established, any or all of these rules may be, for their infraction there is but one real remedy, the sword; for although public opinion may be and often is appealed to with considerable force, in cases of violation of international morality, yet such appeal is not always attended with success, and at best it affords but a precarious defence against the acts of

It has no sanction.

[1] *Law of Nations*, p. 2.

powerful wrong-doers. Therefore, thirdly, of the body of International Law we never can predicate that its rules are commands; we cannot assert that they shall be obeyed, because they have through long observance grown into a sort of law; we can only say they ought to be obeyed because of their long observance and of their consequent utility. Hence, fourthly, neither the law of God, nor positive rules of morality, nor the law of nature (whatever that may be) can be considered as the source or foundation of International Law, or as exercising any absolute necessary influence upon international relations. We say an absolute necessary influence for the existence of certain moral rules, which nations ought to observe, cannot be denied.

Its rules not commands.

Law of nature not its source.

Meanwhile it remains to add a few words upon the Sphere of International Law, and upon what some writers call its Sources, others its Foundation, but what, to speak correctly, is its Evidence; that is, the places where the acts of nations which recognise and give rise to reciprocal rights exist.

Its sphere.

Between International Law and Public (or Municipal) Law there is this strong line of demarcation[1]—that whereas in the latter the social body is separated into two distinct legal or moral personages (the Sovereign and the People), and their mutual relationship is an object of interest to that law; in the former the whole social body is united into one sovereign independent state, and only its relations with other such bodies are the subject of its investigations[2]. Now in those relations the acts of which such bodies are capable can be arranged in three divisions. In the first class are comprised actions which, though morally right and praiseworthy, cannot be enforced; in the second, actions which are morally right and whose performance can be compelled by coercion; in the third class are found actions which are morally wrong and which may be prohibited and prevented by resistance, or any forcible means. The actions comprised in these two last divisions

[1] Schmalz, Liv. I. ch. I. p. 6. French edit. 1823.

[2] Reddie's *Enquiries into International Law*, p. 140.

form the sphere and the rules on which the settlement of difficulties connected with them depends, are the component parts of International Law as distinct from International Morality.

Its evidence. An important question therefore arises, viz. How are we to ascertain these rules? Are there places where such information exists as may throw light upon them? In other words, where are we to look for the evidence of these rules? "The Law of Nations," says Sir William Stowell, "is fixed and evidenced by general, ancient, and admitted practice, by treaties and by the general tenor of the laws, ordinances and formal transactions of civilized states[1]." According to this great authority therefore the evidence of International Law is to be found in the history, the practice, and the contracts of nations. His opinion however, in addition to the defect of want of precision, is open to another objection—that of want of completeness. Accordingly, Mr Wheaton extends the list and enumerates the following, as composing the evidence of the Law we are engaged upon.

First. Text writers of authority whom he calls, with some exaggeration, the witnesses of the sentiment and usages of civilized nations.

Secondly. Treaties of peace, alliance, and commerce.

Thirdly. Marine ordinances of particular states[2].

Fourthly. The adjudications of international tribunals.

Fifthly. The written opinions of official jurists given confidentially to their own governments.

Sixthly. The history of wars, negociations, treaties of peace, and other transactions relating to the public intercourse of nations.

To this enumeration by Mr Wheaton of the sources from which information in disputed questions of international transactions can be drawn, a few words of explanation may be added. And, in the first place, it is clear that the sub-

[1] Le Louis, 2 Dodson, 249.

[2] Marshall, *On Insurance*, 4th edit. p. 324.

ject-matter of International Law may, with great convenience, be arranged into two classes: that of the customary and that of the conventional rules of which it is composed. For whilst, to use Lord Stowell's words, "a great part of the Law of Nations stands on no other foundation than that of usage and practice[1]," another and not unimportant part consists of the express contracts of nations with each other.

Its twofold division.

For the customary branch then of the law we are now examining we must seek for evidence in the decisions of judges, in the confidential opinions of jurists given to their governments, and in the marine ordinances of particular states. Whilst the evidence of the conventional branch is confined to treaties, whether of peace, alliance or commerce. And, secondly, with respect to the other evidence spoken of by Mr Wheaton, viz. the opinions of text writers, and the history of wars, negotiations, treaties of peace and other public transactions, it is clear that whilst the former are matter of opinion only, mere statements of private views, and therefore, except as speculative views, deprived of authority, though as speculation often very valuable; the latter are extremely useful as shewing the state of parties, the current of public opinion, and the mode of discussing and settling grave and perplexing questions at the particular times recorded.

Customary rules.

Conventional rules.

Text writers, &c.

We have alluded to the different views of writers on various points of International Law. In no part is that difference more striking, or their views more confusing, than in discussions about the elements of this law, and in the relation of what is called Natural to International Law.

Its elements.

Now what are the elements of which this law is composed?

First[2], those rules of international conduct which are framed in accordance with the Divine or Natural Law and which are often known as international morality; and

International morality.

[1] *The Flad Oyen*, Robinson, 140.

[2] *Ed. Rev.* Vol. LXXVII.

International Law.

secondly, those rules that are dictated by public opinion and established by consent and usage, forming the positive law of nations and known as International Law proper.

Their relative value.

That the latter set of rules is the most useful and practical part of the law we are enquiring into there can be no doubt; yet it would be improper to separate from it its moral branch and not to uphold its importance, and to remember that the happiness of mankind demands the recognition of national quite as much as it does of individual morality. At the same time, to assert that this law as a system is identical with the law of nature, or that it is founded upon a primary divine law, is as absurd as to hold with Hobbes[1] that organized nations assume the personal characters of individuals, and that the moral rules by which both ought to be governed are the same. These two branches then form together a system rendered perfect by the application of one to the other,] and therefore to separate national morality from International Law proper would be as productive of harm as to encourage the suggestion that governments are not as strictly bound by the obligations of truth, justice, and humanity in relation to other powers, as they are in the management of their own local concerns.

Difference between States and Individuals.

[It has been asserted by other writers than Hobbes, that states or bodies politic are in so many respects like individuals that the same standard of right and the same index to their duties will do for both[2]. Yet a little reflection shews the weakness of this analogy, for the negative precepts of international morality, the absence of any common protective law, the binding nature of all their engagements, and the powerlessness of moral sanctions, shew how incomplete is the resemblance that nations bear to individuals.

Utility, its value.

Whatever doubt therefore there may be as to the value of Utility as the true index to the duties of individual men, there can be none as to its value in that respect for nations, and to ascertain the principles and details of international morality we

[1] *De Cive, Imperium*, c. XIV. § 4.

[2] *Edinburgh Review*, Vol. LXXVII.

must apply not the rules which ought to govern the conduct of individuals, but those rules, if we can find them, which on the whole best promote the happiness of mankind.]

International Law, so far as it is in accordance with principles of justice, truth, and humanity, is equally binding in every age, and upon all mankind. But the Christian nations of Europe, and their descendants across the Atlantic, by the vast superiority of their attainments in arts, and science, and commerce, as well as in policy and government; and, above all, by the brighter light, the more certain truths, and the more definite sanction, which Christianity has communicated to the ethical jurisprudence of the ancients, have established a system of law peculiar to themselves. They form together a community of nations, united by religion, manners, morals, humanity, and science, and united also by the mutual advantages of commercial intercourse, by the habit of forming alliances and treaties with each other, of interchanging ambassadors, and of studying and recognising the same writers and systems of public law.

After devoting the present chapter to a cursory view of the history of International Law, we shall enter upon the examination of the European and American code of International Law, and endeavour to collect, with accuracy, its leading principles, and to discuss their practical details.

**Law of Nations in ancient Greece.**

This law, as understood by the European world, and by America, is the offspring of modern times. The most refined states among the ancients seem to have had no conception of the moral obligations of justice and humanity between nations, and there was no such thing in existence as the science of International Law. [In ancient Greece, from the earliest to the latest period of its history, we find nothing to lead us to the conclusion that the intercourse of state with state, whether in peace or war, was regulated by any systematic legal rules. In peace, or rather in the short intervals of actual cessation from hostilities, there was as little desire among the neighbouring states of which Greece was composed to understand each other's institutions and laws as there was thought of recognising the existence of any of those general or universal rights and obligations that have been found so convenient in modern times for facilitating the international relations of the civilized world; whilst war was disfigured by a ferocity and an absence of legal restraint that are happily unknown to later days. In the so-called heroic ages, we know from Homer[1] the extent to which piracy was carried, and the fact that the pirate's business had very little taint of dishonour attaching to it. Thucydides too speaks of the reign of Minos as an era in civilization, when by his efforts the Ægean was cleared from the swarm of pirates that infested its shores. Nor was piracy confined to those early days: in later times the practice was avowed by powerful Greek cities, and even the fleets of Athens, glorious as was her naval renown, did not disdain occasionally to imitate the Phocæans and relieve the dulness of life by a little maritime robbery[2]. But in addition to this scourge, the ferocity with which hostilities were carried on, the customary devastation by which it was marked, the entire absence of humanity to the conquered, the want of faith in the observance of conventions, and the deep-rooted existence of slavery as a domestic institution, shew that whatever progress civilization had made in Greece, its influence was not productive of anything like a system of International Law based upon honour, justice and equity. And however eloquent was the language and earnest the attempt of philosophers like Plato and Aristotle to maintain the superiority of equity and faith over lawless force, to urge the claims of right against might, such attempts and such language were vain. As far then as the progress of International Law is concerned, the history of Greece presents little that is interesting or valuable,

[1] *Odyss.* XV. 385, 426; XVII. 425; III. 71—74. Thucyd. I. § 8.

[2] Justini *Historiæ*, Lib. XLIII. 3.

whatever interest and value it may have in the history of civilization and of man[1].

Were it worth while to dwell at further length upon the subject, we might notice two features—the right of citizenship with the international conventions relating to it, in which, though the resemblance is but slight, something like the modern notion of private International Law appears; and the influence of the Amphictyonic Council[2], whose object has been stated, with a want of accuracy that needs correction, to have been the institution of a law of nations among the Greeks, and whose efforts it has been as incorrectly asserted were directed to the checking of violence and the settlement of contests between Grecian states by a pacific adjustment. Whereas in truth the council of the Amphictyonic league was but a collection of deputies from certain associated states meeting twice a year at Thermopylæ and at Delphi, for the protection and cultivation of a common worship, a religious rather than a political assembly. In so far as it was a place of union for many of the scattered and otherwise unsympathizing states of Greece, where Dorians and Ionians met and deliberated on some matters of common concern, an idea of brotherhood and of federal unity might have been started, and to that extent the Amphictyonic Council would be national and international, but beyond that its international influence did not go. What it neither did nor attempted to do was to introduce regulations by which state might associate with state and city with city on terms of mutual forbearance; to maintain the principles of honour, justice and regard for plighted faith; to soften the ferocity of war, and to check the violence and settle

The Amphictyonic League.

[1] The reader is directed to Laurent's admirable work, *L'Histoire de l'Humanité*, for full information on the subjects above mentioned. The following passages deserve notice, Tome XI. Livres Premier et Troisième.

[2] For the influence of the Amphictyonic Council valuable information is given in Laurent, *L'Histoire de l'Humanité*, Tom. II. ch. iv. p. 86; for its history in Grote's *History of Greece*, Vol. II. p. 328 &c.; in Smith's *Dictionary of Greek and Roman Antiquities*, sub verb. "Amphictyons," and Freeman's *History of Federal Government*, Vol. I. ch. iii.

the contests between Grecian states. The very oath that was imposed upon its members shews how narrow was the circle of interests within which the league lay[1]; the destruction of Crissa attests the iniquity and cruelty of its acts[2]; and its nullity as a political institution in the best days of Greece is marked by the absence of any allusion to it in the pages of Thucydides, Xenophon, Polybius, and Aristotle.

No Law of Nations in Rome.

If from Greece we turn to Rome, we shall find amidst all the striking differences of habits, manners, thought and action that separate these two great nations of antiquity, none more striking than the devoted cultivation of law as a science and its influence upon all their inner life by which the Romans are marked; yet in spite of the perfection to which law thus cultivated as a science and practised as an art attained, a perfection that has resulted in its "having become the national guide to future ages," and in spite of the large debt which the jurisprudence of nearly every country of Europe owes to the Roman code—that great exemplar of modern legal systems—we may safely affirm that the jurisprudence of ancient Rome is not the nidus out of which modern International Law sprung. Political history, the art of war, the science of government, are all illustrated in the annals of Rome from its earliest to its latest period; and in all these points of contact with the foreign people and nations whom they came across, the Romans have left records enough for us to understand the policy which actuated them, and from these records later times have learnt valuable lessons: but of those relations between foreign states which, whether peaceful or warlike, in later days have produced rules and regulations that have materially improved the happiness of man by softening the cruelties of war and enhancing the blessings of peace, the Romans, in the imperial as much as in the republican time, took no heed. In respect of other nations, when Rome was

[1] Æschin. *de Falsa Legatione*, 121.

[2] Æschin. *c. Ctesip.* 125.

mistress of the world, international rules appealing to justice and equity, and observant of honour and faith, had no existence; and the Jus Gentium was nothing more than a synonym for the law of nature, or a fictitious system which served as a foundation for a new set of equitable as opposed to old common law regulations.

Reasons why.

The reason for this is simple. In the first place, International Law rests upon two great maxims—that nations are mutually independent, and that they are equal—but the history of Rome shews the exaggerated notions of Roman superiority, as well as the constant aim of the Roman people, to destroy all other power, sovereignty and independence than their own.

In the next place, the chronic state of war, and the lust of conquest, which marks the history of Rome, were unfavourable to the growth of anything like that friendly union among states which is productive not only of reciprocal rights and obligations, but of reciprocal esteem.

And lastly, the entire submission of the rest of the world to the Roman empire, whether as subjects or allies, effectually extinguished every vestige of independent national life, and consequently prevented all chance of the creation of International Law. To use D'Hautefeuille's words, "there was only one nation in the world, there could be no other law than what that nation sanctioned."

But it has been asserted that the proofs of the existence of a law of nations among the Romans are visible in the following facts—the institution of a college of heralds and of a fecial law; the recognition of a Jus Gentium, a jurisprudence common to all nations; and the ameliorating influence of humanity, justice and law upon their military operations: we shall examine each of these very briefly, and shew how slight foundation there is for such an assertion.

The Jus Feciale.

What then was the Jus Feciale, what were the functions of the College of Fecials, what was the influence exerted by its members upon the foreign relations of Rome? Much error and much exaggeration have appeared in the accounts that have been written in old and adapted in later days on this subject. According to Cicero[1] (in whose time the fecials and their grotesque forms had lost much of their hold upon Roman life) by the fecial law (jus feciale) was decided whether a war was equitable or inequitable; according to Plutarch and Dionysius of Halicarnassus[2], to the fecials was referred the question of the justice or injustice of a war, on their voice hung the question of peace or war, and it was their peculiar office to settle by arbitration if possible differences that otherwise would end in hostilities. These views have been implicitly adopted by more modern authorities. Thus Grotius[3] has stated that the old Romans first took counsel of the college of priests called Fetiales before they declared war. Bossuet[4] has upheld the superior merits of the godless pagan over the followers of Him who preached peace and good will on earth, in the proof which this holy institution shews of an earnest desire for peace. Whilst Ward, following Vattel, thinks that modern jurisprudence might learn a lesson of moderation and equity from this part of Roman law, deeming the "very existence of a college of heralds, to preside over and expound rules expressly drawn up for their conduct towards foreigners, a proof that the Romans were a people far advanced in the law of nations considered as a science[5];" nor have some eminent writers of our own times distinguished with sufficient accuracy the true position of the Fetiales and the meaning of that Jus which has been ascribed to them; for in one place[6] we read of the Fetiales as being really judges of the legality of a war; in another of the Jus Feciale, or the law of negotiation and diplomacy, being the classical expression for Inter-

[1] *De Off.* I. 2. 36.

[2] Plutarch, *Numa*, XII. Dionys. Hal. *Ant. Rom.* II. 72.

[3] *De Jure Belli et Pacis*, II. 23. 4.

[4] *Discours sur l'histoire Universelle*, 3 partie, VI.

[5] Vattel, II. 14. 209. Ward, *Law of Nations*, Vol. I. p. 184.

[6] Rein in the *Real-Encyklopädie der Classischen Alterthumswissenschaft*, T. III. p. 467.

national Law; whilst one common mistake is, that the Roman law of peace and war was contained in a sort of Fecial jurisprudence[1]. It is unnecessary to examine the whole history of this remarkable institution, whether the College of Fecials owes its origin to a king (Numa or Ancus Martius) as some assert, or whether it was copied by the Romans from some of the ancient tribes that surrounded them, is of little consequence here; nor does it much matter what was the precise number of its members, or what its constitution and form, it is sufficient to know that it was a college of priests charged with the duty of observing those formalities in war which ancient custom had prescribed, and that the fecial law was the collected edition (though never published) of the formal regulations which were observed in declaring war, in carrying it on, and in concluding treaties[2].

The functions of the Fetiales were various. First of all there can be no doubt that they were the interpreters of this Jus Fetiale, deciding all disputed points that arose out of it, and explaining its forms and ceremonies[3]; but the next and not the least remarkable part of the duties cast upon them was that of acting as advisers to the chief magistrate in the state, not on the justice or injustice of a probable war, or upon the advisability or non-advisability of commencing hostilities, but of the proper mode in which war should be declared. Their answer was given in the shape of a decree, and it is a fact which points strongly to the conclusion that they were nothing but heralds, and mere ministers, without the power of originating laws or influencing the national policy[4]; that no instance is recorded of their having been consulted on the policy of a war, of their having dissuaded the people from a war as unjust, or of their having ever been consulted upon the policy of

[1] Maine, *Ancient Law*, p. 53.

[2] Cic. *de Legg.* II. 14; *De Off.* III. 29.

[3] Cic *de Legg.* II. 14; Livy, 31. 8.

[4] See Osenbruggen, *de Jure belli et pacis Romanorum*, p. 25, and Laurent, *Etudes sur l'histoire de l'humanité*, Tom. III. p. 16 et sq.

the rules and regulations by which foreigners were permitted to reside in Rome.

Of the Fecial law itself, if law it can be called, so little has come down to our time that no satisfactory explanation of it can be given. One rule however has been cited by Cicero, and noticed by other writers, which as a leading principle deserves a slight notice. "No war was justum unless preceded by a formal demand of reparation, or unless regularly and solemnly declared[1]." Now, all that seems to be meant by this phraseology is, that unless two particular forms were closely adhered to, and performed with all due ceremony, any hostilities that took place were not justa—that is legal. Those forms were first a demand upon the offending nation to do what was right, to make reparation for injuries, or restoration of property seized, called "rerum repetitio," which was done in a set speech, and with solemn ceremony, by the chief of the Fetiales, the Pater Patratus, with a time granted for deliberation—about thirty-three days. Upon the expiration of that period without a satisfactory answer, the people in the comitia tributa (who had been informed by the Fetiales of what they had done, and how their mission had been received) deliberated on peace or war; and then, if war was decided on, the second form followed, for the Fecials were instructed to declare it; which they did in the name of the Senate of the Roman people, hurling a spear into the enemy's territory. As far therefore as war is concerned, the functions of this college of priests were few and simple; to receive the commands of the Roman people; to act upon them by performing the ceremonies prescribed and hallowed by custom; to decide as Judges upon difficulties that might arise out of the rerum repetitio; and to make the war legal or just by pronouncing the consecrated formula.

But the duties of the Fecials were not confined to the declaration of hostilities or to times of war. From various

[1] Cic. *de Off.* I. XI. 36; *De Leg.* II. IX. 21; Varro, *de ling. Lat.* V. § 86; Dion. Hal. *Ant.* II. 72.

passages in the classical authorities it would appear that they were entrusted with the task of drawing up in proper form the treaties or fœdera that were agreed to be entered into by the Roman people, and this not only in the Kingly period of Rome, but under the Republic[1]; whilst a no less important business was committed to their hands, that of protecting the sanctity of ambassadors, and of seeing that such persons themselves did nothing contrary to law[2].

From the Fecial Law, and its absence of resemblance to anything like a system of International Law, we proceed to consider that which in name, but in name only, means a law of nations.

"It is almost unnecessary," says a modern writer of distinction[3], "to state that the confusion between Jus Gentium, or law common to all nations, and International Law is entirely modern;" but as the confusion has existed it is as well to know what was the precise meaning and what the peculiar province of the Roman Jus Gentium. Now, if we pass over the tripartite arrangement of Ulpian, and refer to Gaius as our authority, we find that the Jus Gentium was practically the same in meaning as the Jus Naturale. An obvious remark however occurs here if such is the case, if the Jus Gentium be no other than the Jus Naturæ; not that jus naturæ, be it noticed, which Ulpian describes as a kind of instinct common to all animals, but that set of rules which all people use in common, and the use of which reason has taught them[4], why were two expressions employed differing in form, and apparently intended to convey distinct meanings, especially as at the time these distinctions were grafted upon the Roman Jurisprudence; "Nature had become a household word in the mouths of the Romans, and the belief

The Jus Gentium.

[1] Livy, 30, 43; Servius *ad Virg. Æn.* XII. 13.

[2] Dion. Hal. *Ant.* II. 72; Varro, *ap. Non. Marcell.* III. 12; Plutarch, *Camillus*, 17 and 18.

[3] Maine's *Ancient Law*, p. 53.

[4] *D.* I. 1. 9.

prevailed among their lawyers that there was a Code of Nature[1]."

The explanation of this will not only help to place this peculiar Roman conception of law in its proper aspect, but will also throw light upon its true position in later Roman Jurisprudence.

In all probability at the outset of Roman history there was but one kind of law, the collection of rules under which the lives, the property, and the contracts of the citizens were protected. Wars took place, kingdoms were established, nations grew up into life, property was held by various individuals; in short all those institutions existed which the Roman lawyers in after days attributed to the Jus Gentium[2], and yet but one law was thought of—the Roman law, and to one class of people only was it applicable, the Roman citizens. Now, when in process of time, a large number of strangers were gathered within the walls of the city, and when many Italian tribes (nations so to speak) had owned the power of Rome, whose members became subject to the state, though not admitted to the right of citizenship, it frequently happened that differences arose between citizens and strangers, or between strangers themselves, to settle which law of some kind was required. What was the law to be resorted to? Not the Jus Civile, or Roman law, for that was rigidly devoted to a particular class, viz. citizens, and formed as it was out of old deep-rooted customs, was too inelastic to be adapted to new combinations and forms. Not the Jus Naturæ, for the influence of that notion was not felt till Greek philosophy had made progress in Roman society. Some device was needed to supply the want, and that was done by the Judges of the court which took under its protection the strangers and their interests, viz. the Prætors. These officials, untrammelled by the harsh rules of the Old Roman law, and free to notice and make use of any of the institutions, laws, and customs of the surrounding tribes, if it suited their purpose—free, that is, to mix their

[1] Maine, p. 56. [2] *D.* 1. 1. 5.

own Jurisprudence and court rules with a foreign element, did so act, influenced probably by the very principle that was afterwards said to lie at the root of the Jus Gentium, that institutions and laws which bore a close resemblance to one another, though brought from foreign parts, must have had a common origin (quasi quo jure omnes gentes utuntur). Thus these new rules which at first were intended to supply a blank in the political administration of Rome, and to remedy a mischief, in time grew into a separate Jurisprudence, requiring a distinct name, and what is still more remarkable, became a stock from which were framed a large number of legal institutions and judicial notions tending to supplement and improve the old law. The Jus Gentium therefore was, as the writer above quoted says, "the sum of the common ingredients in the customs of the old Italian tribes who sent successive swarms of immigrants on to Roman soil, a system forced on the attention of the Romans by a political necessity, at first loved as little as the foreigners, from whose institutions it was derived and for whose benefit it was intended, but in process of time swelling into larger proportions and becoming a great though imperfectly-developed model to which all law ought as far as possible to conform[1]."

This therefore is clear, that neither in the Fecial Law, whatever that was, nor in the Jus Gentium, do we find the germs of the modern system of International Law.

But, lastly, the practice of war among the Romans, from the earliest to the latest period of their existence as a great and warlike nation, exhibits no proof of the ameliorating influence of humanity, justice, or law upon it. It would be an easy but a valueless labour to collect instances without end of the cruel and treacherous spirit which actuated the ancient Romans in their incessant wars, and of their utter disregard for those laws of war which, if there be any meaning in the passage of Sallust presently to be referred to, they were supposed to possess. Two

The practice of war.

[1] Maine, ch. iii. pp. 48—53.

examples will suffice. During the second Punic War (which was waged about 200 or 220 years before the birth of our Saviour) Syracuse was besieged, and after a long and vigorous defence fell. The Roman general, Marcellus, was neither an ungenerous leader nor a cold-blooded butcher; indeed, as Niebuhr asserts, his humanity is generally set forth by the ancients as quite exemplary; and yet Syracuse was given up to slaughter and pillage, its most eminent citizens were butchered, the rest of the inhabitants were driven out and compelled to tear the grass from the earth to appease their hunger, many of them were sold into slavery, all that was in the town became the prize of the soldiery or of the state, and Rome was enriched with the noble specimens of art that had made Syracuse renowned in her day. Nor was this all, Agrigentum suffered the same fate two years later, and from having been once a peerless city, famed for its magnificence and the opulence of its inhabitants, sunk into ruin and utter insignificance; and in each case be it noticed, treachery of the worst description achieved that victory which the Roman arms alone could not.

"The taking of Syracuse," says Niebuhr, "is of the same date as that of Capua, and both of these events may show us how little the wars of the ancients are like those of our own days[1]." Again, at a much later period, when the Emperor Augustus, towards the end of his reign, was consolidating his power and carrying the Roman eagles across the Weser and to the Elbe, a Roman general, famed for his humanity quite as much as for his courage and soldierly qualities, Nero Claudius Drusus, met the Germans in the field and not only defeated them with great slaughter, but laid waste whole districts, carried off the women and children into slavery, and hunted the men down like wild beasts.

Instances like these are enough to mark the fierce spirit of conquest and the barbarous international customs of the Romans without any additional exemplification such

[1] *Lectures on Roman History*, Vol. II., Bohn's Edition, 1852, p. 119.

as is to be found in their haughty triumphs, in their gladiatorial shows, when wretched captives were "butchered to make a Roman holiday," in their cunning interpretation of treaties, in the barbarous doctrine of law maintained in Justinian's time[1], that prisoners of war became slaves jure gentium, and that the consequence of capture, even in time of peace, was slavery and loss of property[2]. "It is impossible," says Chancellor Kent, "to conceive of rules of national law more directly calculated to destroy all commercial intercourse and to maintain eternal enmity among nations." May we not add, it is equally impossible to conceive that modern rules of international law were derived from Rome.

But in the midst of this ferocity some redeeming features are visible; thus, for instance, prisoners of war might purchase their liberty, and were sold only when unransomed[3]; hence in the course of time grew up the more humane custom of allowing the exchange of prisoners; captives were not maltreated by the Romans, as the Athenians were at Syracuse by Greek conquerors, always excepting kings and generals, who were, at least in Cicero's day, butchered without mercy, after having been led in triumph through the city[4]. Nor were the inhabitants of the conquered country entirely deprived of their lands, some small portion was allowed to remain in their hands, on condition of their paying *rent* for the same as tenants (coloni)[5].

The Jus Belli.

That there was too something like a law of war, intended to soften its fierceness, we learn from Sallust and Cicero. The first of these writers, in that admirable and finished piece of composition in which he tells the tale of the war against Jugurtha[6], is narrating the siege and cap-

[1] J. I. 3. 4. [2] *D.* 49. 15. 5. 2.

[3] Niebuhr, *History of Rome*, III. p. 252; Livy, X. 31, XXX. 43.

[4] Idem dies et victoribus imperii et victis vitæ finem fecit. Cic. *Verr.* II 5, 30.

[5] Livy, II. 41, VIII. 4; Cic. *Verr.* Act. II. Lib. III. cap. 6.

[6] Cap. xci.

ture of the Numidian town Capsa by Marius, and in describing the brutalities that ensued, the slaughter of the young men, the sale into slavery of the rest of the inhabitants, and the sack of the town, mentions them as deeds contrary to the law of war (contra jus belli), but forced on Marius by necessity, and pardonable on account of the untameable nature and faithless disposition of the inhabitants. The second, in his oration for Balbus[1], whilst enlarging upon the greatness, the eloquence, and the learning of Cn. Pompey (who was counsel with him and Crassus in the case), speaks of him as eminently distinguished for an acquaintance with all the learning relating to the law of war and peace. Now from the passage here quoted, and from another one in the *De Officiis*[2], as well as from one or two places in the *Digest* and elsewhere, we gain some insight into the matter that was comprised in this part of the Roman law. Thus we find that one important portion of it was taken up, at least in old times, with the rules prescribed by the Fecials, many of whom, like Scævola, were as famed for their knowledge of law as for their high position in the state—that in other parts of it are given clear definitions of war and peace[3], and explanations of the condition of citizens during hostilities, of the position and rights of lawful enemies, of Postliminium, and of the regulations relating to military service; for if we are to place any credence in the story told by Cicero[4], of Cato the Elder, no person was justified in joining in a campaign and fighting with the troops engaged therein unless he was a miles, (a soldier bound by the sacramentum, or oath of obedience,) whilst the law relating to truces, foreign treaties, public conventions and sponsions, formed no small or unimportant head of the Roman jus belli et pacis.

Such then, as far as light is thrown by the scattered fragments to be found in the Corpus Juris Civilis and the allusions dispersed through the classical authorities

[1] Cap. vi. [2] Lib. I. cap. ii.

[3] *D.* 49. 15. 12. and 24; 50. 16. 118.

[4] *De Off.* I. cap. ii.

on this part of the jurisprudence of Rome, such are the vestiges of her law of peace and war; and whilst we see the trace of regular law in this as in other phases of Roman life, we see how easily and wilfully it was set at nought; and we find that, closely allied as modern codes and legal systems are to the old Roman laws, in all the various matter that is comprised within the limits of International Law the Roman Jus belli et pacis has left nothing on which the foundation of the modern system can be said to rest; nay, has left no vestige of any systematic treatise on the subject, save a bare notice of a lost work by Varro, a Liber Humanarum, vaguely alluded to by Aulus Gellius[1]. Yet that the Roman law did exercise an influence upon International Law we shall have occasion to notice a little way further on.]

International Law in the middle ages.

The irruption of the northern tribes of Scythia and Germany overturned all that was gained by the Roman law, annihilated every restraint, destroyed all sense of national obligation, and threw civil society for a time into the violence and confusion of the barbarous ages. Mankind seemed to be doomed to live once more in constant distrust or hostility, and to regard a stranger and an enemy as almost the same. Piracy, rapine, and ferocious warfare, deformed the annals of Europe. The manners of nations were barbarous, and their maxims of war cruel. Slavery was considered as a lawful consequence of captivity. Mr Barrington[2] has cited the laws of the Wisigoths, Saxons, Sicilians, and Bavarians, as restraining, by the severest penalties, the plunder of shipwrecked goods, and the abuse of shipwrecked seamen, and as extending the rights of hospitality to strangers. But, notwithstanding a few efforts of this kind to introduce order and justice, and though municipal law had undergone great improvement, the law of nations remained in the rudest and most uncultivated state, down to the period of the 16th century. In many instances, shipwrecked strangers were made prisoners and

[1] Aul. Gell. I. cap. 25.

[2] *Observations on the more ancient Statutes, Magna Charta*, c. XXX.

sold as slaves, without exciting any complaint, or offending any public sense of justice. Numerous cases occurred of acts of the grossest perfidy and cruelty towards strangers and enemies. Prisoners were put to death for their gallantry and brave defence in war. There was no reliance upon the word and honour of men in power. Reprisals and private war were in constant activity. Instances were frequent of the violation of embassies, of the murder of hostages, the imprisonment of guests, and the killing of heralds. The victor in war had his option in dealing with his prisoners, either to put them to death, or reduce them to slavery, or exact an exorbitant ransom for their deliverance. So late as the time of Cardinal Richelieu, it was held to be the right of all nations to arrest strangers who came into the country without a safe conduct[1].

The Emperor Charlemagne made distinguished efforts to improve the condition of Europe, [by vigorous measures for the promotion of trade and commerce, by opening roads, establishing lighthouses, facilitating communications along the Danube and between that river and the Rhine,] by the introduction of order and by the propagation of Christianity[2]; and we have cheering examples, during the

[[1] Ward's *History of the Law of Nations*, Vol. I. ch. 7, 8, 9; Vol. I. p. 274 (note Z). The reader will find in the Introduction to Pardessus's admirable work on the maritime laws of Europe, *Collection des lois Maritimes*, Tome I. from p. lx., a most interesting account of the state of commercial enterprize in the civilized world at the period here spoken of. He is also referred to the first volume of Duer, *On Insurance*, Lecture II. p. 28, for information on the same subject. In the second and third volumes of Meyer's treatise, *Sur l'esprit, origine, et progrès des Institutions Judiciaires*, a clear and concise account of the judicial institutions of England, France, and Germany during the same period of time is given; and from Guizot's well-known *Lectures on Civilization in Europe*, especially in the 2nd, 4th, 7th, 8th, 9th, and 11th lectures; from Hallam's *History of Europe during the Middle Ages*, and from the Introduction to Robertson's *History of Charles the Fifth*, no small insight into the manners, customs, and social feelings that characterized Europe during the early part of the Middle Ages, can be obtained.]

[[2] The benefits conferred by Charlemagne upon the opening civilization of Europe are concisely stated in Martin's *Histoire de France*, Tome I., in Pardessus's *Collection des lois Maritimes*, Tome I. Introduction, and in Sir Jas. Stephen's *Lectures on French History*, Vol. I.]

darkness of the middle ages, of some recognition of public law, by means of alliances, and the submission of disputes to the arbitrament of a neutral power. Mr Ward enumerates five institutions, existing about the period of the eleventh century, which made a deep impression upon Europe, and contributed in a very essential degree to improve the law of nations[1]. These institutions were, the feudal system, the concurrence of Europe in one form of religious worship and government, the establishment of chivalry, the negotiations and treaties forming the conventional law of Europe, the settlement of a scale of political rank and precedency, [to which must be added the crusades.]

Of all these causes of reformation, the most weight is to be attributed to the intimate alliance of the great powers as one Christian community. The influence of Christianity was very efficient towards the introduction of a better and more enlightened sense of right and justice among the governments of Europe. [Indeed, as Laurent says, the idea of a system of International Law is due to Christianity. For how could there be any legal tie between man as an individual and men as people and nations, until the consciousness of a common nature was acknowledged, until the gulf which separated the free man from the slave was filled up, until the contempt for or hatred of the stranger as barbarian or enemy was removed, until man's nature was changed and war ceased to be regarded as a glorious pastime or as an ordinary occupation, and until an equitable system of independent states was substituted for one huge overgrown empire ever striving to draw all neighbours within its grasp and to maintain unlimited rule[2]?] Christianity taught the duty of benevolence to strangers, of humanity to the van-

Influence of Christianity.

[1] Ward's *History of the Law of Nations*, Vol. I. 322—328.

[[2] *Histoire du droit des gens*, Laurent, Tome IV. livre III. ch. 1; *Le droit maritime*, par Cauchy, Tome I. p. 205. Sociantur gentes unitate religionis magis quam aut alterius communione aut fœderis pactione (Albericus Gentilis, *De Jure Belli*, I. 3, c. 15).]

quished, of the obligation of good faith, and of the sin of murder, revenge, and rapacity. The history of Europe, during the early periods of modern history, abounds with interesting and strong cases, to shew the authority of the church over turbulent princes and fierce warriors, and the effect of that authority in meliorating manners, checking violence, and introducing a system of morals which inculcated peace, moderation and justice. The church had its councils or convocations of the clergy, which formed the nations professing Christianity into a connexion resembling a federal alliance, and those councils sometimes settled the titles and claims of princes, and regulated the temporal affairs of the Christian powers. The confederacy of the Christian nations was bound together by a sense of common duty and interest in respect to the rest of mankind. It became a general principle of belief and action, that it was not only a right, but a duty, to reduce to obedience, for the sake of conversion, every people who professed a religious faith different from their own. To make war upon infidels was, for many ages, a conspicuous part of European public law; and this gross perversion of the doctrines and spirit of Christianity, had at least one propitious effect upon the Christian powers, inasmuch as it led to the cultivation of peace and union between them, and to a more free and civilized intercourse. The notion that it was lawful to invade and subdue Mahometan and Pagan countries, continued very long to sway the minds of men; and it was not until after the age of Grotius and Bacon, that this error was entirely eradicated. Lord Coke[1] held, that an alliance for mutual defence was unlawful between Christians and infidels or idolaters: Grotius was very cautious as to the admission of the lawfulness of alliances with infidels, having no doubt that all Christian nations were bound to assist one another against their attacks[2]; Lord Bacon[3] thought it a matter of so much doubt, as to propound it seriously as a question,

[1] 4 *Inst.* 155.

[2] Grotius, Bk. II. c. 15, § 11, 12.

[3] Bacon's *Works*, Vol. III. p. 538, fol. edition, 1738, "Of an Holy War."

whether a war with infidels was not first in order of dignity, and to be preferred to all other just temporal quarrels; and whether a war with infidels might not be undertaken merely for the propagation of the Christian faith, without other cause of hostility. [Whilst even so late as the commencement of last century we find the enemies of the Christian name almost classed with robbers, upon whom war might be made without special cause or without the observance of ordinary forms[1].]

[The influence of Feudalism upon International Law is rather of a general than of a special nature, viz. that of its influence upon civilization and society, for to Feudalism with its tendency to localization society is indebted for its powerful development of individual character, for self-reliance, for energy in action, for an inclination towards great deeds and noble thoughts, and, above all, for the right of personal resistance which it inspired and to which the political fortunes of Europe have been so much indebted. Of Feudalism.

Nor in estimating the benefits conferred by Feudalism upon later times must we forget the part it played in breaking up the old Roman spirit of universal conquest, substituting for it distinct and various nationalities, and in introducing the Federative form of government; for as the great writer[2] on this part of European history, with truth, says, "Feudalism as a whole was in fact a confederation in which each separate possessor of a fief was invested with all the rights and privileges of sovereignty." But while such are the general benefits it conferred upon civilization, there are two of its characteristic features bearing more directly upon International Law that deserve notice, the right of private war and the notion of territorial sovereignty. The former of these, which became universal throughout Europe during the height of the Feudal system, from a merely isolated and lawless custom

[[1] See a commission, given by the Emperor, Charles the Sixth, to two ships of war in 1718. Callender's *Voyages*, Vol. III. p. 472.]

[2] Guizot.

of obtaining revenge for wrongs by armed force, grew into a law marked with all the forms and ceremonies of a settled legalized system[1]. The latter, though not dating immediately from Feudalism, was an important offshoot of it, through that which was one of its undoubted characteristics, viz. the tie between personal duties and personal rights and the ownership of land. How this Feudal notion of territorial sovereignty bears upon modern International Law is one of those interesting problems which have been so admirably worked out by the author of *Ancient Law*, who traces the postulate, "That sovereigns should be related to each other, like the members of a group of Roman proprietors" (branching out as it does into the two-fold shape of the territoriality of sovereignty and the absolute ownership of territory implied in this term) to its Feudal source, and to whose pages we refer the reader for a more detailed account of this Feudal phenomenon[2].

Whilst Feudalism was acting in the way thus described upon civilization and society, all who have studied its history, and are familiar with its peculiar institutions, will acknowledge that much of the benefit it conferred upon the world was counterbalanced by the exaggerated tendency to isolated life which it inspired, and by the overweening and dangerous importance of the Feudal aristocracy; that society must have been injured by the continuance of these evils is self-evident, but that their continuance was directly adverse to the influence of law upon the intercourse of nations is equally evident. A corrective therefore was needed, and one was found in those extraordinary movements of religious zeal which disturbed the eleventh and twelfth centuries.—By depressing the Feudal nobility, who exhausted their resources to provide for these expeditions to the East, the emancipation of the lower orders of society was assisted; by the diminution of the number of lords, who rushed madly into them, the power of the Crown was restored; by the distress

Of the Crusades.

[1] See Ward's *Law of Nations*, Vol. I. ch. II.

[2] Chapter iv.

produced among the superior classes, who were compelled to barter privileges for money, many Feudal burdens were removed, and large towns grew in wealth and power; by the crowds that followed the banners of the Cross, and the wealth they took with them, maritime commerce received an immense impetus, and through commerce maritime law; and lastly, by the alliances that these expeditions produced among the different sovereigns and people of Europe, as well as by the contact of the Western with the Eastern world, the intercourse of nations with each other was immensely benefited, and prospects of International Law greatly influenced;] nor must we leave out of sight the decided influence of the crusades upon chivalry, which itself had a very beneficial effect upon the laws of war, for chivalry introduced declarations of war by heralds, and to attack an enemy by surprise was deemed cowardly and dishonourable. It dictated humane treatment to the vanquished, courtesy to enemies, and the virtues of fidelity, honour, and magnanimity in every species of warfare.

Of Chivalry.

Of the Civil Law.

The introduction and study of the civil law must also have contributed largely to more correct and liberal views of the rights and duties of nations. [How and in what direction it influenced International Jurisprudence we purpose to consider.]

[Before the fall of the Roman empire there was no necessity for International Jurisprudence; whilst the Roman domination was almost universal throughout the civilized world, whilst along the shores of the Mediterranean, then the great resort of commercial enterprise, Roman arms were supreme, and whilst nearly every seat of commerce was in Roman hands, the free progress of trade and the independent intercourse of nations were almost impossible; those who trafficked with the Romans were their vassals; those who were not vassals were in the position of allies to whom but little respect was shewn. But after the invasion of Italy all was changed, and one important consequence of the disruption of the Roman empire into a multitude of states and nations, differing in manners, language, and religion, was the necessity for something like a common system of International Law. The new comers into Italy, in all probability, did not lose sight of the countries they had once inhabited, and now had left for the fertile plains of Italy, and though these backward looks were neither frequent nor strong, still they were strong enough to keep alive the relations that had once existed, and to prepare the way for international intercourse, and eventually for international regulations. But whilst the Romans had confined themselves to the Mediterranean as the arena for commercial enterprise, their northern invaders, hardy navigators and daring tempters of the perils of the deep, sought new seas and opened up new shores, extending consequently their foreign relations. In this revolutionary crisis, however, one peculiar and somewhat singular fact appeared, that the barbarian conquerors instead of overthrowing the old Roman law, and substituting for it their own laws and customs, were content to leave the conquered inhabitants of Italy in possession not only of a portion of their native soil but of their own codified law. While therefore all else was overwhelmed by the wave of barbaric immigration, that poured with terrific force upon Italy, jurisprudence did not sustain the same fatal shock, remaining intact through the vitality of the Roman laws, which thus became its prop and mainstay. The Roman law then was universally received by the philosophers of the day as the expression of common sense and reason. By the lawyers it was cultivated as the source of legal wisdom, and as the training-ground of juridical science, whilst the legislators of the European world of civilization transplanted its eternal principles into the codes and systems which were being formed, and thus though the name of Roman had fallen into contempt, and was sunk in degradation, the Roman law and its influence passed on from generation to generation, and from land to land. It was under such circumstances then that the commercial energies of the world were awakening into new life, calling into existence great and powerful towns, and introducing a continuous and enlarging intercourse of state with state. One result of such an interchange of international relations soon happened, viz. the necessity of some common system of law to settle the disputes that might arise in the course of such intercourse. An appeal to the law therefore was made, and that appeal was met as was natural, by resorting to the great written code which had for so many years been the standard of authority throughout the greater part of the world, whilst those who now set themselves to supply what was wanted were men who knew of no system of positive International Law, and had been brought up in the study of the Roman Digest and Code. With the maxims and dicta embodied in those books they were familiar, beyond those books their learning did not reach, or rather disdained to go, and therefore when the international disputes that an active commercial spirit must engender were referred to their arbitration they applied the legal rules with which they were familiarized, and thus it came to pass that one portion of International Law in its infancy, and for many a long year to come, was dependent on, and perhaps it may be said shackled by, the Roman law; hence too we may account for the error of those who attribute the increasing ardour in the pursuit of the study of International Law to a revival of the study of Roman law in the 12th century, consequent upon the discovery of a copy of the Pandects at the siege of Amalfi. On this exploded legend it is not necessary to dwell; it is enough to assert that the influence of the Roman law was never lost. Still it is an undoubted fact that the 12th century was remarkable for an increased devotion to its study, and that, to use Mr Dugald Stewart's words, "it shot a strong and auspicious ray of intellectual light across the surrounding darkness, improving men's tastes, enlarging their views, and invigorating their reasoning powers[1];" nay, doing more than that, di-

[1] Introduction to the *Encyclopædia Britannica.*

rectly tending to accelerate the progress of order and civilization, not only by ameliorating and systematizing legal science, but by furnishing the parent stock on which were grafted those branches of pure ethics and liberal politics which have resulted in such compilations as those of Alberic Gentilis, Grotius, and his successor[1].]

On Treaties. The influence of treaties, conventions, and commercial associations, was still more direct and visible in the formation of the great modern code of public law. They gave a new character to the law of nations, and rendered it more and more of a positive or instituted code. Commercial ordinances and conventions contributed greatly to improve and refine public law, and the intercourse of nations, by protecting the persons and property of merchants in cases of shipwreck, and against piracy, and against seizure and arrest upon the breaking out of war. Auxiliary treaties were tolerated, by which one nation was allowed to be an enemy to a certain extent only. Thus, if, in time of peace, a defensive treaty had been made between one of the parties to a subsequent war and a third power, by which a certain number of troops were to be furnished in case of war, a compliance with this engagement implicated the auxiliary as a party to the war, *only so far* as her contingent was concerned. The nations of Europe had advanced to this extent in diplomatic science as early as the beginning of the 13th century, exhibiting a refinement that was totally unknown to the ancients. Treaties of subsidy shewed also the progress of the law of nations. The troops of one nation, to a definite extent, could be hired for the service of one of the belligerents, without affording ground for hostility with the community which supplied the specific aid. The rights of commerce

[1 On this subject generally the reader will find some valuable information in the "Discours Preliminaire" to Mons. D'Hautefeuille's work, *Sur les Droits et Devoirs des Nations neutres;* and in the 4th and 9th chapters of Maine's *Ancient Law* he will see an admirable account of the function of the Law of nature in giving birth to modern International Law, and the influence of the Roman Law upon that Law.]

began to be regarded as under the protection of the law of nations[1], and Queen Elizabeth complained of the Spaniards, that they had prohibited commerce in the Indian seas, contrary to that law.

Law concerning shipwrecks.

The efforts that were made, upon the revival of commerce, to suppress piracy, and protect shipwrecked property, shew a returning sense of the value and of the obligations of national justice. The case of shipwrecks may be cited, and dwelt upon for a moment, as a particular and strong instance of the feeble beginnings, the slow and interrupted progress, and final and triumphant success, of the principles of public right. Valin[2] imputes the barbarous custom of plundering shipwrecked property, not merely to the ordinary cupidity for gain, but to a more particular and peculiar cause. The earliest navigators were almost all pirates, and the inhabitants of the coasts were constantly armed against their depredations, and whenever they had the misfortune to be shipwrecked, they were pursued with a vindictive spirit, and deemed just objects of punishment. The practice of plundering shipwrecks [is attributed by Valin, in accordance with the opinion of Selden, though against that of Loccenius, to the Rhodians, from whom it is said to have passed to the Romans; but Pardessus, (to whom every inquirer into the history and progress of commerce, and of the laws by which it has been developed and protected, owes a debt of gratitude,) shews that the cruel custom of plundering the shipwrecked stranger, the ἀσύλητον γένος of the more polished Greeks, is not attributable to any particular nation, nor to any special cause. During the period when the semi-barbarous tribes of the world were in a chronic state of war, and when piracy was an honourable employment, it was not likely that more mercy should be shewn to the

[[1] In the 1st Vol. of Anderson, *On Commerce*, will be found a treaty between Edward III. and certain towns in Flanders (cited from Rymer's *Fœdera*, Vol. v. p. 38) for carrying on trade, and for other purposes stipulated therein, notwithstanding their earl was at war with England.]

[2] *Com. sur Ord.* Tom. II. Livre IV. Titre IX.

shipwrecked stranger than to others who needed help and pity; but in process of time the custom of pillaging, and even of killing the *ναυαγὸν ξένον*, which from the testimony of Xenophon (*Anab.* VII. c. 5), and Herodotus (IV. § 103), we know was in practice, was changed, and more humanity was exhibited towards the victims of storms and tempests. To lay the sin of plundering wrecks upon the Rhodians rather than on any other nation of antiquity is neither warranted by history nor even by the passage in Selden; that the sin did exist is certain, and that the efforts to restrain it were very feeble and gradual and mixed with much positive injustice is certain also.] The goods cast ashore first belonged to the fortunate occupant, and then they were considered as belonging to the state. This change from private to public appropriation of the property rendered a returning sense of right and duty more natural and easy. [The Emperor Constantine, or Antonine (for there is some doubt as to which it was)], had the honour of being the first to renounce the claim to shipwrecked property in favour of the rightful owner[1]. But the inhuman customs on this subject were too deeply rooted to be eradicated by the wisdom and vigilance of the Roman lawgivers. The legislation in favour of the unfortunate was disregarded by succeeding emperors, and when the empire itself was overturned by the northern barbarians, the laws of humanity were swept away in the tempest, and the continual depredations of the Saxons and Normans induced the inhabitants of the western coasts of Europe to treat all navigators who were thrown by the perils of the sea upon their shores as pirates, and to punish them as such, without inquiry or discrimination.

The Emperor Andronicus Comnenus, who reigned at Constantinople in 1183, made great efforts to repress this inhuman practice. His edict was worthy of the highest

[1] Vinnius *in Inst.* 2. 1. 47, note 5, [and see also Gothofred's *Note upon the Code*, II. 5. 1.]

praise, but it ceased to be put in execution after his death[1]. Pillage had become an inveterate moral pestilence. It required something more effectual than papal bulls, and the excommunication of the church, to stop the evil. The revival of commerce, and with it a sense of the value of order, commercial ordinances, and particular conventions and treaties between sovereigns, contributed gradually to suppress this criminal practice, by rendering the regulations on that subject a branch of the public law of nations. Valin says, it was reserved to the ordinances of Lewis XIV. to put the finishing stroke towards the extinction of this species of piracy, by declaring that shipwrecked persons and property were placed under the special protection and safeguard of the crown, and the punishment of death without hope of pardon, was pronounced against the guilty[2].

Treatment of prisoners.

The progress of moderation and humanity in the treatment of prisoners is to be imputed to the influence of conventional law, establishing a general and indiscriminate exchange of prisoners, rank for rank, and giving protection to cartel ships for that purpose. It is a practice of no very ancient introduction among the states of Europe, and was not of very familiar use in the age of Grotius, succeeding

[[1] This edict will be found in Loccenius, *De Jure Maritimo*, Lib. I. c. 7, n. 14, and in Pardessus, *Collection des lois Maritimes*, Tome I. ch. 5.]

[2] [On this subject the reader may consult Pardessus, *Collection des lois Maritimes*, Tome I. ch. 1; Selden, *De Dominio Maris*, Lib. I. ch. 25; Macculloch's *Commercial Dictionary*, Article, "Wrecks;" and in the following texts he will see the legislation upon this subject between the 6th and the 15th centuries:

The Roman Law is contained in the following passages of the *Digest*: *D.* 7. 7. 7; 12. 4. 2; 12. 41. 1. 8 and l. 44; 47. 2. 43. 11; 47. 9. 3; as well as in the Code, II. 5, and in the Compilation, called the *Jus Navale Rhodiorum*, Lib. III. cap. 9—51. The Græco-Roman Law will be found in the *Basilica*, Lib. LIII. Tit. iii. Both of these last-named compilations are published in the 1st Vol. of Pardessus's *Collection des lois Maritimes*.

The Law in vogue in the time of the Crusades appears in the *Liber Assisarum*, cap. 41; whilst in the *Röles d'Oleron*, Arts. 2, 4, and 36—44, the *Consolato del Mare*, cap. 183 and 207, the *Statutes of Wisby*, Lib. III. Part iii. ch. 4, and in several of the Hanseatic Statutes, all of which sets of laws are published in the 1st and 2nd Vols. of Pardessus's *Collection*, appears the legislation on wrecks between the 12th and 15th centuries.]

the older practice of ransom. From the extracts which Dr Robinson gives from Bellus, who was a judge or assessor in the armies of Charles V. and Philip II., he concludes, that no practice so general, and so favourable to the conduct of prisoners, as a public exchange in time of war, was known in the 16th century[1]. The private interest of the captor in his prisoner continued through that period; and the practice of ransom, founded on the right of property claimed by the captor, succeeded to the Greek and Roman practice of killing prisoners, or selling them as slaves.

Admission of ambassadors.

The custom of admitting resident ministers at each sovereign's court was another important improvement in the security and facility of national intercourse; and this led to the settlement of a great question, which was very frequently discussed in the 15th and 16th centuries, concerning the inviolability of ambassadors. It came at last to be a definitive principle of public law, that ambassadors were exempted from all local jurisdiction, civil and criminal; though Lord Coke considered the law in his day to be, that if an ambassador committed any crime which was *contra jus gentium*, he lost his privilege and dignity as an ambassador, being punishable as any other private alien, and that he was even bound to answer civilly for his contracts that were good *jure gentium*, but for anything that was *malum prohibitum*, and not *malum in se jure gentium*, he was not bound[2].

Grotius.

Thus stood the law of nations at the age of Grotius (A.D. 1625). It had been rescued, to a very considerable extent, from the cruel usages and practices of the northern barbarians. It had been restored to some degree of science and civility by the influence of Christianity, the study of the Roman law, and the spirit of commerce. It had grown greatly in value and efficacy, from the intimate connexion and constant intercourse of the modern nations of Europe, who were derived from a common origin, and were go-

[1] 3 *Rob. Rep.* Appendix A. p. 2.

[2] 4 *Inst.* 153. [Triquet *v.* Bath, 3 Burrows, 1478. Taylor *v.* Best, 14 Common Bench, 487.]

verned by similar institutions, manners, laws, and religion. But it was still in a state of extreme disorder, and its principles were little known and less observed. It consisted of a series of undigested precedents, without order or authority. Grotius has, therefore, been justly considered as the father of the law of nations; and he arose like a splendid luminary, dispelling darkness and confusion, and imparting light and security to the intercourse of nations. [Yet brilliant as he was, and powerful as has been the light he has cast upon this branch of ethics and jurisprudence, it would be unjust to pass over unnoticed the name of one who fairly deserves to share with him the honour of having founded the school of public law in Europe. The treatise, *De Jure Belli*, by Alberic Gentilis is, it is true, inferior in many respects to the great work of Grotius, whom he preceded by a few years; but it is a remarkable production, not only for the classical learning displayed in it, but for the historical information it conveys, and for the commonsense tone of many of its chapters. That his labours were of real practical value to others is clear from Grotius's own acknowledgment, as well as from the similarity of arrangement in the two works[1].] It is said by Barbeyrac[2], that Lord Bacon's works first suggested to Grotius the idea of reducing the law of nations to the certainty and precision of a regular science. But Grotius has himself explained the reasons which led him to undertake his necessary, and most useful, and immortal work[3]. He found the sentiment universally prevalent, not only among the vulgar, but among men of reputed wisdom and learning, that war was a stranger to all justice, and that no commonwealth could be governed without injustice. The saying of Euphemus in Thucydides he perceived to be in almost every one's mouth, that nothing which was useful was unjust. Many persons, who were friends to justice in private life,

Alberic Gentilis.

Grotius.

[1 Ayala's treatise on the rights of war was the first systematic book on the subject, preceding that of Gentilis by seven years, viz. 1582.]

2 *Pref. to Puff.* sec. 29.

3 *Proleg. De Jur. Bell.*

made no account of it in a whole nation, and did not consider it as applicable to rulers. He perceived a horrible licentiousness and cruelty in war, throughout the Christian world, of which barbarians might be ashamed. When men took up arms, there was no longer any reverence for law either human or divine, and it seemed as if some malignant fury was sent forth into the world with a general license for the commission of all manner of wickedness and crime[1].

The object of Grotius was to correct these false theories and pernicious maxims, by shewing a community of sentiment among the wise and learned of all nations and ages in favour of the natural law of morality. He likewise undertook to shew that justice was of perpetual obligation and essential to the well being of every society, and that the great commonwealth of nations stood in need of law, the observance of faith, and the practice of justice. His object was to digest in one systematic code the principles of public right, and to supply authorities for almost every case in the conduct of nations; thus he had the honour of reducing the law of nations to a system, and of producing a work which has been resorted to as the standard of authority in every succeeding age. The more it is studied, the more will our admiration be excited at the consummate execution of the plan, at the genius and erudition of the author. There was no system of the kind extant that had been produced by the ancient philosophers of Greece or by the primitive Christians; whilst the treatises of some learned moderns on public law were most imperfect, and exceedingly defective in illustrations from history, and in omitting to place their decisions upon the true foundations of equity and justice[2]. Grotius, therefore, went purposely into the details of history and the usages of nations, resorting to the testimony of philosophers, historians, orators, poets, civilians, and divines, be-

[1] *Proleg.* sec. 3 and 28.

[2] *Proleg. of Grot.* sec. 36, 37, 38.

cause they were the materials out of which the science of morality was formed; and when many men, at different times and places, unanimously affirmed the same thing for truth, it ought to be ascribed to some universal cause[1]. His unsparing citation of authorities, in support of what the present age may consider very plain and undisputed truths, has been censured by many persons as detracting from the value of the work. On the other hand, the support that he gave to those truths, by the concurrent testimony of all nations and ages has been justly supposed to contribute to that reverence for the principles of international justice which has since distinguished the European nations[2].

Puffendorf.

Among the disciples of Grotius, Puffendorf has always held the first rank, but his work, largely as it enters into the principles of natural law, is of very little practical value in teaching us what the law of nations is at this day. [Whatever merits it may have as a treatise on moral philosophy, as an exponent of International Law it has few or none, and to the same limbo of forgotten authors may be remitted the works of Wolfius, Burlamaqui, and Rutherforth.] Bynkershoeck's treatise on the law of war has always been received as of great authority on that particular branch of International Law, the subject being ably and copiously discussed. [His learning and power of research, the practical turn of his mind, his exegetical skill and the happy art with which he combined the two schools of law of his day, the philosophical and the positive, long made Bynkershoeck a favourite and trusted

Bynkershoeck.

[1] "Omni in re consensio omnium gentium lex naturæ putanda est." Cic. *Tuscul. Quæst.* Lib. I. cap. 13.

[[2] In the 2nd Vol. of Hallam's *Literature of Europe* (3rd edition, 1847), Part III. ch. 4, sec. 3, the reader will find a most useful and elaborate analysis of Grotius's work, *De Jure Belli et Pacis*. In Lerminier's *Histoire du Droit*, ch. 8, he will see its merits and influence ably criticized. In the 77th Vol. of the *Edinburgh Review* appears a short but vigorous examination of the claims of Grotius to his high fame and reputation, in an excellent article on the Law of Nations, by Nassau William Senior; and in the 4th and 9th chapters of *Ancient Law* Dr Maine has well discussed the doctrines of Grotius, his theory of a Law of Nature, and the use he makes of the Roman Law in establishing it.]

authority, and though it may be that he is too exclusive in his references to the ordinances of his own country, yet this defect is not sufficient to detract from the high reputation he has gained.] The most popular and the most elegant writer on the law of nations is Vattel, whose work is an abbreviated and improved edition of the large and systematic treatise of Wolf. [The great merit of Vattel lies in the easy pleasant style of his book, which has been cited more freely than that of any other public jurist, and is still the statesman's manual and oracle, but he is deficient in philosophical precision; the classification of his work is faulty, the selection of topics far from judicious, and their discussion sometimes tedious and diffuse, nor does he sufficiently support the general doctrines of International Law by historical proofs and precedents; yet Vattel's book will never fail to command notice as an excellent summary of the rules of law that are applicable to most of the great questions raised by the mutual intercourse of states and nations, or to deserve approval for the honesty and high moral tone reflected in its pages.] The summary of the law of nations, by Professor Martens, is a treatise of great practical utility, based as it is upon the information he had gained from history and from the treaty engagements of the great nations of Europe. That his excellent manual on the law of nations is not free from errors and imperfections is undoubtedly true—errors arising partly from the exaggerated importance he attached to treaties, and imperfections caused by the limited scope of his work, yet he deserves the credit of being one of the first, if not the first writer, who had issued a readable work for students on a subject that for a long time had worn a most uninviting dress. Since the age of Grotius, the code of war has been vastly enlarged and improved, and its rights better defined, and its severities greatly mitigated. The rights of maritime capture, the principles of the law of prize, and the duties and privileges of neutrals, have grown into very important titles in the system of national law. We now appeal to more accurate,

Vattel.

Martens.

Modern improvements in the Law of Nations.

more authentic, more precise, and more commanding evidence of the rules of public law, by a reference to the decisions of those tribunals to whom, in every country, the administration of that branch of jurisprudence is specially intrusted. We likewise appeal to the official documents and ordinances of particular states which have professed to reduce into a systematic code, for the direction of their own tribunals and for the information of foreign powers, the law of nations on those points which relate particularly to the rights of commerce and the duties of neutrality. But in the absence of higher and more authoritative sanctions the ordinances of foreign states, the opinions of eminent statesmen, and the writings of distinguished jurists, are regarded as of great consideration on questions not settled by conventional law. In cases where the principal jurists agree, the presumption will be very great in favour of the solidity of their maxims; and no civilized nation, that does not arrogantly set all ordinary law and justice at defiance, will venture to disregard the uniform sense of the established writers on International Law. England and the United States have been equally disposed to acknowledge the authority of the works of jurists writing professedly on public law, the binding force of the general usage and practice of nations, and the still greater respect due to judicial decisions recognising and enforcing the principles of International Law. And as in England the decisions of Kent, Story, and other American judges, and the writings of Kent and Wheaton have received the notice which their learning and skill entitled them to receive, so in America in all foreign negotiations and domestic discussions of questions of national law, the most implicit respect has been paid to the practice of Europe and the opinions of her most distinguished civilians. In England, the report made in 1753 to the king, in answer to the Prussian memorial, is very satisfactory evidence of the obedience shewn to the great standing authorities on the law of nations. And in a case which came before Lord Mansfield in 1764, in the King's

Bench[1], he referred to a decision of Lord Talbot, who had declared that the law of nations was to be collected from the practice of different nations and the authority of writers; and who had argued from such authorities as Grotius, Barbeyrac, Bynkershoeck, Wiquefort, &c. in a case where British authority was silent. The most celebrated collections and codes of maritime law, such as the *Consolato del Mare,* the Röles of Oleron, the laws of the Hanseatic league, and, above all, the marine ordinances of Lewis XIV., are also referred to, as containing the most authentic evidence of the immemorial and customary law of Europe.

Importance of the study.

[That the study of International Jurisprudence has not been neglected since Martens published his *Précis du Droit des Gens,* is attested by the large and increasing number of writers who have devoted their energies to the investigation of the various topics comprised in it. Of these writers the names of many are familiar to the generality of students of International Jurisprudence; their fame is too well established, their works too well known, and the special merits of each too well understood to require criticism or comment here. It is sufficient to mention the names of Schmalz, of Klüber and of Heffter; of De Rayneval, De Hautefeuille, Ortolan, Cauchy, and Cussy; Lampredi, Azuni, and Count Mamiami; of Oke-Manning, Wildman, Reddie, Phillimore, Twiss; and of Kent, Wheaton, and Halleck, to shew that in Germany, France, Italy, England and America the science of International Jurisprudence has not been allowed to stagnate or decay, or that there is any lack of materials for the statesman, the advocate, and the student, to prosecute his enquiries or pursue his studies in this department of law[2].]

[1] Triquet *v.* Bath, 3 Burr. 1478.

[[2] For full information as to the scope and plan of the treatises of most of the authors above-mentioned, the reader is referred to Mr Reddie's work on *Maritime International Law,* and to the 2nd Vol. of *Papers of the Juridical Society;* Professor Katchenowsky's Articles.]

The dignity and importance of this branch of jurisprudence cannot fail to recommend it to the deep attention of the student: and a thorough knowledge of its principles is necessary to lawyers and statesmen, and highly ornamental to every scholar who wishes to be adorned with the accomplishments of various learning. Many questions arise in the course of commercial transactions which require for their solution an accurate acquaintance with the conventional law of Europe and the general doctrines of the prize tribunals. Though we may remain in peace, there is always war raging in some part of the globe, and we have at the present moment[1] neutral rights to exact, and neutral duties to perform, in the course of our American trade. A comprehensive and scientific knowledge of International Law is highly necessary, not only to lawyers practising in our courts, but to every gentleman who is animated by liberal views and a generous ambition to assume stations of high public trust. It would be exceedingly to the discredit of any person who should be called to take a share in the councils of the nation, if he should be found to be deficient in the great leading principles of this law; and no one will venture to assert that elementary learning of the law of nations is not only an essential part of the education of an English lawyer, but is proper to be academically taught. The object, therefore, of some succeeding chapters, will be to discuss all the leading points arising upon the rights and duties of nations in the several relations of peace, of war, and of neutrality[2].

[1] 1864.

[[2] "International Law is gradually gaining ground in Europe. Great and useful discoveries are made in it. Unequal as may be our talents for the great task lying before us, we should never despair of ameliorating and reforming the International Law of Christian communities." Professor Katchenowsky, *Papers of the Juridical Society*, Vol. II. p. 576.]

## CHAPTER II.

### OF THE RIGHTS AND DUTIES OF NATIONS IN A STATE OF INDEPENDENCE, OF INTERVENTION, AND OF RECOGNITION[1].

---

A VIEW of the external rights and duties of nations in peace will lead us to examine the grounds of national independence, the extent of territorial jurisdiction, the rights of embassy and of commercial intercourse.

Equality and Independence of Nations.

In the whole range of the matter discussed in public International Law no proposition has been more explicitly announced or more implicitly accepted than this: that nations are equal in respect to each other, and entitled to claim equal consideration for their rights, whatever their relative dimensions or strength may be, or however they may differ in government, religion, or manners.

Intervention or Interference.

As a necessary consequence of this equality it follows not only that each nation has a right to govern itself as it thinks proper, but that no one nation is entitled to dictate to another a form of government or religion or a course of internal policy; nor is any state entitled to take cognizance or notice of the domestic administration of another

[[1] Vattel, Bk. II. c. 4; Martens' *Précis du Droit des Gens,* Tome I. Liv. iv. c. 1; Klüber, *Droit des Gens,* I. p. ii. c. ii; Schmalz, Livre v. c. iv; Heffter, §§ 27 and 31; Gerard de Rayneval, Tome I. Liv. ii. c. 1; Phillimore, *International Law,* Vol. I. pt. 3; *Wheaton on International Law,* by W. B. Lawrence, Vol. I. pt. 2. cc. 1, 2 and 3.]

state, or of what passes within it between the Government and its own subjects. The Spaniards, as Vattel observes, violated all rule of right when they set up a tribunal of their own to judge the Inca of Peru according to their laws. Had he broken the law of nations in respect to them they would have had a right to punish him, but when they undertook to judge of the merits of his own interior administration and to try and punish him for acts committed in the course of it, they were guilty of the grossest injustice. [Whatever value in other respects the histories of the two great nations of antiquity, Greece and Rome, may have, they possess little or none by way of illustration of International Law; and certainly to no part of International Law does this remark apply so exactly as to the present topic, viz. the equality and independence of nations. Among the Greeks the right of one state to interfere in the internal concerns of another seems never to have been questioned,—whilst the policy of the ancient Romans was to lose no chance of turning the contentions of other nations to their own advantage, by an interference in which the pretence that they were taking part with the oppressed against the oppressor was but a cloak to their real object, viz. conquest and dominion[1]. In this way they dissolved the Achæan league and destroyed the last vestige of Grecian freedom, having, after the defeat of Philip and the conquest of Macedon, made a pretentious proclamation of independence, and a specious gift of liberty franchises and laws to Greece[2], which they seized the earliest opportunity to set at nought.]

But it is unnecessary to ransack ancient history for instances of unwarrantable and flagrant violation of the independence of nations. Abundant examples can be found in the history of our own times. The interference of Russia, Prussia, and Austria in the internal affairs of Poland, first dismembering it of large portions of its territory and then finally overturning its constitution and

[1] Niebuhr's *Lectures*, Vol. II. p. 150, Bohn's edition, 1852.

[2] Livy, Lib. xxxiii. cc. 32, 33.

destroying its existence as an independent power, was an aggravated abuse of national right. There were several cases prior to or contemporary with the most violent periods of the French revolution, which were unjustifiable invasions of the right of independent nations to prescribe their own forms of government and to deal in their discretion with their own domestic concerns. Of these instances two of the most memorable are the invasion of Holland by the Prussian arms in 1787, and of France by the Prussian arms in 1792, whilst the wars that were fomented or declared against all monarchical forms of government by the French rulers during the earlier stages of the revolution, and the inflammatory language of their decrees, [at once attest the intemperate nature of that revolution and the contempt of republican France for the soundest principles of International Law]. [Nor were these evil examples confined to the turbulent times of revolution or to democratic governments. Indeed, so numerous have been the instances of intervention and interference among the great European nations on various pretexts, that we shall be justified not only in enumerating the principal interventions that have taken place between the year 1818 and the present time, but in examining somewhat closely the subject of intervention or interference and interposition. And here it is well to bear in mind the distinct meaning of these expressions, for much of the vagueness and confusion that have been imported into discussions connected with this subject may be traced to the want of precision in its terminology. By Intervention then, or Interference, for the terms are synonymous in the limited signification we are about to give them, is meant an actual forcible interference (whether by arms or by a hostile attitude only short of armed force) in the internal affairs of another state[1]; and by Interposition, which, as we shall shew by and by, is not Intervention so much as war, is meant the taking part by one state in a quarrel between two portions of another state or between two other states,

Distinction between Intervention or Interference and Interposition.

[1] Speech of Earl Russell at Blairgowrie, see *Times*, Sept. 28, 1863.

whether by or without invitation, and of each of these two operations we shall have instances in the following narrative.

Congress of Aix-la-Chapelle.

We begin with the year 1818, because that year saw at Aix-la-Chapelle the foundation of an overpowering alliance between the five great European States, constituting, as Mr Wheaton observes, a sort of superintending authority over the international affairs of Europe, and established with the intention of introducing a perpetual system of intervention. "The close alliance of the monarchs who became parties to the political system established in 1815," says the declaration of the five powers, "affords Europe the most sacred pledge of its future tranquillity;" "the sovereigns engage to be observant of the great principles they profess to recognize as the foundation of their compact, in the various conferences which may from time to time be held either between themselves or their respective ministers; whether the conference in question be devoted to a common deliberation upon their own affairs, or whether they concern matters in which other governments shall have formally requested their mediation, the same disposition which is to guide their own deliberations and govern their own diplomatic transactions shall also preside at these conferences, and have for its constant object the general peace and tranquillity of the world[1]."

The events of nearly half a century have put an interpretation on these words, and shew us how far Europe has had cause to rejoice over this sacred pledge of its future tranquillity—how far the deliberations of the great powers have had for their constant object the general peace of Europe, and how many of these powers have waited for the formal request of mediation before venturing to interfere in the affairs of their neighbours. The first fruits of this pacific policy were soon produced. Two years after the Congress of Aix-la-Chapelle, an opportunity was given for testing its principles. On the restoration of

Revolution in Spain, 1820.

[1] *British and Foreign State Papers*, 1818—19, Vol. VI. p. 18; *Annual Register* for 1819, Appendix, p. 135.

the Spanish monarchy, after the fall of Napoleon, a Constitution had been framed by the Cortes and laid before the king. This Constitution he rejected, as one that not merely limited his position, but reduced him to a state of dependence upon the Cortes. Not content, however, with the rejection of the Constitution, and with the dissolution of the body by which it was framed, Ferdinand proceeded to the utmost length of despotism, and reigned for six years with absolute authority, supported by an Inquisition, the Jesuits, and a restricted press. But so unbearable and odious became his tyranny, that various attempts were made to restrain it—attempts that at last, by the aid of an insurrectionary party in the Spanish army, were crowned with a temporary success. The spirit of revolution, which is catching, soon spread to a country that from years of trouble, bad government, and frequent changes, was ripe for revolt. Naples had not long before the period we are speaking of been united to the kingdom of Sicily, but discontented with the Constitution imposed upon them, and eager for a more liberal form of government, the people rose against the crown. A military revolution broke out at Naples, extorting from the king the acceptance of the Spanish Constitution and a united Parliament for Naples and Sicily. Alarmed lest the revolutionary doctrine thus started in Naples should be productive of mischief to Austrian domination, Metternich put in practice the principles announced at Aix-la-Chapelle, and, summoning the five powers to council, a Congress was held first at Troppau[1], and afterwards at Laybach, the result of which was a circular despatch from Austria, Prussia, and Russia, justifying their proceedings on the ground of the existence of a vast conspiracy against all established power and conceded rights in Europe, and announcing their intention to oppose all pretended reforms produced by revolution, and to protect the peace of Europe against the horrors of uni-

Revolution in Naples, 1820.

The despatch of the Three Powers, 1821.

[1] *British and Foreign State Papers*, 1820—21, Vol. VIII. pp. 1128—1205; *Annual Register* for 1820, Part II. Appendix to Chron. pp. 723—746; *Annual Register* for 1821, Chap. XII.

versal anarchy and fanatical innovation[1]. The answer of the British Government to this despatch, dated the 10th of January, 1821, was a strong dissent from the general principles adopted at Troppau and Laybach. It declared the system of measures proposed to be in direct repugnance to the fundamental laws of Great Britain, and the principles on which those measures rested to be such as could not be safely admitted as a system of International Law, leading, if adopted, to more frequent and extensive interference in the internal transactions of states than was reconcileable with the efficient authority and dignity of independent sovereigns; and then were added these emphatic words: "That no government was more prepared than their own, 'to uphold the right of any state or states to interfere where their own security or essential interests were seriously endangered by the internal transactions of another state. That the assumption of the right was only to be justified by the strongest necessity, and to be limited and regulated thereby. That it could not receive a general and indiscriminate application to all revolutionary movements, without reference to their immediate bearing upon some particular state or states; that its exercise was an exception to general principles of the greatest value and importance, and as one that only properly grows out of the circumstances of the special case; and exceptions of this description could never, without the utmost danger, be so far reduced to rule, as to be incorporated into the ordinary diplomacy of states, or into the institutes of the Law of Nations.'"

Answer of Great Britain, Jan. 10, 1821.

The deliberations of the monarchs at Troppau and Laybach were followed by an armed interference in Naples and Piedmont, and the endeavour of the people in the former place to obtain a Constitution at the hands of their king was at once put down by an Austrian army, by whom the revolutionary spirit was rudely quenched. In the meanwhile the movement in Spain, at first confined to the scattered efforts of a few battalions of soldiers,

Intervention in Naples and Piedmont.

Affairs in Spain, 1820–1822.

[1] *British and Foreign State Papers*, Vol. VIII. p. 1128.

became general; and when the royal troops themselves joined the now popular cause, the issue ceased to be doubtful, and the king was compelled to accept the Constitution, summon the Cortes of 1812, and grant other reforms, not the least beneficial of which was the abolition of the Inquisition and of the Monastic orders. But the Church, alarmed and irritated at measures that tended to limit its wealth and influence, resolved upon opposition. An Apostolical Junta was established on the frontiers of Portugal, the peasantry were organized into roving bands of guerillas, and the efforts of the Constitutional party to establish order, and form a strong government, were defeated by the intrigues of Spanish exiles, supported by France. At length matters came to a crisis, a forcible attempt to overthrow the Constitution by some battalions of the royal guards was defeated by the militia of Madrid, and an equally unsuccessful invasion by the troops of the so-called regency, whose head-quarters were at Urgel, near the French frontier, ended in the flight of the regency to France. At this stage of affairs the European powers were again summoned to Verona to debate, and again their fears led them to resort to the sword for the establishment of "the peace and tranquillity of the world," and to put down reform by force of arms. The British government, however, remained true to the principles it had enunciated on the former occasion, and whilst denouncing the assumed right of requiring changes in the internal institutions of independent states, with the menace of hostile attack, pointed out the true object of the alliance of Great Britain with the other powers, viz. the continuance of the order of things established by the Peace of Paris, shewed how vague and unfounded were the fears of a Spanish invasion of France, or of any project to undermine her political institutions, and maintained that so long as the struggles and disturbances of Spain should be confined within the circle of her own territory, they could not be admitted by the British government to afford any plea for foreign interference.

Congress of Verona, 1822.

The resolutions adopted at Verona were carried into effect, and on the retirement of the Cortes with the King of Spain to Seville, and thence to Cadiz, a powerful French army crossed the Spanish frontier, under the command of the Duc D'Angoulême; Cadiz was invested, and after a short siege, fell. Thus, by the help of French arms, the cause of despotism was triumphant, the right of the Spanish nation to select its own form of government was set at nought, and the second armed interference in the internal affairs of a state since the year 1818 again served to illustrate the doctrines of the alliance of Aix-la-Chapelle[1]. Intervention in Spain.

The proceeding that stands next in order of time differs so widely from those just described, that it cannot come within the category of Interventions proper. It is unnecessary to dwell upon the events that led to the armed assistance of Great Britain to Portugal in the year 1826. The cause for the demand of aid was the hostile aggression of Spain, in whose territory large military expeditions were being formed to support the pretensions of Don Miguel to the crown of Portugal, and that not by the connivance merely, but with the direct encouragement of the Spanish authorities. The appearance of British troops in Lisbon therefore was a demonstration in favour of an old and faithful ally, "claiming, in virtue of ancient obligations of alliance and amity between the two crowns, aid against a hostile aggression from a neighbouring state[2],' and whilst the force which landed on Christmas-day in Lisbon, amid the cheers of the people, was not there at the bidding of a Congress of powers from fear of revo- Affairs Portugal, 1822.

[1] For the British documents relating to the Congress of Verona, see *Annual Register* for 1823, Public Documents, pp. 93—151; for M. de Jouffroy's Report to the French Government, and the Circular to the Austrian, Prussian, and Russian Ministers, *British and Foreign State Papers*, 1822—23, Vol. x. pp. 953 and 921; for Vicomte de Chateaubriand's Despatch to Mr Canning, 23 January, 1823, and Mr Canning's reply, *Annuaire Historique* (Leseur), 1823, p. 708, *Annual Register*, 1823, Pub. Doc. 110.

[2] *King's Message to Parliament*, Dec. 1826, *Parliamentary Debates*, New Series, XVI. 335.

lution or reform, "or to rule, or dictate, or prescribe Constitutions, but to defend and preserve the independence of an ally[1]," as soon as its duty was accomplished, and all fear of hostile incursions had vanished, returned at the end of eighteen months without having fired a shot, and having prevented the disturbance of the peace of Europe.

Affairs in Greece.

In the following year the third intervention of the European powers took place. The cause was one that excited the enthusiasm of the civilized world and lent a false lustre to the doctrine of Intervention. The revolutionary movements in Europe which in the year 1820 had roused the fears of Austria, Prussia and Russia, and produced the armed intervention in Spain and Italy, had extended to a country ripe for revolt. For nearly 400 years Greece had had reason (if we are to believe the story of her wrongs) to lament over the evil chance that had doomed her to fall beneath the yoke of Turkey, and to suffer the bigoted sway of Moslem rulers. The Congress of Vienna had raised a hope, destined to be soon overthrown, that feelings of pity for the oppressed might rouse the great powers to extend some sympathy to Greece and procure some relief for her misery, but the time had not yet come for intervening in the affairs of Turkey, or interposing between the Porte and one of its subject dependencies. And, as if to increase in a tenfold degree the bitter feeling arising out of this disappointment, the cession of Parga came like a thunderbolt upon the Greeks, leaving them without hope of external aid and driving them in their despair to insurrection. The story of the six years that ensued between the commencement of the revolt, under the leadership of Ipsilanti and Vladimaruk, in Moldavia and Wallachia in 1821, and the battle of Navarino in 1827, forms a brilliant and romantic chapter in modern history, in which the almost hopeless weakness and the desperate valour of the insurgents are

[1] Speech of Canning, *Parliamentary Debates*, 1826—27, New Series, XVI. 369.

in striking contrast to the overpowering strength and the bloodthirsty vengeance of their opponents. But however inviting it might be to relieve the dryness of a legal treatise with so romantic an episode, it is beyond the limits of this work and beside its purpose to narrate these events. Suffice it to say, that after six years of insurrection, chequered by some wonderful successes and overpowering reverses, in which defeat on land was almost counterbalanced by victory at sea, and when the power of Turkey was, by the superiority of its Egyptian forces, on the point of being established, the cause of Greece was recognized by Europe as worthy of protection, and after a protocol between England and Russia, on the 4th April, 1826[1], a treaty was signed between England, France and Russia in the following year, which brought those powers into direct contact with the Porte, as the allies of the Greeks and the upholders of their resistance. In that document the three powers, first announcing their desire to put an end to the sanguinary struggle that had so long been going on, to the consequent anarchy, and the piracy resulting from the disputed possession of the sea, upon the earnest invitation of the Greeks, declared their object to be the re-establishment of peace, which was called for by the interests of Europe no less than by humanity, proffered their mediation to the Ottoman Porte, and demanded an armistice on certain bases, adding this important article to the treaty, that it would be necessary for them to take immediate measures for forming a connection with the Greeks, and that if the armistice were refused the contracting parties would use all the means which circumstances might suggest in order to obtain the immediate effects desired. To this document the Turkish government replied in an able state paper, dated 9th June, 1827, in which they gave among others the following reasons for rejecting the terms of the treaty. They declared first, that whilst it was

Treaty between England, France, and Russia, 1826.

Reply of the Porte.

[1] *British and Foreign State Papers*, 1826—27, Vol. XIV. pp. 629—639.

an undoubted principle that no state has a right to interfere in the private affairs of another, it is as undoubted that every independent state is entitled to unrestricted power over the regulations it may frame for the government of its subjects. That the Greeks from a very ancient period were tributary subjects of Turkey, and that being in rebellion against their sovereign ruler they were amenable to the consequences thereof, viz. punishment; that the repression of rebellion belongs as of course to the sovereign state; that in this instance the rebellion was confined in its limits to a small part of the Ottoman empire; and that neither armistice nor mediation were terms that could apply to the case of a rebellion against the sovereign authority, but only to that of a rupture between two independent powers. The consequences of this answer are too well known to need detail. The appearance of the fleet of the allied powers in the Bay of Navarino, the resistance and destruction of the Turkish fleet, the occupation of the Morea by a French force under General Maison, and the eventual independence of Greece, are prominent facts in the history of our own times.

The Revolt in Greece, its distinct features.

The narrative of the Greek rebellion, in all its picturesque detail and brilliant colouring, deserves a leading place in the history of the 19th century, but its peculiar value in a treatise on International Law is derived from the light it throws upon the doctrines of Intervention and Recognition. As however we shall have in other parts of this work to state and examine these subjects and the principles on which they are founded, it is unnecessary now to do more than to point out a few of the leading features of the event just recorded. In the first place, the all-important point for notice is the fact that the contest was one caused by the revolt of subjects against the sovereign state.

Secondly, that, though that contest lasted for nearly seven years, an actual present independence was never achieved.

Thirdly, that the sovereign state, so far from abandoning the struggle for supremacy, had almost restored it; whilst lastly (and this seems to be the chief, nay, only possible ground for forcible intervention when remonstrance failed), that the commerce of neutrals was so seriously endangered by the piracy resulting from the disputed possession of the Levant, and the general anarchy consequent upon the prolonged contest, as to require more vigorous measures of repression than the Porte was master of.

The intervention of the Three Powers.

But the intervention of Great Britain, France and Russia, was based on three grounds. First, in order to comply with the request of one of the parties; secondly, on the ground of humanity, in order to stay the effusion of blood; and, thirdly, in order to put a stop to piracy and anarchy. If the recognition of the Greek insurgents and the intervention in their favour are to be looked upon as precedents, it is fitting that all the facts connected with them should be investigated, all the documents examined, and a careful distinction made between the policy and the legality of what was done. And then, in spite of the vigorous defence of the British minister of the day, it is difficult to withhold our assent from the judgment passed by an able writer of our own time upon the event[1], when he says that "The emancipation of Greece was a high act of policy above and beyond the domain of law. As an act of policy it may have been and was justifiable; but it was not the less a hostile act, which if she had dared Turkey might properly have resented by war[2]."

The year 1830 was fruitful of remarkable events, not the least of which were the great revolutionary outbreaks in the neighbouring countries of France and Belgium. In

[1] *Letters of Historicus*, p. 6.

[2] For the history of the Greek revolution, see Alison's *Continuation of the History of Europe*, Vol. III.; Gordon's and Finlay's *Greek Revolution*. For the documents and State papers, see *British and Foreign State Papers*, 1826—30, Vols. XIV.—XVII.; *Parliamentary Debates*, New Series, Vols. XV. XVIII. XIX. XXII.—XXV.

the former a change of dynasty was one of the consequences of the revolution, and a new king was seated on the throne whose watchword was Non-Intervention[1]. In the latter two remarkable results took place, a startling change in the territorial arrangement made by the treaty of Paris and assented to at the Congress of Vienna, and an armed interposition by the great powers for the purpose, as was alleged, of preserving the peace of Europe. By the treaty of Paris the two neighbouring countries of Flanders and Holland had been united under one crown on a foundation in appearance firm and lasting, in reality slight and ephemeral. Whatever other causes might have been at work to produce the separation between the two portions of these united states, there can be no doubt that the immediate impulse to the outbreak was given by the recent revolution in Paris, and by the existence of a strong French party in Brussels[2]; when, therefore, on the 25th Aug. 1830, a slight and apparently temporary disturbance was excited and the cry of Reform was raised, what at first seemed to be nothing more than a short and insignificant émeute grew into alarming proportions, and the little wave of riot swelled into an overflowing torrent of revolution, sweeping through most of the towns of Flanders and carrying all before it.

Affairs in Belgium, 1830.

The revolt ere long assumed a national aspect, and soon the cry was changed from reform into separation. Then followed the visit of the Prince of Orange to Brussels to treat with the revolutionary party; the visit of a deputation of Belgians with a long list of grievances to the king; the attempt on the king's part at conciliation, which was at once rejected; the appeal to arms and the entry of Prince Frederick into Brussels at the head of 9000 men, who were forced to retreat from that city and take refuge in Antwerp; the establishment of a provisional government, by whom the dethronement of Frederick William and the separation of Belgium from Holland were

[1] Louis Blanc, *Hist. de dix Ans*, Vol. II. p. 146.

[2] Louis Blanc, *Hist. de dix Ans*, Vol. II. p. 91.

pronounced; and finally, after the surrender of all the fortresses save the citadel of Antwerp, which the Dutch still retained, the determination of the five great European powers (to whom both parties had appealed) to attempt a settlement of these troubles by a conference of ambassadors.

On the 5th October, 1830, the king of Holland formally requested the assistance of Great Britain and the other four powers parties to the treaty of Vienna, in carrying out the principles they had therein established[1]. The reply of Lord Aberdeen was a refusal to interfere by force of arms, but an announcement that a conference would be held in London for the purpose of remedying the derangement caused by the troubles in Belgium to the system established by the treaties of 1814 and 1815. Accordingly the conference was summoned, and after several preliminary meetings a protocol[2] was published in which the five powers declared their intentions as follows: "In forming by the treaties in question the union of Belgium and Holland, the powers who signed these treaties had in view the establishment of a just equilibrium in Europe, and the assurance of the maintenance of general peace. Unhappily the events of the last four months have shewn that the full and complete amalgamation which the powers desired to produce in those countries had not been obtained, that it would henceforth be impossible to effectuate that purpose, that thus the very object of the union of Belgium and Holland was destroyed, and that henceforth it becomes indispensable to recur to other arrangements in order to accomplish the intention, the means of executing which this union ought to serve. The conference will be occupied with discussing and concerting such new arrangements as may be most proper for combining the future independence of Belgium with treaty stipulations, with the interests and security of

Protocol, 20th Dec. 1830.

[1] *British and Foreign State Papers*, 1830—31, Vol. XIX. p. 749, &c.

[2] 20 Dec. 1830. *British and Foreign State Papers*, 1830—31, Vol. XIX. p. 749.

other powers, and with the preservation of European equilibrium."

Holland and Belgium. London Conference.

To this act, which a modern writer[1] has denounced as a deliberate rending in pieces by the five powers of the work they had so carefully put together in 1814, and a barefaced spoliation under cover of the high-sounding phrases equilibrium and general peace, the king of Holland gave a most reluctant assent; nor was the adhesion of the Belgian provisional government to its terms so cheerfully yielded as it would have been had all reference to treaty-obligations been omitted[2]. Armed, however, with this mutual consent the conference proceeded with its deliberations, and after communicating to both the rival parties the bases of the intended separation, (which both accepted,) on the 19th February, 1831, published another protocol in which, first enunciating the great principle of public law which underlies all such acts as these, viz. "*that treaties do not lose their power whatever be the changes which may be effected in the internal organization of nations*[3]," the plenipotentiaries discussed most carefully the situation of affairs at the time when the settlement of Belgium was made, and the principles and motives which were borne in mind by and influenced the five powers in their protocol of Dec. 20th, 1830[4]; in fact, this important document was an elaborate excuse for the interference of the great powers. The next step was the treaty of the 15th November, 1831[5], between Great Britain, Austria, France, Prussia and Russia, and Belgium, relative to the separation of Belgium from Holland, in which it was provided[6] that orders should be transmitted to both parties to evacuate the territories, towns, fortresses, and places which were to change domination, and deliver them to commissioners,

[1] Mons. Louis Blanc.

[2] *British and Foreign State Papers*, 1830—31, Vol. XIX. p. 665.

[3] 19th Protocol. *British and Foreign State Papers*, 1830—31, Vol. XIX. p. 780.

[4] *British and Foreign State Papers*, 1830—31, Vol. XIX. p. 741.

[5] *British and Foreign State Papers*, 1830—31, Vol. XIX. p. 645.

[6] Articles, 24th and 25th.

and that the courts of Great Britain, Austria, France, Prussia and Russia should guarantee to his majesty the king of the Belgians the execution of all the articles of the treaty[1].

Holland and Belgium. London Conference.

Up to this point affairs had gone though somewhat slowly, not unsmoothly, but the prospect of that harmonious settlement which it was thought the treaty might offer was soon in danger, for on the 2nd December complaints were addressed to the London conference by the Belgian government of the hindrance offered by Holland to the free navigation of the Scheldt and Meuse, to the proposed evacuation of territory, and to the free use of existing roads; whilst on their part the Dutch authorities vigorously replied to this remonstrance, and pointed out various difficulties in the way of the working of the treaty, as well as objections to the treaty itself. On the 20th June the plenipotentiaries, who had in the meanwhile received an unexpected and an unwelcome criticism upon the treaty in the shape of a counter project from the Dutch government, dated the 31st January, 1832, found themselves compelled to express their surprise and sincere regret not only at the delay thus caused, but at a project that to them appeared altogether unpracticable; and at length, after long correspondence and patient debate, the endurance of two at least of the five powers failed, and the plenipotentiaries again met in conference[2]; the result was a protocol in which the decision of England and France for the employment of coercive measures for overcoming the resistance of the Dutch government came in conflict with that of Austria, Prussia, and Russia, who, objecting to the use of force for obtaining the carrying out of the treaty, proposed to refer the matter to the court of Berlin. To this proposition, however, Great Britain and France could not agree, being convinced that whatever regret they might have at the non-

English and French Protocol, Oct. 1832.

[1] As to this guarantee clause, see Lord Aberdeen's speech, *Parliamentary Debates*, 1831—32, 3rd Series, Vol. IX. 850.

[2] Oct. 7, 1832.

concurrence of the other powers in effective measures, unless decisive steps were taken their labours would be fruitless[1].

Upon this divergence of opinion, then, in the minds of the counsellors to whom the settlement of this important matter had been referred, the whole complexion of affairs was changed, and England and France stood alone in the resolution to carry into execution "a treaty invested with the sanction of the five courts, the nonfulfilment of which was exposing Europe to increasing and continual dangers." Within three weeks a convention was signed between these two powers, by which the king of the Netherlands was called upon to withdraw all his troops from the territories which ought to form the kingdom of Belgium, on pain, in case of noncompliance, of an embargo on all Netherland vessels in the ports of their respective dominions, a blockade of the coasts of Holland, and the entry of a French corps into Belgium for the purpose of compelling the evacuation of the territory.

Convention between England and France, 1832.

At this stage of proceedings then we may close the narrative of this remarkable fact in the history of Intervention, for the actual display of force, the siege and capture of Antwerp by a French army, and the appearance of an English squadron in the Scheldt, necessarily resulted from the declarations thus publicly announced. We have dwelt at so much length upon this Belgium affair because it is confessedly one of the most important examples of the subject of Interference; one that has been appealed to in later days as an example to be followed, one to which during the whole period of the discussions upon it the most determined opposition was offered, and one as remarkable for the valuable and skilful state documents by which it is illustrated, as for the peculiar features that distinguish it from every other intervention that the last forty years have witnessed. Among those features the following deserve notice.

[1] In the 20th vol. of the *British and Foreign State Papers*, 1831—32, will be found all the diplomatic correspondence relative to the affairs of Belgium.

In the first place, Belgium was a subject-portion of the king of the Netherlands' dominions, not by force of arms or by original acquisition, but by the deliberate counsel and order of the European powers.

Intervention in Belgium—its peculiar features.

Secondly, there existed so complete a dissimilarity in language, habits and religious sentiment between the two people, that soon expressed discontent at the annexation ripened into positive hatred.

Thirdly, The Dutch government early in the contest felt an inability to maintain its authority, and at once requested the aid of the powers who were parties to the treaty of Vienna to repress the rebellion.

Fourthly, both parties agreed to refer their quarrel to the same kind of tribunal as that which had adjudged the annexation in a conference of the great powers, by whom the separation was decreed.

Fifthly, the efforts of the plenipotentiaries to produce a peaceable settlement were impeded by Holland.

Sixthly, armed intervention was not thought of till nearly every effort at friendly mediation had failed; and, lastly, it is clear, that whilst neither of the intervening powers had anything to fear from the existence of a united kingdom of Holland and Belgium, so neither desired any gain nor received any advantage by the erection of two separate and distinct kingdoms. There were but two possible solutions of the difficulty; one was to leave the combatants to themselves, the other to interfere in behalf of one or the other. It is very doubtful whether, all things considered—the inability of Holland to crush the revolt, the unsettled state of Europe at the time, and the peculiar position of Belgium—the first would have been politic, the resort to arms under the circumstances was not an unnatural step; and to the powerful attack which was made upon the English minister, even at this distance of time, Lord Grey's reply seems cogent. "What was to be done? Was a union of two countries to be kept up where the dispositions of both were so uncongenial, and which was originally founded on a vicious principle?

Could the strife for separation be allowed to continue and hazard the peace of Europe, or was Belgium to be united to any other foreign power? I hold the principle of non-interference," said his lordship, "as strongly as I have ever done, but I am not prepared to say there may not be proper exceptions to the rule. In the present case, however, there has been no interference on our part, for the people were left to their own free choice of a government under the sanction of the five great powers[1]."

The three years that followed 1830 were equally distinguished by interventions in other quarters, based on a very different policy to that just discussed, and distinguished, at least one of them, by no such redeeming features as those we have already specified. The interference of Austria in the Legations, and in some of the minor Italian states in the years 1831 and 1832, to put down a determined effort of the inhabitants of Bologna, Modena, Reggio, Ancona, and Parma, to obtain recommended and promised reforms need not be noticed in detail[2]. The deliberations at Laybach, where the independence of the Italian states was handed over to the tender mercies of Austrian superintendence, bore their fruit in this second armed Austrian intervention, and though the pretence wore as usual the desire to support "legitimate authority against the horrors of anarchy," yet the fear of an extension of the revolutionary movement to Lombardy was not less an exciting cause.

Austrian Intervention in Italy, 1831–32.

By an overpowering display of force the revolt in the Italian states was put down, but the spirit of reform was not trampled out. The inhabitants of the Legations and of Parma, it is true, saw that their worst enemy, the Austrian, was ever ready to crush any efforts they might make to alter and improve their form of government, and

[1] Jan. 26, 1832. *Parliamentary Debates*, 3rd Series, Vol. IX. 840 and 862.

[2] Joint note of the five Powers to the Pope, May 21, 1831. *Annuaire Historique*, XIV. 534, 538.

[3] For a full account of the events connected with it, see Alison's *History of Europe*, Vol. IV. ch. 25, and V. ch. 29; *Annual Register*, 1831, and 1832; Louis Blanc, *Hist. de dix Ans*, Vol. III.; and *Edinburgh Review*, Vol. LV.

learnt from their ruler[1] "that the sacrifices they had suffered would remind them that (one at least of) the Powers who guaranteed the integrity and independence of the Holy See would never be indifferent to what was going on among them;" but they also learnt that other powers were not indifferent to their condition; they saw an armed French intervention close upon the heels of the Austrian one[2], "bringing the mission of peace and a guarantee for their interests." They knew that Austria and the Holy See had been informed[3] "that whenever a government calls in the aid of an ally France would insist upon the right of counterchecking that aid and of interfering by force;" and they read the dignified language of the British Government when the British minister was withdrawn from Rome. "Foreign occupation, on which the court of Rome relies, cannot be indefinitely prolonged, nor can auxiliary force suppress the discontent of a whole population; and even if such means were likely to succeed it is not the kind of pacification which the British Government intended to help to bring about[4]."

Turkey and Egypt 1832—33.

Contemporaneous with these events an intervention of another kind was taking place in a country where intervention had just been productive of great disaster. Scarcely had the contest between Turkey and her Greek subjects come to the termination we have recorded when another not less fierce or unfortunate followed. It is unnecessary to recount the origin and progress of the struggle between the Porte and its too powerful subject, Mehemet Ali, the Viceroy of Egypt; suffice it to say that so terrible

[1] Proclamation of the Pope. *British and Foreign State Papers*, 1831—32, Vol. XIX. p. 1428.

[2] French Proclamation at Ancona. *British and Foreign State Papers*, 1831—32, Vol. XIX. p. 1428.

[3] Declaration of the French Minister of Marine. *Annual Register*, for 1832.

[4] *British and Foreign State Papers*, 1832—33, Vol. XX. p. 1367. *Annual Register*, 1831, 1832. Lesur, *Annuaire Historique*, 1832, Ch. VII. *Times*, March 10, 1832. *Parliamentary Debates*, *House of Lords*, March 14, 1832. 3rd Series, Vol. XI.

Turkey and Egypt 1831–32.

was the blow inflicted by his step-son, Ibrahim Pasha, at the battle in the plains of Homs, on the 7th July, 1832, and so fatally decisive the military incidents following the battle, that the Sultan was compelled to apply to England for assistance. That application came at a time when, owing to the late period of the Parliamentary session and to the complicated state of our foreign relations, we were unable to give a favourable answer. Driven therefore back upon his own resources, the Sultan having collected fresh levies tried again the issue with the sword, and with a result as unfavourable as the last; the battle of Konieh ended the war, and ended the Sultan's hope of retrieving his fortunes. Without an army, without resources, and with every prospect of the enemy making his appearance in triumph at Constantinople, there was nothing left but a fresh appeal to foreigners for help. This time the appeal was made to a power that was only too willing to lend its aid, and that had long been looking out for such a chance. General Mouravieff had already made one offer of Russian protection which had been declined, but under the alarming pressure of the defeat at Konieh the Sultan stooped to accept the proffered assistance; and though obliged at first to withdraw his request under the double influence of the indignation of his subjects and the remonstrances of the French Chargé d'Affaires, his fears again drove him to the Russian alliance, and at the very time when peace was about to be concluded and the Egyptian trouble settled, a Russian fleet was moved up towards the Dardanelles, and a powerful Russian force dispatched with officious haste to the Asiatic shores of the Bosphorus. Nor was this all; in return for the intervention so weakly asked and so promptly granted, in return also for an apparent frank and ready withdrawal of troops and ships, the treaty of Unkiar Skelessi was concluded[1]; its object being the protection of the two contracting parties against all attacks, each engaging to give

[1] July 8, 1833. *British and Foreign State Papers*, 1832—33. Vol. xx. p. 1176.

to the other effective aid and assistance, and by a secret article (not communicated to England for more than six months) Turkey stipulating when required to close the Straits of the Dardanelles to all foreign vessels save Russian. Well might England and France express their indignation at such results of intervention, and say, "The treaty appears to produce a change in the relation between Turkey and Russia to which other European states are entitled to object;" and with reason did they declare "that if the Treaty should hereafter lead to the armed interference of Russia in the internal affairs of Turkey they would hold themselves at liberty to act in any manner which circumstances might appear to require[1]." A remonstrance and threat which bore fruit twenty years later.

Intervention in Portugal 1834.

The countries that now claim our notice in this history of Interventions are Portugal and Spain. We have already had occasion to tell of the assistance rendered by Great Britain to the royal cause in the former of these kingdoms, and the reason for such assistance, namely, the attempt of Don Miguel to seat himself upon the throne—its result was, as was then said, to put a stop for the time to that attempt, but not to stamp out the embers of civil war. At the close of the year 1833 the cause of Don Miguel, which had been carried on with sufficient success to be productive of infinite trouble, was on the decline, and the power of the queen was in the ascendant; and though her opponent was in possession of a large extent of country, yet were his resources so weakened and his forces so shattered, that what hopes he once had of victory were almost gone, and the royal arms were so completely triumphant, that in the following year the civil war was brought to a close, and the authority of the queen, Donna Maria, acknowledged throughout Portugal. At the same time Spain had been the scene of troubles greater, because the revolt in favour of the pretender Don Carlos was more widely extended, and because there was

[1] Lesur, *Ann. Hist.* 1833, p. 443.

some shew of right in his claim. "In each of the kingdoms there was an infant queen supporting her cause by favouring popular privileges, with an uncle for her rival, as a representative of more despotic principles of government[1];" towards each sovereign there was a common feeling of favour on the part of Great Britain and France; and as the cause of both was the same there was a natural tendency on both sides to a close intimacy. It was not long then ere a political alliance cemented this mutual inclination, an alliance to which the two great countries we have just mentioned were also parties, and which from the fourfold union thus produced bore the title by which it is so well known, namely, the Quadruple Alliance[2]. In the preamble of that treaty it was declared "that the Queen Regent of Spain and the Regent of Portugal on behalf of their respective sovereigns, being impressed with the conviction that an immediate and vigorous exertion of joint efforts was necessary to put a stop to hostilities and to produce the blessings of internal peace, had come to the determination of uniting their forces in order to compel the Infant Don Carlos of Spain and the Infant Don Miguel of Portugal to withdraw from the Portuguese dominions. In consequence of such agreement they had addressed themselves to the King of Great Britain and Ireland, and the King of France, who being animated with the desire to assist in the establishment of peace in the Peninsula as well as in every other part of Europe (his Britannic Majesty moreover taking into consideration the special obligations arising out of his ancient alliance with Portugal), consented to become parties to the proposed undertaking, and after naming their plenipotentiaries agreed on the articles of the treaty." By the first and second articles both the powers immediately interested entered into engagements for mutual assistance. By the third, his Majesty the King of the United Kingdom of

The Quadruple Alliance.

[1] *Annual Register*, 1834, Vol. LXXVI. p. 392.

[2] April 22, 1834.

Great Britain and Ireland engaged to co-operate by the employment of the naval force in aid of the co-operations to be undertaken by the troops of Spain and Portugal; whilst in the fourth article his Majesty the King of the French engaged, in the event of the co-operation of France being deemed necessary, to do whatever might be settled by consent between himself and his allies.

The result of the moral effect of the Quadruple Alliance, and, what was more important, of the combined forces of the two queens, was the expulsion of both pretenders from Portuguese territory; but whilst in Portugal the revolution was utterly annihilated by the defeat and capitulation of Don Miguel, in Spain the standard of revolt was still raised. Don Carlos having reappeared in Navarre, a demand was made by the ambassadors of Spain and Portugal upon England and France for an extension of the terms of the treaty to Spain; and, on the compliance of those two powers with such demand, an additional engagement was entered into, by which it was arranged: first, that the King of France should undertake such measures as should seem best calculated to prevent the introduction of any kind of help from French territory contiguous to Spain, of men, arms, or munitions of war[1]; and secondly, that Great Britain should furnish all such supplies of arms and munitions of war, in addition to a naval force, as might be claimed by the Queen of Spain. In furtherance of this engagement the British Government not only supplied a large amount of arms and a naval force, but by an order of council suspending the operation of the Foreign Enlistment Act[2], permitted the enrolment of a body of men to take service with the crown of Spain under the command of Colonel, now General Sir De Lacy Evans. In the English House of Commons, a keen discussion was raised upon the policy and legality of these proceedings. Lord Mahon, in moving for a copy of the order in council

Revolution in Spain 1834.

Intervention of Great Britain.

[1] August 18, 1834.

[2] June 10, 1835. *British and Foreign State Papers*, Vol. XXIII. p. 738.

and of the correspondence between the Spanish Government and the Secretary of State for Foreign Affairs, took exception to the armed support thus rendered, to the changed character of the war, from a dispute about succession to a struggle for freedom, and to the atrocious cruelties with which it was marked; and urged that even if an armed assistance was justifiable, it should be direct, and not, as in this case, that of mercenary troops.

Debate on the Intervention in Spain 1835.

Sir Robert Peel, who followed on the same side, after calling in question the policy of such an act as this, which for the first time in the recent history of this country admitted of direct military intervention in the internal affairs of another nation, objected to a statement that had been made by Lord Palmerston in the course of the debate, to the effect that the permanent interests of this country would be promoted by the firm establishment of the Queen of Spain on the throne, characterizing it as a doctrine that might be carried too far, and would open a pretext for one nation interfering in the domestic concerns of another. "The general rule," said Sir Robert, "on which England has hitherto acted is non-intervention, the only admissible exception to it being cases where the necessity is urgent and immediate, affecting, either on account of vicinage or some special circumstances, the safety and vital interests of the State; to interfere on the vague ground that British interests would be promoted by intervention, or the plea that it would be for our advantage to re-establish a particular form of government in a country circumstanced as Spain was, is to destroy altogether the general rule of non-intervention, and to place the independence of every weak power at the mercy of a formidable neighbour."

Lord Palmerston, in defending the policy of the measures adopted, having first shown that this, so far from being a case of interference of foreigners in the internal affairs of Spain (i.e. the sending armies not under the order and disposition of the Spanish Government), was a mere permission to English subjects to enter the service of the Queen of Spain, went on to explain the aim and intention of the Quadruple Alliance, and after pointing out that this interference was founded on a treaty, added these words:—"In the case of a civil war proceeding either from a disputed succession or from a long revolt, no writer on National Law denies that other countries have a right, if they choose to exercise it, to take part with either of the two belligerents. Undoubtedly it is inexpedient to exercise that right except under circumstances of a peculiar nature. The right however is general; if one country exercises it another may. The present measure establishes no new principle and creates no danger as a precedent[1]." Such is the diplomatic and Parliamentary history of this memorable incident in the account of British Interventions—memorable for several reasons. First, because of the strong expression of opinion as to the propriety and policy of an indirect as well as a direct armed interference in the internal affairs of another state by England. Secondly, on account of the clear declaration of what is and ought to be the conduct of England in the matter of intervention, uttered by a statesman of acknowledged power, ability and experience[2]. Thirdly, because of the nice distinction drawn between such a special form of interference as was here adopted and intervention in its usual shape; and lastly, on account of the opinion announced by the English foreign minister as to the general right of a neutral to take part with one or other of the belligerents in a civil war.

Affairs of Turkey and Egypt 1838.

The survey of the political history of Europe in connection with intervention leads us from the West to the "splendour and the havoc of the East," from the petty distractions caused by rebellious princes in Spain and Portugal to grave events in which the issue of peace or war between the two greatest powers of Europe hung in the balance. We have seen the result of the resistance of

[1] *Parliamentary Debates*, 3rd series, Vol. XXVIII. pp. 1133—1163.

[2] Sir R. Peel.

Mehemet Ali to the authority of the Porte, in a successful campaign followed by a peace hastily concluded and fatal to the prestige and political position of Turkey. We are now brought to the year 1838, when the long-suppressed wrath of the Sultan, defying every pacific suggestion of England and France, burst out with irrepressible fury. Nor were the actual situation and future prospect of affairs in Turkey such as to be productive of calm consideration to one of a less fiery temperament than Mahmoud. Blow upon blow had fallen upon him, limiting his territory, crippling his resources, and humbling his pride. When therefore after the loss of Greece and of Algiers, with rebellion in Servia and a Russian protectorate in Wallachia and Moldavia, he learned that his vassal, the Pasha of Egypt, already raised to the dignity of a rival, had refused to pay the usual tribute, he could restrain himself no longer; in spite of the peace of Kutaya[1] by which he was bound, the earnest remonstrance of England and France, and the probability of danger from the fatal advantages given to Russia through the treaty of Unkiar Skelessi, a large Turkish force was massed along the eastern bank of the Euphrates, war was declared on the 8th June, 1839, and a campaign was the result, as disastrous to the Turkish arms as that of 1833. But ere the news of the battle of Manasch, and the base defection of the Turkish fleet at Alexandria, could reach the ears of Mahmoud he was no more. Abdul Medjid succeeded him on the throne, to whom terms of peace were offered by Mehemet Ali.

The London Conference 1839.

In the middle of the deliberations a communication was made, on the part of the five great European powers, that they had resolved to discuss and settle the Eastern question; on the proposition, it is said, of France. At the same time Marshal Soult addressed a note to the courts of the four powers[2], in which he declared that the union of the great powers, which then was as complete as possible, was prepared to use all means within their reach to maintain that essential element of the balance of power, the

[1] 1833. [2] June 17, 1839.

independence of the Ottoman monarchy. In consequence of this determination a conference was established in London; there the five ambassadors met, and from their deliberations it was hoped and believed a friendly and just settlement of the Eastern question would be the result. But an event of the utmost importance for that settlement, and, for a time, of the utmost importance to the peace of Europe, protracted the negotiations, and threatened to break them off altogether. That event was the disagreement between England and France, as to the propriety of taking coercive measures against Mehemet Ali. It would be impossible to detail at the length they deserve the causes of this disagreement; but so early as Jan. 1840[1], at a time when the sittings of the London conference were being held, two most important debates took place in the Chamber of Deputies upon a paragraph in the Royal Speech which alluded to the happy effects of an amicable understanding between France and Great Britain, in arresting the course of hostilities tending to compromise the safety of the Ottoman empire. In those debates very strong opinions were expressed as to the interested motives that led England to oppose the growing power of Mehemet Ali, as to the necessity of not allowing Egypt to be sacrificed to Turkey, and as to the advisability of upholding the Pasha of Egypt; whilst in the course of them Monsieur Thiers, who at that time was not in office, though insisting upon the advantages of a firm alliance between England and France, and the importance of maintaining the integrity of the Ottoman empire, asserted that there was a visible coldness on the part of England towards France, arising from the fact that the latter power was supposed to espouse the cause of Mehemet Ali, and to be willing to give him the whole of Syria, whereas England wished him to have only a part. "If," says Mons. Thiers, "the proposals to curtail the power of Mehemet Ali and divide Syria are persisted in, I

Debates in the French Chamber of Deputies 1840.

[1] *Annual Register*, Vol. LXXXII. p. 161. 1840; Lesur, *Annuaire Historique*, 1840. Ch. I.

shall advise my country not indeed to come to a rupture, but to retire within herself and await the course of events." Shortly afterwards, in consequence of an adverse vote upon another question, the Soult ministry fell, and Mons. Thiers became Minister for Foreign Affairs. In the meanwhile the London conference still held its sittings, but the split that was thus foreshadowed by the Opposition members of the Chamber of Deputies grew wider and wider, till at length that event happened which took both countries by surprise, startled Europe from its dream of peace, and kindled a flame of indignation in France. The Convention of London of the 15th July, 1840, made its appearance without the signature of France. By it, after announcing the resolve of the Sultan and the four powers to unite their efforts, in order to determine Mehemet Ali to conform to the arrangement come to[1], it was declared that in the event of his refusal to accept the arrangement offered, measures should be concerted and taken between all the parties to the Convention to carry it into effect; that force should be used to cut off the communication by sea between Egypt and Syria, and to prevent the transport of troops, horses, arms, and warlike stores of all kinds, and that the naval commanders of the Austrian and British squadrons in the Mediterranean should afford all possible assistance to the subjects of the Sultan. By a separate article (15th July) the conditions on which the arrangement was to be based were stated, and a term of ten days allowed to Mehemet Ali for acceptance.

The Convention of London 15th July, 1840.

It is unnecessary to pursue at any further length the remainder of the narrative, the anger of France on the publication of the Treaty, the refusal of Mehemet Ali to accept its terms, the capture of Sidon by the British squadron, under Sir Robert Stopford, and the bombardment of St Jean d'Acre; and the still greater anger of France on the announcement of this fierce and rapid display of force on the part of England. But as a most

[1] Art. 2.

The Armed Intervention of Great Britain in Egypt.

remarkable event in the history of armed intervention, and as a memorable crisis in the affairs of this century, the Turkish difficulty of 1839 and '40 is worthy of a prominent place in modern history. To the political and diplomatic student it is attractive on account of the able debates, and still more able state documents, with which the policy of the ministries of England and France is illustrated and defended. In the clear and admirably-reasoned note of Lord Palmerston dated the 31st of August, 1840, the early propositions and counter-propositions of France, the actual position of the contending parties, the narration of the correspondence between the courts of England and France, the general aspect of the Eastern question and its bearing upon the politics of Europe, the attitude of Austria, Prussia and Russia, the mistaken policy of France, and the defence of the line adopted by England, are sketched with that vigorous power that belongs only to a master-hand; whilst the reply of Mons. Thiers is, at least, not inferior in the arts that make a state-paper effective, however much Englishmen may condemn its inconsistent tone and somewhat quibbling spirit. Nor were the debates upon the Ottoman question in the French House of Assembly and the English House of Parliament less remarkable for the skill and eloquence with which each of these great statesmen defended his own policy; the advisability of upholding the cause of the Egyptian Pasha on the one hand, on the other the necessity of preserving the integrity and independence of the Ottoman empire. With the political portion of the Eastern question of 1840 a writer on International Law has but slight business: the attraction it has to him consists more in the light it throws upon the important subject of Intervention than in the position it occupies in the history of the foreign policy of England; yet read the story for what purpose one may, it is impossible not to be struck with the perplexing nature of a transaction that, while it led France to maintain two opposite interests, the integrity of Turkey and the integrity of Mehemet Ali, led England to insist upon restoring a rebellious province to the rule of the very power from whom but a few years before it helped to tear away another rebellious province, and brought Russia into the field as the warmest upholder of the integrity of a state it was longing to crush within its iron grasp. Then as to the legality or propriety of the Intervention, at least, on the part of England. In the face of the sentiments expressed by her to the counsellors of Verona, and the doctrine laid down by Lord Liverpool in 1822, that no Government can interfere with another except in cases where its own security is menaced, it might not perhaps be easy to assign a satisfactory, ostensible reason. Nor would it be very easy to apply the test proposed by one of the ablest writers of our own time, even if the test were a correct one, "that in the case of a protracted civil war in which the contending parties are so equally balanced that there is no probability of a speedy issue, or, if there is, the victorious side cannot hope to keep down the vanquished but by severities repugnant to humanity and injurious to the permanent welfare of the country, it is admitted that intervention to make the contest cease and a reconciliation take place on equitable terms of compromise is warrantable[1]." For, in the first place, so far from there being a protracted contest and no prospect of a speedy issue, Turkey was on the point of concluding peace when the five powers interfered; next, the interfering powers were not united in their view of the terms on which the reconciliation was to be based; thirdly, the armed intervention took place because one of the contending parties refused to submit to terms that it thought not equitable; and lastly, except for the dangerous proximity of Russia to Turkey, as far as England was concerned there was no great apprehension of disturbed security. It is difficult too to reconcile the policy that could bear with the atrocious cruelties of Russia towards Poland and the flagitious spoliation of Cracow, and yet intervene by force in favour of Greece and Turkey in the cause

Legality of the Armed Intervention of Great Britain in Egypt.

[1] J. S. Mill, *Fraser's Magazine*, Vol. LX. p. 774.

of humanity and on grounds of justice; yet there are times when theory and doctrine are displaced by what is called the stern logic of facts, and therefore the existence of the Treaty of Unkiar Skelessi, the actual knowledge of Russian intrigues secretly but vigorously at work to secure such a hold upon Turkey as might turn the Dardanelles into a Russian harbour, and the imminent danger to Turkey and consequent imminent prospective gain to Russia from the increasing strength of Ibrahim Pasha, backed as he was by France, might be assigned as cogent reasons for Lord Palmerston's policy of rapid effective action.

British Intervention in Portugal 1847.

In the year 1847 a powerful opposition had succeeded in carrying on hostilities in Portugal with so much success that the Queen was compelled to accept the offer of British mediation, and propose such terms to the rebellious Junta as the representatives of Spain, France, and Great Britain might advise. On the refusal of those terms a British naval force was despatched to Oporto, and, by that means as well as by the help of a Spanish armed contingent, the rebellion was destroyed. The defence of the ministerial policy again fell to Lord Palmerston, and well and eloquently did he contend that, in spite of the dissatisfaction caused by the course pursued, it was justified by the occasion and fortified by the strong claims the Portuguese Government had upon England, its old natural ally[1]. "The object of our interference," said his Lordship, "was a recall of the Parliament, in which the people could state their grievances and restore the battles of political party to the legitimate arena of the Senate. In consequence of these views the intervention was not confined to the forcible termination of the rebellion. The London conference insisted on the formation of a new ministry prepared to concede liberal measures of reform to the country."

Seventeen years have elapsed since this comparatively bloodless and certainly fortunate intervention, and in that

[1] *Parliamentary Debates*, 3rd Series, Vol. XCIII. pp. 1202—1214; Protocol of Conference, 21st May, 1847, *British and Foreign State Papers*, 1846—47, Vol. XXXV. p. 1110.

short period we have witnessed other events of this nature far more bloody and involving far weightier consequences; but we have little more than space for an enumeration.

Austrian Intervention in Italy 1849.

In 1849 Austria, to use the words of a British Minister, "having under the shelter of a treaty with a weak prince advanced her military posts from the banks of the Po to the frontiers of the Papal and Tuscan States, had, with her usual contempt for the sovereign rights of states, interfered by arms to put down the successful attempts of the people of those states to secure the full enjoyment of conceded reforms[1]." In the same year a powerful body of troops was despatched by order of the Republican Government of France to maintain the cause of the Pope against his revolted subjects in Rome[2]. From the instructions to Admiral Cécille, from the correspondence that took place between the Roman triumvirate and M. Lesseps, from the proclamation of General Oudinot, and from the letter of Pio Nono to that General published in the *Annuaire Historique* for 1849, we learn the real meaning, as well as the ostensible purpose of this intervention; and were anything wanted to put that affair in its true light it would be found not only in these words of the author of the *Annuaire Historique*;—"French intervention in Rome was in accordance with the immemorial policy of France in Italy, at Ancona, and at Civita Vecchia; the liberal intervention of a French army having prevented the despotic intervention of an Austrian one[3];" continued (be it noticed) rather in consequence of the danger of leaving the government of the Pope free than of the wishes of the parties directly interested;—but also in the reply of M. Thouvenel in 1861 to the Austrian and Spanish offers of armed assistance in favour of the temporal power of the Pope[4].

French Intervention in Rome.

[1] Hon. R. Abercromby, *British and Foreign State Papers*, 1848—49, Vol. XXXVII. p. 871.

[2] 19th April, 1849.

[3] *Ann. Hist.* 1849, Ch. XIV., and *Annual Register* for 1849, Vol. XCI. p. 299.

[4] *Annuaire des deux Mondes*, 1861, pp. 265—270; Wheaton's *International Law*, edd. 1863. Vol. I. p. 141. Reference should also be made to Prince Metternich's despatch to Lord Palmerston, 23rd July, 1848, and to the despatches of M. Drouyn de Lhuys, 17th and 18th

Austria and Hungary 1849.

Whilst Austria was exhibiting her contempt for her neighbour's rights of sovereignty, carrying out the doctrines of the Holy Alliance and producing counter Intervention on the part of France, she herself, in the year we are now speaking of, was compelled to ask for aid against her own subjects in Hungary from a power which was always ready to render armed help to oppressed monarchs. With the details of the deadly struggle between the Austrian Imperial Government and her Hungarian subjects we have nothing to do, nor with the causes that led to a campaign so disastrous to Austrian arms and so glorious to those of the rebellious state. All that falls to our lot to notice is that, in the month of April 1849, Hungarian independence was proclaimed by a national diet sitting at Debreczin; and after repeated defeats the position of affairs became so menacing for Austria that she, who had arrogated to herself the right of upholding thrones, putting down insurrection, and intervening when she pleased, was compelled to implore the aid of Russia, and obtain an armed interposition between herself and a portion of her own people. The reasons which Russia gave for rendering the assistance asked for, and it may be added the traditional spirit which actuates that power on occasions of this kind, are to be found in a manifesto published by the Czar[1]. "The Emperor," said that document, "is sorry to quit the passive and expectant position hitherto maintained, but still he remains faithful to the spirit of his former declaration, for in granting to every state the right to arrange its own political constitu-

Russian Interposition.

April, 1849, *British and Foreign State Papers*, 1848—49. Vol. XXXVII. pp. 136, 866. During the passing of this work through the press two most important documents have made their appearance, viz. the convention between the governments of France and Italy, dated Sept. 13, 1864, in which by the 2nd article an engagement is made by the former power for the withdrawal of her troops from the Pontifical States; and a despatch addressed by the Italian Minister Plenipotentiary at Paris to the Minister for Foreign affairs at Turin, dated Sept. 15, 1864, in which it is pointedly declared that the convention is the consequence of the principle of non-intervention, the future policy of Italy towards Rome. (*Times* Newspaper, Oct. 28, 1864.)

[1] 8th May, 1849. *Annual Register*, 1849. Vol. XLI. p. 333.

tion according to its own mind, and refraining from interfering with any alterations of their form of government which such states might think proper to make, his Majesty reserves to himself full liberty of action in case the re-action of revolutions near him should tend to endanger his own safety or the political equilibrium on the frontiers of his empire[1]."

Russia and Turkey 1850.

An obscure dispute in 1850 between the Greek and Latin Churches concerning the guardianship of the Holy Places in Palestine led to the interference of Russia in the internal affairs of Turkey, to the armed interposition of England and France in behalf of the latter power, and to a war that ended most disastrously for the reputation, the influence and the material progress of Russia. By a firman published in March 1852 the right to the key of the church of Bethlehem was conceded to the Latins, in deference to the terms of various treaties that had been made in favour of France; in answer to this, M. D'Orzeroff, the Russian ambassador at Constantinople, made a formal declaration of the claim of his country to the protection of the orthodox, that is the members of the Greek church in Turkey, under and by virtue of the treaty of Kainardji[2] (1774), a claim, in fact, of a protectorate over a large number of the subjects of another sovereign, and an interference of the most audacious kind in the internal affairs of another state. Nor was that all; in addition to an advance of troops to

Lord Palmerston on the Hungarian Question.

[1] In an important debate on the Hungarian revolt, in the British House of Commons, Lord Palmerston, after pointedly describing the Hungarians as a nation, and the question at stake as that of an attempt to maintain a separate nationality and a distinct kingdom, said that "the duty of England on such an occasion is not to remain passive spectators of events that in their immediate consequences affected other countries, but in their remote and certain consequences are sure to come back with disastrous effect upon ourselves, but so far as the courtesies of international intercourse may permit us it is our duty, especially when an opinion is asked, to state our opinions, founded on the experience of this country. We are not entitled to interpose in any manner that will commit this country to embark in these hostilities." *Hansard*, 3rd Series, Vol. CVII. p. 807.

[2] The treaty is to be found in the *Annual Register* for 1854, *State Papers*, p. 462.

the Moldavian frontier, in order to give weight to the claim, Prince Menschikoff was sent as Plenipotentiary to Constantinople, charged with a secret treaty, which he strove by violent threats to force upon the Sultan, and which, had it been accepted, would have completely settled the fate ot Turkish independence; but the Porte, warned by the danger that threatened it, and unmoved by the demeanour and language of Prince Menschikoff, was firm in its rejection of the terms proposed by him. The consequence was the departure of that personage from Constantinople, the breaking off of communication between Russia and Turkey; and an armed interference on the part of the former by the occupation of the Danubian Principalities, followed by the treacherous and cruel assault upon the Turkish fleet at Sinope. At this stage two other powers took upon themselves the duty of rescuing Turkey from the iron grasp that was closing upon her, and of interposing in her behalf. On the 29th January, 1854[1], the Emperor of the French addressed an autograph letter to the Emperor of Russia, in which, after reviewing most clearly and most temperately the position of affairs, and pointing out the danger to Europe involved in the course pursued by the Czar, he shewed that the occupation of the two Principalities was an act which had transferred the question from the region of discussion to fact, whilst "the sound of the cannon-shot at Sinope reverberated painfully in the hearts of all those who in England and France respected national dignity." Two days later (31st January, 1854), in answer to a despatch of Count Nesselrode's to Baron Brunnow (dated 16th January), and written for the purpose of explaining and defending the occupation of the Principalities and the attack upon Sinope, Lord Clarendon declared[2] that a duty had been imposed upon her Majesty's Government by Russia. Turkey was the aggrieved and weaker power, a portion of her territory had been forcibly occupied and retained, while

Russia and Turkey, 1853.

[1] *Annual Register*, 1854, Vol. 96, p. 243; Lesur, *Annuaire Historique*, 1854, p. 40.

[2] *Annual Register*, 1854, *State Papers*, p. 502.

military preparations upon a scale of the greatest magnitude were being made by Russia. In defending Turkey from the imminent danger that threatened her Her Majesty's Government upheld that fundamental principle of European policy involved in the maintenance of the Ottoman Empire, that has been repeatedly proclaimed by the great Powers of Europe[1]. On the 12th March, 1854, a treaty of alliance between France, Great Britain, and Turkey was signed in answer to the Turkish demand of assistance; and on the 21st April the terms of the alliance between France and Great Britain were published[2], in which the main objects of the armed assistance thereby agreed to be rendered were declared to be the restoration of Ottoman independence, violated by the occupation of the Principalities, and the maintenance of the European equilibrium, endangered by the attempts of Russia to absorb a part of European Turkey. The events that followed till peace was made belong to the historian, and are out of the domain of International Law.

The Italian movement, 1860.

In the year 1860 Italy, having scarcely recovered from the excitement produced by the Franco-Sardinian campaign of 1858, and the emancipation of Lombardy from the Austrian yoke, which had so long kept down the spirit of Italian freedom, was again disturbed. The oppressive rule of Francis II. in Naples, which was continued in spite of the remonstrance and warning of the English government, attained a point beyond the endurance of his subjects. An insurrection broke out at Palermo in Sicily, and soon spread through the island. The cause of the insurrection received so stirring an accession by the arrival of General Garibaldi with 2000 men from Genoa, that the troops of the King of Naples were worsted in several encounters. Palermo was taken and the Neapolitan general forced to capitulate. On the 26th July, 1860[3], Lord John Russell addressed a despatch to Lord Cowley, the British minister in Paris: it was a reply to M. Thouvenel's request that England and

[1] *Annuaire Historique*, 1854, Appendice, pp. 38—41.

[2] *Annual Register*, 1854, *State Papers*, p. 534.

[3] *Annual Register*, 1860, *Public Documents*, pp. 282—286.

France should conjointly prevent Garibaldi from crossing the Straits, and stated that the British government would not depart from the principle of non-intervention; that if France interfered alone England would merely disapprove and protest against her course, and that it was for the Neapolitans only to say whether they would reject or receive Garibaldi. On the 7th Sept. his lordship again addressed a despatch to Lord Cowley, in which, after discussing and vindicating the past, present and future conduct of England, and the peculiar position of France in Italy, he declared, "that an armed intervention to stop Garibaldi's expedition was objectionable for one special reason, viz. that it would contradict the principle which Great Britain had long professed, of not interfering in the internal concerns of foreign countries." On the 9th Oct. 1860 the insurgents received a new ally in the person of Victor Emmanuel, king of Piedmont: the grounds on which he proposed to intervene by force of arms[1] in the strife between the people of Southern Italy and their ruler were declared (in the manifesto with which he addressed them) to be "his desire to maintain order, and his wish to make the will of the people respected." Whilst the insurrection in the South had attained the proportions just described, movements of an equally violent and, in the end, successful nature had been going on in another part of Italy. The inhabitants of the Papal States, who had risen in insurrection against their ruler had proclaimed Victor Emmanuel their king. An attempt having been made by the Pope to put down the rebellion by means of a body of foreign mercenaries under General Lamoricière, General Fanti, the Piedmontese commander in the Romagna, announced his intention of occupying Umbria and the Marches, "if the Papal troops attempted to repress by force any manifestation of the inhabitants in the national sense." This was followed up by a despatch of Count Cavour to Cardinal Antonelli, dated the 7th Sept. 1860[2],

Intervention of the King of Piedmont.

[1] *Annual Register*, 1860, *Public Documents*, p. 290.

[2] *Annual Register*, 1860, p. 230.

declaring that Sardinia would feel herself justified in invading the Papal States unless the Pope disbanded the mercenaries in his pay; and as the Cardinal's reply was a strong refusal, an armed intervention was made by Sardinia, grounded on the danger that threatened the north of Italy from the events that were passing in the Papal States[1], on the wish of the inhabitants themselves to get rid of a government maintained solely by foreign troops, and on the obligation that Sardinia was under to Italy to direct the national movement, and to Europe to stay anarchy and disorder in Italy. A short campaign resulted in the annexation, by their own desire, of the revolted states to the kingdom of Piedmont and Sardinia. The judgment passed by the British government upon the affair is fully expressed by Earl (then Lord John) Russell[2]. "There are two questions," said his lordship, "involved in this matter. First, whether the people of Italy had a right to demand help from Sardinia in order to throw off the yoke of a government they disliked. Secondly, whether the King of Sardinia was justified in aiding their cause with his arms." These depend on the following motives: that the government of the King of the two Sicilies was so injurious to the welfare and happiness of the inhabitants that its overthrow was a necessary preliminary to any improvement; and that the only chance for the independence of Italy since 1849 was the establishment of a strong and powerful government. Under these influences clearly the best course to be adopted was to leave the choice to the Italians themselves, and as the matter resolved itself into this question: "Have the people of Naples and of the Roman states taken up arms against their government for good reasons?" the answer of her Majesty's government to it was, that the Italian people were the best judges of their own affairs; a view that, after some hesitation and a little by-play with the King of

Reply of Lord J. Russell.

1 Count Cavour's circular despatch, 12th Sept. 1860.

2 Despatch to Sir James Hudson, Oct. 27, 1860; *Annual Register*, 1860, *Public Documents*, p. 294.

Naples, was adopted by France, whose minister, M. Thouvenel, had already discussed[1] in an amicable spirit the four propositions submitted by England for the purpose of carrying out the principle of non-intervention in Italy, and whose despatch[2] of the 8th Feb. had laid down the position that the question at issue between the Pope and the Legations was not a religious but a purely political one[3]. The last case of intervention by force in the internal affairs of a country which we have to notice is that of England, France and Spain in Mexico. The cause of that intervention is stated in the preamble to the convention of the 31st Oct. 1861 between the three powers[4]. It declares that the sovereigns of these countries feeling themselves compelled by the arbitrary and vexatious conduct of the authorities of the Republic of Mexico, have agreed to demand from those authorities more efficacious protection for the persons and properties of their subjects, as well as a fulfilment of the obligations contracted towards their majesties; and then, in order to limit the intervention to the purposes thus specified, it is agreed, in the second article, that the parties to the treaty shall not employ coercive measures for the purpose of acquiring territory[5], or any special advantage, and shall not exercise any influence of a nature to prejudice the right of the nation to choose its own government[6]; and with the view of showing their bona fides in the transaction they were engaging in, the three Powers, by a common note, dated the 30th Nov. 1861, invited the United States to join them in their efforts to

Affair of Mexico, 1861.

1 30th Jan. 1860. See *Ann. des Deux Mondes* for 1860, p. 755.

2 *Ann. des Deux Mondes*, 1860, pp. 739—741.

3 An important conference between Austria, Prussia, and Russia was held at Warsaw, in which the two latter powers refused to give any pledge of material support to Austria in case she were attacked in Venetia. *Annual Register*, 1860, p. 235.

4 See also the despatch of Sir C. Wyke. The Queen's Speech on opening Parliament, Feb. 1, 1862.

5 *Annual Register*, 1861, p. 216.

6 The same intention was strongly proclaimed in the instructions to the Admiral commanding the French Fleet in the Gulf, Feb. 1862.

obtain a redress of their grievances, an invitation which was rejected by the United States[1]. Eventually England and Spain, after sending ships of war and troops to Vera Cruz, and issuing with France a joint proclamation to the Mexicans, withdrew from further co-operation in consequence of the presence of General Almonte with the French army, and the refusal by the French minister, M. de Saligny, to accede to a conference proposed by the Juarez government[2]. Thereupon General Lorencey, who was in command of the French troops, issued a proclamation to the Mexicans[3], calling upon them to join his army in the consolidation of order and the regeneration of the country, and carried on hostilities which, if at first attended with but partial success, resulted at last in the substitution of a government of order for a tyranny as cruel as it was powerless for good, and in the establishment of an imperial throne guaranteed by France and supported by the good wishes of England, who, though she had withdrawn from the expedition when its design was changed, yet did not look with disfavour upon the attempt of France to establish a monarchy through whose agency order and regular government would be for the benefit of Mexico and the advantage of Europe[4].

In this account of Interventions since the year 1818, it will be seen that two very recent and memorable events have been omitted—the so-called intervention of France in Italy in 1854, and the so-called interventions of Austria and Prussia in Schleswig Holstein in the years 1848 and 1863. Of the former of these events it is scarcely necessary to say more than that the alliance of France with Italy and the armed assistance rendered by her in the war that was declared against the Sardinian people by Austria was as far removed from intervention as the alliance of England with the other powers and the armed resistance made by her in 1815, to the invasion of the Netherlands by France; for, as has been already pointed out, if war is declared between two countries, there is nothing illegal in another

France and Italy, 1854.

[1] Mr Seward's reply, 4th Sept. 1861.

[2] Earl Russell's despatch, 22nd May, 1862. *Annual Register*, 1862, p. 215.

[3] 16th April.

[4] Lord Palmerston, *House of Commons Debate*, Feb. 1864.

country hitherto neutral, renouncing its neutrality by joining one side or the other and taking part in the war. But as regards the question of Schleswig Holstein and the hostile attitude of Austria and Prussia towards Denmark, a few words of explanation are required in order to shew that it is only a confusion of terms to call these events Interventions. And first it must be remembered that Denmark was a member of the Germanic Federative Diet and had a vote therein for Holstein, and next that although Schleswig has never been ostensibly a part of the Confederation, much embarrassment has been caused to Denmark on account of Schleswig through its German population and their appeals to the Diet: if too we bear in mind the existence of the difficult and technical question of the succession to the Danish crown so far as Schleswig and Lauenburg were concerned, and the equally difficult question of the policy of retaining a constitution for Schleswig and Holstein which had become unsuited to the changed order of things, it must be admitted that there was no small opening for the claim advanced by the states of the Germanic Confederation to act in the way they have done against Denmark. Mons. Heffter, in his very clear statement of the principles on which International Law as a science is based, in examining the received doctrine as to Intervention, admits as an exception to the rule of non-Intervention the case of Federal ties which, as he says, may afford a sufficient excuse for opposing changes or introducing changes in the administration of one of the Federal states, or for resorting to measures rendered necessary for the purpose of maintaining the Federal ties. Thus the Germanic Diet enjoys the right of Intervention in the affairs of the Confederation so far as relates to all that concerns its institutions and guaranties[1]. But it would be much more simple and correct to look upon an event of the kind above noticed, not as an exception to the rule about non-Intervention, but as a matter of a different kind altogether, as the case viz. of a Sovereign body exercising its authority over a member of the body. And therefore we have not discussed the Schleswig Holstein affair in our history of Interventions[2].

Schleswig Holstein.

Such is the narrative of the most remarkable events in the history of interference or intervention since the year 1818, laid before the reader for the purpose of enabling him to contrast with the declarations of statesmen and the opinions of legists the facts of history, and to obtain, if possible, some definite and rational rule.

[1] Heffter, *Droit des Gens*, § 45, p. 102.

[2] In addition to Dr Twiss's pamphlet on the Schleswig Holstein difficulty of 1848, the reader is referred for full information to a very recent work, *Denmark and Germany since* 1815, by Charles A. Gooch.

In discussing the subject of intervention, it may be examined under three aspects, Historical, Juridical and Moral; but before noticing the two last topics, it will be well to advert to the distinction laid down some few pages back between intervention or interference and interposition, and to remember that while much confusion has arisen from applying the term intervention to a large class of cases that are related to it but by a slender analogy, by confining it to its strict meaning, that of interference in the internal affairs of a state, we shall be able to lay down some general principles, and shall also get rid of many of the so-called justifications for armed interventions, by which writers have endeavoured to account for the existence of intervention as an exception to what they hold to be the only proper rule, viz. non-intervention[1].

Intervention in its Juridical aspect.

In considering the juridical aspect of the subject, first we must bear in mind that sovereignty or independence and non-intervention are closely, almost inseparably, connected; for if a sovereign state is supreme within itself, if, in order to maintain its self-preservation, it may erect fortifications within its territory, levy troops, and maintain naval forces uncontrolled, save by the correspondent rights of other states, and unquestioned, unless its levies and its

[1] Halleck *on International Law*, Chap. IV. § 7, citing Chateaubriand's speech on the Spanish war of 1823, by whom the rule is thus well and correctly laid down, "with reference to the question whether a government of one country has a right to interfere in the affairs of another, those who consider it as depending on civil right are of opinion that no one government has a right to interfere in the affairs of another. I adopt in the abstract these principles: I maintain that no government has a right to interfere in the internal affairs of another government—for if this principle be not admitted, and above all by all people who enjoy a free constitution, no nation could be in security; and every one would constitute himself judge and might say to his neighbour, Your institutions displease me, change them, or I declare war. Modern jurists seeing however that cases might occur in which it is impossible to abstain from intervention without putting the state in danger have introduced an exception"—"No government has a right to interfere in the affairs of another government except in the case where the security and immediate interests of the first government are compromised."

fortifications cause fair grounds for alarm to neighbouring powers; if too it may increase its dominions and power, by acquisition of new territories, by settlement of new countries, by improving its revenues, in short, by all fair and lawful means[1]; if its jurisdiction within its own territories as to controversies, to crimes, and to rights arising therein is exclusive of all control[2], and if no other state can by its law or acts interfere with persons or matters belonging to it[3], then must it be admitted that Intervention by one state in the internal affairs of another is an infraction of conceded rights, an act of high injustice, and a gross breach of law; and therefore we may lay this down as a principle, that non-intervention in the internal affairs of a state is a rule that admits of no exception whatever, so long as that state confines itself, in its acts, to the strict limits of its own territory. But whilst we insist that interference in the internal affairs of a state is never justifiable, never lawful, we purposely restrain it to the case of a state confining its revolutions and its reforms to the limits of its own territory; for when once those limits are transgressed and an overt act is committed, or where, to use Mr Canning's language, "a nation attempts to propagate first her principles, and afterwards her dominion by the sword, or encourages the subjects of another to resist authority, or assists rebellious projects," then it not only stands to reason that a hostile attitude on the part of the state so injured is lawful, but that such hostile attitude, even though carried to the extent of interfering in the internal affairs of the assailant, and making forcible changes in her government, is not an act of intervention, but a justifiable act of war; "for every circumstance which gives a

[1] Wheaton, *Elements*, Part II. Chap. I.

[2] Vattel, Book II. Chap. VII. §§ 84, 85. Story's *Conflict of Laws*, Chap. I. § 8, and case of Schweighauser and Dobree, *Jefferson's Correspondence*, Vol. 3, p. 277.

[3] See a case in the collection of *Arrêts de la Cour de Cassation*, par Sirey, 1849, I. p. 81, to the effect that French tribunals have no jurisdiction over engagements contracted between a Frenchman and a foreign government; and Duke of Brunswick v. King of Hanover, 1 *House of Lords' Cases*, p. 1.

state a just cause of war, gives it at the same time a just cause of intervention[1]."

If, then, we limit the term intervention in the way above described, it will not be difficult to dispose of the so-called exceptions to the rule, and to account for them without calling them justifications for intervention—justifications that have been sought for and investigated with much care by recent writers, to whose pages we must refer our readers[2], contenting ourselves with this remark, that while intervention in the internal affairs of a state is illegal, is immoral, and is unsafe as a mere matter of expediency, when two parts of a state are fairly divided and are at warlike issue within their own territories, or when two neighbouring states are at war, there is nothing unlawful in a neutral state taking part in the quarrel or in the war[3], but then it does so at its own peril; it renounces its neutrality, fairly embarks in hostilities, and its act is not an act of intervention, but a breach of neutrality, an act of war or hostile interposition; and therefore the following conclusions of M. Heffter are as sound in law as they are in logic; that when troubles or changes have happened in any country of such a kind as to menace the existence or interests of neighbouring states, measures of prevention, of precaution, and of friendly negociation only are permissible. That where hostilities have broken out

[1] Marten's *Précis du droit des Gens*, T. I. L. III. Chap. II. § 74, note par M. Ch. Vergé, p. 203, ed. 1858. Vattel, Book II. Chap. I. § 18.

[2] Wheaton, Vol. I. ed. of 1863, by W. B. Lawrence. Phillimore's *Internat. Law*, Vol. I. §§ 390—395. Halleck's *Internat. Law*, Chap. IV. §§ 7—10. Heffter, §§ 44—46.

These justifications, which are given in a collected shape in the passages of Phillimore and Halleck above cited, will on examination be found to be either something very different from interference properly so called, or else to be directly opposed to the doctrine expressed and approved by Chateaubriand "that no government has a right to interfere in the affairs of another government except in the case where the security and immediate interests of the first government are compromised."

[3] See Lord Palmerston's Speech on the Spanish question, *Parliamentary Debates*, 3rd Series, Vol. XXVIII. p. 1163; and Wheaton's *Elements*, ed. 1863, Vol. I. p. 10.

between two states, others have the right to take necessary steps to prevent the derangement of political equilibrium, either by friendly intercession, limiting the object and extent of the war, or by defensive alliances establishing a counterpoise, or by armaments sufficient for the protection of individual interests; and that however blameworthy may be the conduct of any sovereign, so long as it does no injury, nor in any way threatens the rights of other sovereigns, it affords no plea for intervention[1].

Intervention in its moral aspect.

Such is the legal aspect of the subject of intervention, properly so called. We add a word or two on the moral one, not with the intention of discussing at length a matter that would demand a far more extensive examination than can here be afforded, viz. the relation between international law and international morality, in its bearing upon intervention; but in order to cite from a most admirable treatise on this topic[2] a summarized view of the mischievous effect of intervention upon the morale of nations. For even when it produces an apparent good, says Professor Bernard (as by removing a tyrant, substituting a humane for a cruel government, or putting a stop to the effusion of blood), it encourages a proneness to violent measures, that are only justifiable in cases of extreme necessity; destroys national self-respect and self-reliance; and interrupts the natural process by which political institutions are matured through the ripening of political ideas and habits.

Seeing, therefore, how injurious to international morality, and how subversive of international law is the notion, that states have a right to interfere in the internal affairs of other states—remembering the cruel injustice and the misery that have been inflicted by powerful states interfering with, and eventually destroying the in-

[1] Guizot, *Mémoires pour servir à l'histoire de mon temps*, T. IV. pp. 4, 5. Mr Canning's *Despatch*, March 31, 1823. *Annual Register* for that year. *Pub. Doc.* 140*.

[2] By Professor Bernard, *On the Principles of Non-Intervention*, a Lecture delivered at All Souls' College, Oxford.

dependence and national life of their weaker neighbours remembering too how often the peace of Europe has been disturbed by wanton acts of intervention begun under the pretence of warding off some impending or probable danger to themselves, and bearing in mind the two prime maxims of International Law, that states are sovereign and independent, and are also members of a community united by a social tie;—it is not too much to say, in the words of the writer above cited, "That the doctrine of non-intervention (in its strict and proper signification) is a corollary from a cardinal and substantial principle of International Law, and, as such, has a prima facie claim to a place in the system; the burden of proof lying with those who would dislodge it[1];" and to add that no form of civil government which a nation may think fit to prescribe for itself can be admitted to create a case of necessity justifying an interference by force; for a nation, under any form of civil policy which it may choose to adopt, is competent to preserve its faith, and to maintain the relations of peace and amity with other powers.]

Assistance to a revolted State.

It is sometimes a grave question whether and how far one nation has a right to assist the subjects of another who have revolted and implored that assistance. It is said indeed by Vattel[2] [that when a people from good reasons take up arms against an oppressor, aiming at the destruction of their liberties and religion, it is but an act of justice and generosity to assist brave men in the defence of their liberties. And therefore whenever matters are carried so far as to produce civil war, foreign powers may assist that party which appears to them to have justice on their side]; and Vattel cites the case of the Prince of Orange as a justifiable interference because the tyranny of James II. had compelled the English nation to rise in their defence and call for his assistance. [But however deep may be our debt of gratitude to those by whose help and means the Revolution of 1688 was happily accomplished,

[1] Professor Bernard, *Lecture on the Principles of Non-Intervention*, p. 9.
[2] Book II. Chap. IV. § 56.

and however close may be the connection between that event and the assurance of our present liberties, we must not shut our eyes to the fact that the conduct of William, if judged by principles of International Law was, above and beyond its spirit, to be avoided as a precedent, and certainly not to be assigned as a good and substantial example of a rule neither founded on reason nor warranted by precedents—a rule too which if admitted into practice would lead to the utter destruction of the doctrine that forbids any interference by one state in the internal affairs of another. "Indeed," as General Halleck says, "even supposing the two parties from the very commencement of the civil war or revolution are to be treated as independent states, it by no means follows that a foreign power may render assistance to the one whose cause it may deem to be just. This would be constituting such foreign power a judge of the justice of the war, whereas if both parties are to be considered as independent states the war is to be deemed in International Law as just on both sides. Moreover, would the justice or injustice of the war be in itself a sufficient reason for the interference of a foreign power? Certainly not[1]."] But the right of interposition in this class of cases must depend upon special circumstances, cannot be precisely limited, and is of the utmost delicacy in its application. It must be submitted to the guidance of eminent discretion and controlled by principles of justice and sound policy. It would clearly be a violation of every principle of law and of morality to invite subjects to revolt who were under actual obedience however just their complaints, or to endeavour to produce discontents, violence, and rebellion in neighbouring states; and under colour of a generous assistance to consummate projects of ambition and dominion. The most unexceptionable precedents are those in which the interference did not take place until the new states had actually been established and sufficient means and spirit

[1] Halleck's *International Law*, Chap. III. § 20.

had been displayed to excite a confidence in their stability.

Assistance to revolted States.

The assistance that England gave the United Netherlands when they were struggling against Spain, and the assistance that France gave to America during the war of revolution, [are examples of this kind of interposition, differing widely from each other, and for their wisdom and policy depending as much upon the circumstances of each case as upon the position of the interposing parties. In estimating the propriety of the conduct of Elizabeth, we must keep three important facts in mind, first the peculiar dangers which surrounded her and threatened the integrity of the country she governed; secondly, the breach between the Catholic and the Protestant forms of religion, rendered more deadly by the recent massacre of St Bartholomew; and thirdly, the undisguised hostility to England of that power by which the united Netherlands was oppressed. Actual war it is true had not broken out at this time between England and Spain, but the relations between the two countries had long been of such an uncertain nature, and the hatred of the Catholic Powers of Europe was so well known and so intense, that no one could tell when the blow might be struck, or with what combinations England might be threatened; hence it was as necessary as it was politic to support the cause of those whose interests were so closely connected, and whose strength might be so serviceable to England; and though the league concluded with the States provided merely for an armed assistance, and that assistance wore the appearance of help from a neutral to an insurgent province, yet was it in reality a treaty of alliance between two Protestant powers, compelled by the most imminent danger to unite in a common resistance to an overwhelming foe.

But the assistance rendered by France to America[1] is an event of a different complexion, and though the struggle for freedom which was then being waged between the American colonies and the mother-country was one that

[1] Marten's *Nouvelles Causes Célèbres*, T. I. Cause quat$^{e}$. p. 370.

America may justly be proud of, and that England can look back upon without any other regret than that of the injustice that gave rise to it, yet the glory surrounding it must not blind the eyes of even the most loyal American to the fact, that at the time when France was at peace with this country she went beyond simple recognition of the American states, and signed a secret treaty of alliance, offensive and defensive, by which mutual assistance was stipulated for,—a step which when brought to light was followed by the recall of the British Ambassador[1].]

[And this brings us to the subject of Recognition, which is of itself too important and lies too close to the domain of Intervention to be dismissed without a short examination of the principles on which it appears to rest. Recognition.

According to Sir James Mackintosh[2], than whom no one has a better claim to speak with authority on this as on many other branches of International Law, there are two kinds of Recognition. One where the independence of a country is explicitly acknowledged by a state which formerly exercised sovereignty over it, the other where the independence of a revolted state is acknowledged by third parties. The first[3] of these requires no explanation and presents no difficulty, for whilst on the one hand it is simply a renunciation of sovereignty, a surrender of the power, or the claim to govern, on the part of what to neutral states had hitherto been the sovereign state; on the other, it is an introduction to the great society of nations of a new state entitled to the same rights, and

[1] See *Debate on Foreign Enlistment Act*, 1819, *Parliamentary Debates*, 1819, Vol. XL. p. 1256; and Wheaton, *Elements of International Law* (edition 1863, by Lawrence), p. 47. France not only (said Mr Canning) recognised the United States before her territory was free and without giving the mother-country any offer of precedency, but though in amity with us at the moment, mixed up with the act of recognition a treaty of alliance to enable them to achieve their independence. *Speech on the Address on the King's Speech*, Feb. 15, 1822, 5th Vol. of his Speeches, p. 322.

[2] *Speech on Spanish-American States*, 15 June, 1824, Mackintosh's *Works*, Vol. III. p. 440.

[3] Canning's *Speech on the Independence of S. America*, June 15, 1824, *Speeches*, Vol. V. p. 299.

bound by the same objections as each one of themselves, and though separated from, yet now on an equality with the state of which it once formed a dependent portion[1].

Recognition of a revolted State.

The latter, however, may present some difficulty from the fact of its being a recognition established not by the original sovereign state but by neutrals at the expense it may be of that state, and at the risk of incurring its displeasure. Hence it is well to ascertain why its demand and concession are important when that concession may be made, and what is the effect of it when made. Its importance does not need much in the way of statement. Arising as it does out of a conflict between two parts of what was once a united body, the one struggling to throw off, the other to retain, obedience, it frequently happens that the contest is of the fiercest and bitterest nature, prolonged to a period that severely tries the patience and forbearance of those who are watching it, and that consequently the conduct of neutrals is observed with the most jealous eyes, and subjected to the most partial judgment. Hence when the time comes for neutrals to listen to the demand for recognition on the part of the insurgent body claiming its right to be received as an independent sovereign power, it behoves them to consider carefully the claim, and to decide upon it not only as a matter of policy, but as a question of law. For, in the first place, recognition is a direct loss to one side, a direct gain to the other[2]. Next, as Lord Lansdowne has shewed, the question of

[1] Heffter, *Droit des Gens*, § 23. The following are some of the most memorable instances of this kind of Recognition. That of Switzerland by the Germanic Empire at the Peace of Westphalia (Art. VI. of the Treaty of Munster). Comte Garden, *Hist. des Traités de Paix*, Tom. I. p. 249. Of Holland in 1609 by Spain at the Peace of Antwerp; and again by Europe generally at the Peace of Westphalia. Comte Garden, *in loc. cit.* Of Portugal by Spain in the Treaty of Lisbon, 1662. Comte Garden, Tom. II. p. 60; for more recent ones see Phillimore's *International Law*, Vol. 2, ch. IV. pp. 21–24; and De Marten's *Droit des Gens*, § 66.

[2] *Parliamentary Debates*, New Series, Vol. X. p. 983. See also the letter of Historicus on Recognition, *Letter* III. p. 25, whose letters on this subject and on that of Intervention cannot be too strongly recommended to the student of International Law.

recognition involves a matter of right, and not one of policy merely; and lastly, the legal as well as the political consequences, the international as well as the national gains, are as important as they are extensive[1]. The question of recognition, therefore, being so important to all parties, to the parent state, to its revolted members and to foreign powers, it becomes a very grave matter to consider what is the proper time for conceding it,—for by whom it is to be conceded is free from any doubt whatever[2], viz. "by the sovereign legislative or executive power of foreign states only, not by any subordinate authority or by the private judgment of their individual subjects[3]; whilst equally free from doubt are the propositions that recognition may be refused while the contest is being carried on between the two parties and the issue is doubtful; that such refusal is entirely conformable to law and consistent with good faith[4]; and that until such recognition of independence takes place courts of justice and private individuals are bound to consider the ancient state of things as remaining unaltered[5].

Recognition of a revolted state.

The question of time, then, is all-important, and here, fortunately, we have an excellent precedent for our guidance. Some fifty years ago a portion of the ancient colonial

Revolt of the Spanish Colonies, 1820.

[1] The following cases, some of which are noticed briefly in the 2nd Vol. of Phillimore's *International Law*, pp. 25 and 26, will illustrate the importance of Recognition in a purely legal point of view:

City of Berne v. Bank of England, 9 Vesey, 347.

Dolder v. Bank of England, 10 Vesey, 352, and 11 Vesey, 283.

Thompson v. Powles, 2 Simon, 194.

Taylor v. Barclay, 2 Simon, 213.

See also Grisarri v. Clement, 2 Bingham, 432.

Jones v. Garcia del Rio, 1 Turner and Rupel, 297.

And De Wutz v. Hendricks, 2 Bingham, 314.

[2] Wheaton, Vol. I. Part I. Chap. II. p. 47.

[3] Phillimore's *International Law*, Vol. II. p. 25. 14 Howard's *Reports* (American), p. 38. 7 Howard, p. 1. 3 Wheaton's *Reports* (American), p. 324; and see also The Manilla, 1 Edwards, Appendix D.

[4] Phillimore, Vol. II. p. 25. Wheaton's *Elements of International Law*, Ed. 1863. Vol. I. Part I. Chap. II. note 19.

[5] Halleck, *International Law*, Chap. III. § 22. Wheaton, *Elements*, Par I. Chap. 2, § 10.

dependencies of Spain threw off their allegiance to the mother-country, and strove, ultimately with success, to establish themselves as sovereign states. In the course of a strife that lasted for more than fifteen years the commercial interests of this country and of the United States of America were materially affected. Some fruitless attempts were made to induce the British Government formally to recognize the insurgent powers as independent states, and at length a petition was presented to the House of Commons by Sir James Mackintosh, on the 15th June, 1824, praying for the recognition of the Spanish Colonies, and submitting that for the following reasons they had established de facto a separate political existence:—

1st. Because no vestige of Spanish dominion in Columbia, Buenos Ayres and Chili was left.

2nd. Because each State enjoyed its own separate and independent Government, and

3rd. Because the revolution had been in progress fifteen years.

In the masterly speech with which he supported the petition, Sir James insisted most strongly on the fact that all substantial struggle for sovereignty had ceased on the part of Spain, whilst it was conceded on all hands that three important circumstances marked the crisis. First, a long protracted resistance; secondly, an appeal from the mother-country to Europe for mediation; and, thirdly, an abandonment of the struggle on her part, entire in some places and almost entire in others. The opportunity, therefore, was ripe for recognition, and accordingly, in the following year, Mr Canning formally recognized the South American republics by negotiating and signing a treaty of amity, commerce and navigation with them, urging at the same time as reasons that hostilities had practically ceased, that the new States were consolidated, and that there was an absolute bona fide possession of an independence as a separate kingdom in the shape of a Government acknowledged by the people and ready to prove its responsibility. In his sound and vigorous letter on the international doctrine of recognition, a writer, whom we have had occasion to refer to before, in criticizing the case of the Spanish colonies, which he cites as a true case of recognition, says, and his statement may fairly be adopted, "As far as any practical rule can be deduced from historical examples, it seems to be this. When a sovereign state from exhaustion or any other cause has virtually and substantially abandoned the struggle for supremacy, it has no right to complain if a foreign state treat the independence of its former subjects as de facto established, nor can it prolong its sovereignty by a mere paper assertion of right. When, on the other hand, the contest is not absolutely or permanently decided, a recognition of the inchoate independence of the insurgents by a foreign state is a hostile act towards the sovereign state, which the latter is entitled to resent as a breach of neutrality and friendship. The true rule is laid down in the old distich, Rebellion until it has succeeded is treason; when it is successful it becomes independence; and thus the only real test of independence is final success[1]." Such was the policy of the British Government at this crisis, and such the rules laid down and acted upon by it in an emergency so weighty as that of recognizing the claim of a revolted dependency to rank as an independent state. By these rules has it been guided, and to that policy has it adhered in a crisis of far greater moment and involving far more serious consequences to this country. The strife that has been waged during the last four years between the Northern and the Southern States of America, among other matters of a perplexing nature, has brought the subject of recognition into a prominent place. In both Houses of Parliament the question was keenly discussed, and in both common sense prevailed over party-feeling and sentiment, and the determination of the Government not to imperil the neutrality of this country by a premature recognition, received the support and approval of the large majority of the members of both Houses. In the House of Lords Lord Derby, in con-

Historicus on Recognition.

[1] *Letters* by Historicus, p. 9.

tending that the time for recognition had not yet come, took his stand upon the rule applied in the case of the Spanish Colonies, "That recognition cannot be conceded until the war is in point of fact at an end, and no struggle is going on for the restoration of the original dominion[1];" whilst in the House of Commons Mr Roebuck's motion for the immediate recognition of the Southern States met with so strong an opposition, that he himself put an end to it by withdrawing the motion[2].

The conduct of the British Government then, in the great contest now going on in America, being in strict conformity with the doctrines of International Law and with the declarations of neutrality made at the outbreak of hostilities, both in the matter of intervention and of recognition; and the government of France having, with equal regard for its duties as a neutral state, abstained from any attempt at intervention or premature recognition[3], it may be well to see what rules the government of the United States has laid down, and to what extent it has acted upon them in emergencies of the same nature.

American doctrines. Intervention.

As far as the subject of intervention is concerned, the language and conduct of the American Government towards European States have ever been uniform: thus Mr Monroe, in his Seventh Annual Message[4], says, "Our policy in regard to Europe, adopted at an early state of the wars which so long agitated that quarter of the globe, remains the same, not to interfere in the internal concerns of any of its powers, to consider the government de

[1] House of Lords, Feb. 1862. Hansard, 3rd Series, Vol. CLXV. p. 31.

[2] House of Commons, June 30, 1863. Hansard, 3rd Series, Vols. CLXXI. p. 1171, CLXXII. p. 661.

[3] Although very desirous of offering to the belligerents the support and good offices of the maritime powers to obtain an armistice, and to endeavour by mediation to arrest the war, the Emperor of the French, persuaded by the reasoning of the British Foreign Minister, that the end proposed was not attainable, abandoned his intentions. See the text of the French and English despatches in the 2nd Vol. of Wheaton's *Elements*, p. 1009.

[4] *Statesman's Manual*, Vol. I. p. 537.

facto as the legitimate government for us, and to cultivate and preserve friendly relations with it." And thus too we find Mr Fillmore denouncing the expedition of Lopez and his companions to Cuba, and saying, "No individuals have a right to hazard the peace of the country, or to violate its laws upon vague notions of altering or reforming governments in other states; this principle, reasonable in itself and in accordance with public law, is engrafted into the codes of other nations as well as our own[1];" and in strict accordance with these views are the doctrines laid down and maintained by the American Jurists. Thus Mr Wheaton, in his admirable treatise, insists strenuously upon the rigid adherence to the principle of non-intervention, and points to the numerous interferences of the European States before the Congress of Aix-la-Chapelle in the affairs of each other, as cases not to be referred to any fixed and definite principle of International Law, and not furnishing any general rule fit to be observed in other apparently analogous cases[2]. General Halleck too, in his very recent and excellent work on International Law, examining the numerous exceptions to the rule, that no state has a right to interfere in the domestic concerns and internal government of another state, comes to the conclusion that this is the only true rule, the so-called exceptions to it being specious attempts upon its integrity, which ought to be at once rejected as unsubstantial and unjustifiable[3].

[1] *Statesman's Manual*, Vol. III. p. 1935. See also President Jackson's message, 21 Dec. 1836; and President Polk's fourth message, Dec. 1848; and the vigorous language and measures of President Taylor in putting down attempts at armed naval assistance by citizens of the United States to the Germans in the Schleswig-Holstein business of 1848. *Statesman's Manual*, Vol. III. p. 1864.

[2] Wheaton's *Elements*, ed. 1863, by W. Beach Lawrence, Vol. I. pp. 117—139. The reader is also referred to a valuable note by the learned Editor for modern American views upon the subject of interventions, or probable interventions, of England and France in any portion of territory which, according to President Monroe's views, form part of the American continent. Wheaton, Vol. I. Part II. Chap. I. note 53, pp. 144—150.

[3] Halleck, *International Law*, ch. IV. §§ 4—96.

American doctrines. Recognition.

Nor are the American authorities, whether they be the declarations of statesmen, or the well-weighed opinions of Jurists, one whit less decided in their tone with reference to the subject of Recognition. Thus we find Mr Wheaton holding that, until the revolution is consummated,—whilst the civil war lasts,—other states may remain indifferent spectators of the controversy, still continuing to treat the ancient government as sovereign, and the government de facto as a society entitled to the rights of war against its enemy; but until the independence of the new state has been formally acknowledged, courts of justice and private individuals are bound to consider the ancient state of things as remaining unaltered[1]; and General Halleck too is even more explicit in stating the rule by which a neutral nation is to be governed in the event of a revolution in a neighbouring state: "whilst the civil war continues," he says, "or while a colony or province is shaking off the bonds of its former government, a foreign state should either remain a tacit spectator, or, if its relations require diplomatic intercourse with the revolted society, it should treat it as a de facto government only, and not as an independent state. But when the contest is virtually determined, and the revolted province or colony has firmly established its independence, foreign powers, without any just offence to the metropolitan country, may recognize that independence, and enter into full diplomatic and commercial relations with the new state as a separate and distinct sovereignty[2]."

United States and the South American Colonies, 1822.

It was in strict accordance with these principles that the Government of the United States, although at an earlier period than the action of the British Government, after carefully weighing all the circumstances, in the year 1822 resolved to consider the Spanish provinces in South America as legitimate powers, which had attained sufficient solidity and strength to be entitled to the rights

[1] Wheaton, *Elements of International Law*, Vol. I. Part I. Chap. II. § 7 and § 10.

[2] Halleck, *International Law*, Chap. III. § 21.

and privileges belonging to independent states[1]. Nor can it be said that, in the war between Mexico and Texas, when, after a long and at times severe struggle, the latter threw off her dependence upon the former, there was any disregard of the principles enunciated and acted upon in former times by the government. The debates in the two Houses of Assembly, in the United States, on the subject of the Recognition of Texas, are an excellent commentary on the doctrines hitherto maintained. It was not without strong opposition and after many discussions, and an adverse expression of opinion by the then President (Jackson), that Congress came to the determination of recognizing Texas. The subject required and received more than ordinary caution[2].

But if we do admit that in this matter the decision of the American government was not otherwise than justifiable and legal, it is impossible to say the same of its conduct in the Austro-Hungarian war of 1849.

United States and Hungary, 1849.

Those who may wish to read the elaborate and able defence of the executive will find it set out at full length in the 6th volume of Webster's Works (pp. 488—506), and into abler hands it could not have fallen than those of Mr Webster; but the following language of President Taylor on the occasion, especially in the parts italicized, does seem so contrary to the true principles of recognition, and so opposite to the policy displayed by the United States authority on other events of a similar nature, that however vigorous the defender, his position is a difficult one:—"During the conflict between Austria and Hungary

1 President's message, 8th of March, 1822, *Statesman's Manual*, Vol. I. p. 518, and *Act of Congress*, 4th of May, 1822, Chap. LII. *American Statutes at large*, Vol. III. p. 678.

2 The History of the Texan question is so fully explained in the debates in Congress, that the reader is referred to the following volumes of the *Abridgement of the Debates of Congress*, New York, 1860, Vols. XII, XIII, XIV. (see the Index). See Webster's *Works*, Vol. VI. p. 414. With the question of its subsequent annexation we have nothing to do here. Mr Everett says of it, "As a question of public law there never was an extension of territory more naturally or justifiably made." Wheaton's *Elements*, Vol. I. p. 49, ed. 1863, note 19.

*there seemed to be a prospect that the latter might become an independent nation.* However faint that prospect I thought it my duty, *in accordance with the general sentiments of the American people, who deeply sympathized* with the Magyar patriots, to stand prepared, *upon the contingency* of the establishment by her of a permanent government, to be the first to welcome independent Hungary into the family of nations. For this purpose, *I invested an agent* then in Europe *with power* to declare our willingness promptly to recognize her independence in the event of her ability to maintain it[1]."

Is it necessary to criticize a document in which two faults at all events are visible, the delegacy of sovereign powers to an agent, and the victory of sympathy and sentiment over reason and law? What would be thought of an English minister who should direct an agent in the Confederate States, to declare the willingness of England promptly to recognize their independence in the event of their ability to maintain it?

Mode in which Recognition takes place.

Such are the tests which two great nations have tacitly agreed to adopt ere they proceed to recognize the independence of a revolted colony or member of a state, and such the history of the events in which those tests have been applied; it is only necessary to add a few words upon the mode in which that recognition may take place, and upon a topic which is not out of place here, viz. the recognition of belligerent rights in a revolted colony or portion of a state. Sir Robert Phillimore says there are two modes of recognition, the virtual and the formal, the former preceding the latter, and taking place through the acknowledgment of the revolted state's commercial flag, or the appointment of consuls to its ports. This he asserts gives no just cause of offence to the old state, and is in no way inconsistent with the continued observance of neutrality between the contending parties. The latter, the formal, is evidenced by the sending of ambassadors, and

[1] President Taylor's *First Annual Message*, Dec. 1849. *Statesman's Manual*, Vol. III. p. 1835.

the entering into treaties with the new state; but with this distinction, and with this view, it is impossible to agree. If the time has come for recognition upon the tests above specified, and if that recognition is to be one of independence, of the establishment in fact of a new state, it surely cannot matter in what form the recognition is made, whether by entering into treaties of commerce, as in the case of England with the Spanish colonies and the United States with Texas, or by an absolute declaration of independence, as in the case of Greece, or by sending ambassadors and consuls; nor, on the other hand, can it be said that the recognizing a commercial flag, or the sending consuls to a country still in revolt, and whose independence is not achieved, is either consistent with the duties of neutrality or void of offence to the old state; for to grant recognition in any way, virtual or formal, while the issue is at all doubtful or the contest not wholly abandoned, is as decidedly an offence against International Law as to refuse it under such circumstances is no offence at all.

Recognition of Belligerent rights.

What then is the duty of neutral nations in the event of a war between two portions of a state? Are they justified in putting both parties on an equality and conceding belligerent rights to one and the other, or are they bound to treat the contest as a rebellion and the revolted province as rebels? Most certainly they are justified in putting them on an equality, for the recognition of belligerent rights, says Mr Lawrence[1], in a colony or a portion of a state in revolt from or in opposition to the metropolis, is not to be confounded with the acknowledgment of the independence of such province or colony. It has been the constant practice of European nations and of the United States to "look upon belligerency as a fact rather than a principle," holding with Mr Canning, "that a certain degree of force and consistency acquired by a mass of population engaged in war entitled that population to

[1] Wheaton's *Elements*, Vol. I. ed. 1863, p. 40, n. 16, by Mr W. B. Lawrence.

be treated as belligerent[1]." Instances too are numerous from the time when the North American colonies threw off the yoke of England down to the period when at an early period of hostilities between the United States and the Confederate States, it was resolved by the governments of England and France to treat the Southern Confederacy in accordance with acknowledged principles as a belligerent[2]. It need hardly be said that the decision, whether it is right and proper thus to accord the privilege of belligerency, is one that rests with the government of the neutral country only; and that until they concede the fact of belligerent rights to the revolted state, the courts of law cannot recognize its acts or flag[3]].

Treaties not affected by change of government.

Nations are at liberty to use their own resources in such manner, and to apply them to such public purposes, as they may deem best, provided they do not violate the perfect rights of other nations, nor endanger their safety, nor infringe the indispensable duties of humanity. They may contract alliances with particular nations, and grant or withhold particular privileges, in their discretion. By positive engagements of this kind, a new class of rights and duties is created, which forms the conventional law of nations, and constitutes the most diffusive, and, generally, the most important branch of public jurisprudence. And it is well to be understood, even at periods when alterations in the constitutions of governments, and revolutions in states, are taking place, that it is a clear position of the law of nations, that treaties are not affected, nor positive obligations of any kind with other powers, or with creditors, weakened, by any such mutations[4]. A state neither loses any of its rights, nor is discharged from any of its duties, by a change in the form

[1] Mr Secretary Canning in answer to a remonstrance of the Porte, cited by Lord John Russell in the House of Commons, 6 May, 1861, Hansard, 3rd Series, CLXII. p. 1565.

[2] Hansard, Vol. CLXII. p. 1566. *Annual Register*, 1861, p. 114. Wheaton, Vol. I. p. 43, note by Mr W. B. Lawrence.

[3] Nueva Anna, and Liebre. 6 Wheaton's *Reports* (American), p. 193.

[4] Affairs of Belgium, 19th Protocol, *British and Foreign State Papers*, 1830—31, Vol. XVIII. p. 779.

of its civil government. The body-politic is still the same, though it may have a different organ of communication. So, if a state should be divided in respect to territory, its rights and obligations are not impaired, and if they have not been apportioned by special agreement, those rights are to be enjoyed, and those obligations fulfilled, by all the parts in common...[Where therefore a change has taken place in the internal form of the government or in the person of the ruler, as far as its foreign relations are concerned the state is unchanged, all its treaties remain in force, its public debts in full existence, its public domain and property pass into the hands of the new government, and the responsibility of that new government for wrongs inflicted upon the subjects or government of other states exists as fully as that of the old one.

Again, where a state has undergone a change by the loss of a part of its territory and subjects, whether through foreign conquest or internal revolt, its identity is not on that account altered, nor are its rights and duties affected, and therefore its claims and debts, its property, rights, and its treaty obligations exist as fully as they did before.

But in the event of a state being divided into two or more independent sovereignties, the obligations which had accrued to the whole before the division are rateably binding on the different parts; for, as Story says, "the division of an empire creates no forfeiture of previously vested rights of property." And so *e contrario* where several separate states are incorporated into one new sovereignty the rights and obligations that belonged to each before the union are binding upon the new state; but, as General Halleck points out, of course the rule must be modified to suit the nature of the union formed and the characters of the act of incorporation in each particular case[1]].

[1] Grotius, *de Jure B. et P.* l. II. c. 9, §§ 8—10. Vattel, Bk. II. ch. 12, §§ 183—197. Bynk. *Quæst. Jur. Pub.* l. II. ch. 10. Rutherforth, Book II. ch. 10, § 15. Heffter, *Droit International,* §§ 24 and 25. Merlin, *Répertoire,* sub verbo, 'Souveraineté.' Phillimore, *on International Law,* Vol. I. §§ 126 and 137. Wildman, *on International Law,* Vol. I. p. 68.

Jurisdiction over adjoining seas.

The extent of jurisdiction over the adjoining seas, is often a question of difficulty and of dubious right. As far as a nation can conveniently occupy, and that occupancy is acquired by prior possession or treaty, the jurisdiction is exclusive. Navigable rivers which flow through a territory, from their sources to their mouths, including the bays or estuaries formed by their junction with the sea-coast adjoining such territory, and the navigable waters included in bays, and between headlands and arms of the sea, belong to the sovereign of the adjoining territory, as being necessary to the safety of the nation, and to the undisturbed use of the neighbouring shores[1]. The open sea is not capable of being possessed as private property. The free use of the ocean for navigation and fishing is common to all mankind, and the public jurists generally and explicitly deny that the main ocean can ever be appropriated. The subjects of all nations meet there, in time of peace, on a footing of entire equality and independence. [In this spirit the two governments of the United States and Great Britain resisted the attempt of Russia, in 1824, to establish an exclusive jurisdiction over the north-west coast of America from Behring's Straits to the 51st degree of north latitude, and to make the Northern Pacific ocean a mare clausum. It is unnecessary to enter into the controversies or to describe at length the terms in which the settlement

And the open sea.

Controversy between Great Britain and United States with Russia respecting Northern Pacific ocean, 1824.

Halleck, *on International Law,* ch. III. §§ 25—28. Wheaton's *Elements,* ed. 1863, Vol. I. p. 52, note 20, "Further Correspondence between Great Britain and Texas," and p. 53, n. 21, for the case of a claim made by a British subject holding Texan bonds upon the United States. See also in the *Annual Register,* Vol. LXXXVII. p. 305, that part of the President's message, Dec. 3rd, 1844, relating to the obligations incurred by the United States towards the creditors of Texas. Treaty of Peace at Zurich, Nov. 10th, 1859, Arts. 9—17. Samwer, *Récueil de Traités,* T. III. p[ie]. II. pp. 519—522 and 527. The following cases are also deserving of notice. Calvin's case, 7 Coke, p. 27. Kelly *v.* Harrison, 9 Johnstone's *Cases in the Supreme Court,* p. 32 (American). Jackson *v.* Lunn, 3 Johnson, *ib.* p. 121, and Terrett *v.* Taylor, 9 Cranch (American), p. 50.

[1] Grotius, l. II. c. 2, § 12,—c. 3, § 7. Puffendorf, l. IV. c. 5, §§ 3 and 8. Vattel, Book I. ch. 22, § 266. Marten's *Précis du D. d. G.* L. I. ch. 1, § 39. Heffter, §§ 66, 67.

of them was embodied[1], the result was a successful vindication of the freedom of the waters of the Pacific ocean and of the interior seas and creeks thereof for navigation, fishery, and trade purposes, in the shape of two conventions, one between the United States and Russia, dated April, 1824, for the period of ten years from that date, and not renewed; the other between Great Britain and Russia, dated February, 1825, for the same period of time, which eighteen years after its signature was re-established by the Treaty of Commerce of June 11, 1843, between these two countries]. No nation has any right of jurisdiction at sea, except it be over the persons of its own subjects, in its own vessels; and so far territorial jurisdiction may be considered as preserved, for the vessels of a nation are, in many respects, considered as portions of its territory, and persons on board are protected and governed by the law of the country to which the vessel belongs[2]. This jurisdiction is confined to the ship; and no one ship has a right to prohibit the approach of another at sea, or to draw round her a line of territorial jurisdiction, within which no other is at liberty to intrude. Every vessel, in time of peace, has a right to consult its own safety and convenience, and to pursue its own course and business, without being disturbed, provided it has not violated the rights of others[3]. As to narrow seas, and waters approaching the land, there have been many and sharp controversies among the European nations concerning the claim for exclusive dominion.

Jurisdiction in the open sea.

Narrow seas.

[1] They will be found in Wheaton's *Elements*, Vol. I. pp. 208—314, ed. 1863, by W. B. Lawrence, where the text of the two conventions is fully set out. See also *Ann. Reg.*, Vol. LXIV. pp. 576—584, and *British and Foreign State Papers*, 1824, 25, Vol. XII. pp. 38 and 595.

[2] Grotius, l. II. c. 3, §§ 10 and 12. Rutherforth, Book II. ch. 9. Vattel, Book I. ch. 19, § 216. Forbes *v.* Cochrane, 2 Barnwell and Cresswell, 448, in which case slaves who had escaped from a country where slavery was recognized by the laws and had got on board a British ship of war on the high seas were held to have become subject to the English laws only (a ship being for this purpose considered as a floating island). By Holroyd, J. p. 464.

[3] *The Marianna Flora*, 11, Wheaton, pp. 42—43.

The questions arising on this claim are not very clearly defined and settled, and extravagant pretensions are occasionally put forward. The subject abounds in curious and interesting discussions, and, fortunately for the peace of mankind, they are at the present day, matters rather of speculative curiosity than of use.

Controversy as to close and open seas.

Grotius published his *Mare Liberum*, against the Portuguese claim to an exclusive trade to the Indies, through the South Atlantic and Indian Oceans, and shows that the sea was not capable of private dominion. He vindicates the free navigation of the ocean, and the right of commerce between nations, and justly exposes the folly and absurdity of the Portuguese claim. Selden's *Mare Clausum* was intended to be an answer to the doctrine of Grotius; he undertook to prove, by the laws, usages, and opinions of nations, ancient and modern, that the sea was in point of fact, capable of private dominion, and poured a flood of learning over the subject. He fell far short of his great rival in the force and beauty of his argument, but entirely surpassed him in the extent and variety of his citations and researches. Having established the fact, conceded by most nations that the sea was capable of private dominion, he showed by numerous documents and records, that the English nation had always asserted and enjoyed a supremacy over the surrounding or narrow seas, and that this claim had been recognised by all the neighbouring nations. Sir Matthew Hale considered the title of the king to the narrow seas adjoining the coasts of England, to have been abundantly proved by the treatise of Selden, and Butler speaks of it as a work of profound erudition[1]. Bynkershoek has also written a treatise on the same contested subject, in which he concedes to Selden much of his argument, and admits that the sea was susceptible of dominion, though he denies the title of the English, on the ground of a want of uninterrupted possession. He said there was no instance, at that time, in which the sea was subject to any particular

Selden's argument.

[1] Harg. Vol. I. *Law Tracts*, 10.

sovereign, where the surrounding territory did not belong to him[1].

Puffendorf's view.

The claim of dominion to close or narrow seas, is still the theme of discussion and controversy. Puffendorf[2] admits that in a narrow sea the dominion of it may belong to the sovereigns of the adjoining shores. [Vattel[3] urges two reasons why the sea near and along the coast may be the subject of property, first because of the various uses to which it may be applied, such as furnishing fish, shells, pearls, amber, &c., for no one can doubt that the pearl fisheries of Bahrem and Ceylon may be lawfully enjoyed as property; and secondly, because a nation may appropriate to herself those things of which the free and common use would be in the former case prejudicial to her]. Chitty, in his work on *commercial law*[4], has entered into an elaborate vindication of the British title to the four seas, surrounding the British islands, and known by the name of the British seas, and, consequently, to the exclusive right of fishing, and of controlling the navigation of foreigners therein. On the other hand, Sir Wm. Scott, in the case of the *Twee Gebroeders*[5], did not treat the claim of territory to contiguous portions of the sea with so much indulgence. He said, "Strictly speaking the nature of the claim brought forward is against the general inclination of the law, for it is a claim of private and exclusive property where a general or at least a common use is to be presumed.......In the sea, out of the reach of cannon shot, universal use is presumed. In rivers flowing through conterminous states a common use to the different states is presumed. Yet in both of these cases there may, by legal possibility, exist a peculiar property, excluding the universal, or the common use[6].

Vattel's. Chitty's. Sir W. Scott's.

1 *Dissertatio de Dominio Maris.* Bynk. *Opera.* Tom. II. 124.

2 *Droit de la Nat. et des Gens*, liv. II. ch. 5, sec. 5—10.

3 B. I. ch. 23.

4 Vol. I. 88—102.

5 3 *Rob. Adm.* 336, and see R. *v.* Forty-nine casks of Brandy, 3 Haggard, *Admiralty Reports*, p. 290.

6 The ability of the writers and the relative merits of the controversy

But the general presumption certainly bears strongly against such exclusive rights." The claim of Russia to sovereignty over the Pacific ocean north of the 51st degree of latitude, as a close sea, was considered by the American government, in 1822, to be against the rights of other nations[1]. It is difficult to draw any precise or determinate conclusion, amidst the variety of opinions, as to the distance to which a state may lawfully extend its exclusive dominion over the sea adjoining its territories, and beyond those portions of the sea which are embraced by harbours, gulfs, bays, and estuaries, and over which its jurisdiction unquestionably extends[2]. All that can reasonably be asserted is, that the dominion of the sovereign of the shore over the contiguous sea, extends as far as is requisite for his safety, and for some lawful end. A more extended dominion must rest entirely upon force, and maritime supremacy. According to the current of modern authority, the general territorial jurisdiction extends into the sea as far as a cannon shot will reach, and no farther, and this is usually calculated to be a marine league [or three miles, the maxim in which this doctrine is embodied being 'terræ finitur dominium ubi finitur armorum vis']; and the Congress of the United States have recognised this limitation, by authorizing the District Courts to take cognizance of all captures made within a marine league of the American shores[3]. The

Dominion over adjoining seas.

American views as to dominion in adjoining seas.

are briefly discussed by Mr Manning, *Law of Nations*, p. 25, and a summary of the whole argument will be found in a note by Mr Butler. Co.-Littleton, 107 (*a*), n. 6, and 260 (*b*), n. 1. See also De Rayneval, *De la Liberte des Mers*, T. II. pp. 1—108. Hautefeuille, *Droits des Nations Neutres*, T. I. tit. i. ch. 1, sect. 4, § 2, and Pistoye et Duverdy, *Prises Maritimes*, T. I. tit. xi. ch. 1.

[1] Mr Adams' Letter to the Russian Minister, March 30th, 1822. Wheaton's *Elements*, Vol. I. ed. by W. B. Lawrence, 1863, p. 307 and p. 314.

[2] Azuni on the *Maritime Law of Europe*, Vol. I. p. 206. Wheaton's *Elements*, Vol. I. pt. 2, ch. 4, § 6. Marten's *Précis du Droits des Gens*, § 31, ed. 1858, by Vergé, n. p. 138.

[3] Bynk. Q. Pub. J. c. 8. Vattel, b. I. c. 23, sect. 289. Act of Congress, June 5th, 1794, ch. 50. Th. Ortolan, *Règles Internationales*, T. I.

executive authority of that country, in 1793, considered the whole of Delaware bay to be within its territorial jurisdiction; resting its claims upon those authorities which admit that gulfs, channels, and arms of the sea belong to the people with whose lands they are encompassed; and it was intimated that the law of nations would justify the United States in attaching to their coasts an extent into the sea, beyond the reach of cannon shot[1].

Considering the great extent of the line of the American coasts, their writers contend that they have a right to claim, for fiscal and defensive regulations, a liberal extension of maritime jurisdiction; nor would it be unreasonable, as they say, to assume, for domestic purposes connected with their safety and welfare, the control of the waters on their coasts, though included within lines stretching from quite distant headlands; as, for instance, from Cape Ann to Cape Cod, and from Nantucket to Montauck Point, and from that point to the capes of the Delaware, and from the south cape of Florida to the Mississippi. It is certain that their government would be disposed to view with some uneasiness and sensibility, in the case of war between other maritime powers, the use of the waters of their coast, far beyond the reach of cannon shot, as cruising ground for belligerent purposes. In 1793 the government of the United States thought they were entitled, in reason, to as broad a margin of protected navigation, as any nation whatever, though at that time they did not positively insist upon more than the distance of a marine league from the sea shores[2];

liv. II. ch. 8. Massé, *Le Droit Commercial dans des Rapports*, &c., T. I. Hautefeuille, *Droits et Devoirs des Nations Neutres*, Tome I. tit. i. ch. 3, § I. De Cussy, *Phases et Causes*, &c. T. I. liv. I. tit. xl. Klüber, ed. 1861, by Mons. D. Ott, § 131, n (*a*).

[1] Opinion of the Attorney-General concerning the seizure of the ship *Grange*, dated 14th of May, 1793, and the Letter of Secretary of State to the French minister, of 15th of May, 1793. *American State Papers*, 1789-94, Vol. I. pp. 72—76.

[2] Mr Jefferson's Letter to M. Genet, November 8th, 1793. *Jefferson's Memoirs*, Vol. III. p. 302.

and, in 1806, they thought it would not be unreasonable, considering the extent of the United States, the shoalness of their coast, and the natural indication furnished by the well-defined path of the Gulf Stream, to expect an immunity from belligerent warfare, for the space between that limit and the American shore. It ought, at least, to be insisted, they urged, that the extent of the neutral immunity should correspond with the claims maintained by Great Britain around her own territory, and that no belligerent right should be exercised within "the chambers formed by headlands, or any where at sea within the distance of four leagues, or from a right line from one headland to another[1]." In the case of the *Little Belt*, which was cruising many miles from shore between Cape Henry and Cape Hatteras, the government of the United States laid stress on the circumstance that she was "hovering on our coasts;" and it was contended on their part, that they had a right to know the national character of armed ships in such a situation, and that it was a right immediately connected with their tranquillity and peace. It was further observed, that all nations exercise the right, and none with more rigour, or at a greater distance from the coast, than Great Britain, and none on more justifiable grounds than the United States[2]. There can be but little doubt, that the more the United States advance in commerce and naval strength the more will their government be disposed to feel and acknowledge the justice and policy of the British claim to supremacy over the narrow seas adjacent to the British isles, because they will stand in need of similar accommodation and means of security.

Case of the Little Belt.

Case of the Le Louis.

In the case of the *Le Louis*[3], it was declared that

[1] Mr Madison's Letter to Messrs Monroe and Pinckney, dated May 17th, 1806. *American State Papers,* Vol. VI. pp. 236—244.

[2] Mr Monroe's Letter to Mr Foster, October 11th, 1811, and President's Message, November 5th, 1811. The whole correspondence on this subject will be found in the *American State Papers,* Vol. VIII. pp. 104—126.

[3] 2 Dodson's *Adm. Rep.* 245, and Append. (C.) 2 Cranch, 187 (American).

maritime states claim, upon a principle just in itself, and temperately applied, a right of visitation and search within those parts of the ocean adjoining their shore [and in the *Anna*[1] the question as to what was shore being raised, upon a capture alleged to have been made within neutral territory, viz. at the mouth of the Mississippi, where lay a number of small mud islands, forming a kind of portico to the land, Lord Stowell held, that the protection of the territory was to be reckoned from these islands, which were the natural appendages of the coast on which they bordered; which the common courtesy of nations has for their common convenience allowed to be considered as parts of their dominion for fiscal or defensive regulations more immediately affecting their safety and welfare, such, for instance, as their hovering laws, which within certain limited distances subject foreign vessels to examination. Indeed, so far back as the time of James I. (according to Sir Leoline Jenkins[2]) it was found necessary to make provision for the protection of English merchant vessels against the danger of foreign ships of war roving or hovering near enough to the coasts and harbours of Great Britain to annoy or threaten them in their outward and homeward voyages. By a royal declaration, published A. D. 1604, in that reign, and by another in the reign of Charles II. in addition to express prohibitions of such roving or hovering, it was enacted, that captures by foreign cruisers, even of enemies' ships, would be restored by the Court of Admiralty, if made within certain limits known as the King's Chambers, that is, parts of the sea cut off by lines drawn from promontory to promontory, within which spaces this country has ever claimed exclusive jurisdiction. Hence, in 1736, a revenue act, known as the "Hovering Act" (9 Geo. II. c. 35), was passed prohibiting foreign goods to be transhipped within four leagues of the coast without payment of dues. Adopting the same principles, the United States

Case of the Anna.

British hovering Laws.

United States Laws.

[1] 5 Robinson, 385.

[2] *Life of Sir L. J.*, Vol. II. pp. 727, 728, 780. Vattel, Book I. ch. xxiii. § 288, and Chitty's *Commercial Law*, Vol. I. pp. 770—775.

government claims exclusive jurisdiction over Delaware Bay, and other bays and estuaries forming portions of their territory, and has made a similar provision for the safety and protection of their revenue laws[1], the exercise of such jurisdiction being declared to be conformable to the laws and usages of nations[2].

Summary of the rules relating to open and close seas.

In reviewing the doctrines of International Law on the subjects just discussed they may be exhibited in a summary shape.

And first, as regards the open sea, or ocean, there can be no exclusive property acquired, inasmuch as it is an element free to all men, and its use is common.

Next, as regards maritime territory, or that portion of the sea which lies near to and washes the coast. A state may claim exclusive jurisdiction in the ports, harbours, bays, mouths of rivers, and adjacent parts of the sea inclosed by headlands belonging to that state, though at the same time it may, if it please, modify this exclusive right by compact[3].

Right to exclude ships of war.

The distance to which that exclusive claim extends is a marine league from the shore along all the coasts of the state, and such claim embraces the straits and sounds bounded on both sides by the territory of the state, so narrow as to be commanded by cannon shot from both shores; but this exclusive claim over straits is qualified to this extent, that though there may be a right to exclude foreign ships of war, yet where these straits are communications between open seas, their navigation ought to be free: hence the legal objections to the attempts of the three northern powers in 1780, 1800 and in 1809, to close the Baltic, and hence on the discussion respecting the closing of the Dardanelles and the Bosphorus in the year 1840, the two principles of excluding ships of war and admitting merchant vessels were kept distinctly apart,

1 Wheaton's *Elements*, ed. 1863, Vol. I. p. 323.

2 Church *v.* Hubbard, 2 Cranch, 187, *American Reports.*

3 Wheaton's *Elements*, ed. 1863, Vol. I. p. 342. Phillimore, Vol. I. Part III. ch. 6—8.

and forcibly insisted upon in the first article of the convention attached to the Treaty of Paris, and hence the objection urged against the maintenance of the dues claimed by Denmark from foreign vessels navigating the Sound—objections resulting in the total abolition of those dues in the year 1857[1]].

Rights of commerce.

As the aim of international law is the happiness and perfection of the general society of mankind, it enjoins upon every nation the punctual observance of benevolence and good will, as well as of justice, towards its neighbours[2]. This is equally the policy and the duty of nations. They ought to cultivate a free intercourse for commercial purposes, in order to supply each other's wants, and promote each other's prosperity. The variety of climates and productions on the surface of the globe, and the facility of communication, by means of rivers, lakes, and the ocean, invite to a liberal commerce, as agreeable to the law of nature, and extremely conducive to national amity, industry and happiness[3]. The numerous wants of civilized life can only be supplied by mutual exchange between nations of the peculiar productions of each; and who that is familiar with the English classics, has not dwelt with delight on the description of the extent and blessings of English commerce, which Addison has given with such graceful simplicity, and such enchanting elegance, in one of the *Spectator's* visits to the Royal Exchange[4]? But, as every nation has the right, and is disposed to exercise it, of judging for itself, in respect to the policy and extent of its commercial arrangements,

[1] Wheaton, Vol. I. pp. 326—339. See notes 108 and 110 for the portion of the treaty of Paris above referred to, and for the discussions relating to the Sound duties. Halleck, ch. VI. §§ 20 and 21. Phillimore, Vol. III. Appendix, p. 828. *British and Foreign State Papers*, 1840-41, Vol. XXIX. p. 703. The text of the Sound dues convention, 13th July, 1857, will be found in Hertslet's *Collection of Treaties*, Vol. X. p. 745.

[2] Vattel, *Prelim.* sect. 12, 13, B. II. ch. i. sect. 2, 3.

[3] Vattel, B. II. ch. ii. sect. 21. *Manual of Political Economy* by H. Fawcett, ch. vii.

[4] *Spectator*, Vol. I. No. 69.

the general freedom of trade, however reasonably and strongly it may be inculcated in the modern school of political economy, is but an imperfect right, and necessarily subject to such regulations and restrictions as each nation may think proper to prescribe for itself. Every state may monopolize as much as it pleases of its own internal and colonial trade, or grant to other nations, with whom it deals, such distinctions and particular privileges as it may deem conducive to its interest[1]. The celebrated English navigation act of Charles II. contained nothing, said Martens, contrary to the law of nations, notwithstanding it was very embarrassing to other countries. When the United States put an entire stop to their commerce with all the world, in December, 1807, by laying a general embargo on their trade, without distinction as to nation, or limit as to time, no other power complained of it, and the foreign government most affected by it, and against whose interests it was more immediately directed, declared to the government of the United States[2], that, "if the embargo was only to be considered as an innocent municipal regulation affecting none but the United States themselves, no foreign state had any concern with it, and the government of His Majesty (the King of England) did not conceive they had the right or pretension to make any complaint of it, and they had made none."

Restrictions on trade.

No nation has a right, in time of peace, to interfere with, or interrupt, any commerce which is lawful by the law of nations, and carried on between other independent powers, or between different members of the same state.

[1] *Puff.* B. IV. ch. 5. sect. 10. *Vattel,* B. I. ch. viii. sect. 92, 97. Martens' *Precis du Droit des Gens,* par Vergé, ed. 1858, §§ 140 and 142. 1 Chitty *on Commercial Law,* 76—81. Mr Canning's Letters to Mr Gallatin, of September 11th and November 13th, 1826; Mr Gallatin to Mr Canning, of September 22nd and December 28th, 1826; and Mr Clay to Mr Gallatin, November 11th, 1826. *British and Foreign State Papers,* 1826—27, pp. 500—589.

[2] Mr Canning's letter to Mr Pinkney, Sept. 23rd, 1808. *American State Papers, Foreign Relations,* Vol. III. p. 231.

The claim of the Portuguese, in the height of their maritime power in India, to exclude all other European people from commerce with Asia, was contrary to national law, and a just cause of war. Vattel called it a pretension no less iniquitous than chimerical[1]. The attempt of Russia to appropriate to herself an exclusive trade in the North Pacific met with a prompt resistance on the part of this country and of the United States, as we have seen; both governments claiming the free right of commerce, whilst the latter power maintained a right for its citizens to carry on trade with the aboriginal natives on the north-west coast of America, who were not under the territorial jurisdiction of other nations, even in arms and munitions of war[2].

**Treaties of commerce.**

Treaties of commerce, defining and establishing the rights and extent of commercial intercourse, have been found to be of great utility; and they occupy a very important title in the code of national law. They were considered, even two centuries ago, to be so conducive to the public welfare, as to overcome the bigotry of the times; and Lord Coke[3] admitted them to be one of the four kinds of national compacts that might, lawfully, be made with infidels. They have multiplied exceedingly within the last century, for it has been found by experience, that the general liberty of trade, resting solely on principles of common right, benevolence, and sound policy, was too vague and precarious to be consistent with the safety of the extended intercourse and complicated interests of great commercial states. Every nation may enter into such commercial treaties, and grant such special privileges, as it thinks proper; and no nation, to whom the like privileges are not conceded, has a right to take offence, provided those treaties do not affect its perfect rights. A

1 B. II. c. ii. sect. 24.

2 Mr Adams' letter to the Russian Minister, March 30th, 1822. Wheaton's *Elements*, ed. 1863, Vol. I. p. 308, and *British and Foreign State Papers*, 1821–22, p. 458, where the whole correspondence on the subject will be found.

3 4 Inst. 155.

state may enter into a treaty, by which it grants exclusive privileges to one nation, and deprives itself of the liberty to grant similar privileges to any other. Thus, in 1703, by what is well known in the history of this country's progress as the Methuen Treaty, England granted a monopoly against herself to the wines of Portugal, on payment of a lower duty than what she charged upon those of France[1]; and the Dutch formerly by a treaty with Ceylon engrossed the cinnamon trade, having succeeded, at a later period, in obtaining with the Chinese a monopoly of the trade of Japan[2], a monopoly that lasted until the year 1852, when the restrictions upon foreign commerce were removed by American diplomacy. These are matters of strict legal right; but it is, nevertheless, in a moral sense, the duty of every nation to deal kindly, liberally, and impartially towards all mankind, and not to bind itself by treaty with one nation, in contravention of those general duties which the law of nature dictates to be due to the rest of the world. [Nor is it less the duty of every nation to protect and favour the progress of commerce by all means in its power, by the removal of unnecessary restrictions and burdens, the destruction of unfair because partial privileges, and the abolition of vexatious protective taxes; and if the material advantages conferred by free trade are great (as is abundantly proved by recent facts in this country) the moral advantages are equally powerful. For what greater moral gains can nations have than increased intercourse, substituting mutual friendships and peaceful aspirations in place of distrusts, jealousy and

Advantages of free trade.

[1] The treaty will be found in Adam Smith's *Wealth of Nations*, Vol. II. p. 370, and in Hertslet's *Collection of Treaties*, Vol. II. p. 24. It ceased to exist in 1831 by the simple process of equalizing the duties on French and Spanish wines. The injurious effects of the treaty are well told in M'Culloch's *Dictionary of Commerce*, Art. "Wine," p. 1400. See also Vattel, by Pradier Fodéré, T. I. liv. I. ch. vii. p. 278, note 1. ed. 1863.

[2] *New American Encyclopædia*, Art. "Japan," p. 724, and *Encyclop. Brit.* Art. "Japan," p. 698. 1 Chitty *on Commercial Law*, 40, 41, 42. See also Hertslet's *Treaties*, Vol. XI. p. 396, for the Treaty of Peace, Friendship, and Commerce between Great Britain and Japan, signed August 26, 1858.

old hatreds, ever leading to war. These are the blessings that commerce brings with it; blessings all the more numerous and the greater in proportion to the freedom of that commerce. Such were the feelings which animated the framers of the old commercial treaty[1] with France of 1786, and such would have been the result of that treaty had the times been more propitious. Such too are the feelings which have prompted those, by whose efforts the work was commenced and brought to fruition, to cement the union of this country and France by the great commercial treaty of January, 1860[2]; let us hope that the result will be proportioned to the magnitude of the work and the earnest devotion of the workers].

Passage over foreign territory.

Every nation is bound, in time of peace, to grant a passage, for lawful purposes, over their lands, rivers, and seas, to the people of other states, whenever it can be permitted without inconvenience; and burthensome conditions ought not to be annexed to the transit of persons and property. If, however, any government deems the introduction of foreigners, or their merchandize injurious to those interests of their own people which they are bound to protect and promote, they are at liberty to withhold the indulgence. The entry of foreigners and their effects is not an absolute right, but only one of imperfect obligation, and it is subject to the discretion of the government which tolerates it[3]. [And therefore it is not only the right

[1] Speech of Mr Pitt in introducing the treaty. *Parly History of England*, Vol. XXVI. 1786–88, page 392, and Chitty's edition of Vattel's *Law of Nations*, Book II. ch. ii. § 21, note 97.

[2] The text of the treaty will be found in the *Annual Register* for 1860, p. 736, and in Hertslet's *Collection of Treaties*, Vol. XI. p. 165; a *résumé* of the opinions of the press of the two countries respecting its merits is given in the *Annuaire des deux Mondes* for 1860, p. 269, and an analysis of it appears in the *Times* newspaper, January 26th, 1860. On the subject of Commercial Treaties the reader may consult with advantage a note to a recent French edition of Vattel by Mons. Pradier Fodéré, T. I. liv. II. ch. ii. § 28, note 1.

[3] Puff. B. III. ch. iii. sec. 5, 6, 7. Rutherforth, B. II. ch. ix. Vattel, B. II. ch. vii. sec. 94; ch. viii. sec. 100; ch. ix. sec. 123, 130; ch. x. sec. 132. 1 Chitty, *Commercial Law*, 84—89.

Restrictions upon the entry and exit of foreigners.

but may sometimes be the duty of states to establish checks upon the transit and sojourn of foreigners, however harsh those regulations may appear, or opposed to old-established policy. Indeed, in two countries where more freedom of entry and exit, and fewer restrictions are to be met with than elsewhere, within the last few years such regulations have been published. Thus during the revolutionary period of 1848, an act of parliament (11 and 12 Vict. c. 20) was passed in Great Britain on the ground of "providing for the due security of the peace and tranquillity of the country," by which power was given to the executive in England and Ireland to remove aliens from the realm[1], and in the United States it was declared, by an order, dated 19th Aug. 1861, "that no person, if a foreigner, should be allowed to land in the United States without a passport from his own government, countersigned by a minister or consul of the United States[2]"]. The state too may even levy a tax or toll upon the persons and property of strangers *in transitu*, provided the same be a reasonable charge, by way of recompense for the expense which the accommodation creates[3]. These things are now generally settled in commercial treaties, by which it is usually stipulated, that there shall be free navigation and commerce between the nations, and a free entry to persons and property, subject to the ordinary revenue and police laws of the country, and the special terms and conditions prescribed by treaty[4].

A nation possessing only the upper parts of a navigable river, is entitled to descend to the sea without being embarrassed by useless and oppressive duties or regulations. It is doubtless a right of imperfect obligation, but one that cannot justly be withheld without good cause. When

[1] See also the *Alien Registration Act*, 6 and 7 Wm. IV. c. 11.

[2] *London Gazette*, Sep. 10, 1861. This order was afterwards rescinded, *London Gazette*, Feb. 28, 1862; but see the "Times," January 2nd, 1865.

[3] Rutherforth, B. II. ch. ix. Vattel, B. II. ch. x. sec. 134. 1 Chitty, *Comm. Law*, 103—106.

[4] De Cussy, *Phases et Causes Célèbres du Droit Maritime*, Liv. I. Tit. II. p. 55.

Navigation of the Mississippi.

Spain, in the year 1792, owned the mouth and both banks of the lower Mississippi, and the United States the left bank of the upper portion of the same, it was strongly contended on the part of the United States, that by the law of nature and nations they were entitled to the navigation of that river to the sea, subject only to such modifications as Spain might reasonably deem necessary for her safety and fiscal accommodation. It was further contended, that the right to the end carried with it, as an incident, the right of the means requisite to attain the end; such, for instance, as the right to moor vessels to the shore, and to land in cases of necessity. The same clear right of the United States to the free navigation of the Mississippi, through the territories of Spain to the ocean, was asserted by the Congress under the confederation[1]. The claim in that case, with the qualifications annexed to it, was well grounded on the principles and authorities of the law of nations, [and settled in accordance with those principles by the treaty of San Lorenzo el Real, 1795; however, after the acquisition of Louisiana and Florida by the United States the navigation of the Mississippi was vested exclusively in that power by the treaty of Ghent in 1814. But the political history of Europe and the various public treaties that form so large a part of that history at once attest the value of this right of free navigation, and exhibit the steady determination of the European states generally to resist attempts at impeding it. The following principles would seem to be now well established. First, that where a navigable river forms the boundary of conterminous states the middle of the channel is taken as the line of separation of the two states, the right of navigation being presumed to be common to both, though this presumption may be rebutted

General principles as to navigation of great rivers.

[1] Instructions given to Mr Jay in 1780, and again in 1785. Diplomatic Correspondence by Sparks, Vol. VII. p. 300. Resolution of Congress of September, 1788. Report of the Secretary of State to the President, March 18, 1792. The whole controversy from its commencement to its termination will be found in Wheaton's *Elements*, Vol. I. Part II. ch. IV. pp. 352–356, ed. of 1863, by W. B. Lawrence.

or destroyed by actual proof of the exclusive title of one of the riparian proprietors to the entire river[1]. Secondly, that the right of navigating a river which flows through the territory of different states is common to all the nations inhabiting its banks. But this right of innocent passage, as it has been sometimes called, may be modified according to the convenience of the parties affected by it, and must be secured by mutual conventions regulating its mode of exercise[2]. Thirdly, that this right of innocent passage draws with it that of using the banks, but here also the mutual convenience of the parties affected by it must be consulted[3]. Fourthly, that where a navigable river separates or runs through several states its navigation is free from the point where it first becomes navigable to the point of its discharge into the sea[4]. Fifthly, that while the free navigation of the rivers running through or bounding several states is maintained, the riparian states may exercise rights of sovereignty in such rivers[5]. And lastly, that whilst the regulations for pre-

[1] Wheaton's *Elements*, ed. 1863, Vol. I. Part II. ch. iv. § 11, and Twee Gebræders, 3 Rob. *Adm. Rep.* 338–340.

[2] Wheaton's *Elements*, Vol. I. Part II. ch. iv. § 12. Heffter, *Droit Internat.* § 77. Halleck, *International Law*, §§ 26–28.

[3] Wheaton, Vol. I. Part II. ch. iv. § 13. Halleck, *International Law*, § 27.

[4] Phillimore, Vol. I. § 144. Heffter, *Droit Internat.* § 77.

[5] [The navigation of the great rivers of Europe has been provided for by two modern treaties, that of Vienna in 1815, and that of Paris in 1856; by the former the Rhine, the Neckar, the Mayn, the Moselle, the Meuse, the Scheldt and the Vistula have been proclaimed free, and several regulations for them provided in the 11th annexe to the treaty. See the Annexe in Hertslet's *Treaties*, Vol. I. p. 2, and in Phillimore, Vol. I. p. 173, n. 3. By the latter the freedom of the Danube has been established. By the treaty of June 4, 1856, made between Great Britain and the United States, and known as the Reciprocity Treaty, the navigation of the St Lawrence, which had been in dispute between those two countries ever since 1826, was settled,—it being agreed in the fourth article of that treaty that the navigation of the St Lawrence and the canals in Canada, the means of communication between the great lakes and the Atlantic Ocean, should be free to the inhabitants of the United States, power being reserved to the British Government to suspend the privilege, and the navigation of Lake Michigan being thrown open to British subjects. (Wheaton's *Elements*, ed.

serving and maintaining the proper navigation of these rivers must be drawn up and established in common by all the states interested in and connected with them, they cannot be changed or altered by any one separate state[1].]

Extradition of foreigners.

When foreigners are admitted into a state upon free and liberal terms, the public faith becomes pledged for their protection. The courts of justice ought to be freely open to them to resort to for the redress of their grievances. But strangers are equally bound with natives to obedience to the laws of the country during the time they sojourn in it, and they are equally amenable for infractions of the law[2]. It has sometimes been made a question, how far one government was bound by the law of nations, and independent of treaty, to surrender, upon demand, fugitives from justice, who, having committed crimes in one country, flee to another for shelter. It is declared by the public jurists[3], that every state is bound to deny an asylum to criminals, and upon application and due examination of the case, to surrender the fugitive to the foreign state where the crime was committed. The language of the authorities is clear and explicit, and the law and usage of nations rest on the plainest principles of justice. It is the duty of the government to surrender up fugitives upon demand, after the civil magistrate shall have ascertained the existence of reasonable grounds for the charge, and sufficient to put the accused upon his trial.

1863, Vol. I. Part I. ch. iv. p. 360, n. 114. *United States Statutes*, Vol. X. p. 1089, and 18 and 19 Vict. c. 3.)

In consequence of a discussion upon certain expressions in the Treaties of 1814 and 1815, relating to the navigation of the Rhine, the convention of March 31, 1831, settled that the navigation of that river should be free from the point where it becomes navigable into the sea, including its two principal outlets, the Leck and the Waal. See for the discussion Wheaton's *Elements*, Vol. I. pp. 348—352.]

1 Heffter, *Droit Internat.* § 77.

2 See *Debate, House of Lords*, March 1853, Hansard, 3rd series, CXXIV. p. 1046. Lord Lyndhurst's speech cited at length in Vol. I. of Phillimore's *International Law*, pp. 415, 416.

3 Grotius, B. II. ch. XXI. sec. 3, 4, 5, and Heineccius's *Com.* h. t. Burlamaqui, Part. IV. ch. III. sec. 19. Rutherforth, B. II. ch. 9. Vattel, B. II. ch. VI. sec. 76, 77. See *Questions de Droit*, tit. *Étranger*, par Merlin, for discussions on this subject in France.

The guilty party cannot be tried and punished by any other jurisdiction than the one whose laws have been violated, and therefore, the duty of surrendering him applies as well to the case of the subjects of the state surrendering, as to the case of subjects of the power demanding the fugitive. The only difficulty, in the absence of positive agreement, consists in drawing the line between the class of offences to which the usage of nations does, and to which it does not apply, inasmuch as it is understood, in practice, to apply only to crimes of great atrocity, or deeply affecting the public safety. The act of the legislature of New York, of the 5th of April, 1822, ch. 148, gave facility to the surrender of fugitives, by authorizing the Governor, in his discretion, on requisition from a foreign government, to surrender up fugitives charged with murder, forgery, larceny, or other crimes, which, by the laws of this state, were punishable with death or imprisonment in the state prison; provided the evidence of criminality was sufficient, by our laws, to detain the party for trial on a like charge. Such a legislative provision was requisite, for the judicial power can do no more than to cause the fugitive to be arrested and detained, until sufficient means and opportunity have been afforded, for the discharge of this duty, to the proper organ of communication with the power that makes the demand[1].

The European nations, in early periods of modern his-

[1] [In the following cases, for which we are indebted to the last American edition of Kent's *Commentaries*, will be found the English and American doctrines generally on the subject of extradition:—

ENGLISH.

R. *v.* Hutchinson, 3 Keble.
Lundy's case, 2 Ventris.
R. *v.* Kimberley, Strange, 848.
East India Company *v.* Campbell, 1 Vesey, 246.
Mure *v.* Kay, 1 Taunton, 34.

AMERICAN.

In the matter of Washburn, 4 Johnson, Ch. Rep. 106.
Commonwealth *v.* Deacon, 10, Sergison and Rawle, 125.
Holmes *v.* Jennison, 14 Peters, 540.
Ex parte Holmes, 12 Vermont *Rep.* 631.]

tory, made provision by treaty for the mutual surrender of criminals seeking refuge from justice. Treaties of this kind were made between England and Scotland in 1174, and England and France in 1308, and France and Savoy in 1378, and the last treaty made special provision for the surrender of criminals, though they should happen to be subjects of the state to which they had fled. Mr Ward[1] considers these treaties as evidence of the advancement of society in regularity and order. [At the present time Great Britain has three extradition treaties. One with France, dated 13th February, 1843, which was followed by the Act 6 and 7 Vict. c. 75; one with the United States, dated August 9th, 1842, followed by the Act 8 and 9 Vict. c. 120; and one with Denmark, dated April 15th, 1862, followed by the Act 24 and 25 Vict. c. 70[2]. The first provides under certain terms specified therein for the mutual surrender of persons seeking an asylum within each other's territories, and being accused of murder, forgery, or of fraudulent bankruptcy. The second provides under certain terms also specified therein for the mutual surrender of all persons charged with the crime of murder, piracy, arson, robbery, and forgery, or utterance of forged paper. The two most remarkable cases in which this latter treaty has been involved are of very recent date, and deserve a short notice. The first of these was in the matter of John Anderson, a fugitive slave, who having in the United States killed one of his pursuers, and taken refuge in Canadian territory, was claimed as a murderer under the Treaty. The case was carried into two of the Canadian courts. In the Queen's Bench, in answer to the argument for the prisoner, that as he was acting only in defence of his liberty there was no evidence on which to found a charge of murder, even if the alleged offence had been committed in Canada, and that therefore he was not within the terms of the Treaty, it was held that he

British extradition treaties.

Case of Anderson.

[1] *Hist. of the Law of Nations*, Vol. II. 318–320.

[2] But on the 5th March, 1864, a convention was signed between Her Majesty and the King of Prussia for the mutual surrender of Criminals.

was liable to be surrendered[1] (Mr J. M'Lean dissenting from the opinion of the majority of the Court). Whilst in the Common Pleas, it was held that the act committed by him did not come within the terms of the Treaty, and in consequence the prisoner was discharged; but between the appearance of these two opposite judgments an application had been made to and granted by the Court of Queen's Bench in England for a writ of *habeas corpus ad subjiciendum*[2], and in consequence of this an act of Parliament was passed, the 25th and 26th Vict. c. 20, by which it was enacted that no writ of *habeas corpus* should issue out of England into a colony having a court authorized to grant the same.

Case of Müller.

The other case was that of Franz Müller, who being charged with, and eventually found guilty and executed in England for the murder of Mr Briggs, on the North London Railway, near Hackney, had escaped from England and was captured in New York[3]. Some attempt was made by the prisoner's counsel to excite popular feeling in New York in favour of the prisoner, on the ground of the strong anti-federal feeling in England, the defence being that the treaty was suspended by the action of the British government; but the case was held to be undoubtedly within the act, and the prisoner was at once remanded to the place where the crime was committed[4].]

[1] In the matter of John Anderson, 20 *Upper Canada Q. B. Reports*, p. 124, and 11 *Canada C. P. Reports*, 1, In Re John Anderson.

[2] 30, *Law Journal, C. L., Q. B.* 129.

[3] See *Times* newspaper, September 9th and 13th, 1864.

[4] [For French views on the subject of extradition reference may be made to Ortolan, *Dipl. de la Mer*, L. II. ch. xiv. § 323. Merlin, *Répert. du Droit*, tit. *Souveraineté.* Massé, *Droit Comm.* T. II. § 44, and a note by M. Vergé to Martens' *Droit des Gens*, ed. 1858, T. I. pp. 267–273. For German views to De Marten, L. III. ch. iii. § 101. Klüber, *Droit des Gens*, § 86, with M. Ott's note, ed. 1861. Heffter, *Droit Internat.* § 63.

English views:—Phillimore's *Internat. Law*, Vol. I. ch. xxi., and Earl Russell's letter to Mr Adams, June 12, 1862. *Official Papers* (North America), No. 4, p. 164.

American:—Wheaton's *Elements*, ed. 1863, Vol. I. Part II. ch. ii. § 13. Story's *Conflict of Laws*, §§ 626—628. Halleck *on International Law*, § 28.]

## CHAPTER III.

### AMBASSADORS AND CONSULS.

---

AMBASSADORS form an exception to the general case of foreigners resident in the country, and they are exempted absolutely from all allegiance, and from all responsibility to the laws of the country to which they are deputed. As they are representatives of their sovereigns, and requisite for negotiations and friendly intercourse, their persons, by the consent of all nations, have been deemed inviolable, and the instances are rare in which popular passions, or perfidious policy, have violated this immunity. Some very honourable examples of respect for the rights of ambassadors, even when their privileges would seem in justice to have been forfeited on account of the gross abuse of them, are to be met with in the ancient Roman annals, notwithstanding the extreme arrogance of their pretensions, and the intemperance of their military spirit[1]. If, however, ambassadors should be so regardless of their duty, and of the object of their privilege, as to insult, or openly attack the laws or government of the nation to whom they are sent, their functions may be suspended by a refusal to treat with them, or application can be made to their own sovereign for their recall, or they may be dismissed, and required to depart within a reasonable time. We have had instances within our own times of all these modes of dealing with ministers who had given offence, and it is not to be denied, that every government has a perfect right to

Dismissal of ambassadors.

[1] Livy, B. II. c. 4, B. XXX. c. 25.

judge for itself whether the language or conduct of a foreign minister be admissible. [Thus in 1793 the United States government demanded the recall of M. Genet, the French minister, for issuing commissions to privateers to commit hostilities on nations at peace with the United States, and for other acts of similar misconduct. In 1809 the recall of Mr Jackson, the British minister at Washington, was insisted upon for alleged imputations upon the honour and veracity of the American government. In 1856 the British minister, Mr Crampton, received his exequatur from the President of the United States for violating their neutrality laws, by enlisting residents in the United States to serve in the British army. And in 1848 Sir Henry Bulwer received his dismissal from the court of Spain, for having insulted that country by reflecting on its internal administration.] The writers on public law go still further, and allow force to be employed to confine or send away an ambassador, when the safety of the state, which is superior to all other considerations, absolutely requires it, arising either from the violence of his conduct, or the influence and danger of his machinations[1].

Inviolability of ambassadors.

This is all that can be done, for ambassadors cannot, in any case, be made amenable to the civil or criminal jurisdiction of the country[2]; and this has been the settled rule of public law ever since the attempt made in the reign of Elizabeth to subject the Scotch ambassador to criminal jurisdiction, and the learned discussions which that case excited[3]. By fiction of law, an ambassador is

[1] Wheaton's *Elements*, ed. 1863, Vol. I. p. 437, n. 146.

[2] Except, says Blackstone, (on the authority of a case in *Rolls Reports*,) he conspires the death of the king in whose land he is, when he may be condemned and executed for treason. R. *v.* Owen, 1 *Rolls*, p. 185. 2 Stephens' *Blackstone*, p. 508.

[3] [Vattel, B. IV. ch. VII. sec. 97—103. Ward's *History*, Vol. II. p. 486—552; in which place, as well as in Phillimore's *International Law*, Vol. II. pp. 177—185, will be found the leading cases on this part of the subject. See also Wheaton's *Elements*, ed. 1863, Vol. I. p. 395, note 131, and the reference there to Mahon's *History of England*, Vol. I. pp. 388—392, ed. 1836, for the account of Count Gyllenborg, the Swedish minister at London.

considered as if he were out of the territory of the foreign power; and it is an implied agreement among nations, that the ambassador, while he resides within the foreign state, shall be considered as a member of his own country, and the government he represents has exclusive cognizance of his conduct, and control of his person. ["He continues still subject," says Mr Wheaton, "to the laws of his own country, which govern his personal status and rights of property, whether derived from contract, inheritance, or testament, and his children born abroad are considered as natives[1]."] The attendants of the ambassador attached to his person, and the effects in his use, are under his protection and privilege, and equally exempt from the foreign jurisdiction, though there are strong instances in which their inviolability has been denied and invaded[2]. [In a recent case the true position and liability of a secretary of legation accredited to the court of England by a foreign sovereign, and acting in the absence of his ambassador as chargé d'affaires, were most elaborately discussed, and it was held, 1st, that such an official was entitled to all the privileges of an ambassador; 2ndly, that he did not forfeit his privilege by engaging in mercantile pursuits here; and 3rdly, that if a foreign minister voluntarily attorns to the jurisdiction of the courts of this country, he is estopped from applying to the courts to stay proceedings on the ground of his privilege; but it seems to have been doubted in the course of the arguments, whether the privileges of an ambassador or foreign minister extend to prevent his being sued in the courts of this

**Officials and servants.**

**Case of Taylor v. Best.**

In Halleck's *International Law*, Ch. IX. § 14, all the authorities on this topic are given.]

[1] Wheaton's *Elements of International Law*, ed. 1863, Vol. I. p. 339, where will be found all the authorities in support of the statement, among them Vattel, *Droit des Gens*, Book IV. ch. VII. §§ 81—125; Martens' *Précis du Droit des Gens*, Liv. VII. ch. V. §§ 214—218; Klüber, *Droit des Gens Moderne*, P. II. Tit. ii. § 203. See also Phillimore's *International Law*, Vol. II. ch. VIII.

[2] Rutherforth, B. II. ch. IX. Ward's *History*, Vol. II. 552, 3. Vattel, B. IV. ch. viii. sect. 113 and 120. United States *v.* Hand, 2 *Wash. Cir. R.* 435.

country, or only to protect him from process which may affect the sanctity of his person, or his comfort or dignity. In the course of the case, the question as to the liability of a domestic servant of an ambassador, when engaging in mercantile transactions, being raised, it was held that the same privilege does not extend to them as to the ambassador; for as Mr J. Maule said, "the privilege is not that of the servant, but of the ambassador; it is based on the assumption that by the arrest of any of his household retinue, his personal comfort and state may be affected. Where these are not interfered with, the ambassador is not affected by the suit, and consequently the servant has no privileges[1]. As to the extent of jurisdiction in the matter of crimes over the personnel of the embassy, there appears to be a difference of opinion among some of our modern jurists. Mr Wheaton and Dr Twiss, following Vattel and the older writers, hold that a foreign minister can exercise criminal as well as civil jurisdiction over the personnel of the embassy, though both acknowledge that the modern usage is to arrest and send offenders for trial to their own country; whilst, on the other hand, Heffter maintains that the old extended jurisdiction of ambassadors over the members of their suite in cases of crime, is circumscribed within very narrow limits in the present day; limited, that is, to the power of arresting the accused, or demanding his extradition, and to the right of examining into the fact of the charge in strict conformity with the judicial regulations of his own country. Heffter, too, holds that at no court of Christian Europe are foreign ministers invested with the right of deciding upon the disputes among their countrymen, or even among those of their suites; their powers being confined exclusively to executing the commissions addressed to them, and with this view Mr W. B. Lawrence coincides[2].] The distinction

Jurisdiction of ambassadors.

[1] Taylor *v.* Best, 14 *Common Bench Rep.* pp. 487 and 524. See also Service *v.* Castenada, 9 Jurist, 524; and 1 Chitty's *Statutes*, p. 27, note (a), ed. 1850.

[2] Wheaton's *Elements*, Vol. I. ed. 1863, p. 398, note 133. Twiss's

between ambassadors, ministers plenipotentiary, and envoys extraordinary, relates to diplomatic precedence and etiquette, and not to their essential powers and privileges[1]; [but as to that precedence and etiquette, uniform rules were laid down by the congress of Vienna, which have been adopted generally, and are to this effect. In the first place, public ministers are divided into four classes. 1. Ambassadors and papal legates or nuncios. 2. Envoys, ministers, or others accredited to sovereigns. 3. Resident ministers accredited to sovereigns. 4. Chargé d'affaires accredited to the minister of foreign affairs. Ministers of the first class have what is called the representative character, that is, they represent the sovereign or state by whom they are sent, and are entitled to the same honours: they are of two kinds, ordinary and extraordinary, the latter term being applied to those who are sent on particular missions. Chargés d'affaires are also of two kinds, being either chargés d'affaires ad hoc, i. e. originally sent and accredited by their governments, and chargés d'affaires per interim, i.e. substituted in the place of the minister of their respective nations during his absence; and in the next place, envoys extraordinary acquire no superiority of rank by their extraordinary mission. Public ministers in each class take rank among themselves according to the date of the official notification of their arrival at the court

Rules laid down by the Congress of Vienna.

*Law of Nations*, Vol. I. p. 307. Heffter, *Droit des Gens*, § 216. See also a note by M. Ch. Vergé to his edition of Martens' *Précis du Droit des Gens*, 1850, T. II. § 219, p. 123.

[1] Vattel, B. IV. ch. VI. Martens, par Vergé, 1858, T. II. § 191. Phillimore's *International Law*, Vol. II. ch. IX. and Wheaton's *Elements*, ed. 1863, Vol. I. p. 380, n. 1. *Chargé d'affaires* is a diplomatic representative or minister of an inferior grade, and a *resident minister*, though of higher rank, seems not to be equal to a *minister plenipotentiary*. Nor is a minister plenipotentiary of equal rank and dignity with an *ambassador*, who represents the person of his sovereign. The United States have always been represented in Europe by ministers plenipotentiary, and they have never sent a person of the rank of ambassador in the diplomatic sense. The Prince of Orange once expressed to Mr Adams his surprise that the United States had not put themselves in that respect on a level with the crowned heads. *Diplomatic Correspondence*, edited by Mr Sparks, Vol. VII. 108.

to which they are accredited; and all distinctions of rank between public ministers arising from consanguinity and family or political relations between their different courts are abolished.]

Refusal to receive ambassadors.

A government may, in its discretion, lawfully refuse to receive an ambassador, without affording any just cause for war, though the act would, probably, excite unfriendly dispositions, unless accompanied with conciliatory explanations. The refusal may be upon the ground of the ambassador's bad character, or former offensive conduct, or because the special subject of the embassy is not proper, or not convenient for discussion; [or, as in the case of Great Britain and the Papal States, because of difference of faith standing in the way of receiving the usual accredited minister of the Pope, an ecclesiastic[1].] A state may also be divided and distracted by civil wars, so as to render it inexpedient to acknowledge the supremacy of either party. And though Bynkershoek says[2], that this right of sending ambassadors belongs to the ruling party, in whom stet rei agendi potestas, placing the right where all foreign governments place it, in the government de facto, which is in the actual exercise of power; [yet no modern writers would contend that when the proportions of the struggle are enlarged, and to use Grotius' words[3], that which was one has become two states, when in fact it is no longer a revolt capable of being repressed, but a civil war waged between two parties, each of whom assumes an attitude of independence, the right of sending ambassadors attaches only to one side. Doubtless it is, as Sir R. Phillimore says, a question of circumstance when the citizen is to be considered as entitled to the privilege of an enemy, but when he has attained that position, he may, if he please, claim the right of sending diplomatic agents to others, but whether such agents shall be received, whether, in fact, they will recognize in this way the new

In the case of civil war.

[1] Rutherforth, B. II. ch. IX. *Annual Register*, 1843, p. 160.

[2] *Quæst. J. Pub.* Lib. II. ch. 3.

[3] L. II. 18. 2.

government, is of course a question of expediency. Hence in a well-known recent case, where two persons, claiming to be ministers plenipotentiary of the Southern Confederate States of America, were stopped and arrested in their passage to Europe upon the high seas, Earl Russell, in his despatch to Lord Lyons, dated January 23rd, 1862, says, "the only distinction, arising out of the peculiar circumstances of a civil war and of the non-recognition of the independence of the de facto government of one of the belligerents, either by the other belligerent or by the neutral power, is this, that for the purpose of avoiding the difficulties which might arise from a formal and positive solution of these questions, diplomatic agents are frequently substituted, who are clothed with the powers and enjoy the immunities of ministers, though not invested with the representative character nor entitled to diplomatic honours[1]."] The state to whom the ambassador is sent may exercise its discretion in receiving, or refusing to receive him.

Whether the Sovereign is bound by acts of his Minister.

It sometimes becomes a grave question, in national discussions, how far the sovereign is bound by the act of his minister. This will depend upon the nature and terms of his authority[2]. It is now the usual course for every Government to reserve to itself the right to ratify or dissent from the treaty agreed to by its ambassador. A general letter of credence is the ordinary letter of attorney, or credential of the minister; and it is not understood to confer a power upon the minister to bind his sovereign conclusively. To do so important an act would require a distinct and full power, containing an express authority to

[1] *North American Papers*, Nov. 4, 1862, p. 234.

[2] The discretion and reserve with which a public minister ought to act in relation to the country in which he resides, is strongly exemplified in the case of the *Sally Ann*. (Stewart's *Vice-Adm. Rep.* 367.) It was held that a license granted by the British minister at New York, after the commencement of the war of 1812, to an American citizen to export provisions to a British island, was inconsistent with his diplomatic character and duty, and void; [the vessel and cargo were given up by the Lords Commissioners of the Treasury on the application of the British Minister to the United States].

bind the principal definitively, without the right of review or the necessity of ratification on his part. This is not the ordinary or prudent course of business. Ministers always act under instructions which are confidential, and which, it is admitted, they are not bound to disclose[1]; and it is a well-grounded custom, as Vattel observes[2], "that any engagement which the minister shall enter into is of no force among sovereigns, unless ratified by his principal," [for as Sir Wm. Scott says, "the ratification may be a form, but it is an essential one, for the instrument in point of legal efficacy is useless without it[3]]." This is now the usage, although the treaty may have been signed by plenipotentiaries.

Consuls.

Consuls are commercial agents appointed to reside in the seaports of foreign countries, with a commission to watch over the commercial rights and privileges of the nation deputing them.

History of the Institution.

[In tracing out the history of an institution which has done more to advance commercial enterprise than any other, it is unnecessary to go back to the records of those old nations whose laws and customs exercised so great an influence upon civilisation prior to the fall of the Roman Empire. For if we are to trust the investigations of one of the soundest and most learned of the historians of mercantile law, Monsieur Pardessus[4], there is not in the commercial regulations or in the jurisprudence of ancient Greece and Rome, anything that resembles the consular jurisdiction and office of modern times, except perhaps the old proxenus of the Greeks, whose duty it was, among other things, to settle the disputes and regulate the transactions of merchants. The origin, or rather the first germ of the office whose history we are now sketching will be found in a quarter where we should be least likely to look for it,

[1] Wicquefort, *L'Amb.* T. I. § 14. Martens' *Précis du Droit des Gens*, ed. 1858, T. II. § 205.

[2] B. IV. ch. vi. § 77.

[3] The *Eliza Ann*, 1 Dodson's *Adm. Rep.* p. 248.

[4] Pardessus, *Collection des Lois Maritimes*, T. I. ch. III. p. 52.

where the influence of the Romanized laws and institutions of Europe had not been felt, and where the necessary alliance of law and commerce could not be perceived and appreciated. It was from the Mussulman rulers of Palestine and Syria, so far back as the beginning of the ninth century, that this institution took its rise, not directly it is true, but through concessions and privileges granted to the Frankish residents, whose commercial pursuits led them to settle in large numbers in those countries, and whose presence and enterprise were of such material advantage to their rulers[1]. What precise shape the concessions thus granted to these foreign merchants, and ere long extended from Syria and Palestine to the whole of the Levant and Barbary, assumed, is not very clear; but that among them was the privilege of having officers whose duty it was to act as agents, referees, and arbitrators, and who gradually obtained a recognized position, is certain from the minute regulations to be found in the Assises de Jerusalem[2] for the Cour de la Fonde, whose jurisdiction had supplanted the old Court of the Reis, or Baillis (established by Godfrey of Bouillon for the benefit of the Syrian merchants), and had become so enlarged as to include a cognizance over all commercial matters; its judges being a mixed body of Franks and Syrians. How important was the agency of these Courts in aiding and furthering the commercial enterprise of the West through a large portion of the East is visible in the large number of documents relating to the establishment of Frankish consuls, and eventually of Frankish towns within the limits of Mussulman rule[3], as well as in the fact that within 300 years from the time of the first concessions to the Franks above mentioned the office and name of consul had become fully recognized in the

[1] Pardessus, T. I. Pref. LXVI. and T. II. Pref. CXXV. See Eginhard, *Chron. ad Annum*, 820 A.D.

[2] See Introduction to the *Assises de la Cour des Bourgeois: Assises de Jérusalem*, publiées par Beugnot, T. II. p. XXIV.

[3] Massé, *Droit Maritime*, T. I. § 348, and Miltitz, *Manuel des Consuls*, T. II. p. 400.

History of the Consular Institution.

West; for so early as A.D. 1060 we find consuls, consuls de marchands and consuls de mer, firmly established in one of those great old towns on the Adriatic, Trani, whose fame is now a thing of the past, but whose laws and commerce once formed an era in the history of the world. From that period the institution thus started into life grew in strength, and spread through all the merchant cities of the Adriatic and the Mediterranean: and whilst in the statutes of Marseilles (A.D. 1255), Lucca (A.D. 1300), and Ancona (A.D. 1397), we find the consul spoken of as an officer of note, in the old statutes of Genoa (A.D. 1316) we meet with an elaborate statement of the duties of the consul; we read of his conseil and staff being prescribed for the town of Caffa, then the principal Genoese establishment in the Black Sea[1]; and in the very title of the finest of all these old maritime codes, the Consolato del Mare[2], we have the influence of the institution visibly stamped upon its pages. The utility of such a mercantile office has been perceived and felt by all trading nations. Nor is there any place in the present day where, in consequence of the demands of foreign commerce and the influx of foreign merchants, such accredited agents are needed, that is without them. At the beginning of the century it was justly complained by an old writer, on the influence of Great Britain as a trading power in the Mediterranean, that she allowed herself to be outrivalled by others in the encouragement to trade, caused by the establishment of consular offices on the shores of that sea[3]; but that reproach has long ago been removed, and in the multitude of her ships and the number of her consular representatives, the trade between the Mediterranean and England shows a startling contrast to the days when Mr. Jackson lamented over the supineness of this country.]

Consuls, their powers and jurisdiction.

Consuls have been multiplied and extended to every

[1] Pardessus, T. IV. p. 429.

[2] Published between 1340 and 1400, probably at Barcelona.

[3] Jackson, *On the Commerce of the Mediterranean*, ch. IV. p. 39 (published 1801).

part of the world where navigation and commerce can successfully penetrate, and their duties and privileges are now generally limited and defined in treaties of commerce, or by the statute regulations of the country which they represent. In some places they have been invested with judicial powers over the disputes between their own merchants in foreign ports; but in the commercial treaties made by Great Britain there is rarely any stipulation for clothing them with judicial authority, except in treaties with the Barbary powers, [the Ottoman Porte and the Emperor of China, for consular privileges, are much less extensive in Christian than in Pagan and Mahommedan countries[1].] In England too it has been held, that a vice-consul is not strictly a judicial officer, that he has there no judicial power[2], [and that the certificate of such a person of the amount of the proceeds of damaged goods is not evidence to prove loss sustained by the deteriorations of such goods insured by policy (but see now the stat. 18 and 19, Vict. c. 42, ss. 2 and 3). So also in America, the doctrine holds that American consuls, having no judicial power, cannot take cognizance of the offences of seamen in foreign ports, nor exempt the master from his own responsibility[3].] It has been urged by some writers, as a matter highly expedient, to establish rules requiring merchants abroad to submit their disputes to the judicial authority of their own consuls, particularly with reference to shipping concerns. But no Government can invest its consuls with judicial power over their own subjects, in a foreign country, without the consent of the Government of the foreign country founded on treaty. Much less can it assume a jurisdiction of this kind in a foreign country, in transactions where one of the parties is not a subject of such Government unless by treaty, by long existing usage, or by a voluntary submission of the party himself, such juris-

[1] Fynn, *On Consuls*, p. 19.

[2] Mansfield, Ch. J., in Waldron *v.* Coombe, 3 Taunton, 162; 1 Chitty, *Commercial Law*, 50, 51. Matthews *v.* Offley, 3 Sumner (American), 115.

[3] Toler *v.* White, Ware's *Rep.* (American), 277.

Consuls, their duties and jurisdiction.

diction has been established and acquiesced in[1]; nor is there an instance, in any nation of Europe, of the admission of criminal jurisdiction in foreign consuls. The laws of the United States, on the subject of consuls and vice-consuls, specially authorize them to receive the protests of masters and others, relating to American commerce, declaring that their consular certificates, under seal, shall receive faith and credit in the courts of the United States[2]. It is likewise made their duty, where the laws of the country permit, to administer the personal estates of American citizens, dying within their consulates, and leaving no legal representative, and to take charge of and secure the effects of stranded American vessels, in the absence of the master, owner, or consignee; to direct a survey of American vessels putting into a port of necessity for repairs; to provide for destitute seamen within their consulates, and to send them at the public expense to the United States[3]. These particular powers and duties are similar to those prescribed to British consuls, and to consuls under the consular convention between the United States and France, in 1788; they are in accordance with the usages of nations, and are not to be construed to the exclusion of others, resulting from the nature of the consular appointment[4]. The former consular convention between France and the United States allowed consuls to exercise police over all vessels of their respective nations, "within the interior of the vessels," and to exercise a species of civil jurisdiction, by determining disputes concerning wages, and between the masters and crews of vessels belonging to their own country. The jurisdiction claimed under the

[1] The *Griefswald*, 1 Swabey's *Adm. Reports*, 430.

[2] Brown *v.* the *Independence*, Crabbe's *Reports*, 54 (American). Johnson *v.* the *Coriolanus*, Crabbe, 239.

[3] *Acts of Congress* of 14th of April, 1792, ch. XXIV. and of Feb. 28, 1803, ch. LXII, and now the important statute on this subject is the "Act to regulate the Diplomatic and Consular System of the United States," Aug. 18, 1856. *United States Stats. at Large*, Vol. XI. p. 52.

[4] 1 Beawes' *L. M.* tit. Consuls, pp. 292, 293. Potter *v.* Ocean Insurance Company, Circuit Court, U. S.

consular convention with France was merely voluntary, and altogether exclusive of any coercive authority[1]; and until a very recent period the United States had no treaty which conceded even such consular functions; however, by the convention of the 23rd February, 1853, with France, which provided for the issue of the necessary *exequatur* (the right to withdraw it for proper reasons being duly reserved), it was decreed that the consuls-general, consuls, vice-consuls, or consular agents, as well as the consular pupils, should enjoy in the two countries all the privileges usually accorded to their office and all the exceptions and immunities which might at any future time be granted to the agents of the same rank of the most favoured nation[2]. The doctrine of the American courts is[3], that a foreign consul, duly recognised by their government, may assert and defend, as a competent party, the rights of property of the individuals of his nation, in the courts of the United States, and may institute suits for that purpose, without any special authority from the party for whose benefit he acts[4]. But the court, in that case, said, that they could not go so far as to recognise a right in a vice-consul to receive actual restitution of the property, or its proceeds, without showing some specific power, for the purpose, from the party in interest. Of course where the sovereign is represented by a resident minister, or ambassador, the consul's power of intervention in behalf of his sovereign ceases.

Consuls, how received.

No nation is bound to receive a foreign consul unless it has agreed to do so by treaty, and the refusal is no violation of the peace and amity between the nations. Consuls are to be approved and admitted in the usual form; and if any consul be guilty of illegal or improper conduct,

[1] Mr Pickering to Mr Pinckney, Jan. 16, 1797. *American State Papers*, 1789—1815, Vol. II. p. 182 (Boston, 1817).

[2] *U. S. Statutes at Large*, Vol. X. p. 992.

[3] Case of the *Bello Corrunes*, 6 Wheaton, 168.

[4] Ship *Adolph*, 1 Curt. *C. C.* 87 (American), and Robson *v.* The Huntress, 2 Wall Ir. *C. C.* 59 (American).

he is liable to have his *exequatur*, or written recognition of his character, revoked, and to be punished according to the laws of the country in which he is consul[1]; or he may be sent back to his own country, at the discretion of the Government which he has offended. The French consuls (and Monsieur Massé says, the same prohibition exists in Austria, Holland, and Russia) are forbidden to be concerned in commerce, a rule that would seem to be somewhat relaxed by the 2nd article of the treaty between the United States and France; and, by the act of Congress of February 28th, 1803, American consuls residing on the Barbary coast are forbidden also; but British and American consuls have been generally at liberty to be concerned in trade; in such cases the character of consul does not give any protection to that of merchant, when these characters are united in the same person[2]. Though the functions of consul would seem to require that he should not be a subject of the state in which he resides, yet the practice of the maritime powers is not strict on this point, and it is usual, and sometimes most convenient, to appoint subjects of the foreign country to be consuls at its ports.

Consuls, how far privileged.

A consul is not such a public minister as to be entitled to the privileges appertaining to that character, nor is he under the special protection of the law of nations. He is entitled to privileges to a certain extent, such as for safe conduct, but he is not entitled to the *jus gentium*. Vattel

[1] This, however, is a position that can scarcely be admitted as consistent with the practice of the British Government.

[2] Beawes' *L. M.* Vol. I. tit. Consuls, p. 291, 1 Chitty, *Commerc. Law*, 57, 58, 3 Rob. *Adm. Rep.* 27. The Indian Chief. Massé, *Droit Commerc.* T. I. § 453; and Arnold and Ramsay *v.* U. Insurance Company, 1 Johnson's *Cases*, 363 (American). The inclination of modern legislation in England however is opposed to the continuance of this liberty to trade, and this privilege, if privilege it can be called, is being gradually discontinued, in consequence of a recommendation of the House of Commons, of July, 1858. See the *Report*, dated 27th July, 1858. No. 482. The prohibition against engaging in mercantile pursuits is now rigidly enforced in the United States by the Act 34th Congress, Sept. 1, ch. 127. *U. S. Statutes*, Vol. XI. p. 52.

Modern English doctrine as to Consuls trading.

thinks[1], that his functions require that he should be independent of the ordinary criminal jurisdiction of the country; that he ought not to be molested, unless he violates the law of nations by some enormous crime; and that if guilty of any crime, he ought to be sent home to be punished. But no such immunities have been conferred on consuls by the modern practice of nations; and it may be considered as settled law, that consuls do not enjoy the protection of the law of nations any more than other persons who enter the country under a safe conduct; nor are they exempted from the operation of the laws of war, so as to lose the character of belligerents if residing as traders in an enemy's country, even though they be neutral, and invested with the office of consul of a neutral state in the place of their residence[2]. In civil and criminal cases they are equally subject to the laws of the country in which they reside[3]. The same doctrine declared by the public jurists, has been frequently laid down in the English and American courts of justice[4]. It seems, however, from some decisions in France mentioned by Mr Warden[5], that foreign consuls cannot be prosecuted

[1] B. II. c. 2, § 34.

[2] Sorensen *v.* the Queen, 11 Moore, *Privy Council Cases*, 141.

[3] Wicquefort's *L'Amb.* B. I. ch. V. Bynk. *De foro legat.* ch. X. Martens' *Summ.* B. IV. ch. III. § 8. Edn. by Wm. Cobbett, published 1802. Beawes, Vol. I. tit. Consuls. Pardessus, *Droit Commerc.* T. IV. pp. 148, 183. Barbuit's Case. Cases temp. Talbot, 281. Valarino *v.* Thompson, 3 Seld. 576 (American).

[4] Barbuit's Case. Cases temp. Talbot, 281. Albrecht *v.* Sussman, 2 Veasey and Beames, 323. Clark *v.* Cretico, 1 Taunton, 106. Viveash *v.* Becker, 3 Maule and Selwyn, 284. Aspinwall *v.* Queen's Proctor, 2 Curteis, 241. The *Falcon,* 6 Robinson, 194. The *Hope,* 1 Dodson, 229. The *Grieswald,* 1 Swabey, 430. The following American cases are on the same subject: The *Anne,* 3 Wheaton, 446. United States *v.* Rovara, 2 Dallas, 297. The *Commonwealth v.* Korsloff, 5 Serg. and Raw. 545. Durand *v.* Halback, 1 Miles, 46. Davis *v.* Packhard, 7 Peters, 276. De la Foret's case, 2 Nott and McCord, 217. See also 1 Chitty's *Laws of Commerce,* 70. Wheaton's *Elements,* Part III. ch. I. § 22. Phillimore's *International Law,* Vol. II. §§ 246—248.

[5] *On Consuls,* pp. 108—116. Chitty, *On Laws of Commerce,* p. 71. Massé *Droit. Commerc.* T. I. § 448. *Code Civil,* Tit. II. ch. I. § 3.

before a French tribunal for acts done by them in France by order of their Government, and with the authorization of the French Government, and that in general a consul cannot be prosecuted without the previous consent of his Government. But if a Frenchman has a demand against the consul or vice-consul of his nation in a foreign country he can only sue him before a tribunal in France. Consular privileges are much less extensive in Christian than in Mohammedan countries, [the result, partly, of the abiding influence of the early concession of commercial privileges and exemptions in favour of Christian merchants in the East, and partly of treaty stipulations; the consequence has been that, whilst in Christian countries consuls have no judicial power or authority, in Turkey these officials are allowed to exercise a jurisdiction, civil as well as criminal, over their fellow-countrymen, even to the exclusion of the local magistrates and tribunals; moreover, they partake very considerably of the character of resident ministers and diplomatic agents. According to Mr Cushing, the United States attorney-general, who has expounded his views in a very able state-paper, it appears, "that the consuls of Christian states in the countries not Christian still retain unimpaired, and habitually exercise, their primitive functions of municipal magistrates for their countrymen, their commercial or international capacity in those countries being but a part of their general capacity as the delegated administrative and judicial agents of their nation. This condition of things came to be permanent in the Levant, that is in Greek Europe and its dependencies, by reason of the tide of Arabic and Tartar conquerors having overwhelmed so large a part of the Eastern empire, and established the Mohammedan religion there; but the result was different in Latin Europe; and this difference in the powers of consuls in these countries was founded on the difference of law[1]." "Hence we find, as a consequence of the extra territoriality of foreign Christians, a complete system of peculiar legal and municipal adminis-

Consular privileges in Mohammedan countries.

[1] *Opinions of Attorney-Generals,* Vol. VII. pp. 346—348.

tration existing in the Levant, consisting of (1) Turkish tribunals for questions between subjects of the Porte and foreign Christians. (2) Consular courts for the business of each nation of foreign Christians. (3) Trial of questions between foreign Christians of different nations in the consular court of the defendant's nation. (4) Mixed tribunals of Turkish magistrates and foreign Christians at length substituted by common consent, in part, for cases between Turks and foreign Christians: and (5) finally, for causes between foreign Christians the substitution also at length of mixed tribunals in place of the separate consular courts; an arrangement at first introduced by the legations of Austria, Great Britain, France, and Russia, and then tacitly acceded to by other foreign Christian legations[1]." In fact, from peculiar circumstances, European consuls in the Levant occupy a position entirely distinct from that of consuls in European countries. "There is," says a writer in an excellent foreign periodical[2], "as much difference between the position and duties of these two sets of officials as between the position and rights of the consulate of the middle ages and of these modern days. European consuls accredited to the Ottoman Porte, and its tributary countries, are looked upon as public ministers, enjoying the prerogatives of ambassadors, and, as such, receiving from the Sultan a diploma of investiture in which they are designated by the title of balios-bey. By virtue of these prerogatives their houses become an inviolable asylum from the pursuit of the local laws and authorities. They are exempt from every custom-house tax and from arrest, are beyond the jurisdiction of Mussulman judges and functionaries, and can grant letters of protection, not only to the individuals immediately attached to their person, but to any one they choose to shield. In the East generally, and in Egypt specially, consuls possess every fundamental right that

[1] *Opinions of Attorney-Generals*, Vol. VII. p. 569.

[2] M. Domenico Gatteschi in the *Revue Historique de Droit Français et Étranger*, 8e. année, p. 533.

public international law has conceded to foreign ministers: viz. personal inviolability, exemption from local jurisdiction, and diplomatic honours[1]." These privileges and this immunity have been received by treaty in countries where love of commerce and respect for Christian merchants were not very conspicuous. We find that in old times consuls resided in the Barbary states under the protection of treaties; and in the empire of Morocco (for the subjugation of Algeria to French rule has altered the political boundaries of that part of the world) consuls reside and exercise their functions under the same kind of protection[2].]

Jurisdiction of the Supreme Court in the U. S.

Considering the importance of the consular functions, and the activity which is required of them in all great maritime ports, and the approach which consuls make to the efficacy and dignity of diplomatic characters, it was a wise provision in the constitution of the United States, which gave to the Supreme Court original jurisdiction in all cases affecting consuls, as well as ambassadors and other

[1] The *exequatur* of European consuls, or permission to enter upon the discharge of his office and functions, is termed *barat* in the Levant.

[2] Shaler's *Sketches of Algiers*, pp. 39, 307. Wheaton's *Elements*, ed. 1863, Vol. I. p. 224 n (74). See also in De Cussy, *Phases et Causes Célèbres*, T. I. p. 40, and following pages, a detailed enumeration of the edicts, ordinances, decrees, and regulations of every nation, and of the treaties concluded between them on the subject of consuls and their duties. The following authorities may also be consulted for the foreign law on this subject. General authorities: De Miltitz, *Manuel des Consuls*, Lond. 1837, 2 Volumes. F. de Cussy, *Réglements Consulaires des Principaux États Maritimes de l'Europe et de l'Amerique*, Leips. et Paris, 1851, and Bursotti, *Guide des Agents Consulaires*, 1837. Special authorities: For France, Laget de Podio, *Nouvelle Juridiction des Consuls de France à l'Étranger*, 1843. Tancoigne, *Le Guide de Chanceliers*, 1843. Moreuil, *Manuel des Agents Consulaires Français et Étrangers*, 1853: and *Dictionnaire des Chancelleries diplomatiques et Consulaires*, 1855. Declercy et Vallot, *Guide pratique des Consulats*, 1851. Dalloz, *Jurisprudence générale*, sub verbo *Consuls*. For the United States, Henshaw, *A Manual for the United States Consuls*, New York, 1849. For Austria, Neumann, *Handbuch des Consulatsweren*, Vienna, 1854. For Prussia, König, *Preussans Consulat-Règlement*, Berlin, 1854. For Portugal, Ribeiro Dos Santos, *Traité du Consulat*, Hamb. 1839. For Sardinia, Magnone, *Manuel des Officiels Consulaires, &c.* 1848.

public ministers, and the federal jurisdiction is understood to be exclusive of the state courts[1].

French regulations.

[The organization of the consular establishment in France depends on the "Ordonnances" of October and November, 1833, the law of the 28th March, 1836, and that of the 8th July, 1852, relating to the jurisdiction of consuls in China.

The consular establishment is composed of consuls, general consuls of the first and second class, vice-consuls, and pupil-consuls; the consular posts being divided into consulates-general and consulates of the first and second class.

In those states where France has no consulate-general, the consular duties are attached to the diplomatic mission; but a comparatively recent decree has provided for the position and duties of vice-consuls, placing them, for certain purposes, on a footing with those of consuls[2].

As the character of consul is, according to French law, incompatible with that of merchant, consuls, pupil-consuls, and chancelier, nominated by the *chef du gouvernement*, are strictly forbidden to engage in any kind of trade, direct or indirect, under the penalty of being recalled. Consuls are authorized to nominate, out of the most respectable French residents in the place, delegates (*agents consulaires*, as they are called), for special purposes, but such right of delegation stops there. The power and duties of consuls vary in each country where they exist according to the legislation of such country. Certain general acts, however, they can do, such as giving passports to their countrymen, legalizing *les actes* drawn up by the public functionaries within the consular district, and discharging all the functions of an officer of the *état civil*. They may act as arbitrators where disputes happen between the subjects of their nation, or between

[1] Commonwealth *v.* Kosloff, 5 Serg. and Raw. 545. Hall *v.* Young, 3 Pickering. 80. Davis *v.* Packard, 7 Peters' *U. S. Rep.* 276. Sartori *v.* Hamilton, 1 Green's *N. I. Rep.* 109 (all American).

[2] 22nd Dec. 1854.

such persons and the inhabitants of the country to which they are commissioned. So far as relates to the French mercantile marine, they act as guardians over French merchant vessels in all the ports of their jurisdiction, subject, however, to the local rules and the authorities of the port where such vessels are lying. They are charged with the surveillance of the flag of France, to see that it is legally employed, and to represent and denounce any attempt to use it improperly. They are to take every possible means to prevent the traffic in slaves, and to see that all anti-slave-trade laws, where such exist, are fully carried out. Where any of their fellow-countrymen are arrested by the local authorities, their duty is to assist them by intercession, if available, and to see that they are humanely treated when in arrest, legally tried, and properly defended. Of course in these matters their duties may be more or less extensive by treaties. So far as the ships of war of their country are concerned, their office is to obtain assistance from the local authorities of the place to pursue and arrest deserters; and they are entitled, in the event of probable danger to the persons and property of their resident countrymen, to demand assistance from the commanders of the naval force or ships of war that may chance to be stationed at or near the place of danger. Lastly, they may be called upon, in the absence of diplomatic ministers, to discuss and settle questions of International Law[1].

British regulations.

The position and duties of consuls, under the administration of the laws of Great Britain, are now more clearly defined and better understood than they were some years back. Recent regulations and statutes have done much to remove the objections which were fairly levelled against the inattention of this country to so important an office in the days when Mr Chitty first published his great work on the laws of commerce[2].

[1] For this sketch of the consular office under French law we are indebted to a note in the last French edition of Vattel, T. I. p. 622, n. 2, by the learned editor, Mons. Pradier Fodéré.

[2] A.D. 1820.

The selection of consuls, which in old times emanated from the merchants themselves, subject of course to the approval of the Crown, now rests entirely with the Secretary of State for Foreign Affairs. And, on appointment, every consul is informed as to his general duties by printed instructions. Of the principal part of these duties the following is an abstract.

Duties of Consuls according to British regulations.

He must make it his particular study to become conversant with the laws and general principles which relate to the trade of Great Britain with foreign parts; must make himself acquainted with the language and laws of the country wherein he resides, and especially with such laws as have any connection with the trade between the two countries; and must do all in his power to protect and promote the lawful trade and trading interests of Great Britain, taking special notice of all prohibitions with respect to exports or imports, and cautioning all British subjects against illicit commerce and the violations of the laws and regulations of the state in which he resides, and of Great Britain. He must give his best advice and assistance, when called upon, to the trading subjects of Great Britain, conciliating the subjects of the two countries, as much as possible, on all points of difference which may fall under his cognizance, and upholding the rightful interests and treaty privileges of British subjects by due representations in the proper quarter; applying to Her Majesty's Consul-General or to Her Majesty's minister, if redress cannot be obtained from the local administration. He must keep Her Majesty's Ministers fully informed of all occurrences of national interest within his consulate respecting commercial matters, as well as, in time of war, respecting the arming, equipment, or sailing of armed vessels belonging to Her Majesty's enemies. He is to inform persons who are liable to be taken by due process of the laws of the country where they are residing that they cannot obtain refuge on board British ships, lying in the ports of such country, from the due execution of its laws. He is to forward, within six months from the date of his arrival at his residence, a general report on the trade, market prices, differential duties, if any, tonnage and port-dues, facilities for warehousing goods, and the trading regulations of the place and district, together with the annual returns of trade, and quarterly returns of corn and grain, from the ports of his consulate. He is to see that every so-called British vessel is furnished with a register, and complies with the provisions of the Merchant Shipping Act, as to her ownership, crew, and other particulars. He is to afford to distressed British seamen[1], and others of Her Majesty's subjects thrown upon the coast, or reaching by chance any place within his district, proper aid and assistance. It is his duty also to furnish intelligence to Her Majesty's ships touching upon the coast, and obtain for them supplies of water and provisions, assist in apprehending deserters, and in recovering all wrecks, cables, anchors, &c. belonging to the Queen's ships, when found at sea by fishermen or other persons, and brought into the port where he resides, paying to such persons the customary salvage[2]. And, lastly, he must not leave his post without permission from the Foreign Office, or from Her Majesty's representative in the country where he resides. But besides these powers and duties there are others no less important prescribed by statute; such as the power to administer oaths, and to be present at the taking of affidavits and affirmations, which on proof of the consul's seal, or signature, are admissible as evidence in this country[3]: and various powers and duties enjoined in several sections of the last Merchant Shipping Act of 1854.[4]

British regulations in the Levant and in Turkey.

An account of the position and duties of the consular office of this country would be incomplete without a brief notice of a very peculiar and extensive jurisdiction con-

[1] As to this, see 17 and 18 Vict. c. 104, §§ 211—213.

[2] See also 17 and 18 Vict. c. 104, §§ 486—496, for the duties of consuls in the matter of salvage service by her Majesty's ships.

[3] 18 and 19 Vict. c. 42. See also 15 and 16 Vict. c. 86, § 22.

[4] 17 and 18 Vict. c. 104; see especially §§ 31, 79, 82, 103—105, 160, 195, 197, 205—213, 229, 232, 267—270, 279, and 486—495.

nected therewith; viz. that of Her Majesty's consuls in the Levant. The history of the rise and progress of that jurisdiction lies in a small compass; and is, in fact, told in the preamble to the Stat. 6 Geo. IV. c. 23. From that it appears that a body corporate and politic had been established by letters patent of James I. with certain rights and privileges, termed "The Governor and Company of Merchants of England trading to the Levant Seas." These letters patent, and their rights, were confirmed and extended by various acts of Parliament, down to so late a period as 59 Geo. III. Some few years afterwards the legislature, thinking "it would be beneficial to the trade of the United Kingdom, and especially that carried on in the Levant Seas, to put an end to these rights and privileges, and to recall the letters patent;" the Act before mentioned[1] was passed to carry out that view, and to vest all the property, estate, and interest of the old Levant Company in the Crown, subject, of course, to the legal and equitable conditions specified in the Act. The consequence of this was the establishment of a direct communication and connection with and between Great Britain and the Ottoman Empire[2], and the passing of another Act[3], followed by an Order in Council, dated 2nd October, 1843, by which doubts as to the exercise of power and jurisdiction by Her Majesty within divers countries and places out of Her Majesty's dominions were removed, and the exercise of power and jurisdiction within such places was continued. In a circular to Her Majesty's consuls in the Levant, dated October 6th, 1843, it was said "that the effect of the Order was to relieve Her Majesty's consuls from the serious responsibility under which they had hitherto acted with regard to matters of jurisdiction, by giving to their proceedings the sanction and authority of law; which, in many instances, had till then been wanting."

Since the appearance of that circular several important

[1] 6 Geo. IV. c. 23.

[2] 6 and 7 Wm. IV. c. 78.

[3] 6 and 7 Vict. c. 94.

Orders in Council have been published, from time to time, in which the whole subject of the British consulate in the Ottoman Empire has been reviewed, and a complete code of rules and regulations drawn up, based upon the provisions of the 6 and 7 Vict. c. 94. The last of these Orders, bearing date the 30th November, 1864[1], however, having repealed the two that immediately preceded it, and having made further provision for the more effectually carrying out the objects of the Act of Parliament, and the Orders consequent upon it, a short analysis of its contents will exhibit the actual extent and condition of Her Majesty's jurisdiction in the Ottoman dominions.

British Orders, 30th Nov. 1864.

I. All the jurisdiction exerciseable under the Order, both civil and criminal, is to be exercised in conformity with the Common Law, the Rules of Equity, the Statute Law, and other law in force in England, and pursuant to the course of procedure observed in England.

II. The constitution of Her Majesty's consular courts is as follows:

(1) There is to be a supreme consular court sitting at Constantinople, or at any other place within the Ottoman dominions approved of by one of Her Majesty's Secretaries of State, presided over by a judge, and having attached to it one law-secretary, and as many officers and clerks as shall seem good to one of Her Majesty's Secretaries of State.

The business of the law-secretary, who also is to hold the office of vice-consul, being to act as registrar of the court, to prosecute in criminal matters under the direction of the judge, to determine certain criminal charges in a summary way, and to settle certain suits and proceedings under the reference of the judge.

(2) In addition to this supreme court, provincial consular courts are established, presided over by Her Majesty's consuls-general, consuls, and vice-consuls.

In civil matters it is prescribed,

First. That every consular court and its officers are

[1] Published *in extenso* in the *London Gazette*, Dec. 2, 1864.

to promote, as far as possible, reconciliation, to facilitate the amicable settlement of suits, and refer, if necessary, suits or proceedings to arbitration.

Secondly. In the event of a trial, where the amount sought to be recovered is £50, or upwards, the suit is, on the demand of either party, to be tried by a jury of five, who may be challenged as in England, whose decision must be unanimous, and before whom all the proceedings must be in English.

Thirdly. In certain cases a provincial court is to hear and determine the matters with assessors. And,

Fourthly. Besides being courts of law and equity, the supreme and other consular courts are to be courts of bankruptcy. The supreme court is to be a court of vice-admiralty, a court for matrimonial causes, and a court of probate; whilst the provincial courts, if held before a legal vice-consul, are to have a vice-admiralty jurisdiction, and also power to grant probate or administration in non-contentious cases.

In criminal matters, the jurisdiction of the consular court extends to every British subject within the district of the court and charged with a crime or offence within the Ottoman dominions, or on board a British vessel within those dominions. And,

First. A consular court is to promote reconciliation and facilitate an amicable settlement of proceedings for assault, or offences not amounting to felony, on certain prescribed terms.

Secondly. Certain classes of criminal cases within the jurisdiction of the supreme courts, or of a provincial consular court, may, by direction of the judge of the supreme court, be heard and determined in a summary way.

Thirdly. Other crimes and offences above the degree of misdemeanour, tried before the judge, or law-secretary of the supreme court, or before a resident legal vice-consul in a provincial court, are to be tried by a jury of five, whose decision is to be unanimous, and before whom all the proceedings are to be in English.

Fourthly. Capital crimes are to be tried only by the judge of the supreme court; and in the case of convictions for murder, judgement of death is to be entered on the record, and a report of this and every other judgement to be sent to one of Her Majesty's Secretaries of State, for his direction as to the punishment actually to be imposed.

III. Provision is made for preventing any prospective breach of the public peace, and for the deportation of offenders, for the registration of residents and others, for dealing with the property of British subjects non-resident and dying within the Ottoman dominions, for offences against the religion established or observed within the Ottoman dominions, and for opportunities to foreigners, so desiring it, to institute proceedings of a civil nature against British subjects, or *vice versâ* to British subjects.

IV. In civil cases, where the amount in dispute is of the value of £50, or upwards, appeals are allowed from the provincial courts to the supreme court; and where the amount or value is of £500, or upwards, from the supreme court to the Queen in council.

In criminal cases, where the trial of the offence has been in a summary way, the supreme consular court may review the decision, in the shape of a special case; and where the trial has been otherwise than a summary one, questions of law may be reserved for the consideration of the supreme court.]

# REGULATIONS

FOR THE

## EXAMINATION OF CANDIDATES BEFORE THE CIVIL SERVICE COMMISSIONERS.

(In force January, 1854.)

---

## FOR HER MAJESTY'S DIPLOMATIC SERVICE.

(*Extracted from the London Gazette of September* 16, 1862.)

### 1. *Nomination, Qualification, and Examination of Candidates for Unpaid Attachéships.*

CANDIDATES for the situation of Attaché in Her Majesty's Diplomatic Service will continue to be nominated by Her Majesty's Secretary of State for Foreign Affairs; and they must be prepared to undergo an examination before the Civil Service Commissioners within six months after their nomination, if they elect to undergo only one examination (which single examination will, in that case, exempt them from any further examination previously to their receiving Commissions as Secretaries), or within three months if they prefer to undergo two examinations as heretofore. In the latter case the second examination may be deferred until the candidate is prepared to undergo it.

Candidates on presenting themselves for examination on their nomination must have completed the twenty-first year of their age, and not have exceeded the twenty-sixth.

In the case of candidates electing to undergo only one examination, such examination will comprise the following matters:—

*a.* Orthography and handwriting.

*b.* General intelligence, as evinced by the manner in which the candidate acquits himself, and specifically by the quickness he may show in seizing the points in papers read to him, or read over by him, once or twice.

*c.* Précis.

*d.* The candidate must satisfy the Examiners that he is thoroughly well grounded in the Latin grammar, and that he is able to construe and parse a portion of some good classical Latin author, and to give the derivations of words.

*e.* An accurate knowledge of French grammar, fluency in French conversation, correctness of translation from French into English, and from English into French, and French composition.

*f.* An accurate knowledge of German grammar, a tolerable degree of fluency in German conversation, and correctness of translation from German into English, and from English into German[1].

*g.* A fair knowledge of the political history of Europe, and of North and South America, from the year 1660 to 1860 inclusive, and of the most important international transactions during that period.

*h.* A general knowledge of geography.

*i.* The first four rules of arithmetic and decimal fractions as given with examples in Colenso's Arithmetic.

*j.* The first book of Euclid.

*k.* A general knowledge of maritime and international law, to be acquired from Wheaton's "Elements of International Law," and the first volume of Kent's "Commentary."

*l.* Candidates will be allowed, at their option, to be examined in Spanish and Italian in addition to the above subjects.

In the case of candidates electing to undergo two examinations, the first examination will comprise the following subjects:—

1. Orthography.
2. Handwriting.
3. Précis.
4. Latin.
5. Arithmetic.
6. Geography.
7. General intelligence, except as regards specific tests.
8. An accurate knowledge of French grammar, correctness of translation from French into English, and such a facility of speaking French as may show aptitude for acquiring fluency after a residence abroad.
9. An accurate knowledge of German grammar.
10. A general knowledge of the political history of Europe, and of North and South America, from 1790 to 1815, comprising an acquaintance with the most important international transactions of that period.

[1] If a candidate going up for his second examination should not, in the interval between the two examinations, have resided a reasonable time, twelve months for instance, in Germany, he shall be at liberty, if he should so desire it, to substitute for conversation in German conversation in some other foreign language besides French.

In either case, candidates who have past the first public examination in classics at one of the Universities in Great Britain or Ireland will be exempted from being examined in Latin[1].

Candidates who shall have elected to undergo two examinations must be prepared to satisfy the examiners, if required to do so, as to their acquaintance with the various matters which come within the single examination (except as regards Latin, geography, and arithmetic, in which such candidates are exempted from being re-examined); and they will, moreover, be required, for their second examination, to draw up a report on the general commercial and political relations of the several countries in which they may have resided; and on the internal policy and administration, the social institutions, and the character of the people of such countries.

If a candidate offering himself for the single examination should fail to satisfy the Commissioners to the required extent, but should evince such a knowledge of the subjects on which he may have been examined, as would have obtained for him a certificate of fitness if he had only offered himself for a first examination, the Commissioners will, in such case, give a certificate as for a first examination; and the candidate will eventually have to present himself again before the Commissioners for the second examination.

### 2. *Period of Service of Attachés.*

The service of Attachés will reckon from the date of the certificate first granted by the Civil Service Commissioners, and will be considered as probationary for four years from that date, during which period the Attachés must have been employed for six months in the Foreign Office, and must also have actually resided at one of Her Majesty's Embassies or Missions abroad, or have been actually employed in the Foreign Office, for a further period of three years. If these conditions as to employment and residence have not been fulfilled at the expiration of four years from the date of the certificate of the Civil Service Commissioners, the probationary period will be prolonged until they have been fulfilled; and it will likewise be prolonged in the case of candidates who may have elected to undergo two examinations, until the final certificate of the Commissioners has been obtained.

[1] In this case the candidate, on going up for examination, must exhibit to the Civil Service Commissioners a certificate from the duly-constituted authorities, Examiners, or others, as the case may be, in each University, that he has passed the first public Examination in Classics, in whatever manner that examination may have been conducted, and to whatever points it may have been directed.

3. *A salary of £150 a-year will be granted, contingently, to Attachés on completion of their Probation.*

A salary at the rate of £150 a-year will be granted to Attachés on the termination of the period of probation, and on the receipt from the Minister under whom they have last served, of a certificate showing that their general character and conduct, during the time they have so served, have been satisfactory; and that, as far as such Minister has the means of forming an opinion, they understand and speak French well, and also one other foreign language.

4. *Abolition of the designation of Paid Attachés. Commissions as Second Secretaries to be granted to Paid Attachés.*

The designation of First and Second Paid Attaché is abolished; and in lieu thereof will be substituted the designation of Second Secretaries, which will be conferred by Commissions under Her Majesty's Sign-Manual.

5. *Commissions as Third Secretaries to be granted to Unpaid Attachés on completion of their Probation.*

Commissions as Third Secretaries will also be granted under Her Majesty's Sign-Manual to persons now serving as Unpaid Attachés, or who shall hereafter be appointed Unpaid Attachés, on the fulfilment of the conditions applicable to such persons, as specified in the present Regulations.

It is clearly to be understood that the aforesaid Commissions of Second and Third Secretaries will not imply appointment to any particular Embassy or Mission; but the holders thereof will be subject to the same conditions and liabilities as to removal from one Mission to another, at the discretion of the Secretary of State, as those to which Attachés of all classes are now liable.

Secretaries of the Second and Third Classes may be indiscriminately attached, either to an Embassy or to a Mission; and the circumstance of having been attached in either of the above capacities to an Embassy will not preclude transfers in the same capacity to a Mission. Moreover, there may be more than one Secretary of either of the above classes attached, at the pleasure of the Secretary of State, to any Embassy or Mission.

6. *Number of Second Secretaries.*

There will be a fixed number of Second Secretaries, determined by the number of First and Second Paid Attachés at the date of the issue of these Regulations.

The Salaries of Second Secretaries will be fixed at the same rates as those now assigned to First and Second paid Attachés in the respective Embassies and Missions; it being understood that such rates have reference to the character of the Embassy or Mission, and not to the services of the Second Secretaries, who may be removed, without claim to compensation, from an Embassy or Mission where the rates are higher, to an Embassy or Mission where the rates are lower.

7. *Rules as to Pensions of the Fourth Class.*

In virtue of Her Majesty's Commissions, the service of Second and Third Secretaries will count for their pensions, under the Act of 2 & 3 Wm. IV, cap. 116, from the date of the issue of their first Commission; but the amount of pension to be assigned to them will be calculated, so long as they are eligible for a pension of the Fourth Class only, for each year that has elapsed since the date of their first Commission, at one-thirtieth part of the last salary of which they were in receipt at the time of the pension being granted; provided that no pension shall continue to be issued to a person not incapacitated by ill-health, medically certified, who may decline active service before he has reached the sixtieth year of his age, after which age no person shall be required to serve as Second or Third Secretary.

8. *Provision for the Transfer of the Junior Members of the Diplomatic Service from one post to another; and Payment of their Expenses of Removal.*

Second or Third Secretaries, and Attachés, as a general rule, will not be employed for more than two years consecutively, irrespective of the periods during which they may have been absent on leave, in the same Embassy or Mission, unless for special public reasons. Secretaries of Embassy or Legation, Second and Third Secretaries, and Attachés, will, on their first appointment, or on any subsequent removal by reason of promotion or otherwise on public grounds, receive such an allowance as shall be sufficient to cover the actual expense of their personal journey by land, or the actual amount paid for their personal passage by sea, either from England to their post, or from one foreign post to another; and in the case of Secretaries of Embassy or Legation, and of second Secretaries, a similar allowance for one servant, if they have one; but no allowance will be made under the head of subsistence during a journey by land; neither will any allowance be made for the expense of the journey or subsistence of the families of any such Secretaries or Attachés. In the event of a passage being afforded to Secretaries or Attachés on board of one of Her Majesty's ships of war, the allowance made will be in conformity with the Admiralty Regulations.

No allowance will be made to the Junior Members of the Diplomatic Service for journeys undertaken for their own convenience, in pursuance of leave of absence; but in all such cases the expense of the journeys from and on returning to their posts will be exclusively at their own charge.

It is understood, moreover, that in the case of any journey of which the expense is to be allowed, Secretaries or Attachés, unless specially excused from doing so, will be bound to take charge of despatches, if required; and, in that case, they will be expected to perform the journey without delaying on the road.

9. *Interchange of Employment between Second and Third Secretaries, and Junior Clerks in the Foreign Office.*

The Secretary of State will, should he see occasion, for the advantage of the public service, allow Second and Third Secretaries, and Attachés, to interchange for a time their duties with Clerks of the three Junior Classes in the Foreign Office; the several parties being bound, for the whole period through which the interchange extends, in every respect to perform the duties and to submit to the obligations attaching to the situation which they may temporarily occupy.

The Secretary of State will, moreover, if he sees reason to do so, direct such temporary interchange of duties to be made, irrespective of the wishes of the parties, between Second or Third Secretaries, or Attachés, and Clerks in the Foreign Office; or he will direct such persons to be employed for a time, at home or abroad, without any interchange, making in either case such an allowance to the parties as he may consider just and reasonable. In the event of any Attaché being so employed in the Foreign Office, the period, over and above the six months which are obligatory as stated in section 2, during which he shall be actually employed in the Foreign Office, shall reckon towards the three years during which he is by these Regulations to reside at an Embassy or Mission abroad.

In the case of temporary interchanges between Secretaries and Clerks, they will respectively rank, during the period for which the interchange shall last, after the Junior in the classes of Secretaries or Clerks to which each of them belongs, the Clerk receiving an acting appointment as Secretary of such class. The same principle will apply in cases of permanent interchange.

If a Clerk in the Foreign Office should be permanently transferred to the Diplomatic Service, or should be temporarily employed with a Special, or with an Ordinary, Embassy or Mission, he will receive a Commission or an acting appointment, as the case may be, as Secretary of the Second or Third Class, according to the length of his service in the Foreign Office; but he will, as regards others then in the same class, enter it as the Junior.

### 10. *Deductions to be made from Salaries of Heads of Missions on Leave of Absence.*

With a view to relieve Heads of Missions on leave of absence on private grounds, the deduction to be made from their salaries will in future be limited, for a period not exceeding sixty days from the date of their departure from their posts, to the sum required to provide for the allowances of the Acting Chargés d'Affaires according to the present Regulations; on the expiration of which period the deduction will be at the rate of one-half of their salaries. Such period of sixty days may either be one of sixty consecutive days, or of sixty days occurring at intervals in the course of one year beginning on the 1st of January.

### 11. *Allowances during War or Interruption of Relations.*

Should an Ambassador, Minister, or Secretary, by reason of war or other interruptions of Diplomatic relations, be withdrawn from active service before his services shall have qualified him for a Diplomatic pension of the class under which he would otherwise come, the Secretary of State will, as he may see fit, assign to any such person a temporary allowance calculated on the rate of pension assigned to the class to which he belongs, regard being had to the length and general character of his services; such allowance being, however, strictly subject to the condition in regard to employment specified in the 7th section of the Act 2 & 3 Wm. IV. c. 116.*

### 12. *Date at which present Regulations shall take effect.*

The foregoing Regulations shall take effect from the 1st day of October, 1862; but Unpaid Attachés appointed previously to the 1st of January, 1861, will be allowed until the 1st of July, 1863, to undergo their second examination, according to the Regulations now in force; and if, on such second examination, they obtain their certificates, they will retain their present precedence, but not otherwise.

All persons nominated as Attachés subsequently to the date of the present Regulations will be subject to the provisions as to examination therein contained.

The condition of employment for six months in the Foreign Office will not be enforced with regard to Unpaid Attachés in the service abroad at the date of these Regulations; but such Unpaid Attachés must have passed both examinations under the existing Regulations; must have actually resided for a period of three years at one or more of Her Majesty's Embassies or Missions abroad, must have completed four years from the time of their entering the service, and must be provided with the certificate from the Head of the Mission under whom they have last served, specified in Clause 3 of these Regulations, before they can receive a commission as Secretary of the Third

Class, or the salary at the rate of £150 a-year assigned to that Class. Those persons who continue in the service, or who shall hereafter enter the service, as Unpaid Attachés, will be denominated "Attachés."

(Signed) RUSSELL.

Foreign Office, September 15, 1862.

---

## FOR CONSULAR APPOINTMENTS.

*(Approved by the Earl of Clarendon, January 1, 1856.)*

PERSONS selected for the Consular service—whenever the circumstance of their being resident in England on their first appointment or of their passing through England on their way to take up such first appointment, may admit of their being subjected to examination —will be expected to satisfy the Civil Service Commissioners—

1st. That they have a correct knowledge of the English language so as to be able to express themselves clearly and correctly in writing.

2nd. That they can write and speak French correctly and fluently.

3rd. That they have a sufficient knowledge of the current language, as far as commerce is concerned, of the port at which they are appointed to reside, to enable them to communicate directly with the authorities and natives of the place: a knowledge of the Italian language being taken to meet this requirement as far as any place situated to the east of the Straits of Gibraltar is concerned; and a knowledge of the German language as regards ports within the Baltic, or countries having ports in the Baltic.

4th. A sufficient knowledge of British Mercantile and Commercial Law to enable them to deal with questions arising between British ship-owners, ship-masters, and seamen. As regards this head of examination, candidates must be prepared to be examined in "Smith's Compendium of Mercantile Law."

5th. A sufficient knowledge of arithmetic for the nature of the duties which Consuls are required to perform in drawing up Commercial Tables and Reports. As regards this head of examination, candidates must be prepared to be examined in "Bishop Colenso's Arithmetic."

Moreover, all persons on their first nomination to Consulships, and after having passed their examination before the Civil Service Commissioners, will be required, as far as practicable, to attend for at least three months in the Foreign Office, in order that they may become acquainted with the forms of business as carried on there.

Limit of Age for Candidates:—25 to 50, both years inclusive.

## CHAPTER IV.

### OF THE DECLARATION AND OTHER EARLY MEASURES OF A STATE OF WAR.

---

IN the preceding chapters we have considered the principal rights and duties of nations in a state of peace; and if those duties were generally and duly fulfilled, a new order of things would arise, and shed a brighter light over the history of human affairs. Peace is said to be the natural state of man, and war is undertaken for the sake of peace, which is its only lawful end and purpose[1]. "Wars," says Lord Bacon[2], "are no massacres and confusions, but they are the highest trials of right when princes and states shall put themselves upon the justice of God for deciding their controversies as it shall please Him to put on either side." The history of mankind is an almost uninterrupted narration of a state of war, and gives colour to the extravagant theory of Hobbes[3], who maintains, that the natural

[1] Cic. *de Off.* I. 11 and 23. Grotius, Book I. Chap. I. Burlamaqui, Part IV. Chap. I. § 4. Vattel, Book IV. Chap. I.

[2] Bacon's *Works*, edited by Basil Montague, Vol. V. p. 384.

[3] *Leviathan*, Part I. Chap. 13. The allusion in the text to an often cited though probably carelessly examined dictum of one of the most vigorous as well as one of the clearest thinkers England can boast of, affords an opportunity for a reference to an admirable exposition of the excellencies and errors of Hobbes as a teacher and guide in the science of Politics by one who himself was a sure and certain light in the science of Jurispru-

state of man is a state of war of all against all; and it adds plausibility to the conclusions of those other writers, who, having known and studied the Indian character, insist, that continual war is the natural instinct and appetite of man in a natural state. It is, doubtless, true, that a sincere disposition for peace, and a just appreciation of its blessings, are the natural and necessary result of science and civilization.

All pacific modes of redress to be exhausted.

The right of self-defence is part of the law of our nature, and it is the indispensable duty of civil society to protect its members in the enjoyment of their rights, both of person and property. This is the fundamental principle of the social compact. An injury either done or threatened, to the perfect rights of the nation, or of any of its members, and susceptible of no other redress, is a just cause of war. The injury may consist, not only in the direct violation of personal or political rights, but in wrongfully withholding what is due, or in the refusal of a reasonable reparation for injuries committed, or of adequate explanation or security in respect to manifest and impending danger[1]. Grotius condemns the doctrine, that war may be undertaken to weaken the power of a neighbour, under the apprehension that its further increase may render him dangerous. This would be contrary to justice, unless we were morally certain, not only of a capacity, but of an actual intention to injure us. We ought rather to meet the anticipated danger by a diligent cultivation, and prudent management, of our own resources. We ought to conciliate the respect and good will of other nations, and secure their assistance in case of need, by the benevolence and justice of our conduct. War is not to be resorted to without absolute necessity, nor unless peace would be more dangerous, and more miserable, than war itself. An injury to an individual member of a state, is a just cause of war, if redress be refused,

dence, the late Mr John Austin: see Vol. I. p. 248 (note) of the recent edition of his works (1861).

[1] Grotius, Book II. Chap. I. and 22 Rutherforth, Book II. Chap. IX. Vattel, Book III. Chap. III. § 26.

but a nation is not bound to go to war on so slight a foundation; for it may of itself grant indemnity to the injured party, and if this cannot be done, yet the good of the whole is to be preferred to the welfare of a part[1]. [It is true that a just war, one that is undertaken for just causes, to repel or avert wrongful force, or to establish a right, cannot be impeached on any grounds, religious, moral, or political. And if it be carried to a successful issue, if force is repelled, wrong redressed, or imperilled rights established, for the evils which in its progress war has necessarily inflicted, there is large compensation. Yet, however large that compensation may be it must take years to remove the evils of war and to efface the traces of misery and sorrow it ever brings with it. It is therefore the bounden duty of every nation to pause before it resolves to renounce all means of obtaining a pacific solution of a difficulty that may arise between it and another state, to remember that the time bestowed upon efforts to avert war and its horrors, however long, is never time misspent, and to remember also that when once the sword is drawn and an appeal to arms is made, not only may the decision be prolonged indefinitely but the issue itself must be doubtful[2].]

Of course if the question of right between two powers be in any degree dubious they ought to forbear proceeding to extremities, for that nation would be condemned by the impartial voice of mankind which voluntarily went to war upon a claim whose legality it doubted. But on political subjects we know that the same rigorous demonstration is not to be expected, as does exist in the physical sciences; for policy is a science of calculations and combinations arising out of times places and circumstances and influenced largely by passing events, and therefore there are times when calm judgment is liable to be overthrown by views of fancied expediency and reason set at nought by passion. But against this frame of mind it behoves all

[1] Grotius, Book II. Chap. XXII—XXV. Rutherforth, Book II. Chap. IX.

[2] See *Annual Register* for 1842, p. 321.

nations earnestly to guard. [In doubtful claims, at all events, nations can never be too deliberate in their resolutions, or too diligent and careful in their examination of facts[1]. Nay, even in disputes where each side fancies it has a strong show of right, and therefore each is only too ready to watch with jealous distrustful eyes the attitude of of the other, it is the bounden duty of each to strive calmly and temperately to investigate all the facts and to exhaust every pacific mode of redress before resorting to arms. Nor is the history of the last thirty years without examples of such conduct on the part of three great nations in the case of claims and reclamations that might have produced terrible wars. Thus on two special occasions, when owing to peculiar circumstances the passions of the two nations were carried to an almost irrepressible point, the good sense and steady attitude of the government of Great Britain and the United States saved the subjects of both from the miseries of war; about the same time too a judicious compromise settled a dispute relating to a question of boundary between the same powers that at one time wore a threatening and hostile look; whilst hostilities that were on the very verge of breaking out between Great Britain and France in consequence of an alleged insult to a British consul in Otaheite were averted by the calm judgment, and the moderation of the statesmen by whom the two countries were ruled. A few words on these events will not be out of place here, because they are all of them most admirable examples of what some writers on International Law have classified as pacific settlements of disputes by way of friendly accommodation and compromise[2].

The case of the Caroline.

The first of the cases we are now engaged on arose out of the insurrectionary troubles that disturbed the Canadas in 1837 and 1838, and is known as the case of the *Caroline,* on account of the capture of a vessel of that name in

[1] Schmalz, *Le droit des Gens Européens traduit par le Comte de Bohm,* Liv. VI. Chap. I. p. 213.

[2] See Halleck, Chapter XII. §§ 3 and 4. Heffter, *Droit International,* § 109. Vattel, Book II. Chap. XVIII. §§ 226, 227.

American territory, followed by the arrest and trial of a British subject at New York, on the ground of implication in that affair. It would of course be out of place here to enter into the history of the events connected with the incident under discussion, and unnecessary, because a very clear and temperate account of the matter is given in Lord Ashburton's letter to Mr Webster, dated July 28, 1842, and to be found in the British and Foreign State Papers, 1841–2, Vol. xxx. p. 195. The only point of interest here lies in the fact, that a small passenger steamer, called the *Caroline,* was used by a number of insurgents and reckless people of the border to carry arms, and to transport armed men from the territory of the United States to that of the Canadas. This vessel the British officer in command (Colonel M^cNab) determined, at all hazards, to capture, expecting to find her moored on British ground, very near an island called Navy Island, on the Niagara River. It happened, however, that the *Caroline* had been moved from her usual moorings to the other shore, which was American territory. Undeterred by this, or by the preparations made to beat off an attack, the attempt was made, and after a short but fierce resistance, the vessel was captured by boarding, and at once carried off. It may be imagined that this most daring act excited intense indignation in New York and Washington, and throughout the United States. Probably the galling circumstance that a small force of volunteers, aided by a few seamen, should have so successfully carried out their plans in spite of a strong and well-armed resistance, and in the sight of American sympathizers with the rebellion, added fuel to a flame that the other fact of the capture taking place in American territory would alone have been sufficient to kindle, and it appeared scarcely possible to avert a war between the two countries, especially when the anger of the people of Great Britain and of the Canadian loyalists was roused by the arrest and imprisonment of Mr Macleod, and his trial on an indictment for murder, alleged to have been made in the attack upon the *Caro-*

Complaints of Great Britain.

*line.* On the side of Great Britain, then, the causes for complaint against the United States Government were, that a lawless expedition was allowed to be organized on American territory, without an effort, on the part of the Executive, to prevent or repress it; that the seditious movements against Canada were supported by bands of American citizens, and armed from American arsenals; and that a British subject was arrested and put upon his trial for a transaction of a public character, sanctioned by the constituted authorities of his Government, in contravention of the universal practice of civilized nations. On the side of the United States it was complained, that the attack upon the *Caroline* went beyond the limits of the law that allows an act of this kind, under the necessity of self-defence, instant, overwhelming, leaving no choice of means, and no moment for deliberation; that it was an attack upon a passenger ship, and on unarmed passengers and crew, and at night; that even if justifiable on the ground of self-defence, it was a violation of the territory of the United States; and that though the case had immediately been brought to the attention of the British Secretary of State for Foreign affairs, an unnecessary delay had taken place in the communication of his decision. Here, then, were complaints, charges, and countercharges, that might have embroiled two great nations, "and produced reprisals, or even general war," to use Mr Webster's words, but, fortunately for both countries, there was an inclination on the part of those who were at the head of affairs, not only to examine all the facts carefully, and to proceed with calm deliberation, but to act with mutual courtesy; and though the matter was in suspense for five years and upwards, on the appointment of Lord Ashburton, as Commissioner, to arrange the Maine Boundary question, it was happily settled. Her Majesty's Government having stated their regret at the violation of territory complained of, and at the omission, or neglect, to explain and apologize for that violation at the time of its occurrence; and having frankly explained the circumstances of the event,

Complaints of the United States.

attributable entirely to the necessity of the case, the Government of the United States expressed their satisfaction at this exhibition of good feeling, and their readiness to receive these acknowledgements and assurances in the conciliatory spirit in which they were offered[1]. Not long after the affair of the *Caroline*, there were fresh complications between the same Governments, in connection with what had often been a topic of animadversion, the slave trade; the case out of which they arose, briefly stated, was this. An American brig, called the *Creole*, of Richmond, Virginia, sailed on the 27th of October, 1841, from Hampton Roads to New Orleans, carrying, among other things, a cargo of slaves. On the 7th of November, while at sea, the slaves rose on the crew, murdered a passenger, wounded the captain and mate, and two of the crew; and, after obtaining possession of the brig, carried her into Nassau, New Providence. At the request of the American Consul, a guard was placed on board, and, after an investigation of the transaction by two magistrates, nineteen of the slaves were placed in confinement until further orders; but the proposition of the American Consul, that they should be sent to America, was refused; and the rest of the slaves, about 113 in all, were set at liberty, on the ground that they became free the moment they landed on British territory, and that England could not recognize the right of dominion claimed by American owners. It is scarcely necessary to say, that there was a furious storm of indignation in the Southern states against Great Britain, and loud denunciations of her, for aiding and abetting piracy and murder; and in a long despatch from Mr Webster to Lord Ashburton, dated August 1842, in which, whilst the facts of the case were not stated, but assumed to be known, it was specially urged, that vessels driven by necessity into a friendly port and detained there, ought to be regarded as still pursuing their original voyage and turned out of their

The case of the Creole.

[1] See *British and Foreign State Papers*, 1840—41, Vol. XXIX. pp. 1126—1142 and 1841—42, Vol. XXX. pp. 195—202.

course only by disaster or wrongful violence; and that if driven into foreign waters by stress of weather or unavoidable force, those on board ought not to be held to be within the territorial jurisdiction of the foreign port. To this despatch, which was couched in a friendly and courteous style, though earnestly pressing for a settlement of this and other questions by a formal Treaty, Lord Ashburton replied in language equally courteous and friendly. While admitting the importance of the case, he pointed out its peculiar circumstances, dwelt on the desire of the British government to respect the laws of their neighbours, and to listen to every possible suggestion of means of averting annoyance and injury, engaged that instructions should be given to the Governor of the British Colonies on the Southern boundaries of the United States, to execute their own laws with careful attention to the wish of their government, to maintain good neighbourhood; and that there should be no officious interference with American vessels driven by accident, or by unlawful violence, into these ports; but pointed out the necessity of referring so important a matter, as the consideration of a Treaty settlement, to the home government. With this reply, Mr Webster declared his government satisfied; and thus, on two occasions, complications, that at one time threatened to end in war, by the forbearance of the leading authorities in Great Britain and the United States, terminated, in what Vattel calls, an amicable accommodation[1].

The Tahiti affair 1842.

In the autumn of 1842, the island of Tahiti had been placed under French protection by Treaty. This was a measure that was so repugnant to the feelings of the islanders themselves, as well as of their Queen Pomaré,

[1] Book II. Chap. XVIII. § 326. Indemnity was accorded in January, 1855, for the loss resulting to the owners of the *Creole* by the umpire appointed under the convention of February 8th, 1853. See *Report of the Proceedings of the Mixed Commission on Private Claims*, compiled by Edward Hornby, Esq. p. 392. For the American view of this affair of the *Creole*, the reader is referred to Wheaton's *Elements*, Vol. I. p. 204 (n) 70, ed. by W. B. Laurence, 1863.

that the ill-will of the former was shown by constant petty outbreaks, and of the latter, by her refusal to hoist the French flag over her own. In consequence of this hostility, the French authorities went to the length of placing a countryman of their own in the seat of power, and Monsieur D'Aubigny was installed as governor in November 1843. This step of course was not one that was likely to make matters smoother, and the breach between the two parties became wider than ever. Whether by design, or from ignorance, the state of ill feeling on the part of the natives to the French, was attributed, by the latter, to the English protestant missionaries in the island; and as it happened that the recently appointed British Consul, Mr Pritchard, had been a missionary, he was pitched upon as the arch agitator, or, to use Captain Bruat's words, "a dangerous man, exercising his influence over the natives against France." On the morning of the 3rd of March 1844, a French sentinel on guard at the harbour was knocked down by a blow of the fist, and an attempt was made to rob him of his musket. That attempt, however, was frustrated, and the would be thief was captured. "Struck with this piece of audacity," says Monsieur D'Aubigny, "and convinced that all our strength lies in our moral superiority over the natives, persuaded too that the best means to put an end to such acts was to seize their director and instigator, I decided on causing Pritchard to be arrested." Accordingly, his arrest was effected at 5 o'clock that evening (the 3rd of March); he was sent to prison, and was only released on condition that he should not be again landed on the Society Islands: he was therefore removed to Valparaiso, and thence to England. Great was the indignation in England when the news of this affair arrived there; how serious the crisis was is visible in the correspondence between Comte de Jarnac, the French Ambassador in England, and Monsieur Guizot. "Such an excitement," says the Count, in a despatch dated August 4th, 1844, "I have never seen caused by any political event since my sojourn here: the public press treat it as a proof of the evident hostility and animosity of our government towards England, whilst Lord Aberdeen, though anxious to preserve a friendly attitude towards me, is evidently much annoyed by this difficulty, and seems fully convinced that satisfaction for it is imperiously required." Sir Robert Peel too, in the House of Commons, declared, "that a gross outrage, accompanied with gross indignity, had been committed upon Mr Pritchard." Fortunately, there was an anxious desire on the part of the French government to investigate calmly the circumstances of the case, and a readiness to listen to reason and justice, rather than to give way to national vanity. Monsieur Guizot, therefore, in acknowledging the gravity of the situation, and urging the importance of calm discussion, after a temperate statement of what he conceived to be the right of the French government, confessed that the arrest of Mr Pritchard had been a hasty act, and expressed to the British authorities the regret of his government for, and their disapprobation of, the circumstances attending it, and their willingness to give him an equitable indemnity; language and proposals that were at once accepted by Her Majesty's government as completely satisfactory[1].

Here, then, we have three occasions on which, by the self-action of the parties concerned, by a cool and candid examination of the subject of dispute, and by a gentle method of terminating differences, three of the greatest countries in the world set examples of forbearance that deserve to be recorded as precedents worthy of imitation.

Compromise.

But there is a second method of bringing disputes to a peaceful termination, produced also by the self-action of the parties concerned, one in which concessions are made on both sides[2]. This is the form of settlement known by the name compromise; and of all the instances that may serve to illustrate it, there are none that better deserve a place in a treatise of this kind, as a precedent,

[1] *British and Foreign State Papers*, 1843—44, Vol. XXXII. 1063—1079.
[2] Vattel, Book II. Chap. XVIII. § 327.

than the settlement of the disputes relating to the Maine boundary. These disputes arose out of the treaty of 1783 between Great Britain and the United States, in which the frontier was arranged to be "a ridge dividing the waters that flow into the St Lawrence from those which flow into the Atlantic." Without describing them, or specifying the desires of both parties[1], it will be sufficient to say that, after a reference by consent to the King of Holland in 1827, whose award in 1831, though by no means favourable to Great Britain, was rejected by the American Government; and after an elaborate enquiry by two Commissions, one in 1839 and another in 1841, sent out by Lord Palmerston to enquire into the merits of the lines claimed respectively by the two parties, it was determined by Sir Robert Peel at the end of 1841, to try the effect of a Special Mission, presided over by a nobleman of high repute in the mercantile world, and of high esteem in the United States. Accordingly, Lord Ashburton left England early in 1842, and at once announced his purpose and the spirit with which he was actuated, in a despatch dated June 13th, 1842. He said, in effect, that any attempt to revive old discussions would be productive of fruitless labour; that the resort to arbitration was useless; and, therefore, that the present effort would have to rest for its success on the alternative of a compromise. To these views Mr Webster expressed his assent, admitting the importance of each side showing a disposition to yield liberally to mutual convenience; and eventually, after a comparatively short, and certainly courteous, correspondence, the boundary was fixed, and a Treaty, agreed to settle it, drawn up. That this was a compromise, a mutual waiver of claims, and certainly on the side of Great Britain a liberal concession, is shewn by the Debates in the Legislative Chambers of both Countries. It is a remarkable fact that, on each side of the Atlantic, the Treaty was

The Maine Boundary.

[1] They will be found at full length in the *Parliamentary Debates*, Hansard, Vol. LXVIII. pp. 599—678, and in the *British and Foreign State Papers*, 1841—42, Vol. XXX. pp. 141—181.

attacked as a settlement productive of injury to the honour and the mutual interests of each country; by Lord Palmerston it was stigmatized as the Ashburton Capitulation, whilst Mr Webster was compelled to deliver a most elaborate defence of the policy of his government in concluding the Convention. To that speech we especially invite attention for two reasons; first, because it contains a most lucid and exhaustive narrative of the events that preceded and led to the Maine Boundary Compromise; and, secondly, because a perusal of it will show that the action of the British Government was as disinterested as it was honest; that their expressed intention of compromising was strictly adhered to, and that they were willing even to yield what, in strict law, they might have retained. "For, if we had gone for arbitration," said Mr Webster, "we should inevitably have lost what the treaty gave to Vermont and New York, because all that was clear matter of cession, and not adjustment of Boundary[1]."

From the settlement of disputes and the averting of war by the self action of nations in the way thus recorded we advance to two other methods of obtaining a pacific solution of difficulties by the help of third parties both of which are deserving of a few words of explanation and illustration.

Mediation. "The approved usage of nations," says Mr Wheaton, "authorizes the proposal of one state of its good offices or mediation for the settlement of the intestine divisions of another state. When such offer is accepted it becomes a just title for the interference of the mediating power[2]. In one very important respect the mediator differs from the arbitrator, viz. in not giving a judgment, but only counsel and advice[3]. Sir James Mackintosh styles him a

[1] See Webster's *Works*, Vol. v. p. 78, &c. The negotiations terminating in the treaty of 1846, in which the Oregon difficulty was formally disposed of, are cited by General Halleck as another modern example of compromise, but as that difficulty is not finally settled we have abstained from entering into it.

[2] Wheaton's *Elements*, Vol. I. Part. II. Chap. II. § 13, ed. 1863.

[3] Garden, *Traité de la Diplomatie*, Tome I. p. 436, note.

common friend who counsels both parties with a weight proportioned to his behalf in their integrity and in their respect for his power[1].

It is the undoubted business of every nation, that has sufficient power and influence to make its voice heard, when there is a danger of peace being disturbed to spare no trouble in efforts to preserve that peace. Hubner, with truth, affirms it to be the greatest duty neutrals have to discharge[2]; and though a modern writer, who professes to be the ardent champion of neutral rights, and who looks with just disfavour upon those who engage in war, maintains that the perils of mediation are greater than the advantages to be derived from it, and that it ends in an interference between two other people that neutrals ought to avoid, yet the practice of modern times happily is at variance with such cold-blooded views; and the expressed opinions of the leading statesmen by whom the peace of Europe in 1856 was settled, are in direct opposition to Monsieur D'Hautefeuille's recommendations[3]. To those who may wish to see an example of the attitude and the diplomatic language of a neutral nation eager to prevent war and pressing its good offices as a mediator between two neighbouring states on the verge of hostilities, we recommend a perusal of the documents containing the offer of Great Britain to mediate between France and Spain in 1823, an offer which though rejected by the former for particular reasons, met with no unfriendly notice from both sides. Nor should the efforts of the Emperor of the French to put a stop to the present destructive war between the Northern and the Southern portions of the United States be forgotten[4]. For although the two powers whose aid

[1] Hansard, Vol. XXX. 326.

[2] Twiss's *Law of Nations*, Vol. II. p. 12, &c. where the reader will find a very complete and clear statement of mediation as distinguished from arbitration. Hubner, *De la Saisie, &c.* Tome I. Part I. Chap. II. § II.

[3] D'Hautefeuille, *Droits et devoirs des nations neutres*, Tome I. Tit. V. § I.

[4] The despatch of the French Minister of Foreign Affairs (Oct. 30, 1862) will be found set out at length in the 2nd Vol. of Wheaton's *Elements*, edn. 1863, by J. P. Lawrence, p. 1009. (Note 167, p. 501.)

he invoked did not consider the time had yet come for any prospect of success from the offer of mediation, yet was the offer itself not the less deserving of the highest commendation. But if we wanted any further proof of the importance and value of mediation as a method of putting a stop to international disputes we have them in two remarkable modern instances. In the 23rd Protocol of the Treaty of Paris (1856) the Earl of Clarendon earnestly pressed upon the conference the necessity of seeking out every expedient calculated to prevent a return of the calamities of war: he pointed out the existence of a clause in the new treaty recommending mediation in the event of disputes between the Porte and the other signing powers, and then proposed to the conference to agree upon a resolution that should have a more general application and become a barrier to conflicts, which frequently only break out because it is not always possible to enter into explanations: in short to initiate a policy of recognized international mediation. The proposition, it is true, owing to the opposition of Austria, did not meet with such an unanimous reception as to allow of its being recorded as an article of the Treaty; but the Plenipotentiaries did not hesitate to express a wish that States should, before appealing to arms, have recourse, as far as circumstances might allow, to the good offices of neutral powers. In the same spirit Earl Russell suggested, and M. De Bismarck accepted the suggestion in the course of the late contest respecting the Duchies of Schleswig and Holstein, that the following principle ought to be laid down as the basis of any future experiment, viz. that all matters of international difference should be referred to the mediation of friendly non-German powers, with a view to a pacific and final settlement[1].

Arbitration. From mediation or the voluntary self-proposed action of a third power, either to prevent impending hostilities or to

[1] Papers relating to Denmark and Germany, laid before Parliament, No. 178, p. 168.

stay the further effusion of blood, we advance to the consideration of Arbitration, or, to use Vattel's words, "that reasonable and natural mode of deciding such disputes as do not directly interest the safety of a nation,—a third power chosen by common agreement." Vattel in enumerating one or two of the leading features of this form of settling difficulties dwells upon the necessity of having a specification of the subject in dispute precisely laid down in the arbitration articles, as well as the demands of one side and the objections of the other; and of the necessity also of the arbitrator's judgment being confined within these precise bounds. "If that is done," says he, "the contending parties are bound to abide by his decision, for if they pretend to evade it they must prove by incontestable facts that it was the offspring of corruption or flagrant partiality[1]." Monsieur Heffter, whose paragraph on this topic contains some very useful hints, states the following as valid grounds of objection to an arbitrator's judgment.

1st. If given without any sufficient agreement to refer, or beyond the terms of the agreement.

2ndly. If given by arbitrators who turn out to be utterly incapable.

3rdly. If the arbitrator or the other (that is the successful) party has not acted in good faith.

4thly. If the parties, or one of them, have not been understood.

5thly. If the judgment relates to things not in dispute. And

6thly. If its terms are absolutely at variance with the rules of justice, and cannot therefore form the object of any agreement[2].

On this statement of grounds of objection two remarks may be made: first, that they should rather be termed *excuses* for not taking up an award that may turn out

[1] Vattel, Book II. chap. XVIII. § 329; see also Klüber, *Dr. des Gens mod. de l'Eur.* § 318, Martens, *Précis du Dr. des Gens mod.*, Tome II. §§ 176 and 327. Phillimore's *International Law,* Vol. III. § 3.

[2] *Droit Internat. Public,* § 109.

different to what was expected; and secondly, that if Vattel's rule, of laying down precisely the subject of the dispute, the propositions, and the counter propositions, be rigidly adhered to, there can be no legal reason (always assuming that a competent, upright, and impartial arbitrator is selected) for setting the award aside. But, as Monsier Vergé[1] says, "Arbitration has of late years lost the important position in international disputes it once occupied, and modern practice shows that whilst its objects are generally only matters of secondary interest, objections not always of the fairest or most substantial kind, can be and are found for refusing to abide by an arbitrator's judgment." Still there are questions that are pre-eminently fitted for arbitration. Thus, in disputes relating to boundaries between states—"The sense of modern times, the law of humanity, the honour of civilized states, and the authority of religion, all require that controversies of this sort which cannot be adjusted by the parties themselves, should be referred to the decision of some intelligent and impartial tribunal[2]." Again, in contested claims made by the subjects of one state for losses occasioned by the alleged misconduct or negligence of another state, or in reclamations by one state against another for violation of neutral territory, the calm decision of a competent and disinterested third power has been a valuable means of obtaining satisfaction. Instances are not wanting in recent times of such modes of settlement. Thus in the case of the claims of the British government for losses sustained by its merchants trading to the coast of Portendic, in consequence of the blockade of that coast by France in 1834 and 1835, reference to His Majesty the King of Prussia was made by the consent of both the powers interested. By his award, dated the 30th November, 1843, France was held to be bound in

The Portendic claims.

[1] In a note to the French edition of Vattel by Pradier Fodéré, Tome II. Liv. II. chap. XVIII. § 229, p. 306.

[2] Webster's *Works*, Vol. II. pp. 325—26, speaking of the Maine boundary question and defending the government for referring the matter to the arbitration of the King of the Netherlands.

equity to pay an indemnity for the alleged losses; the amount of compensation and mode of payment being left to two commissioners (one English and one French) and an umpire. Again in the case of the reclamations made by the United States government upon that of Portugal for the destruction of the privateer, *General Armstrong*, in Fayal Harbour, in 1814, by an English squadron, being in effect a violation of neutral territory, the matter was referred to the arbitration of the Emperor Louis Napoleon, at that time President of the French Republic, who by his award dated the 30th November, 1852, having ascertained that the first shot was fired by the American commander, that the protection of the Portuguese government was not appealed to until the fight had commenced, and that consequently the American captain had himself violated the neutral territory of the Portuguese sovereign, held that on these grounds that sovereign not responsible for the result of the conflict, and consequently no indemnity to be due to the American government[1].]

Case of *The General Armstrong.*

Assistance by Treaty.

If one nation be bound by treaty to afford assistance, in a case of war between its ally and a third power, the assistance is to be given whenever the *casus fœderis* (or case of the alliance) occurs; [in other words, whenever the engagements thus contracted come in force; and the nation so bound is under an obligation to act in consequence of the alliance]. But a question will sometimes arise, whether the Government which is to afford the aid, is to judge for itself of the justice of the war on the part of the ally, and to make the right to assistance depend upon its own judgment. Grotius is of opinion that treaties of that kind do not oblige us to participate in a war which appears to be manifestly unjust on the part of the ally; and it is said to be a tacit condition annexed to every

[1] This award, as well as that of the king of Prussia above mentioned, will be found in the *British and Foreign State Papers*, 1852—53, pp. 1377—1380. Mr Lawrence has also commented on the *General Armstrong* decision in a note (217) to his last edition of Wheaton's *Elements*, Vol. II. Part IV. chap. III. § 11. p. 720.

treaty made in time of peace, and stipulating to afford succours in time of war, that the stipulation is only to apply to a just war. To give assistance in an unjust war, on the ground of the treaty, would be contracting an obligation to do injustice, and no such contract is valid[1]. But to set up a pretext of this kind in order to avoid a positive engagement is extremely hazardous, and it cannot be done, except in a very clear case, without exposing the nation to the imputation of a breach of public faith. In doubtful cases, the presumption ought rather to be in favour of our ally, and of the justice of his war[2].

The doctrine that one nation is not bound to assist another, under any circumstances, in a war clearly unjust, is similar to the principle in the feudal law, to be met with in the *Book of Feuds,* compiled from the usages of the Lombards, and forming part of the common law of Europe, during the prevalence of the feudal system. [A vassal was bound to assist his lord in a just war; but though bound to defend him, might, if he pleased, abstain from helping him in offensive operations where the war was unjust[3].]

A nation which has agreed to render assistance to another, is not obliged to furnish it when the case is hopeless, or when giving the succours would expose the state itself to imminent danger. Such extreme cases are tacit exceptions to the obligation of the treaty; but the danger must not be slight, remote, or contingent, for this would be to seek a frivolous cause to violate a solemn engagement[4]. In the case of a defensive alliance, the condition of the contract does not call for the assistance, unless the ally be engaged in a *defensive* war, for in a defensive alliance, the nation engages only to defend its ally, in case he be attacked, and even then

[1] B. 2. ch. XV. § 13; XXIV. § 4. Bynk. *Qu. Jur. Pub.* Lib. I. c. 9. Vattel, B. II. ch. XII. § 168; B. III. ch. VI. §§ 86, 87.

[2] Wheaton's *Elem. of Int. Law,* Vol. I. Part III. ch. II. § 15, ed. 1863, by W. B. Lawrence.

[3] *Feud.* Lib. II. tit. 28, § 1.

[4] Vattel, B. III. c. VI. § 92.

we are to enquire whether he be not justly attacked[1]. The defensive alliance applies only to the case of a war first commenced, in point of fact, against the ally, and the power that first declares, or actually begins the war, makes what is deemed, in the conventional law of nations, an *offensive* war[2]. The treaty of alliance between France and the United States, in 1778, was declared, by the second article, to be a defensive alliance; and that declaration gave a character to the whole instrument, and consequently the whole guaranty, on the part of the United States, of the French possessions in America, could only apply to future defensive wars on the part of France. Upon that ground the Government of the United States, in 1793, did not consider themselves bound to depart from their neutrality, and to take part with France in the war in which she was then engaged[3]. The war of 1793 was first actually declared and commenced by France, against all the allied powers of Europe, and the nature of the guaranty required the United States to look only to that fact.

[As there are points of contact in treaties of alliance and of guarantee, especially with reference to the *casus fœderis*, a few additional remarks upon each of these international engagements will not be out of place here.

Treaties of Alliance.

In defensive alliances (for these remarks are confined to them), although the *casus fœderis*, as we have seen, depends first on the justice and next on the defensive character of the war; yet, whilst on the one hand the presumption of the justice of his quarrel in doubtful cases always is in

1 Vattel, B. III. c. VI. §§ 79, 83, 90.

2 A war may be *defensive* in its principles, though *offensive* in its operation, as where attack is the best mode to repel a menaced invasion, and the *casus fœderis* of a *defensive* alliance will apply. He who first renders the application of force necessary is the aggressor, though he may not be the one who first actually applies it. Vattel, B. III. ch. VI. §§ 91, 100. *Edin. Review*, No. 89, pp. 244, 5.

3 See *Pacificus*, written in 1793, by Mr Hamilton, then Secretary of the Treasury, and the *Instructions from the Secretary of State to the American Ministers to France, July* 15th, 1797. See also Wheaton's *Elements*, Vol. I. Part III. ch. II. § 15, p. 490, note 165, ed. 1863, by W. B. Lawrence, for a *résumé* of the discussion.

favour of the confederate, on the other this restriction of the obligation applies only to instances of clear and manifest injustice, and is never to be resorted to as a pretence for evading treaty obligations; and therefore even where the ally who appeals to the alliance, and calls for aid, has been wrong in the first instance, yet if he has made an offer of reasonable satisfaction, and that offer has been rejected by his enemy, the *casus fœderis* comes in force, and whatever has been promised in the treaty of alliance is due in the *casus fœderis*[1]. Where, therefore, the war is unaggressive, just, or inevitable, the allied state is bound in law and honour to render the assistance stipulated; for no matter what shape the danger, provided it be real, may assume, whether marked by open hostilities or confined to instigations to revolt and mutiny on the part of the enemy, whether the authority of the sovereign be denounced as an usurpation, the well-affected portion of his subjects being treated as enemies, the ill-affected as friends; or whether when the insurrection has broken out, money, provisions, arms, and military stores be supplied by another power to further the rebellious movement, in all these events the *casus fœderis* will arise, and the injured state may call upon its ally for the succour agreed upon by the treaty[2].

France and the United Provinces, 1665.

Nor are there wanting in the public history of Europe excellent illustrations of the points above mentioned. Thus, so far back as the year 1665, when the United Provinces called upon France, at that time their ally, to assist them in their contest with England, the answer they received was that the English Government had announced its intention of proving that the Dutch were the transgressors, "in which event," said France, "the *casus fœderis* would not arise[3]."

[1] Grotius *de J. et B.* Lib. II. ch. XV. § 13; ch. XXV. § 4. Bynk. *Q. J. P.* Lib. I. ch. IX. Vattel, Book III. ch. VI. §§ 86, 87. Wheaton's *Elements*, Vol. I. Part III. ch. II. § 15.

[2] *Edinburgh Review*, Vol. XLV. p. 243.

[3] *Flassan*, III. p. 537. It must however be acknowledged that this was a somewhat shabby, and, as it turned out, interested evasion of treaty obligations.

Again, a hundred years or so later, when Great Britain, then in alliance with the states of Holland, appealed to the three treaties of alliance made in 1678, in 1709 and 1713, and in 1717 respectively, and invoked the aid of the states in consequence of the attack of France upon Minorca, then forming part of the possessions of Great Britain, the Dutch Government contended first that the *casus fœderis* had not arisen, Great Britain having been the aggressor, and next that the hostilities commenced by France were the consequence of hostilities previously commenced in America. Each of these objections Lord Liverpool, in what Mr Wheaton has characterized with truth as an irresistible reply, demolished in turn, pointing out the true nature of these alliances. "It is not presumed," said he, "that they who framed these treaties meant that either party should be obliged to support every act of violence or injustice which his ally might be prompted to commit through views of interest or ambition, but on the other hand they were cautious of affording too frequent opportunities to pretend that the case of the guarantees (that is, the *casus fœderis*) did not exist, and of eluding thereby the principal intention of the alliance; both these inconveniences were equally to be avoided." Again, with reference to the second objection, ("and his answer to that," says Mr Wheaton, "illustrates the good faith by which these contracts ought to be interpreted"), "If the reasoning on which this objection is founded," he urges, "were admitted, it would alone be sufficient to destroy the effects of every such treaty, and to extinguish that confidence which nations mutually place in each other on the faith of defensive alliances; it points out to the enemy a certain method of avoiding the inconvenience of such an alliance; it shows him where he ought to begin his attack[1]." Great Britain and Holland, 1709.

We have already had occasion in a former chapter to Portugal, 1826.

[1] *Discourse on the Conduct of the Government of Great Britain in respect to Neutral Nations*, by the Earl of Liverpool. See also Wheaton's *Elements*, Vol. I. Part III. ch. II. § 15, pp. 483—485, ed. 1863, by W. B. Lawrence.

notice the conduct and attitude of the British Government towards Portugal when in 1826 it was reminded of the ancient and still continuing treaties of alliance by which the two countries were bound together, and its assistance was demanded against the hostile designs of the Spanish court. We cited it then as a so-called instance of intervention, we cite it now as a proper and valuable illustration of the rule "that in defensive alliances every wrong which gives to one ally a just cause of war entitles him to succour from the other ally." It will be sufficient to quote the following words of Mr Canning, who after narrating the various treaties of alliance between the two countries, said "This being the state of our relations when the Regency of Portugal, in apprehension of the coming storm, called on Great Britain for aid, the only question we had to consider was whether the *casus fœderis* had arisen. In our opinion it had[1]."

In generalizing upon the subject of treaties of alliance one rule stands out in clearer relief than any of the others, and that is "that when once an engagement of this kind is contracted, if the *casus fœderis* can be shewn to arise, that engagement ought to be fulfilled at all risks." It is no answer to the demand for help to say that the assistance cannot be rendered nor the promised succour given because there will be imminent danger in so doing[2]. National honour, and that faith which is the foundation of all contracts, demand that treaties be strictly observed. If there is any prospect of danger arising out of their obligations the right course is to abstain from entering into them at all, but if they are entered into, then the danger must be set against the gains, and the maxim will apply, *qui sentiunt commodum sentire debent et onus.*

Guarantees. It remains to add a few words on the subject of guarantees, that is, additional agreements (pacta accessoria) entered into by some powerful state or states, for the pur-

[1] *Parliamentary Debates,* XVI. 356.

[2] Vattel holds a contrary opinion, Book III. ch. VI. § 92.

pose of maintaining the integrity of a province or territory, the political existence or sovereignty of a state, the right of succession to a throne, or the terms and conditions of a treaty of peace—in fact being in themselves a kind of treaty in which help is promised in the shape of money[1] or arms to some one or more contracting powers. Such an undertaking however gives the guaranteeing state no right to interfere unasked in the execution of a treaty, for that would be to substitute for the mere act of guaranty, the power of interfering in the internal affairs of a state. On the other hand it lays no absolute obligation on the guaranteeing state to assist that one of the contracting parties in whose favour it may be bound, in the events of disputes between the contracting parties themselves—and most certainly, as a modern writer[2] urges, it lays no obligation upon and gives no right to the guaranteeing state or states to interfere in favour of or against subjects who may, by force of arms even, be attempting to make political changes or to alter a form of government[3].

Guaranty conventions are of frequent occurrence, and may be said have proved a fruitful source of trouble in the public history of Europe, from the time of the treaty of Westphalia in 1648, down to the treaty of Paris in 1856[4]. It is unnecessary to examine or even to enumerate them; many of them will be found in the modern editions of Vattel, Klüber, and Wheaton, and in the works of Phillimore and Twiss. Those who may be desirous of investigating the subject with reference to Great Britain will find,

[1] See the guaranties of Russia, England and France to Greece under the Convention of 7 May, 1832. *British and Foreign State Papers*, Vol. XIX. 1831-32, p. 33.

[2] Twiss on *International Law*, Vol. I. § 230, p. 320.

[3] See Protocols Nos. 10 and 13, *Treaty of Paris*, 1856. *Parliamentary Papers*, Vol. LXI. pp. 42 and 51.

[4] The guaranteeing clause of the Treaty of Westphalia is in Art. XVII. See a short commentary on it in Schœll. *Hist. des Traités de Paix*, T. I. Part I. ch. I. sect. 4, § 3, and a notice of the various treatises on it in *Ompteda Literatur*, II. 619 f. The guaranteeing clauses of the *Treaty of Paris*, 1856, are Arts. VII. XXVII. XXVIII.

in the Return to an Address of the House of Commons, August 9, 1859,—"Copies of such parts of all Treaties and Conventions now existing, and still obligatory, as contain an engagement of guaranty, under which this country is in any way, or on any contingency bound[1]."]

Declaration of war.

In the old republics of Greece and Italy, the right of declaring war resided with the people, who retained, in their collective capacity, the exercise of a large portion of the sovereign power[2]. Among the ancient Germans it belonged also to the popular assemblies[3], and the power was afterwards continued in the same channel, and actually resided in the Saxon Wittenagemote[4]. But in the monarchies of Europe, which arose upon the ruins of the feudal system, this important prerogative was generally assumed by the king, as appertaining to the duties of the executive department of government. Many publicists[5] consider the power as a part of the sovereign authority of the state, of which the legislative department is an essential branch. There are, however, several exceptions to the generality of this position; for in the limited monarchies of England, France, and Holland, the king alone declares war, and yet the power, to apply an observation of Vattel to the case, is but a slender prerogative of the crown, if the parliaments or legislative bodies of those kingdoms will act independently, since the king cannot raise the money requisite to carry on the war without their consent. The wild and destructive

[1] For full information on the subject of defensive alliances and guarantees the reader may consult Vattel, Book II. ch. XII. §§ 172—197, and ch. XVI., and Book III. ch. VI. §§ 87—101. Martens' *Précis du Droit des Gens*, Tit. ii. Lib. VIII. ch. VIII. § 338. Klüber, §§ 148, 149, 157, 158, 159, ed. 1861, par M. A. Ott. Heffter, *Droit des Gens*, §§ 96 and 97. Twiss on *International Law*, Vol. I. §§ 228—232. Phillimore, Vol. II. Wildman, *Institutes of International Law*, Vol. I. pp. 164—170. Wheaton's *Elements*, Vol. I. Part III. c. II. §§ 12—15. Halleck, §§

[2] Thirlwall's *Greece*, ch. VIII. XI. Niebuhr's *History of Rome*, Vol. II. p. 184, ed. 1822. Fuss's *Roman Antiquities*, §§ 146—177 (Oxford 1840).

[3] Tacit. *de M. G.* c. II. Menzel's *Hist. of Ger.*, Vol. I. Part I. Bohn's ed.

[4] Millar's *View of the English Government*, B. I. ch. 7.

[5] *Puff.* B. VIII. ch. VI. § 10. Vattel, B. III. ch. I. § 4.

wars of Charles XII. led the states of Sweden to reserve to themselves the right of declaring war; and in the form of government adopted in Sweden in 1772[1], the right to make war was continued in the same legislative body. This was the provision in those ephemeral constitutions which appeared in Poland and France the latter part of the last century; and as evidence of the force of public opinion on this subject, it may be observed, that in the constitution proposed by Bonaparte, on his reascension of the throne of France in 1815, the right to levy men and money for war, was to rest entirely upon a law, to be proposed to the House of Representatives of the people, and assented to by them. In the United States, the power of declaring war, as well as of raising the supplies, is wisely confided to the legislature of the Union, the presumption being that nothing short of a strong case deeply affecting essential rights, and which cannot receive a pacific adjustment, after all reasonable efforts shall have been exhausted, will ever prevail upon Congress to declare war. [In Great Britain, on the other hand, the right of making peace or war is the sole prerogative of the Crown, like all the other great prerogatives of the Crown, exercised by the advice and upon the responsibility of the State, and subject to the check of Parliamentary censure or impeachment[2].]

Declaration of War. Ancient custom.

It has been usual to precede hostilities by a public declaration communicated to the enemy. It was the custom of the ancient Greeks and Romans to publish a declaration of the injuries they had received, and to send a herald to the enemy's borders to demand satisfaction, before they actually engaged in war; and invasions, without notice, were not looked upon as lawful[3]. War was declared with religious

[1] Art. 48. But this free constitution of Sweden was overturned before the end of the year 1772, and a simple despotism established in its stead.

[2] See *Institutions of the English Government,* by Homersham Cox, M.A. Book III. ch. II. § 2.

[3] Schömann, *Antiq. Juris Publ. Græcorum,* Pars VI. §§ 1—4, pp. 364—371. Livy, B. I. ch. XXXII. Cic. *de Off.* B. I. ch. XI. Osenbrüggen, *De Jure belli et pacis Romanorum,* ch. I.

preparation and solemnity. According to Ulpian[1], they alone were reputed enemies against whom the Roman people had publicly declared war. During the Middle Ages, a previous declaration of war was held to be requisite by the laws of honour, chivalry, and religion. Lewis IX. refused to attack the Sultan of Egypt until he made a previous declaration to him by a herald at arms, and one of his successors sent a herald with great formality to the Governor of the Low Countries, when he declared war against that power in 1635[2]. But, in modern times, the practice of a solemn declaration made to the enemy, has fallen into disuse, and the nation contents itself with making a public declaration of war within its own territory, and to its own people. The jurists are, however, divided in opinion, in respect to the necessity or justice of some previous declaration to the enemy in the case of offensive war. Grotius[3] considers a previous demand of satisfaction, and a declaration, as requisite to a solemn and lawful war; and Puffendorf[4] holds acts of hostility, which have not been preceded by a formal declaration of war, to be no better than acts of piracy and robbery. Emerigon[5] is of the same opinion; and he considered the hostilities exercised by England in the year 1755, prior to any declaration of war, to have been in contempt of the law of nations, and condemned by all Europe. Vattel strongly recommends[6] a previous declaration of war, as being required by justice and humanity; citing the fecial law of the Romans as worthy of imitation for giving such moderation and religious solemnity to a preparation of war.

Bynkershoek has devoted an entire chapter to this question[7], maintaining, that a declaration of war is not re-

[1] *Dig.* 49. 15. 24. Cicero says, that under the Roman kings it was instituted law, that war was unjust and impious, unless declared and proclaimed by the heralds under religious sanction. *De Repub.* Lib. II. XVII.

[2] Emerigon, *Traité des Ass.* ch. XII. § XXXV. p. 561. Translated by J. Meredith, ed. 1550, p. 437.

[3] Book I. ch. III. § 4.

[4] B. VIII. ch. VI. § 9.

[5] *Traité des Ass.* Tom. I. p. 563.

[6] B. III. ch. IV. § 51.

[7] *Quæst. J. Pub.* B. I. ch. II.

quisite by the law of nations, and that though it may very properly be made, it cannot be required as a matter of right. The practice rests entirely on manners and magnanimity, being borrowed from the ancient Romans. All that he contends for is, that a demand of what we conceive to be due should be previously made. We are not bound to accompany that demand with threats of hostility, or to follow it with a public declaration of war; and he cites many instances to show, that within the two last centuries, wars have been frequently commenced without a previous declaration. Since the time of Bynkershoek, it has become settled by the practice of Europe, that war may lawfully exist by a declaration which is unilateral only, or without a declaration on either side. It may begin with mutual hostilities[1]. Since the Peace of Versailles in 1763, formal declarations of war of any kind seem to have been discontinued, and all the necessary and legitimate consequences of war flow at once from a state of public hostilities, duly recognised, and explicitly announced, by a domestic manifesto or state paper. In the war between England and France in 1778, the first public act on the part of the English government, was recalling its minister, and that single act was considered by France as a breach of the peace between the two countries. There was no other declaration of war, though each government afterwards published a manifesto in vindication of its claims and conduct. The same thing may be said of the war which broke out in 1793, and again in 1803; and, indeed, in the war of 1756, though a solemn and formal declaration of war, in the ancient style, was made in June, 1756, vigorous hostilities had been carried on between England and France for a year preceding. In the war declared by the United States against England in 1812, hostilities were immediately commenced on their part as soon as the act of Congress was passed, without waiting to communicate to the English Government any notice of their intentions.

Modern custom.

[1] Sir Wm. Scott, 1 Dodson's *Adm. Rep.* 247.

But, though a solemn declaration, of previous notice to the enemy, be now laid aside, it is essential that some formal public act, proceeding directly from the competent source, should announce to the people at home their new relations and duties growing out of a state of war, and at the same time apprize neutral nations of the fact, to enable them to conform their conduct to the rights belonging to the new state of things[1]. As Vattel says, War is often at present published and declared by manifestoes, and just as treaties of peace operate from their date to annul all hostile acts, so these manifestoes operate from their date to legalize [and distinguish them from naked wrongs, for which under certain circumstances reparation may be claimed[2]].

Manifestoes.

[In modern times, too, documents of this kind are used as formal and solemn justifications to the rest of the world of the conduct and ulterior views of the belligerent immediately interested; they will therefore be generally found to contain other matters than a simple declaration of war, and to be intended not so much for a warning to the subjects of the belligerent nation of the fact of war as for an appeal to public opinion. The fact itself, thanks to the publicity given to the discussions and debates of nations on subjects of international importance by the press, and by the improved condition of international intercourse, is often known long before the last manifesto or declaration appears; and it not unfrequently happens that warlike intentions are proclaimed by other preliminaries than manifestoes or declarations, as for instance by the recall of ambassadors, by the tender of an ultimatum, or by peremptory language followed by hostile acts. Thus the war between Austria and Sardinia in 1859, was commenced by a peremptory demand upon Sardinia to disarm, followed by a warlike address of the Emperor of Austria to his troops and an invasion of Sardinian terri-

Recent Wars in Europe.

[1] Twiss' *Law of Nations*, Vol. II. § 36.

[2] Vattel, B. III. c. IV. § 64. Wheaton's *Elements*, Vol. II. P. IV. ch. I. § 8, p. 526, ed. 1863, by W. B. Lawrence. Klüber, *Droit des Gens Mod.* §§ 238, 239.

tory[1]. That between Denmark and the German Confederation in 1864[2], was heralded by the tender of an ultimatum, in which the recall of the common constitution of Nov. 18 was insisted upon; this was followed a few days afterwards by the advance of troops and the occupation of Schleswig[3].]

In the United States

As war cannot lawfully be commenced on the part of the United States without an act of Congress, such an act is, of course, a formal official notice to all the world, and equivalent to the most solemn declaration. [But the war between that power and Mexico in 1846 was commenced by a conflict of armed forces in the disputed territory, and an act of Congress was not passed till after such commencement[4]. Again, the immediate outbreak of hostilities between the Northern or Federal and the Southern or Confederate States of America was preceded by acts on the part of the latter that amounted to such a defiance of constituted authority as almost to amount to a declaration of war[5]. On the 20th Dec. 1860, a convention was passed in South Carolina declaring the union between that and the other states dissolved. That line of conduct was imitated by six other states on the 4th March, 1861, the then president, Mr Buchanan, having meanwhile, in his message of December, 1860, denounced the act of Secession to be rebellion, and declared that such an emergency was to be met not by a declaration of war, for Congress had no power to declare and make war against a state, but by punishment. His successor, President Lincoln[6], in

[1] *Annual Register*, 1859, p. 223.

[2] *Times* Newspaper, January 19, 1864.

[3] For other instances of hostilities commenced before any declaration of war, see De Cussy, *Phases et Causes Célèbres*, T. I. pp. 182, and 362.

[4] Twiss, *On the Law of Nations*, Vol. II. ch. II. § 36, p. 69, citing Halleck's *International Law*, p. 354.

[5] *Annual Register*, 1859.

[6] [Whose cruel death by the hand of an assassin it is our melancholy duty to record while these pages are passing through the press. Let an Englishman here add his humble tribute of respect to the memory of a President whose firmness and zeal in the discharge of the duties of his office were only equalled by the kindness of his heart and the honesty of his purpose.]

his inaugural address, 4th March, 1861, whilst differing in some important points from the views of his predecessor, declared his intention to maintain the constitution and laws of the Union without bloodshed, violence, or any attempt at invasion or force among the people anywhere. This declaration was followed by an effort on the part of the Confederate States to treat with the government at Washington; that however failed, and the Southern commissioners were refused an audience on the ground that the states whom they represented did not constitute a foreign power with whom diplomatic relations ought to be established. On 12th April, 1861, the first shot was fired in the attack upon Fort Sumter, and on the 15th a proclamation was issued by the President of the United States calling out the militia to suppress the combinations of the seceding states, and to cause the laws to be executed. This was met by an act of Congress of the Confederate States passed on the 6th of May, recognizing a state of war with the Federal States[1].]

State of War binds subjects.

When war is duly declared, it is not merely a war between this and the adverse government in their political characters. Every man is, in judgment of law, a party to the acts of his own government, and a war between the governments of two nations is a war between all the individuals of the one, and all the individuals of which the other nation is composed. Government is the representative of the will of all the people, and acts for the whole society. This is the theory in all governments;

[1] [As to the effect of the Act of Congress of the 5th July, 1861, and the Proclamation of President Lincoln of the 16th August, 1861, upon the contest then commenced between the two divided portions of the United States, and the consequences resulting therefrom to neutral States as well as to the belligerents themselves, see the case of Peter Miller and other claimants of the bark *Hiawatha v.* United States, decided in the Supreme Court in December, 1862, and cited at full length in the Supplement to the last edition of Wheaton's *Elements of International Law*, Vol. II. Supplement, pp. 12—33. The whole subject of the Declaration of War as a proper mode of commencing hostilities is thoroughly discussed by Dr Twiss. See *Law of Nations*, Vol. II. ch. II. §§ 35—41.]

and the best writers on International Law concur in the doctrine, that when the sovereign of a state declares war against another sovereign, it implies that the whole nation declares war, and that all the subjects of the one are enemies to all the subjects of the other[1]. Very important consequences concerning the obligations of subjects are deducible from this principle.

Enemy's Property within the country.

When hostilities have commenced, the first objects that naturally present themselves for detention and capture, are the persons and property of the enemy, found within the territory on the breaking out of the war. According to strict authority, a state has a right to deal as an enemy with persons and property so found within its power, and to confiscate the property, and detain the persons as prisoners of war[2]. No one, says Bynkershoek, ever required that notice should be given to the subjects of the enemy, to withdraw their property, on pain of forfeiture. The practice of nations is to appropriate it at once, without notice, if there be no special convention to the contrary. But, though Bynkershoek lays down this, as well as other rules of war, with great harshness and severity, he mentions several instances arising in the 17th, and one as early as the 15th century, of stipulations in treaties, allowing foreign subjects a reasonable time after the war breaks out, to recover and dispose of their effects, or to withdraw them. Such stipulations have now become an established *formula* in commercial treaties[3].

[1] Grotius, B. III. c. III. § 9; c. IV. § 8. Burlamaqui, P. IV. c. IV. § 20. Vattel, B. III. c. V. § 70; and see Esposito *v.* Bowden, 7 E. and B. 781.

[2] Grotius, B. III. c. IX. § 3; c. XXI. § 1. Bynk. *Quæst. Pub. J.* lib. I. c. II. and VII. Martens, lib. VIII. c. IV. § 274, ed. par Vergé, 1859.

[3] See also in Wildman's *International Law*, Vol. II. ch. I. pp. 12—14, various instances of the same principle in treaties to which Great Britain was a party. A liberal provision of this kind is inserted in the treaty of amity and commerce between the United States and the Republic of Columbia, which was ratified at Washington, May 27, 1825; see also the Treaties between the United States and Venezuela, May 27, 1836; and the United States and Chili, May 1832, Art. 23, where the protection is a permanent one.

Emerigon[1] considers such treaties as an affirmance of common right, or the public law of Europe, and the general rule laid down by some of the later publicists is in conformity with that provision[2]. The sovereign who declares war, says Vattel, can neither detain those subjects of the enemy who are within his dominions at the time of the declaration of war, nor their effects. They came into the country under the sanction of public faith. By permitting them to enter his territories, and continue there, the sovereign tacitly promised them protection and security for their return. He is, therefore, to allow them a reasonable time to retire with their effects, and if they stay beyond the time, he has a right to treat them as disarmed enemies, unless detained by sickness, or other insurmountable necessity, and then they are to be allowed a further time. It has been frequently provided by treaty, that foreign subjects should be permitted to remain, and continue their business, notwithstanding a rupture between the governments, so long as they conducted it innocently; and when there was no such treaty, such a liberal permission has been often announced in the very declaration of war[3]. Sir Michael Foster[4] mentions several instances of such declarations by the King of Great Britain; and he says that aliens were thereby enabled to acquire personal chattels, and to maintain actions for the recovery of their personal rights, in as full a manner as alien friends.

Enemy's Persons and Property protected by Special Laws.

Besides those stipulations in treaties, which have softened the rigours of war by the civilizing spirit of commerce, many governments have made special provision, in their own laws and ordinances, for the security of the persons and property of enemy's subjects, found in the country at the commencement of war[5].

[1] T. I. ch. XII. § 35, Meredith's edition, 1850, p. 468.

[2] Vattel, B. III. c. IV. § 63. Azuni, P. II. ch. IV. Art. 2, § 7. *Le Droit Public de l'Europe*, par Mably, Œuvres, T. VI. p. 334.

[3] Vattel, B. III. c. IV. § 63.

[4] *Discourse of High Treason*, pp. 185, 186.

[5] By the Spanish decree of February, 1829, making Cadiz a free port,

It was provided by *Magna Charta*[1], that, upon the breaking out of war, foreign merchants found in England, and belonging to the country of the enemy, should be attached, "without harm of body or goods," until it be known how English merchants were treated by the enemy; and "if our merchants," said the charter, "be safe and well treated there, theirs shall be likewise with us." It has been deemed extraordinary that such a liberal provision should have found a place in a treaty between a feudal king and his barons; and Montesquieu[2] was struck with admiration at the fact, that a protection of that kind should have been made one of the articles of English liberty. But this provision was confined to the effects of alien merchants, who were within the realm at the commencement of the war, and it was understood to be confined to the case of merchants domiciled there[3]. It was accompanied also with one very ominous qualification, and was at least equalled, if not greatly excelled, by an ordinance of Charles V. of France, a century afterwards, which declared that foreign merchants, who should be in France at the time of the declaration of war, should have nothing to fear, for they should have liberty to depart freely, with their effects[4]. The spirit of the provision in *Magna Charta* was sustained by a resolution of the judges, in the time of Henry VIII., when they resolved, that if a Frenchman came to England before the war, neither his person nor goods should be seized[5]. The statute of staples, of 27 Edw. III. c. 17, made a still more liberal and precise enactment in favour of foreign merchants residing in

it was declared that in the event of war, foreigners who had established themselves there for the purposes of commerce, becoming alien enemies by means of the war, were to be allowed a proper time to withdraw, and their property was to be sacred from all sequestration or reprisal. [Cf. Phillimore's *International Law*, Vol. III. ch. I. §§ 78, 79.]

1 Ch. XXX.

2 *Esprit des Loix*, XX. 14. See Barrington on the Statutes, p. 25.

3 Hale's *P. C.* 93.

4 Henault, *Abreg. Chron.* T. I. 338.

5 Broke's *Abridgement Tit. Property*, pl. 38. Jenk. *Cent.* 201, case 22.

England when war commenced between their prince and the King of England. They were to have convenient warning of forty days, by proclamation, to depart the realm, with their goods; and if they could not do it within that time, by reason of accident, they were to have forty days more to pass with their merchandise, and with liberty, in the mean time, to sell the same[1]. The act of Congress of the 6th July, 1798, c. 66, was dictated by the same humane and enlightened policy. It authorized the President, in case of war, to direct the conduct to be observed towards subjects of the hostile nation, being aliens, and within the United States, and in what cases, and upon what security, their residence should be permitted; and declared, in reference to those who were to depart, that they should be allowed such reasonable time as might be consistent with the public safety, and according to the dictates of humanity and national hospitality, "for the recovery, disposal, and removal of their goods and effects, and for their departure[2]."

Modern American Practice.

But however strong the current of authority in favour of the modern and milder construction of the rule of national law on this subject, the point seems no longer open for discussion in America; and it has become definitely settled in favour of the ancient and sterner rule, by the Supreme Court of the United States[3]. The effect of war upon British property, found in the United States, on land, at the commencement of the war, was learnedly discussed, and thoroughly considered, in the case of *Brown;* and the Circuit Court of the United States, at Boston, decided[4], as upon a settled rule of the law of nations, that the goods of the enemy found in the country, and all the vessels and cargoes found afloat in the ports of the United

1 [This was followed by a similar enactment in the reign of Henry V. statute 4 Hen. V. c. 5. See Coke's 2 *Institute,* 205.]

2 *Statutes at Large,* Vol. I. p. 577, (American).

3 Brown *v.* the United States, 8 Cranch, 110. See also *Ib.* 228, 229. [Wheaton's *Elements,* Vol. II. Part IV. ch. I. § 9, p. 530, Ed. 1863.]

4 The cargo of the ship *Emulous,* 1 Gallison, 563.

States at the commencement of hostilities, were liable to seizure and confiscation; the exercise of the right resting in the discretion of the sovereign of the nation. When the case was brought up, on appeal, before the Supreme Court of the United States, the broad principle was assumed, that war gave to the sovereign full right to take the persons, and confiscate the property of the enemy, wherever found; and that the mitigations of this rigid rule, which the wise and humane policy of modern times had introduced into practice, might, more or less, affect the exercise of the right, but could not impair the right itself. Commercial nations have always considerable property in the possession of their neighbours; and, when war breaks out, the question what shall be done with enemy's property found in the country, is one rather of policy than of law, and is properly addressed to the consideration of the legislature, and not to the courts of law. [The Supreme Court therefore proceeded to reverse the sentence of the court below, holding that an express act of Congress (which at that time had not been passed) was necessary in order to render effective the belligerent right to confiscate enemy's property found in the United States at the commencement of the war, and that its confiscation was not in consequence of the declaration of war, without further legislation.]

Though this decision established the right, contrary to much of modern authority and practice, yet a great point was gained over the rigour and violence of the ancient doctrine, by making the exercise of the right to depend upon a special act of Congress.

The practice, so common in modern Europe, of imposing embargoes at the breaking out of hostility, has, apparently, the effect of destroying that protection to property, which the rule of faith and justice gives to it, when brought into the country in the course of trade, and in the confidence of peace. Sir William Scott, in the case of the *Boedes Lust*[1], explains this species of embargo to be

Hostile Embargoes.

[1] 5 Rob. 233.

an act of a hostile nature, and amounting to an implied declaration of war, though liable to be explained away and annulled, by a subsequent accommodation between the nations. The seizure is at first equivocal, and if the matter in dispute terminates in reconciliation, the seizure becomes a mere civil embargo, but if it terminates otherwise, the subsequent hostilities have a retroactive effect, and render the embargo a hostile measure, *ab initio*. [The property taken is liable to be used as the property of persons trespassers *ab initio*, and guilty of injuries which they have refused to redeem by any amicable alteration of their measures.] This species of reprisal for some previous injury, is laid down in the books as a lawful measure, according to the usage of nations[1]; but it is often reprobated, and it cannot well be distinguished from the practice of seizing property found within the territory upon the declaration of war. It does not differ in substance from the conduct of the Syracusans, in the time of Dionysius the Elder, (and which Mitford considered to be a gross violation of the law of nations,) for they voted a declaration of war against Carthage, and immediately seized the effects of Carthaginian traders in their warehouses, and Carthaginian richly laden vessels in their harbour, and sent a herald to Carthage to negotiate[2]. But this act of the Syracusans, near four hundred years before the Christian era, was no more than what was the ordinary practice in England, according to the observation of Lord Mansfield, in Lindo *v.* Rodney[3]. "Upon the declaration of war or hostilities, all the ships of the enemy," he says, "are detained in our ports, to be confiscated, as the property of the enemy, if no reciprocal agreement is made, [but they are only to be condemned in a prize court[4]"].

[1] Vattel, B. II. ch. XVIII. §§ 342, 344. Martens, Lib. VIII. ch. III. § 268, Ed. par Vergé, 1858.

[2] Mitf. *Hist. of Greece*, Vol. V. pp. 402—4, and Grote, Vol. X. p. 671.

[3] Doug. 613. See also the Santa Cruz, 1 Rob. 63.

[4] [It is scarcely necessary to point out the distinction between these two cases. In the Syracusan case, which is rightly characterized as a gross

Seizure in transitu.

Another question respecting the effect of a declaration of war upon property, arose in the case of the *Rapid*[1]. It was held, that after the commencement of war, an American citizen could not lawfully send a vessel to the enemy's country, to bring home his own property, without rendering it liable to seizure *in transitu,* as enemy's property. Every thing that issues from a hostile country, is, *prima facie,* the property of the enemy, and a citizen cannot lawfully be concerned in any commercial intercourse with the enemy. The English courts were formerly inclined to allow goods in the enemy's country, at the beginning of the war, to be brought home; but it is now the settled law, that it cannot be done safely, without a license from the government[2]. [The rule however has been limited to this extent, that if a British subject be domiciled in a neutral state, he may legally trade even with the enemies of Great Britain, for as a domiciled member of a neutral state he has all the privileges of neutrality[3].]

Confiscation of debts.

The claim of a right to confiscate debts, contracted by individuals in time of peace, and which remain due to subjects of the enemy at the declaration of war, rests very much upon the same principles as that concerning enemy's tangible property, found in the country at the opening of the war; though the objection to the right of confiscation, in this latter case, appears to be much stronger. In for-

violation of law, and it might be added of honour, there was more than a mere contingent seizure after a declaration of war or any hostile conduct on the part of the Carthaginians, there was, as Mr Grote's text shews, an audacious and cruel act of robbery; but the seizure specified by Lord Mansfield, in accordance with the practice of this country, was neither an unusual nor a sudden and unprovoked one, it was also contingent upon the conduct of our enemy, and, as the concluding words of Lord Mansfield shew, it did not necessarily import condemnation, because that had to be decided by the only proper tribunal, a prize court.]

[1] 8 Cranch, 155. See also the St Lawrence, 8 Cranch, p. 434.

[2] Bell *v.* Potts, 8 Term, 548. The *Harp,* 1 Rob. 196. The *Ocean,* 5 Rob. *Rep.* 90. The *Juffrow Catharina, Ib.* 141.

[3] Bell *v.* Reid 1 M. and S. 726. The *Danaous,* cited in 4 Rob. 225. [See also Tudor's leading cases in *Mercantile Law,* p. 690 (note to the *Hoop*) where all the cases on this point are collected.]

mer times the right to confiscate debts was admitted as a doctrine of National Law, and Grotius, Puffendorf, and Bynkershoek, pronounce in favour of it[1]. It had the countenance of the civil law[2], and even Cicero, in his *Offices*[3], when stating the cases in which promises are not to be kept, mentions that of the creditor becoming the enemy of the country of the debtor. Down to the year 1737, the general opinion of jurists was in favour of the right; but Vattel says, that a relaxation of the rigour of the rule has since taken place among the sovereigns of Europe, and that, as the custom has been generally received, he who should act contrary to it, would injure the public faith, for strangers trusted his subjects only from a firm persuasion that the general custom would be observed[4]. There has frequently been a stipulation in modern treaties, that debts should not be confiscated in the event of war; and as these conventional provisions are evidence of the sense of the governments which are parties to them, so the general inclination in modern times tends to show that the right of confiscation of debts and things in action, is against good policy, and ought to be discontinued. The treaty between the United States and Colombia contains such a provision; but that between the United States and Great Britain in 1795, went further, and contained the explicit declaration, that it was "unjust and impolitic" that the debts of individuals should

[1] Grotius, B. I. ch. I. § 6; B. III. ch. VIII. § 4. Puff. Lib. VIII. ch. VI. XIX. XX. Bynk. Lib. I. ch. 7. Lord Hale also laid it down to be the law of England. 1 Hale's *P. C.* 95.

[2] *Dig.* XLI. 1, l. 5, § 7, l. 51, and XLIX. 15. [The passages here quoted do not bear out the dictum to the extent laid down in the text, but the practice of the ancient Romans certainly cannot be said to be opposed to the view thus ascribed to them by the learned author.]

[3] Lib. III. c. 25, § 29.

[4] Vattel, B. III. ch. V. § 77. [M. Massé's remarks on this passage in Vattel's work deserve to be read, they are too long for insertion here, but the writer successfully points out the mischievous consequences of maintaining a principle, that of confiscation, as Vattel does, in the face of the acknowledged opposition it met with in practice. Massé, *Droit Comm.* T. I. p. 117.]

be impaired by national differences. A very able discussion of this assumed right to confiscate debts, was made by General Hamilton, in the numbers of *Camillus*, published in 1795. He examined the claim to confiscate private debts, or private property in banks, or in public funds, on the ground of reason and principle, on those of policy and expediency, on the opinion of jurists, on usage, and on conventional law; and his argument against the justice and policy of the claim was exceedingly powerful. He contended that it was against good faith for a government to lay its hands on private property, acquired by the permission, or upon the invitation of the government, and under a necessarily implied promise of protection and security[1]. Vattel says, that every where, in case of a war, funds credited to the public are exempt from confiscation and seizure. Emerigon[2] and Martens[3] make the same declaration. The practice would have a very injurious influence upon the general sense of the inviolability and sanctity of private contracts; and with debtors who had a nice and accurate sense of justice and honour, the requisition of government would not be cheerfully or readily obeyed. Voltaire has given[4] a striking instance of the impracticability of confiscating property deposited in trust with a debtor, and of the firmness of Spanish faith. When war was declared between France and Spain, in 1684, the

1 [The arguments of M. Massé are equally vigorous to the same effect. Massé, *Droit Commercial dans ses rapports avec le Droit des Gens*, T. I. p. 117, et seq. Heffter has also discussed the question in a somewhat elaborate argument and from the same point of view. Heffter, *Le Dr. Int. Pub.* § 132. See also Twiss *on the Law of Nations*, Vol. II. pp. 100—108, and Wheaton's *Elements*, Vol. II. Part IV. ch. I. §§ 11 and 12, pp. 532—543, ed. 1863 ]

2 *Des Ass.* T. I. ch. XII. § 35, pp. 552—555. Meredith's *Transl.* pp. 438, 439.

3 B. VIII. c. IV. § 279, ed. par Vergé. [A reference to this passage however will show that Martens admits the lawfulness of confiscating public debts, but denies its expediency; his editor M. Vergé in a learned and able note takes him to task for the opinion thus laid down, and cites the example of England and the language of General Hamilton above referred to as opposed to so faithless a practice.]

4 *Essai sur les Mœurs et l'Esprit des Nations.*

king of Spain endeavoured to seize the property of the French in Spain, but not a single Spanish factor would betray his French correspondent[1].

Rule of the United States.

Notwithstanding the weight of modern authority, and of argument, against this claim of right on the part of the sovereign, to confiscate the debts and funds of the subjects of his enemy during war, the judicial language in the United States is decidedly in support of the right. In the case of Brown *v.* The United States[2], already mentioned, Judge Story, in the Circuit Court in Massachusetts, laid down the right to confiscate debts, and enemy's property found in the country, according to the rigorous doctrine of the elder jurists; and he said the opinion was fully confirmed by the judgment of the Supreme Court in Ware *v.* Hylton[3], where the doctrine was explicitly asserted by some of the judges, reluctantly admitted by others, and denied by none. Chief Justice Marshall, in delivering the opinion of the Supreme Court, in the case of Brown, observed, that between debts contracted under the faith of laws, and property acquired in the course of trade on the faith of the same laws, reason drew no distinction, and the right of the sovereign to confiscate debts, was precisely the same with the right to confiscate other property found in the country.

[1] The English Court of K. B. declared in the case of Wolff *v.* Oxholm (6 *Mau. and Selw.* 92), that an ordinance of Denmark in 1807, pending hostilities with England, which sequestered debts due from Danish to English subjects, and caused them to be paid over to the Danish government, was not a defence to a suit in England for the debt, and that the ordinance was not conformable to the usage of nations, and was void. It was observed by the Court, that the right of confiscating debts, contended for on the authority of Vattel, B. II. c. xviii. § 344, B. III. c. v. § 77, was not recognised by Grotius (see Grot. lib. III. c. VII. § 4, and c. VIII. § 4), and was impugned by Puffendorf (B. VIII. c. VI. § 22), and others; and that no instance had occurred of the exercise of the right, except the ordinance in question, for upwards of a century. [As to this, see Wheaton's *Elements*, Vol. II. P. IV. ch. I. § 12, who doubts, though with no very good reason, the soundness of the judgment. See ex parte Boussmaker, 13 Vesey, Junior, 71, and Furtado *v.* Rogers, 3 Bos. and Pull. 191.]

[2] 8 Cranch, 110.

[3] 3 Dallas, 199.

This right, therefore, was admitted to exist as a settled and decided right *stricto jure*, though at the same time it was conceded to be the universal practice to forbear to seize and confiscate debts and credits. It may, therefore, be laid down as a principle of public law, so far as the same is understood and declared by the highest judicial authorities in the United States, that it rests in the discretion of the legislature of the Union, by a special law for that purpose, to confiscate debts contracted by their citizens, and due to the enemy; but, as is asserted by the same authority, this right is contrary to universal practice, and it may, therefore, well be considered as a naked and impolitic right, condemned by the enlightened conscience and judgment of modern times[1].

If property should have been wrongfully taken by the state before the war, and be in the country at the opening of the war, such property cannot be seized, but must be restored; because to confiscate that species of enemy's property, would be for the government to take advantage of its own wrong. The celebrated *Report* of the English law officers of the crown in 1753, *in Answer to the Prussian Memorial*, stated, that French ships taken before the war of 1741, were, during the heat of the war with France, as well as afterwards, restored by sentences of the admiralty courts to the French owners. No such property was ever attempted to be confiscated; for had it not been for the wrong done, the property would not have been within the king's dominions. And yet even such property is considered to be subject to the rule of vindictive retaliation: for as Sir Wm. Scott observed, in the case of the *Santa Cruz*[2], it was the constant practice of England to condemn property seized before the war, if the enemy condemns—and to restore, if the enemy restores; [and this rule,

[1] The practice of Great Britain with reference to the payment of debts due to an enemy in time of war is well illustrated by the debate upon the Russo-Dutch Loan in the year 1854, a short account of which will be found in Twiss's *Law of Nations*, Vol. II. pp. 112—114.

[2] Rob. *Rep.* 63 (?).

which is not without precedent or authority, both American and French, applies to the case of re-captures of the ships and cargoes of allies or co-belligerents[1]].

Trading with the Enemy.

One of the immediate and important consequences of the declaration of war, is the absolute interruption and interdiction of all commercial correspondence, intercourse, and dealing, between the subjects of the two countries. The idea that any commercial intercourse, or pacific dealing, can lawfully subsist between the people of the powers at war, except under the clear and express sanction of the government, and without a special license, is utterly inconsistent with the new class of duties growing out of a state of war[2]. [This interdiction is based on views of public policy alone, resting solely on the judgment of the state, and being adhered to out of regard to the welfare of the nation rather than on account of any special jealousy of private enterprise]: it flows necessarily, from the principles already laid down, that a state of war puts all the members of the two nations respectively in hostility to each other; and that to suffer individuals to carry on a friendly or commercial intercourse, while the two governments were at war, would be placing the act of government, and the acts of individuals, in contradiction to each other. It would counteract the operations of war, throw obstacles in the way of the public efforts, and lead to disorder, imbecility, and treason[3]. Trading supposes the existence of civil contracts and relations, and a reference to courts of justice; and it is therefore, necessarily, contradictory to a state of war. It affords aid to the enemy in an effectual manner, by enabling the merchants of the enemy's country to support their government, and it facilitates the means of conveying intelligence, and carrying on a traitorous correspondence with the enemy.

*Act of Congress*, 3rd March, 1800, ch. 14, American *Statutes at Large*, Vol. II. p. 16, and Valin, T. II. p. 262. See also chapter 6 infra.

[2] The *Hoop*, Rob. 196. Esposito *v.* Bowden, 7 E. and B. 793.

[3] 1 Duer, *On Insurance*, p. 555. The *Julia*, 1 Gall. 601—3. The *Jonge Pieter*, 4 Rob. 79.

These considerations apply with peculiar force to maritime states, where the principal object is to destroy the marine and commerce of the enemy, in order to force them to peace[1]. It is a well settled doctrine in the English courts, and with the English jurists, that there cannot exist, at the same time, a war for arms, and a peace for commerce. The war puts an end at once to all dealing and all communication with each other, and places every individual of the respective governments, as well as the governments themselves, in a state of hostility[2]. [And as it places every subject or citizen in hostility to the adverse party, and as each individual is bound by his personal efforts to assist his own government and to counteract the measures of the foe, so every mode of intercourse with the public enemy, whether by personal communication, correspondence, or otherwise, that can possibly tend to relieve him from the pressure of hostilities or aid him in the prosecution of the war, is a violation of duty, and is strictly prohibited[3].] This is the doctrine of all the authoritative writers on the law of nations, and of the maritime ordinances of all the great powers of Europe[4]. It is also the received law of the United States, and frequent decisions in accordance with it by the Congress of the United States during the revolutionary war, and again by the Supreme Court of the United States during the course of the war of 1812, have attested its truth; nor is it easy to conceive of a point of doctrine more deeply or extensively rooted in the general

[1] Chitty, *On Commercial Law*, Vol. I. 378.

[2] Potts *v.* Bell, 8 Term, 548. [This case and that of the *Hoop*, 1 Rob. 196, further establish that it is illegal for a subject in time of war without licence to bring from an enemy's port even in a neutral ship goods purchased in the enemy's country after the commencement of hostilities although not appearing to have been purchased from an enemy; in effect, that trading with the inhabitants of the enemy's country is trading with the enemy (per Willes J.) in Esposito *v.* Bowden, 7 E. and B. 780. See also Reid *v.* Hoskins, 4 E. and B. 979 and 6 E. and B. 953.] Willison *v.* Patteson, 7 Taunt. 439.

[3] The *Hoop*, 1 Robinson, 199, 200.

[4] Duer, *On Insurance*, Vol. I. p. 553, ed. 1845.

maritime law of Europe, and in the universal and immemorial usage of the whole community of the civilized world[1].

Contracts with an Enemy.

It follows, as a necessary consequence of the doctrine of the illegality of all intercourse or traffic, without express permission, that all contracts with the enemy, made during war, are utterly void. The insurance of enemy's property is an illegal contract, because it is a species of trade and intercourse with the enemy. The drawing of a bill of exchange, by an alien enemy, on a subject of the adverse country, is an illegal and void contract, because it is a communication and contract[2]. The purchase of bills on the enemy's country, or the remission and deposit of funds there, is a dangerous and illegal act, because it may be cherishing the resources and relieving the wants of the enemy. The remission of funds, in money or bills, to subjects of the enemy, is unlawful. The inhibition reaches to every communication, direct or circuitous. All endeavours at trade with the enemy, by the intervention of third persons, or by partnerships, have equally failed, and no artifice has succeeded to legalize the trade, without the express permission of the government[3]. Every relaxation of the rule tends to corrupt the allegiance of the subject, and prevents the war from fulfilling its end. The only exception to this strict and rigorous rule of international jurisprudence, is the case of ransom bills, and they are contracts of necessity, founded on a state of war, and engendered by its violence. It is also a further consequence of the inability of the subjects of the two states, to commune or carry on any correspondence or business together, that all commercial partnerships existing between the subjects of the two parties, prior to the war, are dissolved by the mere force and act

1 See also *Act of Congress*, July 6, 1812, II. Stats. at large, 784.

2 But see Antoine *v.* Morehead, 6 Taunton, 237, where a bill of exchange drawn on England by a British prisoner in France for his own subsistence and endorsed to an alien enemy, was held to be a valid contract.

3 Willison *v.* Patteson, ut sup. The *Indian Chief*, 3 Rob. 22. The *Jonge Pieter*, 4 Rob. 79. The *Franklin*, 6 Rob. 127. The *Nayade*, 4 Rob. 251.

of the war itself; though other contracts, existing prior to the war, are not extinguished, but the remedy is only suspended, and this from the inability of an alien enemy to sue, or to sustain, in the language of the civilians, a *persona standi in judicio*[1]. The whole of this doctrine respecting the illegality of any commercial intercourse between the inhabitants of two nations at war, was extensively reviewed, and the principal authorities, ancient and modern, foreign and domestic, were accurately examined, and the positions which have been laid down established, in the case of *Griswold* v. *Waddington*[2], decided in the Supreme Court of New York, and afterwards affirmed on error, [where it was held that a war between two powers *ipso facto* dissolves a partnership created before the war between two subjects of each belligerent, each residing in his own country. Mr Duer, in approving of the doctrine as applied to partnerships, thinks that in the case of other contracts a war suspends their existence without dissolving the obligation, the distinction arising from the nature of the contracts, which in one case are executory, in the other productive of a vested right[3].]

This strict rule has been carried so far in the British admiralty, as to prohibit a remittance of supplies even to a British colony, during its temporary subjection to the enemy, and when the colony was under the necessity of supplies, and was only very partially and imperfectly supplied by the enemy[4]. The same interdiction of trade

Trade with the Enemy. British rule,

[1] [See De Wahl *v.* Braune, 1 Hurlstone and Norman, 178, where it was held that the wife of an alien enemy cannot maintain an action in her own name made either before or during coverture; but see also Alcinous *v.* Nygren, 4 E. and B. 217, where the same principle as is above laid down in the text was held, that though by the law of England an alien enemy cannot *flagrante bello* maintain an action upon a contract entered into before the war, when peace is restored he will be well entitled to sue.]

[2] 15 Johnson's *Rep.* 57. 16 Johnson, 438, S. C. See Esposito *v.* Bowden, 7 E. and B. 785.

[3] Duer, *On Insurance*, Vol. I. p. 478.

[4] Case of the *Bella Guidita*, in 1785, cited in the case of the *Hoop*, 1 Rob. *Rep.* 174.

applies to ships of truce, or cartel ships, which are a species of navigation intended for the recovery of the liberty of prisoners of war. Such a special and limited intercourse is dictated by policy and humanity, and it is indispensable that it be conducted with the most exact and exclusive attention to the original purpose, as being the only condition upon which the intercourse can be tolerated. All trade, therefore, by means of such vessels is unlawful, without the express consent of both the governments concerned[1]. It is equally illegal for an ally of one of the belligerents, and who carries on the war conjointly, to have any commerce with the enemy. A single belligerent may grant licenses to trade with the enemy, and dilute and weaken his own rights at pleasure, but it is otherwise when allied nations are pursuing a common cause. The community of interest, and object, and action, creates a mutual duty not to prejudice that joint interest; and it is a declared principle of the Law of Nations, founded on very clear and just grounds, that one of the belligerents may seize, and inflict the penalty of forfeiture, on the property of a subject of a co-ally, engaged in a trade with the common enemy, and thereby affording him aid and comfort, whilst the other ally was carrying on a severe and vigorous warfare. It would be contrary to the implied contract in every such warlike confederacy, that neither of the belligerents, without the other's consent, should do any thing to defeat the common object[2].

[1] The *Venus*, 4 Rob. 355. The *Carolina*, 6 Rob. 336. The *Rose in Bloom*, 1 Dodson, 60.

[2] The *Nayade*, 4 Rob. 251. The *Neptunus*, 6 Rob. 403. The *Aina*, 1 *Eccl. and Admiralty Reports* (Spinks) 315. The subjects that are discussed in the text, beginning with that of enemy's persons and property within the country of the other belligerent and ending with that of contracts with an enemy, will be found treated at more or less length in the following modern works. Heffter, *Droit Intern.* §§ 120—128. Phillimore, Vol. III. §§ 67—75 and 87—89. Twiss, Vol. II. ch. I. §§ 11, 12, and ch. III. Wildman, Vol. II. ch. I. Wheaton's *Elements*, Vol. II. Part IV. ch. I. §§ 9—15. Halleck's *International Law*, ch. XV. §§ 8—20.]

[In nearly all the topics above discussed, considerable changes and relaxations of the ancient harshness have been introduced by the orders and regulations issued at the commencement of the late Russian war.

as altered by the Russian War, 1854—56.

Enemy's persons and property.

In answer to a deputation of Russian merchants who waited on Lord Clarendon in March 1854, his Lordship stated "that the British government were disposed to respect the persons and property of all Russian subjects residing as merchants in this country to the full extent promised by the Emperor of Russia towards British subjects; and that all necessary measures should be adopted to enable them to remain unmolested in the quiet prosecution of their business[1]." By a notice published in the *Moniteur*, it was announced that the subjects of Russia might continue their residence in France under the protection which the laws provide for foreigners on condition that they respected those laws; whilst the same protection was accorded by the Russian declaration of the 7th April, 1854, to all British and French subjects resident in Russia. The following important answer of Lord Clarendon to a question proposed by merchants interested in the Russian trade, whether produce of Russia brought over the frontier by land and shipped from thence by British or neutral vessels would be subject to seizure and confiscation, still further illustrates the present policy of this country with reference to commercial intercourse with the enemy. After stating that the question turned not on the place of origin, nor the mode of conveyance of the property but on the true ownership or interest, or risk in and destination of it, Lord Clarendon went on to say that, if shipped at neutral risk or after having become *bonâ fide* neutral property, it would not be liable to condemnation whatever its destination, but if it still remained enemy's property, notwithstanding it was shipped from a neutral port and in a neutral ship, it would be condemned whatever its destination. If it were British property or

[1] 24th March, 1854.

shipped at British risk, it would be condemned should it be proved to be really engaged in a trade with the enemy. "If there has been a *bonâ fide* and complete transfer of ownership to a neutral (as by purchase in a neutral market) the goods will not be liable to condemnation, notwithstanding they may have come to that neutral market from the enemy's country either over land or by sea[1]."

Exemption of neutral goods and neutral ships.

Then came the adoption by England and France of the principle "free ships free goods," the complete adhesion to the rule exempting neutral goods in enemy's vessels from confiscation, and the Order in Council of the 15th April, 1854, allowing all vessels under a neutral or friendly flag, to import into and to export from any port or place in her Majesty's dominions to any port or place not blockaded, all goods and merchandize, and any cargo not contraband of war or requiring a special permission; thus largely relaxing, nay almost entirely removing the old restrictions upon trade with the enemy, and allowing such trade indirectly and through the medium of a neutral flag.

Nor are the rules and orders bearing upon the subject of the seizure of enemy's merchant shipping less remarkable for the liberal policy they have sanctioned. Thus by English and French orders bearing date the 24th, 28th and 29th of March respectively, protection was given to Russian vessels which had left Russian ports before the time fixed in the Order, and a delay of six weeks was granted such vessels to quit the ports of England and France, or where they had left the ports of Russia previous to the declaration of the war that they might enter and complete their cargoes; and by an order of the 15th April, 1854, the former one of the 29th of March was still farther extended. Not less liberal were the regulations published

[1] *Times Newspaper*, March 25th, 1854, and see as to this doctrine the *Jonge Pieter*, 4 C. Rob. 84.

by Russia on the same subject, being in fact conceived in almost the same terms as those above described[1].

Embargo.

As regards Embargo the order of the 29th of March declared that a general embargo or stop should be made of all Russian ships or vessels whatever within any of her Majesty's dominions, together with all persons and effects on board except such as came under the special circumstances of the exempting order of the 29th of March above specified. With reference to the confiscation of debts, the law of Great Britain has always pursued "a policy of a liberal and wise character," holding that the right of the original creditor to sue for the recovery of a debt is not extinguished but only suspended by the war, reviving again when peace is restored. Whatever prerogative the Crown may have to confiscate debts due from individuals before the commencement of the war, it has never adopted such a course of proceeding as to confiscate any debt due to an alien enemy from any of its subjects; "nor," as Lord Alvanley said in Furtado *v.* Rodgers, "is it very probable that such a course of proceeding will ever be adopted[2]."—And therefore when, some little time after the commencement of the present war in America, by an act of the Confederate Congress of August 21, 1861, property of whatever nature save public stocks and securities held by an alien enemy was declared confiscated, Earl Russell, after appealing to the principle laid down by Mr Wheaton[3] as being in direct opposition to such conduct, and pointing out the peculiar application of that principle to the case of a civil war between different parts of the confederation, during whose union the subjects of foreign states were invited and induced to settle in its various states without any ground for contemplating such a disruption, protested in the strongest language against an act as rare

Confiscation of debts.

[1] See them described at length in the second volume of Wheaton, pp. 534, 535, note (173), ed. 1863, by W. B. Laurence.

[2] 3 Bos. and Pull. 201. Ex parte Boussmaker, 13 Vesey 71.

[3] Wheaton's *Elements*, Vol. II. Part IV. ch. I. § 9 apud finem.

in modern practice, as it was grossly unjust and faithless in principle[1].]

Judicial decision on Public Law.

In the investigation of the rules of the modern law of nations, particularly with regard to the extensive field of maritime capture, the courts of the United States generally and freely refer to the decisions of the English courts. These latter courts are in the habit of taking accurate and comprehensive views of general jurisprudence, and have been deservedly followed by those of the United States, on all the leading points of national law. The United States possess a series of judicial decisions made in England, and in their own country, in which the usages and the duties of nations are explained and declared with that depth of research, and that liberal and enlarged inquiry, which strengthen and embellish the conclusions of reason. They contain more intrinsic argument, more full and precise details, more accurate illustrations, and are of more authority, than the loose *dicta* of elementary writers. When those courts in the United States, which are charged with the administration of international law, have differed from the English adjudications, they must take the law from domestic sources; but such an alternative is rarely to be met with, and there is scarcely a decision in the English prize courts at Westminster, on any general question of public right, that has not received the express approbation and sanction of American national courts. "We have attained the rank of a great commercial nation (says Mr Chancellor Kent) and war, on our part, is carried on upon the same principles of maritime policy, which have directed the forces and animated the councils of the naval powers of Europe. When the United States formed a component part of the British empire, our prize law and theirs was the same; and after the revolution it continued to be the same, as far as it was adapted to our circumstances, and was not varied by the power which was capable of chang-

[1] *Parliamentary Papers*, 1862. *Corresp. relating to the Civil War*, p. 108.

ing it." The great value of a series of judicial decisions, in prize cases, and on other questions depending on the law of nations, is, that they liquidate, and render certain and stable the loose general principles of that law, and show their application, and how they are understood in the country where the tribunals are sitting. They are, therefore, deservedly received with very great respect, and as presumptive, though not conclusive, evidence of the law in the given case. This was the language of the Supreme Court of the United States, so late as 1815[1], and the decisions of the English High Court of Admiralty, especially since the year 1798, have been consulted and uniformly respected by that court, as enlightened commentaries on the law of nations, and affording a vast variety of instructive precedents for the application of the principles of that law. They have also this to recommend them: that they are pre-eminently distinguished for sagacity, wisdom, and learning, as well as for the chaste and classical beauties of their composition.

Many of the most important principles of public law have been brought into use, and received a practical application, and been reduced to legal precision, since the age of Grotius and Puffendorf; and it is acknowledged in the United States that resort must be had to the judicial decisions of the prize tribunals in Europe, as well as in their own country, for information and authority on a great many points, on which all the leading text-books have preserved a total silence. The complexity of modern commerce has swelled, beyond all bounds, the number and intricacy of questions upon national law, and particularly upon the very comprehensive head of maritime capture. The illegality and penal consequences of trade with the enemy; the illegality of carrying enemy's despatches, or of engaging in the coasting, fishing, or other privileged trade of the enemy; the illegality of transfer of property *in transitu*, between the neutral and belligerent; the rules

[1] 9 Cranch, 198.

which impress upon neutral property a hostile character, arising either from the domicil of the neutral owner, or his territorial possessions, or his connexion in a house in trade in the enemy's country, are all of them doctrines in the modern international law, which are either not to be found at all, or certainly not with any fulness of discussion, and power of argument, anywhere, but in the judicial investigations to which reference has been made, and which have given the highest authority and splendour to this branch of learning.

# CHAPTER V.

## OF THE VARIOUS KINDS OF PROPERTY LIABLE TO CAPTURE.

---

Enemy character, how acquired.

It becomes important, in a maritime war, to determine with precision what relations and circumstances will impress a hostile character upon persons and property, and the modern international law of the commercial world is replete with refined and complicated distinctions on this subject. It is settled, that there may be a hostile character merely as to commercial purposes, and hostility may attach only to the person as a temporary enemy, or it may attach only to property of a particular description. This hostile character, in a commercial view, or one limited to certain intents and purposes only, will attach in consequence of having possessions in the territory of the enemy, or by maintaining a commercial establishment there, or by a personal residence, or by particular modes of traffic, as by sailing under the enemy's flag or passport. This hostile relation, growing out of particular circumstances, assumes, as valid, the distinction which has been taken between a permanent and a temporary alien enemy. A man is said to be permanently an alien enemy, when he owes a permanent allegiance to the adverse belligerent, and his hostility is commensurate in point of time with his country's quarrel. But he who does not owe a permanent allegiance to the enemy, is an enemy only during the existence and continuance of certain circumstances.

A neutral, for instance, said Ch. J. Eyre[1], can be an alien enemy only with respect to his acts done under a local or temporary allegiance to a power at war, and, when his temporary allegiance determines, his hostile character determines also.

Possession of the soil impresses character.

It was considered by Sir Wm. Scott, in the case of the *Phœnix*[2], and again in the case of the *Vrow Anna Catharina*[3], to be a fixed principle of maritime law, that the possession of the soil impressed upon the owner the character of the country, so far as the produce of the soil was concerned, wherever the local residence of the owner might be. The produce of a hostile soil bears a hostile character for the purpose of capture, and is the subject of legitimate prize when taken in a course of transportation to any other country. The enemy's lands are supposed to be a great source of his wealth, and, perhaps, the most solid foundation of his power; and whoever owns or possesses land in the enemy's country, though he may in fact reside elsewhere, and be in every other respect a neutral or friend, must be taken to have incorporated himself with the nation, so far as he is a holder of the soil, and the produce of that soil is held to be enemy's property, independent of the personal residence or occupation of the owner. The reasonableness of this principle will be acceded to by all maritime nations, and it was particularly recognised as a valid doctrine by the Supreme Court of the United States, in Bentzon *v.* Boyle[4], [where, in strict accordance with and reliance upon the principles laid down by Lord Stowell in the two cases above-mentioned, it was held that the produce of an enemy's colony or other territory is to be considered as hostile property, so long as it belongs to the owner of the soil, whatever may

[1] Sparenburg *v.* Bannatyne, 1 Bos. and Pull. 163.

[2] 5 Rob. *Rep.* 21.

[3] 5 Rob. *Rep.* 161.

[4] 9 Cranch, 191. [The reader will find this case cited at full length by Mr Wheaton in the 2nd Vol. of the *Elements of Internat. Law*, Part IV. Ch. I. § 21. pp. 576—580, Edn. 1863, by W. B. Lawrence. See also the *Dree Gebroeders*, 4 Rob. 232.]

be his national character in other respects, or wherever may be his place of residence.]

If a person has a settlement in a hostile country by the maintenance of a commercial establishment there, he will be considered a hostile character, and a subject of the enemy's country, in regard to his commercial transactions connected with that establishment. The position is a clear one, that if a person goes into a foreign country, and engages in trade there, he is, by the law of nations, to be considered a merchant of that country, and a subject to all civil purposes, whether that country be hostile or neutral, and he cannot be permitted to retain the privileges of a neutral character during his residence and occupation in an enemy's country[1]. This general rule has been applied by the English courts to the case of Englishmen residing in a neutral country, and they are admitted, in respect of their *bonâ fide* trade, to the privileges of the neutral character[2]. In the case of the *Danous*[3], the rule was laid down by the English House of Lords in 1802, in unrestricted terms, and a British born subject, resident in Portugal, was allowed the benefit of the Portuguese character, so far as to render his trade with Holland, then at war with England, not impeachable as an illegal trade. The same rule was afterwards applied[4] to a natural born British subject domiciled in the United States, and it was held, that he might lawfully trade to a country at war with England, but at peace with the United States.

Domicile the test of national character.

This same principle, that for all commercial purposes, the domicil of the party, without reference to the place of birth, becomes the test of national character, has been repeatedly and explicitly admitted in the courts of the

[1] Wilson *v.* Maryat 8. T. R. 31. M[c] Connell *v.* Hector, 3 Bos. and Pull. 113. The *Indian Chief*, 3 Rob. 12. The *Anna Catharina*, 4 Rob. 107. The *President*, 5 Rob. 277. The *Matchless*, 1 Hagg, *Adm. Rep.* 103, 104. [O'Mealey *v.* Wilson, 1 Campb. 482. Albrecht *v.* Sussmann, 2 Ves. and B. 323. The *Aina*, 1 Spinks (*Ecc. and Adm.*) 315.]

[2] M[c]Connell *v.* Hector, 3 Bos. and Pull. 113. The *Emanuel*, 1 Rob. 249.

[3] Cited in 4 Rob. 255, note.

[4] Bell *v.* Reid, 1 Maule and Selw. 726.

United States. If he resides in a belligerent country his property is liable to capture as enemy's property, and if he resides in a neutral country he enjoys all the privileges, and is subjected to all the inconveniences, of the neutral trade. He takes the advantages and disadvantages, whatever they may be, of the country of his residence[1]. This doctrine is founded on the principles of national law, and it accords with the reason and practice of all civilized nations. *Migrans Jura amittit ac Privilegia et immunitates domicilii prioris*[2]. A person is not however to be permitted to acquire a neutral domicile, that will protect such a trade in opposition to the belligerent claims of his native country, if he emigrates from that country *flagrante bello*. [Vattel denies the right of emigration in a war in which his country is involved. In the *Dos Hermanos* this doctrine was upheld as well settled law, and, in his remarks upon it, Mr Duer says, that the ground of the doctrine is that there rests upon every subject or citizen a moral obligation not to abandon his country in time of war without the express sanction of the government. "It is for these reasons," says the learned author here referred to, "that the principle in question has been sanctioned by many of the most approved writers on the law of nations, and although not expressly approved, as far as I can discover, by any decision of the English Admiralty, I doubt not that its authority would be promptly admitted and followed by the court." Mr Arnould, too, cites the principle with approval "as founded on a decision that seems thoroughly well founded[3]."]

[1] Case of the sloop *Chester*, 2 Dallas, 41. Murray *v.* Schooner *Betsey*, 2 Cranch, 64. Maley *v.* Shattuck, 3 Cranch, 488. Livingston *v.* Maryland Ins. Co. 7 Cranch, 506. The *Venus*, 8 Cranch, 253. The *Frances*, 8 Cranch, 363. [*San Jose Indiano* and cargo, 2 Gallison, 28. The judgment in the case of the *Venus* is cited at full length in Wheaton's *Elements*, Vol. II. pp. 565—572. Edn. 1863, by W. B. Lawrence.]

[2] Voet, *Com. ad Pand.* Tom. I. 347, § 99.

[3] The *Dos Hermanos*, 2 Wheaton, 76. [Vattel, Bk. I. Ch. XIX. §§ 220 223. 1 Duer, *On Insurance*, 523. 1 Arnould, *On Insurance*, 113.]

The only limitation upon the principle of determining the character from residence, is, that the party must not be found in hostility to his native country. He must do nothing inconsistent with his native allegiance, and this qualification is annexed to the rule by Sir William Scott in the case of the *Emanuel,* and the same qualification exists in the French law, as well since as before their revolution[1]. It has been questioned whether the rule does not go too far, even with this restriction; but it appears to be too well and solidly settled to be now shaken.

Limitation of the test from residence.

It has been a question admitting of much discussion and difficulty, arising from the complicated character of commercial speculations, what state of facts constitutes a residence, so as to change or fix the commercial character of the party. [Mr Wheaton, whose remarks on this subject deserve to be cited, says, "that the text writers are deficient in definitions and detail as to what species of residence constitutes such a domicile as will render the party liable to reprisals. Their defects are supplied by the precedents furnished by the British courts, which, if they have not applied the principle with undue severity in the case of neutrals, have certainly not mitigated it in its application to that of British subjects resident in the enemy's country on the commencement of hostilities." He then reviews at considerable length the leading cases on the subject, and winds up with an extract from Sir W. Scott's judgement in the case of the *Indian Chief*[2], to the effect that the character that is gained by residence ceases by non-residence, and is an adventitious one, no longer adhering to the subject of it from the moment he puts himself in motion to quit the country *sine animo*

What is residence.

[1] 1 Rob. *Rep.* 249. *Code Napoleon,* Articles 17. 21. [For a description of these Articles, the reader is referred to Macardé, *Explication du Code,* 5ième edn. T. I. Tit. I. ch. ii. § 1. pp. 114—120; and Deslombes *Cours de Code Napoléon,* T. I. pp. 209—226.] Pothier's *Traité du droit de Propriété,* No. 94.

[[2] Wheaton's *Elements,* Vol. II. Part. IV. Chap. I. § 16, p. 559.]

*revertendi*[1]. From these precedents then the following positions may be specified.] First, that the most important test is the *animus manendi*. The presumption arising from actual residence in any place, is, that the party is there *animo manendi*, and it lies upon him to remove the presumption, if it should be requisite for his safety[2]. If the intention to establish a permanent residence be ascertained, the recency of the establishment, though it may have been for a day only, is immaterial. If there be no such intention, and the residence be involuntary or constrained, then a residence, however long, does not change the original character of the party, or give him a new and hostile one[3]. But the circumstances requisite to establish the domicil, are flexible, and easily accommodated to the real truth and equity of the case. Thus it requires fewer circumstances to constitute domicil in the case of a native subject, who returns to reassume his original character, than it does to impress the national character on a stranger[4]. The *quo animo* is, in each case, the real subject of inquiry, and when the residence exists freely, without force or restraint, it is usually held to be complete, whether it be an actual or only an implied residence.

The animus manendi.

[Secondly, to use Lord Stowell's language, "Of the few principles that can be laid down generally *time* is the grand ingredient in constituting domicile. It is the great agent in this matter (of domicile); which is to be taken in a compound ratio of time and the occupation, with a great preponderance on the article of time. Be the occupation what it may it cannot happen, save with few

Time.

[[1] Wheaton's *Elements*, Vol. II. Part IV. Ch. I. § 17, p. 561. Citing the *Harmony*, 2 Rob. 324. *The Indian Chief*, 3 Rob. 12, and proceedings of the commissioners under the treaty of 1794, between Great Britain and the United States. See also the *Matchless*, 1 Hogg. *Adm. Rep.* 103.]

[2] The *Bernon*, 1 Rob. 86.

[3] The *Diana*, 5 Rob. 60. The *Ocean*, 5 Rob. 90. [Bromley *v.* Heseltine, 1 Campbell, 76. See also Lord *v.* Colvin, 28 *Law Journal Equity*, 373; and 4 Drewry, 366.]

[4] *La Virginie*, 5 Rob. 99.

exceptions, that mere length of time shall not constitute domicile[1]."

But, thirdly, *permanency* is another important element in the affixing a national character by means of residence, for, as Lord Stowell observes in the *Diana*, "mere recency of establishment will not avail if the intention of making a permanent residence was fully fixed upon the party;" and therefore it follows that] when the residence is once fixed, and has communicated a national character to the party, it is not devested by a periodical absence, or even by occasional visits to his native country[2]. Nor is it invariably necessary, that the residence be personal, in order to impress a person with a national character. The general rule undoubtedly is, that a neutral merchant may trade in the ordinary manner to the country of a belligerent, by means of a stationed agent there, and yet not contract the character of a domiciled person. If however the principal be trading, not on the ordinary footing of a foreign merchant, but as a privileged trader of the enemy, such a privileged trade puts him on the same ground with their own subjects, and he would be considered as sufficiently invested with the national character by the residence of his agent. Sir William Scott, in the *Anna Catharina*[3], applied this distinction to the case of a neutral invested with the privileges of a Spanish merchant and the full benefit of the Spanish character; and this case has been followed to its fullest extent in the United States, [where, to use Mr Duer's words, "in language that reflects the spirit and emulates the style of the illustrious judge whose doctrines he adopts and defends, Mr Justice Story asserts the principle to be deduced from the case, viz. that where a person is engaged in the ordinary or extraordinary commerce of an enemy's country upon the

Permanency.

Privileged trader.

[[1] The *Harmony*, 2 Rob. 324. See also the *Anne Green* and cargo, 1 Gallison, 284.]

[2] The *Junge Ruiter*, 1 Acton, 116. The *Nereide*, 9 Cranch, 414. (Marshall, Ch. J.). The *Friendschaft*, 3 Wheaton, 14.

[3] 4 Rob. *Rep.* 107. See also the *Portland*, 3 Rob. 41.

same footing and with the same advantages as native resident subjects, his property *so employed* is to be deemed incorporated into the general commerce of that country, and subject to confiscation, be his residence what it may[1]."] It affords a sample of that piercing and unwearied investigation which the courts of admiralty have displayed, in unravelling the intricate process by which an enemy's trade was attempted to be protected from hostile seizure, and in the application of sound principles of national law to new and complex cases. On the same ground it has been decided[2], that an American consul general in Scotland, committing his whole duty to vice-consuls, was deemed to have lost his neutral character by engaging in trade in France; and it is well settled, that if a foreign consul carries on trade as a merchant, in an enemy's country, his consular residence and character will not protect that trade from interruption by seizure and condemnation as enemy's property[3].

The national character reverts.

A national character acquired by residence may be thrown off at pleasure by a return to the native country. It is an adventitious character, and ceases by non-residence, or when the party puts himself in motion *bonâ fide* to quit the country *sine animo revertendi*, and such an intention is essential in order to enable the party to reassume his native character[4]; and so it has been decided by the Supreme Court of the United States, that a neutral leaving a belligerent country with his family at the commencement of war (he having been domiciled in such country) might carry with him the property which he had acquired there. His neutral character, as to his person and property, reverting as soon as he sails from

[1] The *Indiano*, 2 Gallison, 268. [1 Duer, *On Insurance*, 527; and 1 Arnould, *On Insurance*, pp. 110—112.]

[2] The *Dree Gebroeders*, 4 Rob. 232.

[3] Vattel Bk. IV. Ch. VIII. § 114. The *Indian Chief*, 3 Rob. 22. Albrecht *v.* Sussman, 2 Vesey and Beamers, 323. Sorenson *v.* the Queen 11 Moore, Privy Council Cases, 141. Arnold and Ramsay *v.* U. I. Company, 1 *Johns. Cases*, 363, (American).

[4] The *Indian Chief*, 3 Rob. 12. The *Friendschaft*, 3 Wheaton, 14.

the hostile port[1]. In the case of the *Venus*[2], the decisions of the English courts on the subject of national character acquired by residence, and on the consequences of such acquired character, were recognised as being founded on sound principles of public law. It was declared, that the law of nations distinguishes between a temporary residence in a foreign country for a special purpose, and a residence accompanied with an intention to make it the party's domicil, or permanent place of abode; and that the doctrine of the prize courts, and the common law courts of England, was the same on this subject with that of the public jurists. As a consequence of the doctrine of domicil, the court decided, that if a citizen of the United States should establish his commercial domicil in a foreign country, and hostilities should afterwards break out between that country and the United States, his property, shipped before knowledge of the war, and while that domicil continued, would be liable to capture, on the ground, that his permanent residence had stamped him with the national character of that country. The hostile character was deemed to attach to the American citizen, only in respect to his property connected with his residence in the enemy's country, and the converse of the proposition was also true, that the subject of a belligerent state, domiciled in a neutral country, was to be considered a neutral by both the belligerents, in reference to his trade. The doctrine of enemy's property, arising from a domicil in an enemy's country, is taken strictly; and equitable qualifications of the rule are generally disallowed, for the sake of preventing frauds on belligerent rights, and to give the rule more precision and certainty. [From this opinion of the court, however, Mr Justice Marshall dissented, contending that a commercial domicile wholly acquired in time of peace ceases at the commencement of hostilites; that the presumption of an intention

Srict construction of the rule as to domicile in enemy's country.

[[1] U. S. *v.* Guillem, 11 Howard's *Rep.* 60. cited in a note by Mr W. B. Lawrence to Wheaton's *Elements*, Vol. II. p. 572.]

[2] 8 Cranch, 253. The *Mary and Susan*, 1 Wheaton's *Rep.* 54.

to return to the native country at the first opportunity is to be entertained, and that this presumption ought to shield the property from condemnation until delay or circumstances destroy that presumption. Mr Duer and Mr Phillips both incline to this opinion; and whilst the former cites the judgement as one deserving of the highest consideration, the latter conceives that the learned judge's views are supported by Lord Stowell's language in the case of the *Ocean*[1].]

Exception in the East.

In the law of nations as to Europe, the rule is, that men take their national character from the general character of the country in which they reside, and this rule applies equally to America. But in the East, says Lord Stowell, from the oldest times an immiscible character has been kept up, foreigners are not admitted into the general body and mass of the society of the nation; they continue strangers and sojourners as all their fathers were—*Doris amara suam non intermiscuit undam;* and trading under the protection of a factory, they take their national character from the establishment under which they live and trade, not acquiring any under the general sovereignty of the country[2].

Trade in the enemy's country impresses hostile character.

National character may be acquired in consideration of the traffic in which the party is concerned. If a person connects himself with a house of trade in the enemy's country, in time of war, or continues, during a war, a connexion formed in a time of peace, he cannot protect himself by having his domicil in a neutral country. He is considered as impressed with a hostile character, in reference to so much of his commerce as may be connected with that establishment. The rule is the same, whether he maintains that establishment as a partner or as a sole trader[3]. The Supreme Court of the United States, refer-

[[1] 1 Duer, *On Insurance*, p. 505. 1 Phillips, *On Insurance*, p. 63, note (*a*). The *Ocean*, 5 Rob. 90.]

[2] The *Indian Chief*, 3 Rob. 22.

[3] The *Vigilantia*, 1 Rob. *Rep.* 1. The *Portland*, 3 Rob. 41. The *Nina*, 1 Spinks 276. The *Indiano*, 2 Gallison, 268. The *Antonia Johanna*, 1 Wheaton, 159. The *Friendschaft*, 4 Wheaton, 105.

ring to the English prize cases on this subject, observed, that they considered the rule to be inflexibly settled, and that they were not at liberty to depart from it, whatever doubt might have been entertained, if the case was entirely new.

Equitable qualification of the rule.

But though a belligerent has a right to consider as enemies all persons who reside in a hostile country or maintain commercial establishments there, whether they be by birth neutrals, or allies, or fellow-subjects, yet the rule is accompanied with this equitable qualification: that they are enemies *sub modo* only, or in reference to so much of their property as is connected with that residence or establishment. This nice and subtle distinction allows a merchant to act in two characters, so as to protect his property connected with his house in a neutral country, and to subject to seizure and forfeiture his effects belonging to the establishment in the belligerent country. So there may be a partnership between two persons, the one residing in a neutral, and the other in a belligerent country, and the trade of one of them, with the enemy, will be held lawful, and that of the other unlawful, and consequently the share of one partner in the joint traffic will be condemned, while that of the other will be restored. This distinction has been frequently sustained, notwithstanding the difficulties that may attend the discrimination between the innocent and the noxious trade, and the rule has been introduced into the maritime law of the United States[1].

[1] The *Portland*, 3 Rob. *Rep.* 41. The *Herman*, 4 Rob. 228. The *Jonge Classina*, 5 Rob. 297. The *San Jose Indiano*, 2 Gall. 268. [On the foregoing subject, that of domicile and national character, the following accessible authorities may be consulted with advantage. English.—*Laws of Maritime Warfare*, by Hazlitt and Roche, pp. 16—43. Phillimore, *On International Law*, Vol. I. §§ 315 et seq. and Vol. III. §§ 474 et seq. where the cases, both English and American, are all cited. Tudor's leading cases in *Mercantile Law*, notes to the *Fortuna* and the *Santa Cruz*, pp. 808—814. Twiss, *On the Law of Nations*, Vol. II. ch. VIII. Westlake's *Private International Law*, §§ 7. 20. 22. 32. 35. 36. 40. 42. 43. 51—53. French.—Dalloz, *Repertoire*, sub verb. 'Domicile.' Merlin, *Repertoire*, sub verb.

Colonial and coasting trade of the enemy.

The next mode in which a hostile character may be impressed, according to the doctrine of the English courts, is by dealing in those branches of commerce which were confined, in time of peace, to the subjects of the enemy. There can be no doubt, that a special license, granted by a belligerent to a neutral vessel, to trade to her colony, with all the privileges of a native vessel, in those branches of commerce which were before confined to native subjects, would warrant the presumption that such vessel was adopted and naturalized, or that such permission was granted in fraud of the belligerent right of capture, and the property so covered may reasonably be regarded as enemy's property. This was the doctrine in the case of *Berens* v. *Rucker*, as early as 1760[1]. But the English rule went further, annexing a hostile character, and the penal consequences of confiscation, to the ship and cargo of a neutral engaged in the colonial or coasting trade of the enemy, not open to foreigners in time of peace, but confined to native subjects by the fundamental regulations of the state. This prohibition stood upon two grounds: 1st. That if the coasting or colonial trade, reserved by the permanent policy of a nation to its own subjects and vessels, were opened to vessels during war, the act would proceed from the pressure of the naval force of the enemy, and its object would be to obtain relief from that pressure. The neutral who should interpose to relieve the belligerent, under such circumstances, would rescue him from the condition to which the arms of his enemy might have reduced him, would restore him to those resources which had been wrested from him by the arms of his adversary, and would deprive that adversary of the advantages which successful

'Domicile.' Massé, *Droit Commercial*, Tom. III. Fœlix, *Droit International Privé*, Liv. I. Tit. I. § 27. German.—Heffter, *Le Droit International Public*, Edn. par Bergson, §§ 58—63. American.—Story's *Conflict of Laws*, §§ 40—49. Wheaton's *Elements of International Law*, Edn. 1863, by W. B. Lawrence, Vol. II. Part IV. pp. 557—585. Halleck's *International Law*, ch. XXIX. Story on *Prize Courts*, by Pratt, 1854, pp. 54—70.]

[1] 1 Wm. Black. *Rep.* 313.

war might have given him. This the opposing belligerent would pronounce a departure from neutrality, and an interference in the war, to his prejudice. 2nd. That if the trade should not have been opened by law, the neutral employed in a trade reserved by the enemy to his own vessels, would identify himself with that enemy, and assume his character. These principles first became a subject of interesting discussion in the war of 1756, and are generally known in England and the United States by the appellation of the Rule of 1756, though the rule is said to have been asserted before that period. Rule of 1756.

In the letter of Puffendorf to Groningius, published in 1701[1], he declares, that the English and the Dutch were willing to leave to neutrals the commerce they were accustomed to carry on in time of peace, but were not willing to allow them to avail themselves of the war to augment it, to the prejudice of the English and the Dutch. The French ordinances of 1704[2] and 1744, it has been considered, were founded upon the basis of the same rule, and regulations were made to enforce it, and to preserve to neutrals the same trade which they had been accustomed to enjoy in peace. There is some evidence, also, that in the reign of Charles II. neutral vessels were considered, both by England and Holland, to be liable to capture and condemnation for being concerned in the coasting trade of the enemy. The Dutch, at that day, contended for this neutral exclusion, on the authority of general reasoning and the practice of nations; and the same rule is said to have been asserted in the English courts, in the war of 1741, and the exclusion of neutral vessels from the coasting trade of the enemy was declared to stand upon the law of nations[3]. But it was in the war of 1756 that the rule awakened general and earnest attention. Mr Jenkinson, in his *Discourse on the conduct of Great Britain in respect*

[1] Puff. *Droit des Gens*, par Barbeyrac, Tom. II. 558, note (z).

[2] 2 Valin, *Com.* 248, 250.

[3] 6 Rob. *Rep.* 74, note, and 252, note. [Courtenay's *Life of Sir Wm. Temple*, Vol. I. p. 433.]

*to neutral nations,* written in 1757, considered it to be unjust and illegal for neutrals to avail themselves of the pressure of war to engage in a new species of traffic, not permitted in peace, and which the necessities of one belligerent obliged him to grant, to the detriment, or perhaps to the destruction of the other[1]. On the other hand, Hubner, who published his Treatise in 1759, is of opinion that neutrals may avail themselves of this advantage, presented by the war, though he admits the lawfulness of the trade to be a question of some uncertainty[2].

English judicial interpretation of the rule.

Thus seemed to stand the authority of the rule of 1756[3], when it was revived and brought into operation by England, in the war of 1793, and again upon the renewal of war in 1803. The rule was enforced by her, under occasional relaxations, during the long course of the wars arising out of the French revolution, and was frequently vindicated by Sir William Scott, in the course of his judicial decisions, with his customary ability and persuasive manner, as a rule founded in natural justice and the established jurisprudence of nations[4]. On the other hand, the

Protests of the United States.

government of the United States constantly and earnestly protested against the legality of the rule, to the extent claimed by Great Britain; insisting, in its diplomatic intercourse, that the rule was an attempt to establish "a new principle of the law of nations," and one which subverted "many other principles of great importance, which have heretofore been held sacred among nations." It insisted,

[1] In the British Memorial addressed to the Deputies of the States General of Holland, December 22, 1758, the injustice of neutrals in assuming the enemy's carrying trade was urged, and it was declared that their *high mightinesses had never suffered such a trade,* and that it had been opposed in all countries in like circumstances.

[2] *De la Saisie des Bâtimens Neutres,* I. ch. IV. § 6. It must not be forgotten that Hübner was an ardent and partial advocate of neutral rights and privileges.

[3] It stood upon loose grounds, in point of official authority, according to the able examination of the documentary evidence of the rule, given in a note to the first volume of Mr Wheaton's *Reports*, app. note 3.

[4] Rob. *Rep.* passim. And see 1 Rob. 296 and 6 Rob. 78 and 255. See also 4 Rob. app. 1—15.

that neutrals were of right entitled "to trade, with the exceptions of blockades and contrabands, to and between all ports of the enemy, and in all articles, although the trade should not have been opened to them in time of peace[1]." It was considered to be the right of every independent power, to treat, in time of peace, with every other nation, for leave to trade with its colonies, and to enter into any trade, whether new or old, that was not of itself illegal, and a violation of neutrality. One state had nothing to do with the circumstances or motives which induced another nation to open her ports. The trade must have a direct reference to the hostile efforts of the belligerents, like dealing in contraband, in order to render it a breach of neutrality.

The rule of 1756, especially in respect to colonial trade, has also been repeatedly attacked by writers in the United States with great ability and learning: and though the rule would seem to have received the very general approbation of British lawyers and statesmen, yet it was not exempted from severe criticism, even in distinguished publications in their country[2]. The principle of the rule of 1756 may, therefore, very fairly be considered as one unsettled and doubtful, and open to future and vexed discussion. The Chief Justice of the United States, in the case of the *Commercen*[3], alluded to the rule, but purposely avoided expressing any opinion on the correctness of the principle. "It is very possible," said the learned author of these commentaries so far back as 1830, "that if the United States should hereafter attain that elevation of maritime power and influence, which their rapid growth and great resources seem to indicate, and which shall prove sufficient

[1] Mr Monroe's *Letter to Lord Mulgrave*, of Sept. 23, 1805, American *State Papers*, Vol. V. p. 297, and Mr Madison's *Letter to Messrs Monroe and Pinckney*, dated May 17, 1806.

[2] [On this subject the following authorities may be consulted. Manning's *Law of Nations*, Chap. V. Phillimore's *International Law*, Vol. III. Ch. XI. Tudor's *Leading Cases in Mercantile Law*, pp. 722—731. Wheaton's *Elements*, Part IV. ch. III. § 27.]

[3] 1 Wheat. 396.

to render it expedient for her maritime enemy (if any such enemy shall ever exist) to open all his domestic trade to enterprising neutrals, we might be induced to feel more sensibly than we have hitherto done, the weight of the arguments in favour of the policy and equity of the rule."

[In Mr Tudor's excellent and carefully digested work, the reader will find most of the decisions that belong to this branch of international law stated and analyzed[1], and in Mr Pritchard's analytical digest of Admiralty cases (1847) will be found all the cases relating to the interdictions on the colonial and coasting trade well classified[2]. It is therefore unnecessary to do more than refer to those authorities, stopping only to notice] a point discussed in the case of the *Polly*[3], whether the fact of a cargo consisting of Spanish colonial produce imported from the Havana (a colony belonging to a belligerent power) in a neutral (American) ship to the United States, and after being landed and duties paid, re-exported in the same vessel to Spain, was sufficient to break the continuity of the voyage from the enemy's colony to the mother country, and legalize the trade by the mere transhipment in the United States. Sir William Scott in that case thought, that landing the goods and paying the duties was a sufficient test of the bona fides of the transaction. Afterwards, however, it was held that merely touching at the neutral port and paying a nominal duty was a mere evasion, and not sufficient to exempt the voyage from the charge of a direct continued and unlawful trade between the mother country and the colony of the enemy[4]. The question is one of intent. Did the animus importandi terminate at the intermediate port, or look to an ulterior port? Was it, under the circumstances, a bona fide im-

The *Polly*.

Effect of breaking the continuity of the voyage.

[1] See the notes to the *Immanuel* and the *Wilhelmina*. Tudor's *Leading Cases on Mercantile Law*, pp. 722—731.

[2] See also Phillimore, *On International Law*, Vol. III. p. 312, and *Manual of the Law of Maritime Warfare*, Hazlitt and Roche, pp. 182—210.

[3] 2 Robinson, 361.

[4] The *Essex* and the *Maria*, 5 Rob. 365—369.

portation, ending at the intermediate port, or a mere contrivance to cover the original scheme of the voyage to an ulterior port? This is the true principle of the cases as declared by Sir William Grant in the *William*, 5 Rob. 385, and recognized in the United States[1].

It is understood that the English and American commissioners at London in 1806 came to an agreement as to the proper and defined test of a bona fide importation of cargo into the common stock of the country, and as to the difference between a continuous and an interrupted voyage. But the treaty so agreed on was withheld by President Jefferson from the Senate of the United States, and never ratified. The doctrine of the English Admiralty is just and reasonable on the assumption of the British rule (of 1793), because we have no right to do covertly and insidiously, what we have no right to do openly and directly. But if that rule be not well founded, all the qualifications of it do not help it; and in the official opinion of Mr Wirt (the Attorney-General of the United States) to the executive department, while he condemns the legality of the rule itself, he approves, as just in the abstract, the English principle of continuity (that is, that landing the goods and paying the duties in the neutral country breaks the continuity of the voyage, and is such an importation as legalizes the trade)[2].

The rules of 1756 and 1793 as affecting the law of marine insurance.

[As the rule of 1756, and that which grew out of it in 1793, have an important bearing upon the law of marine insurance, a few words on this topic will not be out of place, before any further remarks are hazarded upon these rules and their future fate. Now if the doctrine exists as an acknowledged rule of law in this country, that where neutrals at the commencement of, or during the continuance of hostilities, engage in such a trade of the enemy (whether colonial or coasting) as is not open to them, or other foreigners, in time of peace, but is confined to native

[1] *Opinions of the Attorneys-General of the United States*, Vol. I. pp. 359—362.

[2] *Opinions of Attorneys-General*, Vol. I. pp. 394—396.

subjects by the fundamental law of the state, their ships and cargo shall be liable to condemnation as prize of war, then all trading of this kind is an attempt to break the law, and insurances to protect it would seem to be void. "There can be no doubt," says Mr Arnould, writing since the Russian war and the treaty of Paris, "that an insurance effected in this country in time of war to protect such privileged neutral trading would be treated as wholly illegal and void by our Courts, on the ground that trading to an enemy's colony, with all the privileges of an enemy's ship, causes a neutral vessel to be regarded as an enemy's

Chavasse *v.* Grazebrook.

ship[1]." But, according to a recent decision by the Lord Chancellor[2], those views must now be materially modified. It is true that the case itself relates to another topic altogether, viz. the legality of the trade in munitions of war and contraband articles by a neutral; but it is conceived that the following passage, in his Lordship's judgment, is so general in its tendency, as to be capable of application to the point now in hand. "In the view of international law, the commerce of nations is perfectly free and unrestricted. The subjects of each nation have a right to interchange the products of labour with the inhabitants of every other country. If hostilities occur between two nations and they become belligerents, neither belligerent has a right to impose, or to require a neutral government to impose, any restrictions on the commerce of its subjects." On the one hand, then, we have the principle laid down as a clear and approved principle of the English prize courts, that neutrals are not to carry on in time of war a trade which is interdicted to them in time of peace: in support of this doctrine we have a large number of cases, and no

[1] Arnould, *On Insurances*, 2nd edition, Vol. II. p. 774, citing Berens *v.* Rucker, 1. W. Bl. 314.

[2] Chavasse *v.* Grazebrook. See the *Times*, April 24, 1865. In mentioning the subject of neutral trade in contraband of war, the Editor seizes the earliest opportunity of drawing the reader's special attention to two Letters on that subject, and on *Marine Insurance on Contraband of War*, by Historicus. See Historicus on *International Law* (London, 1863), pp. 121—145.

modern case calling in question the propriety and expediency of retaining it. On the other, we have the strongly expressed dissatisfaction with the principle of writers on the continent, as well as on the other side of the Atlantic; we have the fact that even at the time when the rule of 1756 was looked upon with high favour, there were many intermissions and relaxations of it, caused by peculiar circumstances and suggested by varying policy; we have the latest opinion just cited of an eminent authority on this as well as other branches of the law of England, delivered not as a mere view of what the law ought to be, but as a judgement ex cathedra of what the relations between neutrals and belligerents now are; and we have also the fact, that the policy of Great Britain in time of peace, as well as in time of war, has undergone a great and beneficial change. That in peace her policy is that of free trade, her ports open to all comers, her colonial trade unrestricted, and her coasting trade free. That in war her inclination and expressed desire are to remove as much as possible from neutral trade the difficulties that war throws in its path[1]. It may be, therefore, that the words of Mr Wheaton are true, in which he says the practical importance of the rule of 1756 is now much diminished, and that if there should be unhappily any occasion to test the truth of Mr Arnould's view of its effect upon marine insurances, the courts will refuse to recognize its existence, and to hold insurances even upon these voyages legal[2].]

Sailing under flag and pass of the enemy.

Sailing under the flag and pass of an enemy, is another mode by which a hostile character may be affixed to property; for, if a neutral vessel enjoys the privileges of a foreign character, she must expect, at the same time, to be subject to the inconveniences attaching to that character.

[1] See the order in Council of the 15th of April, 1854, allowing neutrals to trade to all ports and places wheresoever situated, that are not in a state of blockade. *B. & F. State Papers*, Vol. XLVI. p. 49. See in the *Edinburgh Review*, No. 203, (Vol. C.) p. 220, an excellent analysis and explanation of this important rule.

[2] See Tudor's *Leading Cases in Mercantile Law*, pp. 730, 731.

This rule is necessary to prevent the fraudulent mask of enemy's property[1]. But a distinction is made, in the English cases, between the ship and the cargo. Some countries have gone so far as to make the flag and pass of the ship conclusive on the cargo also; but the English courts have never carried the principle to that extent, as to cargoes laden before the war. The English rule is, to hold the ship bound by the character imposed upon it, by the authority of the government from which all the documents issue. But goods which have no such dependence upon the authority of the state may be differently considered; and if the cargo be laden in time of peace, though documented as foreign property in the same manner as the ship, the sailing under a foreign flag and pass has not been held conclusive as to the cargo[2]. The doctrine of the courts in the United States has been very strict on this point, and it has been frequently decided there, that sailing under the license and passport of protection of the enemy, in furtherance of his views and interests, was, without regard to the object of the voyage, or the port of destination, such an act of illegality as subjected both ship and cargo to confiscation as prize of war[3] [and rendered void an insurance made on such a voyage]. The federal courts placed the objection to these licenses on the ground of a pacific dealing with the enemy, and as amounting to a contract that the party to whom the license is given, should, for that voyage, withdraw himself from the war, and enjoy the repose and blessings of peace. The illegality of such an intercourse was strongly condemned; and it was held, that the moment the vessel sailed on a voyage, with

English doctrine.

[1] See the *Industrie*, Spinks, (Ecc. and Adm.) Reports, 444. The Spinks (do.) *Primus* E. 353; and Story on *Prize Courts*, by Pratt, pp. 61—63.

[2] The *Elizabeth*, 5 Rob. 2. The *Vreede Scholtys*, cited in the note to 5 Rob. 5.

[3] The *Julia*, 8 Cranch, 181. The *Aurora*, Ib. 203. The *Hiram*, Ib. 444. The *Ariadne*, 2 Wheaton, 143. The *Caledonia*, 4 Wheaton, 100. Colquhoun *v.* New York Firemen Insurance Company, 15 Johnson, 352. Ogden *v.* Barker 18 Johnson, 87, and see 1 Peters, C. C. Rep. 410.

an enemy's license on board, the offence was irrevocably committed and consummated, and that the *delictum* was not done away even by the termination of the voyage, but the vessel and cargo might be seized after arrival in a port of the United States, and condemned as lawful prize[1].

Assignments *in transitu.*

Having thus considered the principal circumstances which have been held by the courts of international law to impress a hostile character upon commerce, it may be here observed, that property which has a hostile character at the commencement of the voyage, cannot change that character by assignment, while it is *in transitu,* so as to protect it from capture. This would lead to fraudulent contrivances, to protect the property from capture, by colourable assignments to neutrals. During peace a transfer *in transitu* may be made, but when war is existing or impending, the belligerent rule applies, and the ownership of the property is deemed to continue, as it was at the time of the shipment, until actual delivery. This illegality of transfer, during, or in contemplation of war, is for the sake of the belligerent right, and to prevent secret transfers from the enemy to neutrals, in fraud of that right, and upon conditions and reservations which it might be impossible to detect[2]. [For if such a rule did not exist, all goods shipped in the enemy's country would be protected by transfers, which it would be impossible to detect; and, therefore, it has been held, as a general rule, that property cannot be converted *in transitu* by an enemy]. So, property shipped from a neutral to the enemy's country, under a contract to become the property of the enemy on arrival, may be taken *in transitu* as enemy's property, for capture is considered as delivery. The captor, by the rights of war, standing in the place of the enemy, [and the capture being considered as delivery, the captor is entitled

[1] Duer, *On Insurance,* Vol. I. pp. 582—589.

[2] *Vrow Margaretha,* 1 Rob. 336. *Jan Frederick,* 5 Rob. 128. See also 1 Rob. 1, 101, 122. 2 Rob. 137. 1 Rob. 16, note. 4 Rob. 32. The *Sechs Geschwistern,* 4 Rob. 100. The *Benedict,* Spinks, 314. The *Caroline,* Spinks, 252. The *Neptune,* ib. 281. The *Rapid,* ib. 80. The *Rapida,* ib. 172.

to a condemnation of the goods passing under such a contract, as of enemy's property[1]]. The prize courts will not allow a neutral and belligerent, by a special agreement, to change the ordinary rule of peace, by which goods ordered and delivered to the master are considered as delivered to the consignee. All such agreements are held to be constructively fraudulent, and if they could operate, they would go to cover all belligerent property, while passing between a belligerent and a neutral country, since the risk of capture would be laid alternately on the consignor or consignee, as the neutral factor should happen to stand in the one or the other of those relations. [In the ordinary course of affairs, as is well known, valid sales of ships and cargoes at sea are frequent; but, in times of war, all property at sea liable to confiscation, owing to hostilities either continued or broken out since its despatch, would be affected by colourable transfers in fraud of the belligerent's rights. It is a general rule, therefore, that transfer of the property, without actual delivery of the subject, is insufficient, under these circumstances, to change the rights and liabilities attaching thereto. Hence it follows, that if the subject of sale and transfer actually reach the hand of the purchaser anywhere, the transitus for this purpose is thereby determined, and the ownership effectually changed. But prize courts investigate claims founded on titles of that kind with great jealousy; and if they find that no reasonable proof in support of the genuineness of the transaction is adduced, or such proof only as is inadequate to satisfy the demand which the practice of the court and its rules require; if, in fact, it turns out that there is no sale but a transfer *in transitu flagrante bello*, all the authorities denounce such a transaction as illegal[2].

Sales and transfers of ships during war.

[1] The *Anna Catharina*, 4 Rob. 107. The *Sally Griffiths*, 3 Rob. 300, in notis. The *Danckebaar Africaan*, 1 Rob. 107.

[2] The *Soglasie*, 2 Spinks, (Ecc. and Adm.) 106; *The Ocean Bride*, Spinks (Prize cases), 72; and see Story on *Prize Courts*, by Pratt, pp. 64, 65.

Transfers of ships during war, or whilst it is imminent, from the enemy to a neutral, are transactions closely scrutinized by prize courts, and on the claimant lies the onus of proving the sale to be bona fide[1]. If bona fide title be shown and the court be satisfied therewith, although it be acquired by gift from an enemy father to a neutral son, the absence of pecuniary consideration, or in case of a sale the fact of part of the money being still unpaid, is not a valid objection[2].]

These rules of maritime jurisprudence are strictly construed.

These principles of the English admiralty have been explicitly recognized and acted upon by the prize courts in the United States. The great principles of national law were held to require, that, in war, enemy's property should not change its hostile character *in transitu;* and that no secret liens, no future elections, no private contracts looking to future events should be able to cover hostile property while sailing on the ocean[3]. Captors disregard all equitable liens on enemy's property, and lay their hands on the gross tangible property, and rely on the simple title in the name and possession of the enemy. If they were to open the door to equitable claims, there would be no end to discussion and imposition, and the simplicity and ce-

[1] See MacClachlan's *Treatise on the Law of Merchant Shipping*, p. 478, and the cases cited in note 7, beginning with the *Christine*, Spinks' *Prize Case*, 82, and ending with the *Soglasie*; Story on *Prize Courts*, p. 63.

[2] The *Benedict*, Spinks' *Prize Cases*, 314, and Sorensen *v.* the Queen, 11 Moore, 118. As to colourable transfers see the *Johanna Christoph*. 2 Spinks, (Ecc. and Adm.) 2; and see also the American view of the subject under discussion, viz. sales and transfers of ships during war, exhibited in the 7th Vol. of the *Opinions of Attorneys-General*, p. 538, where Mr C. Cushing's explanation of the law will be found to be identical with the English authorities. Mr Lawrence has collected some of the more recent cases, American and English, in a note (182) to Wheaton's *Elements*, Vol. II. p. 581, edn. 1863, and contrasted the doctrines enunciated in them with the somewhat opposite doctrine of the French law on this subject; cf. Pistoye et Duverdy, *Traité des Prises Maritimes*, T. II. pp. 1 et 502.

[3] The *Frances*, 1 Gallison, 445. 8 Cranch, 335, 359. S. C. And see the whole subject discussed in Vol. III. p. 539 of *The Opinions of Attorneys-General* (American).

lerity of proceedings in prize courts would be lost[1]. All reservations of risk to the neutral consignors, in order to protect belligerent consignees, are held to be fraudulent, and these numerous and strict rules of the maritime jurisprudence of the prize courts, are intended to uphold the rights of lawful maritime capture, and to prevent frauds, and preserve candour and good faith in the intercourse between belligerents and neutrals. The modern cases contain numerous and striking instances of the acuteness of the captors in tracking out deceit, and of the dexterity of the claimants in eluding investigation.

[1] The *Josephine*, 4 Rob. 25. The *Tobago*, 5 Rob. 218. The *Marianna*, 6 Rob. 24. The *Aina*, 1 Spinks, 81. The *Ida*, 1 Spinks, 26. And the *American cases* ubi sup.

# CHAPTER VI.

## OF THE RIGHTS OF BELLIGERENT NATIONS IN RELATION TO EACH OTHER.

---

THE end of war is to procure by force the justice which cannot otherwise be obtained; and the law of nations allows the means requisite to the end. The persons and property of the enemy may be attacked, and captured, or destroyed, when necessary to procure reparation or security. There is no limitation to the career of violence and destruction, if we follow the earlier writers on this subject, who have paid too much deference to the violent maxims and practices of the ancients, and the usages of the Gothic ages. They have considered a state of war as a dissolution of all moral ties, and a license for every kind of disorder and intemperate fierceness. An enemy was regarded as a criminal and an outlaw, who had forfeited all his rights, and whose life, liberty, and property, lay at the mercy of the conqueror. Every thing done against an enemy was held to be lawful. He might be destroyed, though unarmed and defenceless. Fraud might be employed as well as force, and force without any regard to the means[1]. But these barbarous rights of war have been questioned, and checked, in the progress of civilization. Public opinion, as it becomes enlightened and refined, condemns all cruelty, and all wanton destruction of life and property, as equally useless and injurious;

[1] Grotius, Bk. III. ch. iv. and v. Puff. lib. II. ch. xvi. § 6. Bynk. *Q. J. Pub.* Bk. I. ch. i. ii. iii. Burlamaq. Part IV. ch. v.

and controls the violence of war by the energy and severity of its reproaches[1].

Ancient rules of war condemned.

Grotius, even in opposition to many of his own authorities, and under a due sense of the obligations of religion and humanity, placed bounds to the ravages of war, and mentioned that many things were not fit and commendable, though they might be strictly lawful; and that the law of nature forbade what the law of nations (meaning thereby the practice of nations) tolerated. He held that the law of nations prohibited the use of poisoned arms, or the employment of assassins, or violence to women, or to the dead, or making slaves of prisoners[2]; and the moderation which he inculcated had a visible influence upon the sentiments and manners of Europe. Under the sanction of his great authority, men began to entertain more enlarged views of national policy, and to consider a mild and temperate exercise of the rights of war, to be dictated by an enlightened self-interest, as well as by the precepts of Christianity. And, though some subsequent writers, as Bynkershoek and Wolfius, contended for the restoration to war of all its horrors, by allowing the use of poison, and other illicit arms, yet such rules became abhorrent to the cultivated reason and growing humanity of the Christian nations. Montesquieu insisted[3] that the laws of war gave no other power over a captive than to keep him safely, and that all unnecessary rigour was condemned by the reason and conscience of mankind. Rutherforth[4] has spoken to the same effect, and Martens[5] enumerates several modes of war, and species of arms, as being now held unlawful by the laws of war. Vattel[6] has entered largely into the subject, arguing with great strength of reason and

[1] De Hautefeuille, *Droits et Devoirs des Nations Neutres*, T. I. tit. III. § 1, and Heffter, *Droit International*, § 125.

[2] Bk. III. ch. iv. v. vii.

[3] *Esprit des Loix*, Bk. XV. ch. ii.

[4] *Inst.* Bk. II. ch. ix.

[5] *Summary*, Bk. VIII. ch. iii. § 3 (translation by William Cobbett, 1802;) and see also the last edition of Martens' *Droit des Gens*, by Vergé, T. II. §§ 273, 274, with Pinheiro Fereira's notes.

[6] Bk. III. ch. viii.

eloquence, against all unnecessary cruelty, or base revenge, and all mean and perfidious warfare; he recommends his benevolent doctrines by the precepts of exalted ethics and sound policy, and by illustrations drawn from some of the most pathetic and illustrious examples[1].

Plunder on land.

There is a marked difference in the rights of war carried on by land and at sea[2]. The object of a maritime war is the destruction of the enemy's commerce and navigation, in order to weaken or destroy the foundations of his naval power. The capture or destruction of private property is essential to that end, and it is allowed in maritime wars by the law and practice of nations. But there are great limitations imposed upon the operations of war by land, though depredations upon private property, and despoiling and plundering the enemy's territory are still too prevalent a practice, especially when the war is assisted by irregulars[3]. Such conduct has been condemned in all ages by the wise and virtuous, and it is usually severely punished by those commanders of disciplined troops who have studied war as a science, and are animated by a sense of duty, or the love of fame. We may infer the opinion of Xenophon on this subject (and he was a warrior as well

[[1] In an admirable Essay on the *Growth and Usages of War*, by Professor Montague Bernard, published in the *Oxford Essays of* 1856, the reader will find all that can be said in favour of the merciful and humane doctrines above eulogized, with a most complete sketch of the changes in the method of conducting war and the changes in sentiment and feeling with regard to the conduct of war, from the earliest well recorded period in the history of war down to the Russian war of 1854.

How far there has been an improvement in the customs and established laws of war since the peace of Westphalia, has been discussed by Mr Wheaton and Mr Nassau Wm. Senior, with opposite opinions, the former in his *History of the Law of Nations*, p. 760, holding that an immense improvement has taken place, the latter, in No. 146 of the *Edinburgh Review* (Vol. LXXII.) contesting that view.]

[[2] For an elaborate examination of the difference between war by land and war by sea, the reader is referred to De Hautefeuille, *Droits et Devoirs des Nations Neutres*, T. I. Tit. iii. Sect. III. § 1.]

[[3] The *Johanna Emilie*, 1 Spink, 14; and see also Tudor's *Leading Cases in Mercantile Law*, p. 804.]

as a philosopher), when he states, in the *Cyropædia*[1], that Cyrus of Persia gave orders to his army, when marching upon the enemy's borders, not to disturb the cultivators of the soil; and there have been such ordinances in modern times for the protection of innocent and pacific pursuits[2].

[1] Lib. v.

[2] Emerigon *Des Ass.* ch. iv. § 9. and ch. xii. § 19 (Meredith's translation, pp. 105 and 364), refers to ordinances of France and Holland, in favour of protection to fishermen; and to the like effect was the order of the British government in 1810, for abstaining from hostilities against the inhabitants of the Feroe islands and Iceland. General Brune stated to the Duke of York, in October, 1799, when an armistice in Holland was negotiating, that if the latter should cause the dikes to be destroyed, and the country to be inundated, when not useful to his own army, or detrimental to the enemy's, it would be contrary to the laws of war, and must draw upon him the reprobation of all Europe, and of his own nation. Nay, even the obstinate defence of a town, if it partake of the character of a mercantile place, rather than a fortress of strength, has been alleged to be contrary to the laws of war. (See the correspondence between General Laudohn and the Governor of Breslau, in 1760. Dodsley's *Ann Reg.* 1760.) So, the destruction of the forts and warlike stores of the besieged in the post of Almeida, by the French commander, when he abandoned it with his garrison by night in 1811, is declared by General Sarrazin, in his history of the Peninsular war, to have been an act of wantonness which justly placed him without the pale of civilized warfare. [In his account of the evacuation of Almeida, General William Napier so far from denouncing General Brennier's act, as wanton and uncivilized, speaks of the whole affair as one that reflected credit upon the strategical skill and the military reputation of that officer, the result of whose successful evacuation was a junction of the garrison with Marmont, provoking a strong remonstrance from the British Commander, Lord Wellington, in a general order to the army. Napier's *History of the Peninsular War*, Vol. III. pp. 520—522. A perusal of the general orders of the Duke of Wellington, when in command of the armies in Spain, will show how war may be conducted vigorously and effectively, and yet with the utmost regard for feelings of humanity. One instance out of many will suffice for special notice:—that instance is the order issued to the army under his command upon the memorable occasion of crossing the frontiers of France and carrying the war into the enemy's country (9th July 1813): "The officers and soldiers must recollect that their nations are at war with France solely because the ruler of the French nation will not allow them to be at peace....They must not forget that the worst of the evils suffered by the enemy in his profligate invasion of Spain and Portugal have been occasioned by the irregularities of the soldiers and their cruelties authorized and encouraged by their chiefs towards the unfortunate and peaceful inhabitants of the country." (See *The*

Vattel condemns very strongly the spoliations of a country without palpable necessity, and speaks with a just indignation of the burning of the Palatinate by Turenne, under the cruel instructions of Louvois, the war minister of Louis XIV.[1] The general usage now is not to touch private property upon land, without making compensation[2], unless in special cases dictated by the necessary operations of war, or when captured in places carried by storm, and which repelled all the overtures for a capitulation. Contributions are sometimes levied upon a conquered country, in lieu of confiscation of property, and as some indemnity for the expenses of maintaining order, and affording protection[3]. If the conqueror goes beyond these limits wantonly, or when it is not clearly indispensable to the just purposes of war, and seizes private

*Dispatches of the Duke of Wellington*, Vol. XI. p. 169.)] When a Russian army under the command of Count Diebitsch had penetrated through the passes of the Balkan to the plains of Romelia, in the summer of 1829, the Russian commander gave a bright example of the mitigated rules of modern warfare, for he assured the Mussulmen that they should be entirely safe in their persons and property, and in the exercise of their religion ; and that the Mussulman authorities in the cities, towns and villages might continue in the exercise of their civil administration for the protection of person and property. The inhabitants were required to give up their arms, as a deposit, to be restored on the return of peace, and in every other respect they were to enjoy their property and pacific pursuits as formerly. This protection and full security to the persons and property of the peaceable inhabitants of conquered towns and provinces, is according to the doctrine and declared practice of modern civilized nations. (See Dodsley's *Ann. Reg.* 1772, p. 37). [An admirable testimony to the discipline of European armies, and to the progress of civilization and humanity in the conduct of war, as evinced by the appearance of the country traversed by the French and Austrian armies in 1859, during the Italian campaign, is rendered by Mr W. B. Lawrence in a note (190) to Wheaton's *Elements*, p. 625, ed. 1863.]

[1] Vattel, Bk. III. ch. ix. § 167.

[2] See Phillimore's *International Law*, Vol. III. p. 135. Twiss, *on the Law of Nations*, Vol. II. p. 118. Halleck, *on International Law*, ch. xix. § 12, p. 456. Wheaton's *Elements*, Vol. II. Part IV. ch. ii. § 5, pp. 596, 597, ed. 1863, by W. B. Lawrence. Hautefeuille, *Des Nations Neutres*, T. II. tit. vii. ch. i. p. 176. Heffter, *Droit International*, § 133.

[3] Vattel, Bk. III. ch. ix. § 165. Halleck *on International Law*, ch. xix. §§ 15—18. Heffter, *Dr. Int.* §§ 135, 136.

property of pacific persons for the sake of gain, and destroys private dwellings, or public edifices, devoted to civil purposes only; or makes war upon monuments of art, and models of taste, he violates the modern usages of war, and is sure to meet with indignant resentment, and to be held up to the general scorn and detestation of the world[1].

Law of retaliation.

Views of the older writers.

Cruelty to prisoners, and barbarous destruction of private property, will provoke the enemy to severe retaliation upon the innocent[2]. Retaliation is said by Rutherforth[3] not to be a justifiable cause for putting innocent prisoners or hostages to death; for no individual is chargeable, by the law of nations, with the guilt of a personal crime, merely because the community of which he is a member is guilty. He is only responsible as a member of the state, in his property, for reparation in damages for the acts of others; and it is on this prin-

[1] Vattel, Bk. III. ch. ix. § 168. In the case of the Marquis De Somerueles (Stewart's *Vice-Adm. Rep.* 482), the enlightened judge of the Vice-Admiralty Court at Halifax restored to the Academy of Arts in Philadelphia a case of Italian paintings and prints, captured by a British vessel in the war of 1812, on their passage to the United States; and he did it "in conformity to the law of nations, as practised by all civilized countries," and because "the arts and sciences are admitted to form an exception to the severe rights of warfare." [A short but able notice of the determination of the British Parliament to recommend the restitution of the works of art in the Louvre at Paris, in 1815, the reasons for that determination, and the views of those who were opposed thereto, will be found in Wheaton's *Elements*, Vol. II. Part IV. ch. ii. § 6, pp. 622—625, ed. 1863, by W. B. Lawrence. On this topic see Halleck's *International Law*, ch. xix. §§ 11—27, and the authorities there cited, especially with reference to the jurisdiction of the English Court of Admiralty over questions of booty and captures made on land by military forces alone, § 27.]

[2] Hence during the progress of the civil war in Spain, in 1835, the government of Great Britain drew attention to the charges of cruelty and sanguinary reprisals, alleged to have been perpetrated by the officers and partisans of Don Carlos, insisting upon the necessity and expediency of conducting the war in a manner more in accordance with feelings of humanity, and more consonant with modern practice: see *British and Foreign State Papers*, Vol. XXIV. (1835—36), pp. 396—416.

[3] *Inst.* Bk. II. ch. ix. and see Wheaton's *Elements*, Vol. II. Part IV. ch. ii. § 4. and Klüber, *Droit des Gens*, Part II. tit. 2. § 2. ch. i. §§ 245—247.

ciple, that, by the law of nations, private property may be taken and appropriated in war. Retaliation, to be just, ought to be confined to the guilty individuals, who may have committed some enormous violation of public law. On this subject of retaliation Professor Martens is not so strict[1]. While he admits that the life of an innocent man cannot be taken, unless in extraordinary cases, he declares that cases will sometimes occur, when the established usages of war are violated, and there are no other means, except the influence of retaliation, of restraining the enemy from further excesses. Vattel speaks of retaliation as a sad extremity, and it is frequently threatened without being put in execution, and, probably, without the intention to do it, and in hopes that fear will operate to restrain the enemy. Instances of resolutions to retaliate on innocent prisoners of war occurred in the United States during the revolutionary war, as well as during the war of 1812; but there was no instance in which retaliation, beyond the measure of severe confinement, took place in respect to prisoners of war[2].

Enlightened conduct of the United States Government in the recent war.

[In the course of the recent contest in the United States, which has been carried on with all the fierceness, but happily with comparatively little of the uncivilized brutality of a civil war, the subject of the treatment of Southern privateersmen, when taken prisoners, has more than once been mooted. Very great loss, it is well known, was inflicted upon the merchants of the Federal States by the depredations of the cruisers who roamed the sea in the service of the Confederate States,

[1] *Summary of the Law of Nations*, Bk. VIII. ch. i. § 3, note, Cobbett's translation (1802). The learned Professor, however, must have seen cause for altering his opinion, for the view above stated does not appear in the last edition of his work, and the whole subject is discussed in a different spirit: see Vergé's ed. 1858, T. II. Liv. VIII. ch. ii. §§ 252, 262.

[2] *Journals of Congress under the Confederation*, Vol. II. p. 245. Vol. VII. p. 9, and 147. Vol. VIII. p. 10. British Orders in Canada of 27th October, and December 12th, 1813, and President's Message to Congress, of December 7th, 1813, and of October 28th, 1814. See *American State Papers*, Vol. IX. p. 276.

burning, sinking, and destroying, wherever they sailed. It may well be conceived that the irritation caused by the losses thus inflicted on the trade of the Federal States was extreme, especially as all this destruction and loss affected only a few private individuals, and had not the slightest influence upon the war itself. It is not surprising, then, if that irritation at times found vent in threats of, and demands for, retaliatory vengeance, or if the government was called upon to treat as pirates those who were thus depredating. Fortunately the authorities at Washington, steadily rejecting the counsel of those who would have turned the war into a series of unrestrained acts of retaliation, and remembering that "the rights of belligerents having been conceded to the rebellious states, they were entitled to make use of all the means and appliances known to modern warfare," refused "to fall back into the barbarism of the middle ages, and resolved to observe in their own conduct those humane usages in the treatment and exchange of prisoners, which modern civilization has shewn to be equally the dictates of humanity and policy." "Let us remember," says Judge Daly, in the memorable and eloquent letter[1] we have been quoting from, "that the great duty we have in hand, viz. to put down this rebellion, imposes on us all the exigencies of war. War, when conducted in accordance with all the strictest usages of humanity, is, as all who have shared in the recent battles know, a sufficiently bloody business; and if we are to add to its horrors by hanging up all who fall into our hands as traitors or pirates, we leave to the South no alternative but resistance to the last extremity[2]."]

Judge Daly's Letter, Dec. 1861.

Regular commissions necessary for carrying on war.

Although war puts all the subjects of the one nation in a state of hostility with those of the other, yet, by the customary law of Europe, every individual is not allowed to fall upon the enemy. If subjects confine themselves to simple defence, they are to be considered

[1] To the Hon. Ira Harris, December 21st, 1861.

[2] Papers presented to both Houses Parliament 1862, *North America*, No. 1.—No. 148.

as acting under the presumed order of the state, and are entitled to be treated by the adversary as lawful enemies, and the captures which they make in such a case are allowed to be lawful prize. But they cannot engage in offensive hostilities without the express permission of their sovereign; and if they have not a regular commission, as evidence of that consent, they run the hazard of being treated by the enemy as lawless banditti, not entitled to the protection of the mitigated rules of modern warfare[1].

Ancient regulations on the subject.

It was the received opinion in ancient Rome, in the times of Cato and Cicero[2], that one who was not regularly enrolled as a soldier could not lawfully kill an enemy. But the law of Solon, by which individuals were permitted to form associations for plunder, was afterwards introduced into the Roman law, and has been transmitted to us as part of their system[3]. During the lawless confusion of the feudal ages the right of making reprisals was claimed, and exercised, without a public commission. It was not until the fifteenth century that commissions were held necessary, and began to be issued to private subjects in time of war, and that subjects were forbidden to fit out vessels to cruise against enemies without license; and there were ordinances in Germany, France, and England, to that effect[4]. In later times it became the practice for maritime states to make use of the voluntary aid of individuals against their enemies, as auxiliary to the public force. Bynkershoek says, that the Dutch formerly employed no vessels of war but such as were owned by private persons, to whom the government allowed a proportion of the captured property, as well as indemnity from the public treasury. Until a very recent period among

Non-commissioned vessels.

1 Bynk. *Q. J. P.* ch. 20. Vattel, Bk. III. ch. xv. § 226. *Journals of Congress*, Vol. VII. 187. Martens, Bk. VIII. ch. iii. § 2.

2 *De Off.* Bk. I. ch. xi.

3 *Dig.* 47. 22. 4. Bynk. *Q. J. P.* Bk. I. ch. xviii.

4 *Code des Prises*, T. I. p. 1. Martens, *on Privateers*, p. 18. Robinson's *Collectanea Maritima*, p. 21; and see Ward's *Law of Nations*, Vol. I. pp. 293—297.

the European maritime states, it was customary to allow vessels to be fitted out and equipped by private adventurers, at their own expense, to cruise against the commerce of the enemy, [a practice that has been resorted to by the Confederate States in their contest with the Federal Government]. They were duly commissioned, and it was said not to be lawful to cruise without a regular commission[1]. Sir Matthew Hale held it to be depredation in a subject to attack the enemy's vessels, except in his own defence, without a commission[2]. The subject has been repeatedly discussed in the Supreme Court of the United States[3], and the doctrine of international law is considered to be, that private citizens cannot acquire a title to hostile property, unless seized under a commission, but they may still lawfully seize hostile property in their own defence. If they depredate upon the enemy without a commission, they act upon their peril, and are liable to be punished by their own sovereign; but the enemy are not warranted to consider them as criminals, and, as respects the enemy, they violate no rights by capture.

Such hostilities, without a commission, are, however, contrary to usage, and exceedingly irregular and dangerous; and they would probably expose the party to the unchecked severity of the enemy, but they are not acts of piracy. Vattel, indeed, says[4], that private ships of war, without a regular commission, are not entitled to be treated like captures made in a formal war. The observation is rather loose, and the weight of authority undoubtedly is, that non-commissioned vessels of a belligerent nation may at all times capture hostile ships, without being deemed, by the rules of international law, pirates. They

English Law as to non-commissioned vessels.

[1] Bynk. *ub sup.* Martens, Bk. VIII. ch. iii. § 27, Cobbett's translation (1802). Judge Croke in the case of the *Curlew*, Stewart's *Vice-Adm. Rep.* 326.

[2] Harg. *Law T.* 245, 246, 247.

[3] Brown *v.* United States, 8 Cranch, 132—135. The *Nereide*, 9 Cranch, 449. The *Dos Hermanos*, 2 Wheaton, 76, and 10 Wheaton, 306. The *Amiable Isabella*, 6 Wheaton, 1.

[4] Bk. III. ch. xv. § 226.

are lawful combatants, but they have no interest in the prizes they may take, and the property will remain subject to condemnation in favour of the government of the captor, as *droits of the admiralty*[1]. It is said, however, that, in the United States, the property is not strictly and technically condemned upon that principle, but *jure reipublicæ;* and it is settled law there that all captures made by non-commissioned captors are made for the government[2]. [The above remarks of the learned author are too important to pass by without some further notice. And first, according to an American writer, whose views have been frequently referred to, there is an apparent contradiction in the language here used; for if private individuals who engage in offensive hostilities on land without a regular commission are liable to be treated as lawless banditti, and if such hostilities on the high seas are exceedingly irregular and dangerous, and expose the party to the unchecked severity of the enemy, then, says General Halleck[3], it is difficult to understand why the enemy is not warranted to consider them as criminals, and why such parties violate no right of capture as respects the enemy. The answer probably is to be found partly in the widely different nature of maritime and land warfare, already discussed, and partly in the fiction, or rather the assumption, that on the sea all the subjects of one belligerent are the enemies of all the subjects of the other, and entitled to do all such acts as war justifies between the belligerent powers themselves. Hence, whilst there may be impediments in the way of a private uncommis-

United States Law.

Subject reviewed.

[1] The *Rebekah,* 1 Rob. 227. The *Melomane,* 5 Rob. 42. The *Charlotte,* 1 Dodson, 220.

[2] *Com. Dig.* tit. Admiralty, E. 3. 2 Wood. *Lec.* 432. The *Georgiana,* 1 Dodson's *Adm.* 397. The brig *Joseph,* 1 Gall. *Rep.* 545. The *Dos Hermanos,* 10 Wheaton, 306. The American Commissioners at the Court of France, in 1778, (Benjamin Franklin, Arthur Lee, and John Adams), in a letter to the French Government, laid down accurately and with precision, the law in the text, as to captures of enemy's property without a commission. *Diplomatic Correspondence,* by J. Sparks, Vol. I. 443.

[3] Halleck's *International Law,* ch. xvi. § 10.

sioned ship retaining the captures it may make, or disposing of them in any way it may please, those impediments arise from the enactments of municipal law, and are not imposed by international law, which in no way affects this question[1]. But, secondly, if a private ship belonging to one of the belligerents attack and capture the vessel of a neutral power, without a commission of war, the case is widely different; here the attacking vessel may be treated as a pirate by the vessel attacked, or by any vessel coming to her aid; and in the event of the neutral being captured, a Prize court would decree a release, on account of the want of a commission[2]; therefore, thirdly, even if Privateering be recognized by a state or nation as a lawful mode of carrying on war, it is also a recognized principle in all codes of maritime law, that to cruise without a commission from some constituted authority, is an illegal act, which, according to the naval instructions of Great Britain of 1730, 1806, and 1826, would render the crew of a vessel so engaged liable to be considered and treated as pirates[3]. Now as the determination that Privateering shall henceforth be abolished, which was propounded at the Treaty of Paris, has not been universally accepted, it is still important to ascertain what does constitute a lawful commission to cruise, at least where there is any doubt as to the competency of the authority granting it; for, in the course of the civil war between the Northern and the Southern States of America, a question was raised in France, by certain insurance offices at Bordeaux, as to the quality of a vessel (the well known *Alabama*), alleged to be cruising under a commission from the President of the Confederate States[4]. Assuming, then,

Privateering.

[1] The *Rebekah*, 1 Rob. 227. The *Melomane*, 5 Rob. 42. See Twiss, *on the Laws of Nations*, Vol. II. § 190, p. 383.

[2] See a case cited by Dr Twiss from *The Life of Sir Leoline Jenkins*, Vol. II. p. 727.

[3] Twiss, *Law of Nations*, Vol. II. p. 385. Phillimore, Vol. III. § 383. See Halleck's *International Law*, ch. XXX. § 22, and the cases there cited.

[4] See *Times* Newspaper, Sept. 12, 1863.

that a belligerent has a right to commission and use private armed vessels, and that the right to issue letters of marque is inherent in the government of every independent state, being a part of its war-making power:—what is the rule in the case of a war between a revolted province and its mother country? How are third powers to act where there is a war between two bodies, neither of whom recognizes the *de facto* political superiority of the other? Are the ships of the mother country alone to be considered as properly commissioned, and are those of her opponent to be treated as pirates? Fortunately the difficulty, if difficulty it be, has been solved by the high authority of the leading law officer of the United States, in a case arising out of the war between Texas and Mexico, in 1836[1]: "When a civil war," says the Attorney-General of the United States, "breaks out in a foreign nation, and part of such nation erect a distinct and separate government, and the United States, although they do not acknowledge the independence of a new government, do yet recognize the existence of a civil war, our courts have uniformly regarded each party as a belligerent nation in regard to acts done *Jure belli;* and the parties concerned in those acts are not treated as pirates. It is true that when persons acting under a commission from one of the belligerents make a capture ostensibly in the right of war, but really with the design of robbery, they will be held guilty of piracy[2]." When, therefore, the existence of a civil war is recognized by a neutral state, where official notice of this fact, and of the intention of such state to preserve its neutrality, has been given to the parent state, where such recognition has been frequently repeated by the executive, and where a proper commission to cruise is proved to exist, there a charge of piracy against the cruiser of the revolted state cannot be established[3].]

[1] For this case, and its comment, we are indebted to Dr Twiss. See Twiss's *Laws of Nations*, Vol. II. p. 387.

[2] *Opinions of Attorneys-General,* Vol. II. p. 1066.

[3] In conformity with these views the Federal Government early in

In order to encourage privateering, it has been usual in Europe, until very recently, and still is so in the United States, to allow the owners of private armed vessels to appropriate to themselves the property, or a large portion of the property, they may capture; and to afford them, and the crews, other facilities and rewards for honourable and successful efforts. This depends upon the municipal regulations of each particular power, and as a necessary precaution against abuse, the owners of privateers are required, by the ordinances of the commercial states, where privateering is recognized, to give adequate security that they will conduct the cruise according to the laws and usages of war, and the instructions of the government, and that they will regard the rights of neutrals, and bring their prizes in for adjudication. These checks are essential to the character and safety of maritime nations[1]. Privateering, under all the restrictions which have been adopted, is very liable to abuse. The object is not fame or chivalric warfare, but plunder and profit. The discipline of the crews is not apt to be of the highest order, and privateers are often guilty of enormous excesses, and become the scourge of neutral commerce[2]. They are sometimes manned and officered by foreigners, having no permanent connexion with the country, or interest in its cause. This was a complaint made by the United States, in 1819, in relation to irregularities and acts of atrocity

the war announced its intention not to treat Southern Privateersmen as pirates.

[1] Bynk. *Q. J. P.* ch. xix. *Journals of Congress*, 1776, Vol. II. 102—114. *Acts of Congress* of 26th June, 1812, ch. cvii., and April 20th, 1818, ch. lxxxiii. § 10. President's instructions to private armed vessels, 2 Wheaton, App. p. 80. Danish instructions of 10th March, 1810, Hall's *L. J.* Vol. IV. 263, and App. to 5 Wheaton, 91. Vattel, B. III. ch. xv. § 229. Martens' *Summ.*, Cobbett's translation (1802), p. 297, note; and see Vergé's edition of Martens (Paris, 1858), T. I. L. VIII. ch. iv. § 289. Ord. of Buenos Ayres, May, 1817, in App. to 4 Wheaton, 28. Digest of the Code of British Instructions, App. to 5 Wheaton, 129. See also 2 Robinson's *Reports*, App. No. viii. p. 9, and Twiss, *On the Law of Nations*, Vol. II. pp. 393—397.

[2] *Reports of the United States Secretary of State*, March 2d, 1794, and June 21st, 1797. *American State Papers*, Vol. III. p. 170.

committed by private armed vessels sailing under the flag of Buenos Ayres[1]. Under the best regulations, the business tends strongly to blunt the sense of private right, and to nourish a lawless and fierce spirit of rapacity. [And even where it is resorted to as a powerful weapon of offence, "and a principal means of annoying a maritime nation," where the strongest motive and the fullest justification for using it are, that it is a valuable protection to a nation possessed of an extensive commerce spread through all seas, but unguarded by large standing fleets[2]; even there it may turn out to be a source of terrible annoyance, for "it is not enough that there be brave and gallant captors, there must be something to be captured;" and if, as Mr Webster most pointedly hypothesized[3], an hypothesis that the recent contest in America has converted into a stern reality, a war between the United States and any state without ships and commerce were existing, who would lose most by the practice of privateering in such a war? "There would be nothing," adds that able lawyer and diplomatist, "for the former to attack, while the means of attacking them would flow to their enemies from every part of the world. Capital, ships and men would be abundant in all their ports, and then commerce, spread over every sea, would be the destined prey." Indeed, as Lord Clarendon well said at one of the Conferences in Paris in 1856, "Privateering is nothing less than an organized and legal piracy, and privateers are one of the greatest scourges of war, fostering a system which the present condition of civilization and humanity requires should be put an end to[4]."] Efforts have been made, from time to time, to abolish the practice. In the treaty of amity and commerce between Prussia and the United

Efforts to put down Privateering prior to the Treaty of Paris.

[1] Mr Adams' *Letter* of 1st January, 1819, to Mr De Forest, and his *Official Report* of 28th January, 1819.

[2] *Works of John Adams*, Vol. VIII. p. 646.

[3] See Webster's *Works*, Vol. III. p. 212.

[4] Papers presented to Parliament, 1856, Paris Conferences. Protocol, No. 22, April 8th, 1856.

States, in 1785, it is stipulated that, in case of war, neither party should grant commissions to any private armed vessel to attack the commerce of the other. But the spirit and policy of maritime warfare would not permit such generous provisions to prevail. That provision was not renewed with the renewal of the treaty. A similar attempt to put an end to the practice was made in the agreement between Sweden and Holland, in 1675, but the agreement was not performed. The French legislature, soon after the breaking out of the war with Austria, in 1792, passed a decree for the total suppression of privateering, but that was a transitory act, and it was soon swept away in the tempest of the Revolution. The efforts to stop the practice have, till recently, been very feeble and fruitless, notwithstanding that enlightened and enlarged considerations of national policy have shown it to be for the general benefit of mankind, to surrender the licentious practice, and to obstruct as little as possible the freedom and security of commercial intercourse among the nations[1].

Treaty of Paris as to Privateering. [Fortunately the subject was renewed and discussed under happier auspices at the Treaty of Paris, for of all the four propositions relating to maritime law, none met with heartier support than that which stands at the head of the Declaration signed by the representatives of Great Britain, Austria, France, Prussia, Russia, Sardinia and Turkey, that "Privateering is and remains abolished." In Europe the adoption of the principle met with almost

[1] Emerigon, *Des Assurances*, T. I. pp. 129—132, citing Mably, *Droit Public de l'Europe*, ch. xii. § 1, p. 308 (edn. 1742), Meredith's translation, ch. iv. § 9, p. 105. See also Cauchy, *Le Droit Maritime Internationale*, T. II. p. 74. *Edinburgh Review*, Vol. VIII. pp. 13—15. *North American Review*, N. S. Vol. II. p. 166. During the war between the United States and Great Britain the legislature of New York went so far as to pass an act to encourage privateering associations, by authorizing any five or more persons who should be desirous to form a company for the purpose of annoying the enemy and their commerce by means of private armed vessels, to sign and file a certificate stating the name of the company and its stock, &c., and that they and their successors should thereupon become a body politic and corporate with the ordinary corporate powers. *Laws*, New York, 38, Sept. 12, Oct. 21, 1814.

universal acceptance[1], and by that adoption it is hoped, nay it must be assumed, that states according to its reception among themselves will on all future emergencies be bound. But in the United States its fate was different. In answer to a requisition made to the government of that country, it was urged by Mr Marcy that the adoption of the rule would give to a nation having a powerful military marine an immense preponderance over one with an equal commercial one, but which had discarded a permanent navy; that it was difficult to define what peculiar class of maritime force should be regarded as privateers, and that the proceedings of the Congress were in the nature of an act of legislation, seeking to change a well-settled principle of international law. The resolution of the United States was declared to be not to surrender the practice, unless, in belligerent operations, the government and nation were entirely separated, and war was confined in its agencies and effects to the former[2]; that is, unless all the private property save contraband of war of the subjects or citizens of one belligerent should be exempt from capture by public armed vessels of the other belligerent. Mr Lawrence, in a review of the arguments contained in Mr Marcy's note and of the conclusion thus arrived at, as in duty bound, gives an unfeigned assent to all that is thus propounded, and thinks with President Pierce that there is no real gain so long as private property is still left to the depredations of armed cruisers. Against the peculiar line of reasoning he adopts in support of his view, and in defence of Mr Marcy's position, we abstain from arguing; though it is not very easy to see what is meant by the assertion, that "the proposition for the abolition of privateering was a mistake in confounding one of the means for the accom-

Mr W. B. Lawrence's Defence of Mr Marcy's note, examined.

[1] The various powers by whom the proposition was accepted will be found enumerated in the *British and Foreign State Papers*, Vol. XLVIII.

[2] President's *Message and Documents*, 1856—7, p. 35; *Statesman's Manual*, Vol. III. p. 2163 et seq.; and *Parliamentary Paper*, North America, No. 3, Appendix, p. 29.

plishment of an object with the end to be obtained." But we must express our strong dissent from the conclusion he draws, that Mr Marcy's proposed addition to the privateer clause "is a legitimate development of the true spirit of the declaration[1]." Mr Lawrence has, we venture to think, here confounded two things entirely distinct. The true spirit, that is the intention of the Declaration, as the exordium or preamble shows, was directly to improve the condition of maritime law, by removing doubts and difficulties that had been the source of endless trouble and ill-will, and indirectly to soften the nature of maritime warfare. To abolish privateering, which, as we have shown by abundant authority, was but a legal name for a most licentious system of robbery, was to act in complete accordance with the spirit of the declaration, by getting rid of one of the worst blots by which maritime law and maritime warfare were disfigured; but the exemption of all property from seizure by public armed vessels is another and totally distinct act, neither connected with the abolition of privateering, nor capable of being developed from it; one that rests on different grounds altogether, and is affected by an entirely distinct line of argument; and one that, however desirable in the interests of commerce and private enterprize, cannot, unfortunately for those interests, be considered apart from views of expediency and state policy.

Further correspondence between Mr Seward and Earl Russell, April, 1861.

On the 24th April, 1861, Mr Seward, Secretary of State, in a circular note to the ministers of the United States in the principal courts of Europe, in referring to the insurrection of a portion of the American people then recently begun, expressed the desire of his government to waive their amendment upon the Declaration of Paris of 1856, and to accept the proposition relating to privateering. Mr Adams, the American minister in London, brought the matter before Earl Russell on the 11th July.

[1] W. B. Lawrence's note to Wheaton's *Elements*, edition 1863, Vol. II. pp. 638, 639.

In a note of the 18th July, Earl Russell signified the assent of the government of England to conclude, instead of an accession to the declaration, a convention to the same effect so soon as he was informed that a similar convention had been agreed on with France. Accordingly Mr Dayton, the American minister in Paris, being informed of this determination, notified to M. Thouvenel that he was in a position to sign a convention embodying the four points contained in the Declaration of Paris. A draft convention was therefore prepared, but prior to its presentment for signature, Earl Russell thought it advisable to add to it the following Declaration: "In affixing his signature, &c....Earl Russell declares by order of Her Majesty, that Her Majesty does not intend thereby to undertake any engagement which shall have any bearing direct or indirect on the internal differences now prevailing in the United States." M. Thouvenel having intimated to Mr Dayton that the French government intended to make a similar declaration, the Convention, with its addition, was referred back to Mr Adams, who thinking first that the presentation of a written declaration, not being part of the Convention, was a novel and anomalous proceeding; and secondly, that, by the terms of the constitution of the United States, the matter was one for the cognizance of the Senate of that power, resolved to submit the whole question to the judgment of the authorities at Washington. This was done, and the result was that Mr Adams was directed by Mr Seward to break off the negotiation altogether, if the declaration were insisted upon; and accordingly the negotiation was broken off and completely at an end. Lord Lyons, in a despatch to Earl Russell, dated December 6th, 1861, enclosing a copy of the papers relating to the business with the President's message, winds up with these words: "From several of the papers now published it appears that it was only an act of common prudence on the part of the governments of Great Britain and France not to accept the accession of this country (the United States) to the Declaration of Paris without stating distinctly what obligations they intended by doing so to assume with regard to the seceded States. Little doubt can remain after reading the papers, that the accession was offered solely with a view to the effect it would have on the privateering operations of the Southern States, and that a refusal on the part of England and France, after having accepted the accession, to treat the Southern privateers as pirates, would have been made a serious grievance if not a ground of quarrel[1]."

Rules and decisions relating to Privateering.

Such is the history of the proposition relating to privateering in the declaration attached to the Treaty of Paris of 1856, and from that history it appears that, as the proposition did not meet with universal acceptance, the rules and decisions relating to privateering must still remain upon the pages of a treatise on International Law. An examination of some of those decisions will show the truth of Mr Justice Story's observation, that the great object of maritime nations has been to restrain and regulate the conduct of privateers[2]. In the first place, then, every vessel claiming to act as a private ship of war must have her commission of war on board, for if without a commission she attacks a ship belonging to a neutral power, she may be treated as a pirate by the vessel attacked, or by any vessel coming to her aid: nor would a prize court adjudge the vessel she may capture good prize to her. Therefore the mere application for a letter of marque is not sufficient to invest her with authority to cruise[3]; and moreover, if at the time of capture the master of the privateer be not on board, the capture is considered as made without a commission, and enures to the government or its special grantee[4]. Nor should it be forgotten that every capture is at the peril of the captors, who are liable to a suit for restitution, and may also be mulcted in costs and damages should they seize without reasonable

1 *Parliamentary Papers*, North America, No. 3 (1862).

2 The *Thomas Gibbons*, 8 Cranch, 428.

3 The *Spitfire*, 2 Rob. 285.

4 The *Charlotte*, 5 Rob. 280.

or justifiable cause[1]. Upon granting letters of marque the rule is for the captain to appear and with two sureties give security for his conduct. How far the liability of the owners and officers extends, whether beyond the amount of the security so given or not, has been variously discussed. Again, in the matter of constructive joint captures, an important difference has been established between public ships of war and privateers, that whereas the former are privileged in being allowed to share in the capture if they are in sight only at the time[2], the latter have not the same benefit of a presumed animus capiendi: for with them that must be demonstrated by some overt act, such as actual intimidation, or actual or constructive assistance, or by some variation of conduct which would not have taken place save with reference to that particular object, and if the intention of acting against the enemy had not been entertained[3]. So too privateers are not within the terms of a capitulation protecting *private property* generally; for, as Lord Stowell said in the case cited below[4], "Privateers are private property in one sense, but they have at the same time a public property impressed on them by their employment; though they are private property, they are still private property employed in the public service." On the other hand, *public property* ceded by capitulation, but not taken possession of by the captors and afterwards seized by a privateer, belongs to the crown, and not to the privateer[5].

In addition to this very brief notice of some of the leading rules of law affecting privateers, there are two or three other points of sufficient importance to demand a short review.

[1] Story, *On Prize Courts*, p. 35.

[2] The *Dree Gebrœders*, 5 Rob. 339.

[3] Bynk. *Q. J. Pub.* L. I. ch. xviii. Talbot *v.* Three Briggs, 1 Dallas, 95. The *Santa Brigada*, 3 Rob. 52. *L'Amitié*, 6 Rob. 261.

[4] The *Dash*, 1 Edwards, 271.

[5] Thorshaven and its dependencies, 1 Edwards, 102.

Status of the commissioned vessels of a revolted nation or colony.

The first we shall advert to will be the following: In the event of a revolt or of a civil war, what ought to be the conduct of neutral nations towards vessels of war which have received a commission from the de facto government of the revolted member or colony? Are they to concede to them the position and privileges of belligerents, and if so, when? At the risk of repeating what has already been said in a former portion of this work, we would remind the reader that "whilst a revolution is going on and the war arising out of it is being waged, foreign nations are not departing in the least from their position of neutrals if they treat the old government as sovereign, and that which is endeavouring to throw off its yoke as a society entitled to the rights of war against its enemy (indeed if they do so, they are acting strictly within the law[1]);" we would also remind him that the recognition of belligerent rights is a very different thing from the recognition of a state as sovereign and independent, and that it not only may be accorded before that independence is achieved, or even near its achievement, but in the practice of nations has usually been so accorded; as, for instance, by France, the Netherlands and Spain in the contest between Great Britain and her North American Colonies, in 1776[2], and again by the United States in the revolt of Texas from Mexico, in 1836. An examination of the state papers connected with both these affairs will show that, however annoying such recognition may be to the parent state or the mother country, as raising her opponent from the position of a mere rebel to the dignity of a rival, there is no real ground for remonstrance against those by whom such recognition is granted, for (to use Mr Forsyth's argument in answer to the Mexican minister[3]), it has never been held necessary, as

[1] Martens, *Droit des Gens*, Liv. III. ch. ii. § 80. Wheaton's *Elements*, Vol. I. Part I. ch. II. § 7, p. 40, edn. 1863.

[2] *Annual Register*, 1776, p. 182, and 1779, p. 249.

[3] Mr Forsyth to Mr Gorostiza, Sept. 20, 1836. *British and Foreign State Papers*, Vol. XXV. p. 1166.

a preliminary to the extension of the rights of hospitality to either party, that the chances of war should be balanced and the probability of eventual success determined. It is enough if one of the combatants has actually declared his independence, and was at the time actually maintaining it. Hence then, whilst it is clear that in the event we are speaking of, viz. a revolt or civil war, it is right and proper for neutral nations to recognize as a belligerent the revolted state or colony, to treat its commissioned vessels of war as cruisers, to admit its privateers and cruisers to their ports, and to respect the immunity of its flag; it is also clear not only that there is nothing unneutral in doing so at the very earliest opportunity, but that such a line of conduct is most prudent and expedient[1]. And here the test laid down by Mr Canning is a sound one, that when a neutral state acknowledges the rights of either of the combatants to visit and detain its vessels for breach of blockade or for carrying contraband of war[2], it necessarily acknowledges that both of them are belligerents. Indeed when the proportions of the contest are so much enlarged that both the combatants come across the path of, and interfere with, neutral states, what are these latter to do? If they do not recognize both as belligerents, but treat one of them as rebels and its cruisers as pirates, they cease to be neutral, and become the allies or partisans of the other. When therefore at the outset of the late rebellion in the United States, there was evidence that that rebellion would assume the proportions of a civil war, in consequence of there being a government de facto established, acts amounting to a declaration of hostilities, an army in the field powerful enough to resist the attack of the loyal troops, a line of coast to be blockaded, and cruisers ready to sally out and depredate upon the open sea; there can be no doubt that the government of Great Britain was not only justified in declaring, but was

[1] The *Hiawatha*, 2 Black's *Reports* (American), p. 636; and the *Santissima Trinidad*, 7 Wheaton, 538 (American).

[2] Lord J. Russell, House of Commons, May 6, 1861.

bound to declare, its neutrality and its resolution to allow to the Southern States a belligerent character; that its conduct in so doing was neither premature nor unjust; and in spite of what an American writer of ability has urged[1], its motive was not to throw protection over Confederate privateers and their crews, or to aid the rebel cause, but to evince its determination to stand neutral, and to act with the impartiality of a neutral in the contest.

Such being the conduct that neutral governments ought to adopt towards a revolted state or colony and its regularly commissioned cruisers, there remains another question connected with, though varying in an important respect from it. What is to be the conduct of a neutral nation towards a vessel of war which has been illegally equipped within its territory, and has subsequently, by a trick or by force, escaped and received a commission from a recognized belligerent? Thus, suppose a war going on between Great Britain and France, America being friendly to both powers with a Foreign Enlistment Act to protect its neutrality. A vessel is built in an American dockyard, and armed, equipped and manned there for the purpose, as is well known, of cruising against British commerce. By trick or fraud, or, to make the case stronger, by a display of force which overpowers that of the American authorities at the port where she is being fitted out, the vessel escapes to sea, receives a commission from France, and then proceeds to cruise and to capture British ships. Some months afterwards she returns to an American port for repairs, and it turns out that the captain who carried her out to sea and commanded her during the whole cruise is not a Frenchman, but an American. Under these circumstances ought the American authorities to respect the immunity of her flag, or to treat her as an unlicensed rover? Are they bound

[1] See Mr Bemis's letter of the 3rd May, 1865, in the *Boston Daily Advertiser*, in answer to a letter of Historicus in the *Times* newspaper, March 22, 1864, as to the advisability and propriety of early recognition, under analogous circumstances, by the United States government itself. See Webster's Works, Vol. III. p. 195. Speech on the Panama Mission.

to prohibit her entrance into their ports, or to punish the captain and the crew for their breach of the Foreign Enlistment Act? ought they to seize the ship, and surrender her to certain claimants who may attach her by suit? Now, if we are to be bound by the authority of the *Cassius*, a well-known and oft-quoted American case, they are bound to recognize her as a commissioned cruiser, to respect her flag, and to give her free ingress, and they may put a stop to the demands of the claimants, restore her to the government which own her as a cruiser, and suffer her to go to sea again, and resume her cruise against British commerce without any hurt to their neutrality. It has been said indeed in two cases decided in the United States court, that the suits against the *Cassius* were taken cognizance of by the Federal courts, and that the vessel was finally condemned; but a careful perusal of the correspondence between Messrs Pickering and Pinckney will show that such was not the case, but that in the month of October, 1796, the question against the *Cassius* was dismissed, the French minister was informed that she was ready to be delivered to his orders, and there the affair rested[1]. With this case then as our authority, as well as the general current of opinion, there can be little doubt that while a neutral nation is bound to maintain strictly her neutrality by preventing illegal equipments of vessels intended to issue from her shores and prey upon the commerce of a friendly power, if by fraud or force a vessel so illegally equipped should escape from her ports, and obtain a commission, such vessel is a lawful cruiser, and is entirely free from the jurisdiction of the neutral nation whose principal regulations she has broken, and as little doubt that if she revisits the ports of that nation she cannot be detained[2].

We now come to the second point that demands a Responsibility of the

[1] *American State Papers*, Vol. II. pp. 137, 415 and 422; and *L'Invincible*, 1 Wheaton's *Rep.* 252 (American).

[2] See the whole subject fully discussed and the case of the *Cassius* completely set out in a letter of Historicus, *Times Newspaper*, April 24th, 1865.

owners of Privateers and of Admirals, Commanders and Captains of Public Ships.

short explanation, that of the responsibility of the owners of privateers for the acts of their captains and crew; but before stating the law thereon, it is as well to contrast it with the rules affecting the liability of admirals of fleets, commanders of squadrons, and captains of public ships of war for wrongful captures and other such torts committed by them and their vessels. Now in respect to public ships the general rule is clear, that for wrongful acts the actual wrong-doer and he only is responsible; that is to say, the individual by whom the act is ordered is liable for the damages, and not his superior in command (assuming that he is not cognizant of, or has not concurred in it), for this simple reason, that he is presumed to be acting within the scope of his general orders[1]. Hence, if a captain of a public ship of war has made a wrongful capture, and neither the admiral of the station has been privy to it nor the commodore of the squadron has given orders for it, each of these persons is exempt from a suit, and the person liable to it, and against whom only it can be brought, is the commander of the capturing vessel[2]. But where the commander of a squadron or the admiral of a fleet or station has been actually present at the time of the act complained of, or co-operated in it or given positive orders about it, each of these persons is liable to individuals for the wrongful acts, the trespasses of those under his command, unless the trespasses are unattended with a conversion to the use of the fleet or squadron, and so enure simply to the benefit of the individual captor[3].

But with regard to the liability of privateers for illegal acts the rule is different, for not only are their

[1] The *Mentor*, 1 Rob. 181.

[2] The *Mentor*, ut sup. and the *Eleanor*, 2 Wheaton (*American Reports*), p. 346.

[3] General Halleck specifies a distinction between the doctrine in England and in the United States; viz. that in the United States the commander of the station or squadron is responsible for acts done under his permissive orders; whereas in England he is only responsible for actual orders. Halleck, *On International Law*, ch. xxx. § 30, p. 745.

masters responsible but their owners also for the damages and costs thus occasioned, and that to the extent of the actual loss and injury, even if it exceed the amount of the bond usually given upon the taking out of the commission.

Bynkershoek's doctrine on this point.

Nor is this a doctrine of modern times. Many of the older writers on International Law have so laid it down, and in accordance with their views it has become fixed in the jurisprudence of Great Britain and the United States;] among others Bynkershoek has discussed this point quite at large, and he concludes that the owner, master, and sureties, are jointly and severally liable, *in solido*, for the damages incurred; and that the master and owners are liable to the whole extent of the injury, though it may exceed the value of the privateer and her equipment, and the sureties are bound only to the amount of the sums for which they became bound. Of course the rule, like most other dogmatic principles, is liable to be modified by municipal regulations, but in the absence of such modifications, and where there is no positive local law on the subject, the general principle is that the liability is commensurate with the injury. The French law of prize was formerly identical with the rule laid down by Bynkershoek, but in the present day that is not the case, for the commercial code of France now exempts the owners of private armed vessels in time of war from responsibility for trespasses at sea beyond the amount of the security they may have given, unless they were accomplices in the tort[1].

French Law.

English Statute Law.

[On the other hand, in Great Britain and the United States the stricter rule has always prevailed. In the former country it is true that in the three statutes on the subject of the limitation of the responsibility of shipowners which preceded the amending and consolidating

[1] *Code de Commerce*, Art. 217. [Massé, *Droit Commercial*, T. I. p. 144, § 168, and T. IV. p. 488, § 2655. See also Pistoye et Duverdy, *Des Prises Maritimes*. T. I. p. 200.]

statute, the Merchant Shipping Act of 1854[1], as well as in that statute, a limitation of responsibility for embezzlement and other wrongful acts to the amount of the vessel and freight has been established, but that is confined to particular specified offences and to ships in the merchant service. In those statutes, nothing is said about privateers in time of war, their owners therefore are not to be included within the benefit of the acts.]

American Law.

In the United States the rule that the liability is commensurate with the injury has been declared by the Supreme Court in the case of Del Col *v.* Arnold[2], and though that case has since been shaken as to other points[3], it has not been disturbed as to the one before us. We may therefore consider it to be a settled rule of law and equity, that the measure of damages is the value of the property unlawfully injured or destroyed, that each individual owner is responsible for the entire damages and not rateably pro tanto, and that a part owner cannot escape from his common liability by pleading compensation pro tanto, or a release of the claimant to him[4]. [Where however the torts complained of are *piratical* acts committed by the officers and crew of the privateer, there the civil liability of the owners is limited to the security given by law, and the loss of their vessel. They are liable only for the conduct of the officers and crew while in the execution *of the business of the cruise*[5], and therefore where a neutral vessel was plundered of her papers by a privateer in consequence of which she was

Measure of damages

For piratical acts.

[1] 7 Geo. II. c. 15, 26 Geo. III. c. 86, and 53 Geo. III. c. 159, repealed and amended by 17 & 18 Vict. c. 104, see Part IX. §§ 502—506.

[2] 3 Dallas, 333. Wheaton, *On Captures*, p. 45.

[3] 1 Wheaton's *Reports*, 259. 1 Paine's *Reports*, 116, to the same point. (American Reports).

[4] The *Karasan*, 5 Rob. 291. The *Anna Maria*, 2 Wheaton (American), p. 327. The reader will find a large collection of authorities, American, Continental, and English, cited in confirmation of the doctrine above stated in Halleck's *International Law*, ch. XXX. § 31, p. 746.

[5] Dias *v.* Privateer *Revenge*, 3 *Washington Circuit Reports* (American), p. 262.

seized by another belligerent and proceeded against as prize, but made a compromise with her captors and paid a ransom and costs, it was held that the owners were not liable for these items (there being no privity to the compromise), nor for any other injurious consequences flowing from the compromise[1].]

Foreign commissions to cruise.

Vattel, though admitting that an individual may with a safe conscience serve his country by fitting out privateers, holds it to be inexcusable and base to take a commission from a foreign prince to prey upon the subjects of a state in amity with his native country[2].

American doctrine

[In the United States ample provision has been made on this subject by decisions of the courts, by treaty, and by municipal regulations], and the principles thereby adhered to may be considered as in affirmance of international law, and as prescribing specific punishment for acts which were before unlawful.

[The courts there have always been ready to discourage captures made in violation of neutrality, or partaking of a piratical character. Thus it has been held that in the case of the capture of a vessel of a country at peace with the United States by another fitted out in their ports, and commanded by one of their citizens, the district courts may inquire into the facts and decree restitution, and that if a privateer duly commissioned by a belligerent collude with such a vessel to carry her prizes and share with her their proceeds, this collusion is a fraud on the law of nations, and the claim of the belligerent must be rejected[3]. It has also been established that if a capture be made by a privateer illegally equipped in a neutral country, the prize courts of such neutral country have

[1] Dias *v.* Privateer *Revenge*, ut supra. N.B. The New York scheme (noticed in a preceding page) of making privateering companies actual corporations or bodies politic, would seem to exempt the members from the personal responsibility ordinarily incident to the owners of privateers.

[2] Bk. III. ch. XV. § 229.

[3] Talbot *v.* Janson, 3 Dallas, 133. *La Conception*, 6 Wheaton, 235.

power, and it is their duty to restore the captured property, if brought within their jurisdiction, to the owner[1].

and Treaty regulations.

By the various treaties with England, France, the Netherlands, Prussia, Spain, and Sweden, between the years 1778 and 1828[2], it was provided that if any citizen or subject of either of the contracting parties should take a commission, or letters of marque, for privateering against the other from any power with whom that other might be at war, the person so offending should be treated as a pirate; and the same provision was introduced into the more recent treaties of 1825 with Columbia, and of 1849 and 1851 with Guatemala and Peru. The treaties with England and France of 1778 and 1794 respectively, having been suffered to expire without the renewal of the above principle by any subsequent act, so far as this branch of privateering regulations between those countries and the United States is concerned, the matter rests now not on special treaty enactments, but upon those ordinary neutrality obligations which international law upholds, and which are enforced by the municipal law by special orders of the respective States.

By two acts of Congress passed June 14, 1797, and April 24, 1818, the subject was also provided for. The title of the former was "an act to prevent citizens of the United States from privateering against nations in amity with, or against citizens of the United States[3]." This, however, was repealed, and to a large extent re-enacted by the later Act[4], the 3rd section of which prohibits the fitting out by any person within the United States, of any ship or vessel to cruise or commit hostilities against the subjects, citizens, or property, of any foreign

[1] The Brig *Alerta v.* Blas Moran, 9 Cranch, 359.

[2] *United States Statutes at large*, Vol. VIII.

[3] *Statutes at large*, Vol. I. p. 520.

[4] *Ibid.* Vol. III. pp. 448—450. These two Acts with the corresponding English Statutes will be noticed at length in another chapter.

power or state, with whom the United States are at peace[1].

French Rules on the same subject.

Similar prohibitions are contained in the laws of other countries[2]. In France the ordonnances of 1650 and 1681 contained very severe denunciations of the conduct we are now speaking of. "We forbid," is their language, "all our subjects from taking commissions from any kings, princes, or foreign states, and cruising under their flags, save by permission of the crown, under pain of being treated as pirates" (and, therefore, of being punished with death). The punishment of death, however, for this offence, was repealed by the ordonnance of 1718, and now by the law of the 10th April, 1825, which regulates this among other maritime matters, the punishment for an illegal arming of this kind (which is still termed piracy) is imprisonment[3].

British regulations.

In Great Britain the doctrine maintained by Vattel (as above cited) has been upheld both by the courts and by the legislature from early times. Thus Molloy[4] says, that if it happen that those to whom letters of marque are granted, instead of taking the ships and goods of that nation against whom the same were awarded, wilfully take or spoil the goods of another nation in amity, this would amount to a downright piracy; and in the life of Sir L. Jenkins[5] we find him denouncing those who thus act, as instruments to irritate friends, undo subjects, and

[1] See W. B. Lawrence's note (192) to Wheaton's *Elements of International Law*, Vol. II. Part IV. ch. ii. § 11, pp. 633—635.

[2] See the Austrian Ordinance of Neutrality of August 7, 1803, Art. 2, 3, and of May 25, 1854. By the law of Plymouth colony in 1682 it was declared to be felony to commit hostilities on the high seas, under the flag of any foreign power upon the subjects of another foreign power in amity with England. Baylies, *Historical Memorial*, Vol. II. Part IV.

[3] Pistoye et Duverdy, *Traité des Prises Maritimes*, T. I. ch. ii. § I. pp. 174—5. The reader will find in the same chapter of this excellent treatise a short account of the legislation of the principal states of Europe on the subject.

[4] Bk. I. ch. ii. § 23, citing Rolle's abridgment, fol. 530, and Moor, 776.

[5] Sir Leoline Jenkin's *Life and Letters*, Vol. II. p. 714.

inflict little or no harm on the enemy. But it is scarcely necessary to refer to cases or to quote expressions of opinion to establish what is an admitted fact, approved by treaty, and now enforced by statute, that it is an illegal act for an English vessel to receive a commission as a cruiser from one of two belligerents, both of whom are at amity with Great Britain.

Such being the state of the law in Great Britain, France, and the United States upon this point, there remains another question which may also be discussed here.

Status of a cruiser commissioned by two different powers.

What is the status of a cruiser furnished with a commission from two different powers? The learned author of these commentaries says,] "that the better opinion is that a vessel so acting is liable to be treated as a pirate." [The view thus adopted by him is based upon the authority of the older jurists: modern writers, however, have dissented from that opinion[1], which is not supported either by the recognized definition of piracy[2], or strengthened by the reason given for it by the author himself, viz. that one of the two commissioning powers may be in amity with a state at war with the other. Now, in such a case as this, where a commissioned cruiser of Great Britain, for example, takes a commission from Denmark (say) to depredate upon the ships and vessels of Prussia, who may be at war with Denmark, though in amity with Great Britain, no one will for a moment think of terming such an act piratical. It would be, undoubtedly, a gross breach of neutrality on the part of Great Britain to allow it, and would come within the terms of the Foreign Enlistment Act, but its consequences would affect not the particular ship but the neutral nation to whom she belonged, who is responsible to other nations for the acts of its commissioned cruisers. And the

[1] Phillimore, Vol. I. § 358.

[2] Piracy is the offence of depredating on the seas without the authority of any sovereign state, or with commissions from different sovereigns at war with each other.

slightest reflection will show that to treat the act as piratical, and the vessel as a pirate, provides a remedy in the case of a weak nation thus injured, of a far less useful nature than a direct appeal to the neutral obligations, and the neutrality laws and declarations of the state by whose vessel she is hindered. At the same time too it should never be forgotten that as a state is not responsible for acts committed by cruisers or privateers illegally fitted out by belligerents in its ports, if there be neither cognizance nor collusion on its part[1], so *à fortiori,* it is not responsible for the acts of unlicensed pirates professing to sail under its flag. On these grounds, therefore, it is expedient not to treat the acts of a cruiser professing to sail under a double commission as piratical[2].]

Prizes.

The right to all captures vests primarily in the sovereign, and no individual can have any interest in a prize, whether made by a public or private armed vessel, but what he receives under the grant of the state. This is a general principle of public jurisprudence, *bello parta cedunt reipublicæ;* the distribution of the proceeds of prizes depends upon the regulations of each state, and unless the local laws have otherwise provided, the prizes vest in the sovereign[3]. But the general practice under the laws and ordinances of the belligerent governments is, to distribute the proceeds of captured property, when duly pressed upon, and condemned as prize (whether captured by public or private commissioned vessels), among the captors, as a reward for bravery, and a stimulus to exertion[4].

Title to Prize when complete.

When a prize is taken at sea, it must be brought, with

1 *American State Papers,* Vol. IV. p. 133.

2 See Wheaton's *Elements,* Vol. I. Part II. ch. ii. § 15, pp. 250—254, edn. 1863, by W. B. Lawence.

3 Grotius, Bk. III. ch. vi. Vattel, Bk. III. ch. ix. § 164. The *Elsebe,* 5 Rob. 173. Home *v.* Earl Camden, 2 H. Blacks. 533. At common law, the goods taken from an enemy belonged to the captor. Finch's *Law,* 28. 178. 12 Mod. 135. 1 Wils. 213.

4 By Lord Loughborough in Brymer *v.* Atkins, 1 H. Blacks. 189—191, in which case will be found a most admirable historical resumé of the Prize Law of England from Charles the Second's reign.

due care, into some convenient port, for adjudication by a competent court; though, strictly speaking, as between the belligerent parties the title passes, and is vested when the capture is complete; and that was formerly held to be complete and perfect when the battle was over, and the *spes recuperandi* was gone. *Voet,* in his Commentaries upon the Pandects[1], and the authors he refers to, maintain with great strength, as Lord Mansfield observed in *Goss* v. *Withers*[2], that occupation of itself transferred the title to the captor, *per solam occupationem dominium prædæ hostibus acquiri.* The question never arises but between the original owner and a neutral purchasing from the captor, and between the original owner and a recaptor. If a captured ship escapes from the captor, or is retaken, or if the owner ransoms her, his property is thereby revested. But if neither of these events happens, the question as to the change of title is open to dispute, and many arbitrary lines have been drawn, partly from policy, to prevent too easy dispositions of the property to neutrals, and partly from equity, to extend the *jus postliminii* in favour of the owner. Grotius[3], and many other writers, and some marine ordinances, as those of Louis XIV. and of Congress during the American war, made twenty-four hours' quiet possession by the enemy the test of title by capture. Bynkershoek[4] says that such a rule is repugnant to the laws and customs of Holland, and he insists, that a firm possession, at any time, vests the property in the captor, and that ships and goods brought *infra præsidia,* do most clearly change the property. But by the modern usage of nations, neither the twenty-four hours' possession, nor the bringing the prize *infra præsidia,* is sufficient to change

[1] T. II. p. 1155.

[2] 2 Burr. 683.

[3] Bk. III. ch. 6, and see Ordonnance of 1681, Liv. III. Tit. IX. Valin, *Des Prises,* ch. vi. p. 84. Azuni, Tom II. Art. ii. ch. iv. § 6. Emerigon, *Des Assurances,* T. I. p. 495.

[4] *Q. J. Pub.* Bk. I. ch. iv. and ch. v. See the *Ceylon,* 1 Dodson, 105. *L'Actif,* Edw. 185, and Martens, *On Recaptures,* ch. viii. p. 242.

the property in the case of a maritime capture[1]. A judicial inquiry must pass upon the case, and the present enlightened practice of the commercial nations, has subjected all such captures to the scrutiny of judicial tribunals, as the only sure way to furnish due proof that the seizure was lawful. The property is not changed in favour of a neutral vendee or recaptor, so as to bar the original owner, until a regular sentence of condemnation has been pronounced by some court of competent jurisdiction, belonging to the sovereign of the captor; and the purchaser must be able to show documentary evidence of that fact, to support his title. Until the capture becomes invested with the character of prize by a sentence of condemnation, the right of property is in abeyance, or in a state of legal sequestration. [The rights of the owner are not barred, and he is entitled to restitution at the hands of whomsoever he may find possessed of the property[2].] It cannot be alienated or disposed of, but the possession of it by the government of the captor is a trust for the benefit of those who may be ultimately entitled. This salutary rule, and one so necessary to check irregular conduct, and individual outrage, has been long established in the English admiralty[3], and it is now every where recognised as the law and practice of nations[4].

[In connexion with some of the principles above discussed, the following comparatively recent case decided in the Supreme Court of the United States deserves — Jecker *v.* Montgomery.

[[1] See Mr Tudor's remarks on the subject here discussed at pp 819—821 of his "Leading cases on Mercantile Law."]

[2] Le Caux *v.* Eden, Douglas, 613, 616. Goss *v.* Withers, ut supra. The *Flad Oyen*, 1 Rob. 135. The *Santa Cruz*, 1 Rob. 50. *L'Actif*, Edw. 185, and Story, *On Prize Courts*, p. 77, by Pratt (1854).

[3] Carth. 423. 10 Mod. 79. 12 Mod. 143. 2 Burr. 624. 3 Rob. 97, in notis.

[4] *Flad Oyen*, 1 Rob. 117. *Henrick and Maria*, 4 Rob. 48. Vattel, Bk. III. ch. xiv. § 216. Heineccii *Opera*, edit. Geneva, 1744, T. II. 310, 361. 5 Rob. 294. Doug. 591. 6 Taunton, 25. 8 Cranch, 226. 4 Wheaton, 298. 2 Dallas, 1, 2, 4.

notice[1]. The facts were, that during the war with Mexico, an American vessel was seized in a port of California by the commander of a vessel of war of the United States upon suspicion of trading with the enemy. She was condemned as a lawful prize by the captain belonging to one of the vessels of war upon that station, who had been authorized by the President of the United States to exercise admiralty jurisdiction in cases of capture, and upon a bill filed by the owners against the captain of the vessel of war, it was held on appeal, *inter alia,* that the condemnation in California was invalid, inasmuch as the prize court there established was not authorized by the laws of the United States, or the law of nations, and, in his judgment, Mr Justice Taney said, "All captures, *jure belli*, are for the benefit of the sovereign under whose authority they are made, and the validity of the seizure, and the question of prize or no prize can be determined in his own courts only upon which he has conferred jurisdiction to try the question. Under the constitution of the United States the judicial power of the general government is vested in one supreme court, and in such inferior Courts as Congress shall from time to time ordain and establish. Neither the President nor any military officer can establish a court in a conquered country, and authorize it to decide upon the rights of the United States or of individuals in prize cases."]

Courts of the Captor's only can condemn government.

The condemnation must be pronounced by a prize court of the government of the captor, sitting either in the country of the captor or of his ally. Prize or no prize is a question belonging exclusively to the courts of the country of the captor. The reason of this rule is said to be[2], that the sovereign of the captors has a right to inspect their behaviour, for he is answerable to other states for the acts of the captor. The prize court of the captor may sit in the territory of the ally [or a consul belonging to the nation of the captors may, within the

[1] Jecker *v.* Montgomery, 13 Howard's *Rep.* 498.

[2] Rutherforth's *Institutes*, Bk. II. ch. ix. seq. p. 596.

territory of the ally, condemn a prize brought into the allied state on the ground that the allied state and that of the captors are considered as forming one community, but it is undoubted law] that no prize court of an ally can condemn[1], and that it is not lawful for a prize court to act in a neutral country. Neutral ports are not intended to be auxiliary to the operations of the power at war, and the law of nations has clearly ordained, that a prize court of a belligerent captor cannot exercise jurisdiction in a neutral country. This prohibition not merely rests on the unfitness and danger of making neutral ports the theatre of hostile proceedings, but stands on the ground of the usage of nations[2].

Condemnation of Prizes lying in a neutral port.

It was for some time supposed that a prize court, though sitting in the country of its own sovereign, or of his ally, had no jurisdiction over prizes lying in a neutral port, because the court wanted that possession which was deemed essential to the exercise of a jurisdiction in a proceeding *in rem.* The principle was admitted to be correct by Sir William Scott, in the case of the *Henrick & Maria*[3], and he acted upon it in a prior case[4]. But he considered that the English admiralty had gone too far, in supporting condemnations, in England, of prizes abroad in a neutral port, to permit him to recall the vicious practice of the court to the acknowledged principle; and the English rule is now definitively settled, agreeably to the old usage, and the practice of other nations. The Supreme Court of the United States has followed the English rule, and it has held valid the

[1] See Abbott, *On Shipping* (last edition), p. 21, citing 2 Robinson, 210, and 2 East, 473.

[2] Glass *v.* the sloop *Betsey,* 3 Dallas, 6. *Flad Oyen,* 1 Rob. 114. Havelock *v.* Rockwood, 8 Term, 268. Oddy *v.* Bovill, 2 East, 475. Answer to the Prussian Memorial, 1753. *L'Invincible,* 1 Wheat. 228. The *Estrella,* 4 Wheat. 298. [The *Comet,* 5 Rob. 285. The *Victoria,* Edwards, 97. Pistoye et Duverdy, *Traité des Prises,* T. II. Tit. VIII. § 3. Halleck's *International Law,* ch. XXXI. § 10.]

[3] 4 Rob. 43.

[4] Note to the case of the *Herstelder,* 1 Rob. *Adm. Rep.* 118.

condemnations, by a belligerent court, of prizes carried into a neutral port, and remaining there. This was deemed the most convenient practice for neutrals, as well as for the parties at war, and though the prize was in fact within a neutral jurisdiction, it was still to be deemed under the control, or *sub potestate*, of the captor[1].

[Hence, in the course of the case above cited[2], in answer to an objection to the authority of the District Court to adjudicate, because the property had not been brought within its jurisdiction; Mr Justice Taney said, "A prize court may always proceed, *in rem*, whenever the proceeds of the prize can be traced to the hands of any person whatever. As a general rule it is the duty of the captor to bring it within the jurisdiction of a prize court of the nation to which it belongs and to institute proceedings to have it condemned. But there are cases where, from existing circumstances, the captors may be excused from the performance of this duty, and may sell or otherwise dispose of the property before condemnation. And where the commander of a national ship cannot, without weakening inconveniently, the force under his command, spare a sufficient prize crew to man the captured vessel; or where the orders of his government prohibit him from doing so, he may lawfully sell or otherwise dispose of the captured property in a foreign country, and may afterwards proceed to adjudication in a court of the United States[3]."]

Ransom. Sometimes circumstances will not permit property captured at sea to be sent into port; and the captor, in such cases, may either destroy it, or permit the original

[1] 6 Rob. *Rep.* 138. Note to the case of the schooner *Sophie.* Smart *v.* Wolf, 3 Term *Rep.* 823. Bynk. *Q. J. P.* Lib. 1. ch. v. by Duponceau, p. 38, note. Hudson *v.* Guestier, 4 Cranch, 293. Williams *v.* Armroyd, 7 Cranch, 423. The *Arabella* and the *Madeira*, 2 Gallison, 368.

[2] Jecker *v.* Montgomery, 13 Howard, p. 115.

[3] On the subject above discussed, viz. the law and regulations relating to Prize, the reader is referred first to the letter of Sir W. Scott and Sir J. Nicholl, Sept. 10th, 1794, prefixed to Story, *On Prize Courts;* secondly, to that work, edited by Pratt (1854); and lastly, to the 17 Vict. c. 18.

owner to ransom it. It was formerly the general custom to redeem property from the hands of the enemy by ransom, and the contract is undoubtedly valid, when municipal regulations do not intervene. It is now but little known in the commercial law of England, for several statutes in the reign of Geo. III. absolutely prohibited to British subjects the privilege of ransom of property captured at sea, unless in a case of extreme necessity, to be judged of by the court of admiralty[1]. A ransom bill, when not locally prohibited, is a war contract, protected by good faith and the law of nations; and notwithstanding that the contract is considered in England as tending to relax the energy of war, and deprive cruisers of the chance of recapture, it is, in many views, highly reasonable and humane. Other maritime nations regard ransoms as binding, and to be classed among the few legitimate *commercia belli.* They have never been prohibited in the United States; and the act of Congress of August 2nd, 1813, interdicting the use of British licenses or passes, did not apply to the contract of ransom[2].

The effect of a ransom is equivalent to a safe conduct granted by the authority of the state to which the captor belongs, and it binds the commanders of other cruisers to respect the safe conduct thus given, and under the implied obligation of the treaty of alliance, it binds equally the cruisers of the allies of the captor's country[3]. From the very nature of the connexion between allies, their compacts with the common enemy must bind each other, when they tend to accomplish the objects of the alliance. If they did not, the ally would reap all the fruits of the

[1] Chitty, *On Comm. Law,* 428. See the Statutes, 22 Geo. III. c. 25, 43 Geo. III. c. 160, 45 Geo. III. c. 72, and 17 Vict. c. 18, §§ 42—44, where the prohibitory enactments against ransom are repeated.

[2] 2 Azuni, *On Maritime Law,* ch. iv. art. 6. 1 Emérigon, ch. xii. § 21. 2 Valin, art. 66, p. 149. Le Guidon, ch. vi. art. 2. Grotius, Bk. III. ch. 19. Goodrich *v.* Gordon, 15 Johnson, 6.

[3] Miller *v.* the *Resolution,* 2 Dallas, 15.

compact, without being subject to the terms and conditions of it; and the enemy with whom the agreement was made, would be exposed, in regard to the ally, to all the disadvantages of it, without participating in the stipulated benefits. Such an inequality of obligation is contrary to every principle of reason and justice[1].

The safe conduct implied in a ransom bill, requires that the vessel should be found within the course prescribed, and within the time limited by the contract, unless forced out of her course by stress of weather, or unavoidable necessity[2]. If the vessel ransomed perishes by a peril of the sea, before arrival in port, the ransom is, nevertheless, due, for the captor has not insured the prize against the perils of the sea, but only against recapture by cruisers of his own nation, or of the allies of his country. If there should be a stipulation in the ransom contract, that the ransom should not be due if the vessel was lost by sea perils, the provision ought to be limited to total losses by shipwreck, and not to mere stranding, which might lead to frauds, in order to save the cargo at the expense of the ship[3].

If the vessel should be recaptured out of the route prescribed by the contract for her return, or after the time allowed for her return, and be adjudged lawful prize, it has been made a question whether the debtors of the ransom are discharged from their contract. Valin[4] says, that, according to the constant practice, the debtors are discharged in such case, and the price of the ransom is deducted from the proceeds of the prize, and given to the first captor, and the residue goes to the second taker. So, if the captor himself should afterwards be taken by an enemy's cruiser, together with his ransom bill, the ransom becomes part of the lawful conquest of the enemy, and the debtors of the ransom are, consequently, discharged[5].

[1] Miller v. Miller, 2 Dallas, 15. Pothier, *Traité du Droit de Propriété*, No. 134.

[2] Pothier, *Ibid.* Nos. 134, 135.

[3] *Ibid.* No. 138.

[4] *Ord. de Prises*, art. 19.

[5] Pothier, *Traité du Droit de Propriété*, Nos. 139, 140.

*Ricard* v. *Bettenham.* Actions on ransom bills.

In the case of *Ricard* v. *Bettenham*[1], an English vessel was captured by a French privateer in the war of 1756, (several years before the first prohibitory statute) and ransomed, and a hostage given as a security for the payment of the ransom bill. The hostage died while in possession of the French, and it was made a question in the K. B. in a suit brought upon the ransom bill after the peace, whether the death of the hostage discharged the contract, and whether the alien could sue on the ransom bill in the English courts. It was shown, that such a contract was valid among the other nations of Europe, that the owner of the bill was entitled to sue upon it, and that it was not discharged by the death of the hostage, who was taken as a mere collateral security, and the plaintiff was, accordingly, allowed to recover. But it has been since decided, and it is now understood to be the law, that, during war, and while the character of alien enemy continues, no suit will lie in the British courts, by the enemy, in proper person, on a ransom bill, notwithstanding it is a contract arising *jure belli*[2]. The remedy to enforce payment of the ransom bill for the benefit of the enemy captor, is by an action by the imprisoned hostage, in the courts of his own country, for the recovery of his freedom. This severe technical objection would seem to be peculiar to the British courts, for it was shown, in the case of *Ricard* v. *Bettenham,* to be the practice in France and Holland, to sustain such actions by the owner of the ransom contract. Lord Mansfield considered the contract as worthy to be sustained by sound morality and good policy, and as governed by the law of nations, and the eternal rules of justice[3]. The practice in France[4], when a French vessel has been ransomed, and a hostage given to the enemy, is for the officers of the admiralty to seize the vessel and her cargo, on her return to port, in order to compel the owners to pay the ransom debt, and relieve the hostage;

[1] 3 Burr. 1734.
[2] Anthon *v.* Fisher, Doug. 649, note. The *Hoop,* 1 Rob. 169.
[3] Cornu *v.* Blackburne, Doug. 641.
[4] Pothier, *De Propriété,* No. 144.

and this is a course dictated by a prompt and liberal sense of justice.

Law relating to Ransom Bills in connexion with

The recapture of the ransom bill, according to Valin[1], puts an end to the claim of the captor. He may be deprived of the entire benefit of his prize, as well as of the ransom bill, either by recapture or rescue, and the questions arising on them lead to the consideration of postliminy and salvage. Upon recapture from pirates, the property is to be restored to the owner, on the allowance of a reasonable compensation to the retaker, in the nature of salvage; for it is a principle of the law of nations, that a capture by pirates does not, like a capture by an enemy in solemn war, change the title, or divest the original owner of his right to the property, and it does not require the doctrine of postliminy to restore it[2]. In France, property may be reclaimed by the owner within a year and a day[3]; but in some other countries (and Grotius mentions Spain and Venice) the rule formerly was, that the whole property recaptured from pirates went to the retaker, and this rule was founded on the consideration of the desperate nature of the recovery.

the *Jus Postliminii.*

The *jus postliminii* was a fiction of the Roman law, by which persons or things taken by the enemy were restored to their former state, upon coming again under the power of the nation to which they formetly belonged. *Postliminium fingit eum qui captus est, in civitate semper fuisse*[4]. It is a right recognised by the law of nations, and contributes essentially to mitigate the calamities of war. When, therefore, property taken by the enemy is either recaptured or rescued from him, by the fellow subjects or allies of the original owner, it does not become the property of the recaptor or rescuer, as if it had been a new prize, but it is restored to the original owner, by right of postliminy, upon certain terms. Moveables are not entitled, by the strict rules of the laws of nations, to the full benefit of postliminy,

[1] Tom. II. Liv. III. Tit. IX. art. 19.

[2] Grotius, Bk. III. ch. ix. §§ 16, 17. Bynk. *Q. J. P.* ch. XV. and XVII.

[3] Valin, *Com.* Tom. II. 261.

[4] *Inst.* I. 12. 5.

unless retaken from the enemy promptly after the capture, for then the original owner neither finds a difficulty in recognising his effects, nor is presumed to have relinquished them. Real property is easily identified, and therefore, more completely within the right of postliminy; and the reason for a stricter limitation of it in respect to personal property arises from its transitory nature, and the difficulty of identifying it, and the consequent presumption that the original owner had abandoned the hope of recovery[1]. This right does not take effect in neutral countries, because the neutral nation is bound to consider the war on each side as equally just, so far as relates to its effects, and to look upon every acquisition made by either party, as a lawful acquisition; with the exception of cases where the capture itself is an infringement of the jurisdiction or rights of the neutral power[2]. If one party was allowed, in a neutral territory, to enjoy the right of claiming goods taken by the other, it would be a departure from the duty of neutrality. The right of postliminy takes place, therefore, only within the territories of the nation of the captor, or of his ally[3]; and if a prize be brought into a neutral port by the captors, it does not return to the former owner by the law of postliminy, because neutrals are bound to take notice of the military right which possession gives, and which is the only evidence of right acquired by military force, as contradistinguished from civil rights and titles. They are bound to take the fact for the law. Strictly speaking, there is no such thing as a marine tort between belligerents. All captures are to be deemed lawful, and they have never been held within the cognizance of the prize tribunals of neutral nations[4]. With respect to persons, the right of postliminy takes place even in a neutral country, so that

[1] Vattel, Bk. III. ch. xiv. § 209.

[2] M'Donough *v.* Dannery, 3 Dallas, 188, 198. The *Josefa Segunda*, 5 Wheaton, 338, 358.

[3] Vattel, Bk. III. ch. xiv. §§ 207, 208.

[4] *L'Amistad de Rues*, 5 Wheaton, 390.

if a captor brings his prisoners into a neutral port, he may, perhaps, confine them on board his ship, as being, by fiction of law, part of the territory of his sovereign, but he has no control over them on shore[1].

In respect to real property, the acquisition by the conqueror is not fully consummated until confirmed by the treaty of peace, or by the entire submission or destruction of the state to which it belonged. If it be recovered by the original sovereign, it returns to the former proprietor, notwithstanding it may, in the mean time, have been transferred by purchase. The purchaser is understood to have taken the property at the hazard of a recovery or reconquest before the end of the war. But if the real property, as a town or portion of the territory, for instance, be ceded to the conqueror by the treaty of peace, the right of postliminy is gone for ever, and a previous alienation by the conqueror would be valid[2].

Mr Wheaton upon the *Jus Postliminii.*

[Upon this subject Mr Wheaton's remarks may also be quoted: he says, "A different rule than that which governs the captor's title to personal property or moveables is applied to real property. The original owner of this species of property is entitled to the benefit of postliminy, and the title acquired by war must be confirmed by a treaty of peace before it can be considered as completely valid. This rule cannot be frequently applied to the case

[1] Vattel, Bk. III. ch. vii. § 132. Bynk. by Duponceau, pp. 116, 117, notes. *Austrian Ord. of Neutrality*, August 7th, 1803, art. 19. See the ordonnance in Martens et Cussy *Recueil de Traités*, T. II. p. 301, and in Neumann, *Traités concl. par L'Autriche*, T. II. p. 83. By one of the provisions of a commercial treaty between Carthage and Rome, in the earliest period of the Roman republic, soon after the expedition of Tarquin, it was stipulated, that if either party should bring into the ports of the other, prisoners taken from an ally, the prisoners might be reclaimed and set free. Polybius, Bk. III. ch. iii. See Hampton's *Translation*, Vol. I. p. 277.

[2] Vattel, Bk. III. ch. xiv. § 212. Wheaton's *Elements*, ed. 1863 by W. B. Lawrence, Vol. II. Part IV. ch. ii. § 17. Martens, Bk. VIII. ch. iii. §§ 11, 12, edition of 1802 by W. Cobbett. See also Martens par Vergé, *Droit des Gens*, T. II. Bk. VIII. ch. iv. §§ 282 (*a*) 283, with Pinheiro Ferreira's *Commentary* (*loc. cit.*), p. 261. Klüber, *Droit des Gens Moderne*, §§ 256—258.

of mere private property, which by the general usage of modern nations is exempt from confiscation. It only becomes practically important in questions arising out of alienation of real property belonging to the government made by the opposite belligerent, while in the military occupation of the country. Such a title must be expressly confirmed by the treaty of peace, or by the general operation of the cession of territory made by the enemy in such treaty. Until such confirmation it continues liable to be divested by the *Jus Postliminii*."]

Right of *Postliminium* after conclusion of Peace.

It is also a rule on this subject, that if a treaty of peace makes no particular provisions relative to captured property, it remains in the same condition in which the treaty finds it, and it is tacitly conceded to the possessor. The right of postliminy no longer exists, after the conclusion of the peace. It is a right which belongs exclusively to a state of war[1], and, therefore, a transfer to a neutral, before the peace, even without a judicial sentence of condemnation, is valid, if there has been no recovery or recaption before the peace. The intervention of peace cures all defects of title, and vests a lawful possession in the neutral, equally as the title of the enemy captor himself is quieted by the intervention of peace[2]. The title, in the hands of such a neutral, could not be defeated in favour of the original owner, even by his subsequently becoming an enemy. It would only be liable, with his other property, to be seized as prize of war[3].

Moveable property how affected by war.

In a land war, moveable property, after it has been in complete possession of the enemy for twenty-four hours, (and which goes by the name of booty, and not prize)[4], becomes absolutely his, without any right of postliminy in favour of the original owner; and much more ought this

[1] Vattel, Bk. III. ch. xiv. § 216.

[2] Schooner *Sophie*, 6 Rob. 138.

[3] The *Purissima Conception*, 6 Rob. 45.

[4] Genoa and its dependencies &c., 2 Dodson's *Adm.* 446. In which case Sir W. Scott said, "It is well known that a land force has no interest in prize properly so called; what a land force takes by itself is not prize but booty."

species of property to be protected from the operation of the rule of postliminy, when it has not only passed into the complete possession of the enemy, but been *bona fide* transferred to a neutral. By the ancient and strict doctrine of the law of nations, captures at sea fell under the same rule as other moveable property, taken on land, and goods so taken were not recoverable by the original owner from the rescuer or retaker. But the municipal regulations of most states, have softened the rigour of the law of nations on this point, by an equitable extension of the right of postliminy, as against a recaption by their own subjects. [By the ordinances of several of the Continental powers the right of restoration on recaption was directly provided for], being generally confined to cases where the property had not been in the possession of the enemy above twenty-four hours.

French regulations.

[In France the first regulation on the subject is to be found in the 61st article of the ordonnance of 1584, the terms of which it is unnecessary to quote, because the article was renewed in the ordonnance of 1681[1]. An article in that ordonnance, in effect, provided that where a French owned vessel (after capture and possession by the enemy for twenty-four hours) was recaptured it should be good prize in the captor's hands, but that if the twenty-four hours' possession had not elapsed, then it should be restored to the owner with all in it on payment of a third (as salvage to the recaptors). In 1803 another marine ordonnance was promulgated, known as the "Arrêté du 2 Prairial, an XI." (22nd May, 1803.) By the 54th article, which was in the main a reproduction of the one just described, it was also enacted that as far as recapture by privateers of vessels owned by Frenchmen, or the subjects of countries in alliance with France was concerned, the vessel, after a twenty-four hours' possession by the enemy, should become the privateers' property (*en totalité*), but before the twenty-four hours' possession had

[1] Liv. III. Tit. IX. Art. 8.

expired the vessel and cargo should be restored to the owner minus a third of their value (as salvage). As far as recaptures by public ships of war are concerned it is there enacted that the vessel and cargo shall be restored on payment of a tenth part of her value if the twenty-four hours have elapsed, and a thirtieth if they have not. It does not appear that any alterations have been made upon this rule of 1803, and, therefore, by the French law there are three points on which the recaptors' title to and profit on ships owned by Frenchmen and their allies (*i. e.* non-neutral ships) depend. 1st, *Time*, viz. the completion or not of the twenty-four hours. 2nd, Quality of the captors from whom the vessel is recaptured, whether pirates[1] or qualified cruisers, and 3rdly, Quality of the recaptors, whether privateers or public ships of war, but as by the treaty of Paris privateering is declared to be abolished, so far as those nations are concerned who were parties to it, and as France was one of those parties it is presumed that the exception in favour of privateers under the above 54th article will have but little value[2].

Spanish regulations.

The modern law of Spain on this subject is regulated by the prize ordinance of the 20th June, 1801, the 38th article of which enacts that when the recaptured ship belongs to a friendly nation, and is not laden for enemy's account, it shall, if recaptured by a privateer, be restored on payment of the sixth of its value as salvage, if by a public vessel on payment of one-eighth, provided that the nation to whom the restored vessel belongs has adopted or agrees to adopt a similar line of conduct towards Spain When, however, the recaptured vessel belongs to Spanish owners, then the test of twenty-four hours' possession is introduced with the same effect as in

[1] This will be found in the 51st article of the Ord. 2 Prairial an XI.

[2] For decisions upon these ordonnances and for a discussion upon their application in the present day the reader is referred to the *Traité des Prises Maritimes* by De Pistoye et Duverdy, T. II. pp. 110—129. See also Emérigon, *Traité des Assurances*, ch. xii. 23. Valin, Liv. III. Tit. IX. Art. 3, and Massé, *Droit Commercial*, T. I. Liv. II. ch. ii. § iii., vi. pp. 337—349.

the French ordonnance, as well as the quality of the recaptors. The salvage payment on restoration from a privateer is fixed at one-third of the value, from a public ship nothing is allowed[1].

Dutch, The Dutch law, which will be found with all its variations, recorded in Sir Robert Phillimore's work[2], regulates restitution on payment of salvage at different rates, according to the length of time the property has been in the Danish, enemy's possession. The Danish law, which is governed by the ordinance of the 28th March, 1810, decrees restoration of Danish or allied property without regard to the time of possession on payment of one-third. That of Portuguese, Portugal allows restitution after the lapse of twenty-four hours on payment of one-eighth where the recapture is made by a public ship, of one-fifth by a privateer. Whilst and Swedish regulations. Sweden disregarding the test of time of possession provides a uniform rate of salvage on Swedish property, viz. one-half the value[3].

From this short conspectus then of the ordinances and rules of the several continental powers thus specified, it would appear that whilst in most of them, some, if not all, of the three tests above-mentioned are prescribed, in none does the right of restoration or recaption depend on condemnation, though, doubtless, what the learned author of this commentary says is correct, that the right continues until sentence of condemnation and no longer, but condemnation will be decreed only upon the right application of the tests so described.]

1 Wheaton's *Elements*, Vol. II. Part IV. ch. ii. § 12, pp. 661, 662, ed. 1863 by W. B. Lawrence. Phillimore, Vol. III. § 412, p. 513, where all the Spanish ordonnances are cited, and where also is noticed the Spanish regulation by which recaptures from Pirates by Privateers after a twenty-four hours' possession give a title to possession to the Privateer. Spain be it also noticed refused to adhere to the Privateer clause of the Treaty of Paris.

2 Vol. III. p. 514, 515.

3 Wheaton's *Elements*, and Phillimore, Vol. III., passages above cited. N.B. Denmark, Portugal and Sweden gave their adhesion to all the articles of the maritime clauses of the treaty of Paris.

Modifications of the Rule as to Postliminy.

Every power is obliged to conform to these rules of the law of nations relative to postliminy, where the interests of neutrals are concerned. But in cases arising between her own subjects, or between them and those of her allies, the principle may undergo such modifications as policy dictates. Thus by English Statute Law, as we shall presently see, the maritime right of postliminy as among English subjects subsists to the end of the war, and restoration to the original proprietor is decreed on certain terms. Nor does the maritime law of England withhold the benefit of the liberal rule of restitution which she thus gives her subjects from her allies, unless it appear that they act on a less liberal principle, in which case her law treats them according to their own measure of justice[1]. The allotment of salvage, on recapture or rescue, is a question not of municipal law merely, except as to the particular rates of it. It is a question of the *jus gentium*, when the subjects of allies or neutral states claim the benefit of the recaption. The restitution is a matter not of strict right, after the property has been vested in the enemy, but one of favour and relaxation; and the belligerent recaptor has a right to annex a reasonable condition to his liberality[2]. Neutral property, retaken from the enemy, is usually restored, without the payment of any salvage, unless, from the nature of the case, or the usages of the enemy, there was a probability that the property would have been condemned, if carried into the enemy's ports, and, in that case, a reasonable salvage ought to be allowed, for a benefit has been conferred[3].

The United States, by the act of Congress of 3rd March, 1800, directed restoration of captured property, at sea, to the foreign and friendly owner, on the payment of reasonable salvage; but the act was not to apply when the pro-

[1] The *Santa Cruz*, 1 Rob. 49. The *San Francisco*, Edw. 279.

[2] The *Two Friends*, 1 Rob. 271. Marshall, *On Ins.* (4th ed. by W. Shee, 1861), p. 436. Abbott, *On Shipping* (by W. Shee), 10th ed. pp. 516, 517. Corner *v.* Blackburne, Doug. 649.

[3] The *War Onskan*, 2 Rob. 299. The *Charlotta*, 5 Rob. 54.

perty had been condemned as prize by a competent court, before recapture; nor when the foreign government would not restore the goods or vessels of the citizens of the United States, under the like circumstances. [Provision was also made by it that in the event of the recaptured vessel appearing to have been set forth and armed as a vessel of war before its capture, or between its capture and recapture, the amount of salvage was to be increased. But by the last prize act[1], 30th June, 1864, in which the whole subject of prize has been recast and by which prize proceedings and the distribution of prize money are regulated, the above-mentioned act of the 3rd March, 1800, has been repealed, and the rule respecting salvage for recaptures is contained in the 29th section, which in effect enacts that upon recaptures if it appear to the board that *the same has not been condemned as prize before its recapture by any competent authority*, the court shall award the amount of salvage according to the circumstances of each case; that if the recaptured property belongs to the United States, it shall be restored to the United States on payment of salvage and costs by the treasury; that if it belongs to persons residing within or under the protection of the United States, it shall be restored on payment of the salvage and costs decreed by the court, and if it belongs to persons resident within the territory and under the protection of a prince or state in amity with the United States, it shall be restored on such terms as would be exacted by the laws of that prince or state, if a citizen of the United States, or in the absence of such laws, on payment of the salvage decided by the court.]

From this statute then, it appears that the *Jus Postliminii* is continued until the property is divested by a sentence of condemnation, and that while the old prize act of 1800 is repealed, by it no reference is made to the proviso in that act respecting the consequences of a setting forth as a vessel of war.

[1] 1 Session, ch. clxxiv.; see *United States Statutes at Large*, Vol. XIII. p. 306.

[But inasmuch as the only penalty for such an act was an increase to the amount of salvage payable on restitution, and as the court has the power by the new act of fixing the amount at its discretion, there is nothing to prevent the court taking such a setting forth into its consideration in order to increase the salvage and costs if necessary.

In contrasting these American acts, so far as salvage is concerned, with the corresponding portions of the English prize statutes, we shall find two important features of difference with respect to the right of postliminy as between owners and recaptors, one that whilst the American acts, as we have seen, continue the right until sentence of condemnation, the English statutes revive it even after a sentence of condemnation; the other, that whereas by the American act of 1800, the consequence of a captured vessel being set forth[1] as a vessel of war on recapture was merely an increase of the owner's liability for salvage—by the English statutes the consequence is condemnation as a prize of war. Those statutes are the following: the 45 Geo. III. c. 72, and 17 and 18 Vict. c. 18. The enactment of the § 9 of the former act was to the effect that if any vessel or goods therein, belonging to British subjects and taken as prize were recaptured, they should be restored to the former owners on payment of a salvage of one-eighth part of their value if recaptured by his majesty's ships, and if by privateers or other ships or vessels under his majesty's protection, of one-sixth part of such value. If recaptured by the joint operation of his majesty's ships and privateers, then such salvage was to be given as should seem just and reasonable to the proper court. But if the vessel so retaken should appear to have been set forth by the enemy as a ship of war, then the same was not to be restored to the former owners, but to be adjudged lawful prize for the captor's benefit. The 17 and 18 Vict. c. 18, in the

[1] For the construction of the term "setting forth by the enemy" in these acts, the reader is referred to the following case, the *Ceylon*, 1 Dodson, p. 115. The *Horatio*, 6 Robinson, p. 320. *L'Actif*, Edwards, p. 185.

9th section was conceived in almost identical words, except that all allusion to privateers was dropped, as they were not to be employed during the Russian war, and that provision was made for the division and distribution of the salvage money in the same manner as in all prize cases; by the 10th section it was declared that all recaptured ships of her majesty's subjects before being carried into an enemy's port might be allowed to prosecute their voyage.]

NOTE. For a critical investigation of the right of Postliminy, as illustrated by the Roman Law and the older commentators on International Law and as exhibiting the philosophical tendencies of the German school of International Jurists the reader is referred to Heffter's work "*Le Droit International Public,* traduit par Bergsen," ed. 1857, §§ 187—190.

See also Story, *On Prize Courts,* ed. by F. T. Pratt, D.C.L. (1854), p. 81, citing the *Santa Cruz,* the *San Francisco,* the *Adeline,* 9 Cranch, 246, and Valin, T. II. p. 262, for the law in the case of the country of the recaptor having no municipal regulations on the subject.

# CHAPTER VII.

## FOREIGN ENLISTMENT ACTS.

---

[IT is proposed in the present chapter to give a short account of the settlement and provisions of the Foreign Enlistment Acts of the United States and of Great Britain, and of the leading decisions upon them.

It is scarcely necessary to draw attention to the importance of the subject in connexion with the relations between neutrals and belligerents in time of war. The history of the recent contest in the United States, the diplomatic correspondence between the authorities at Washington and London, and the well-known case of the *Alexandra*, will bear sufficient testimony to that fact; and, as from what has been said in the former chapter, the law relating to privateering is materially influenced by the municipal regulations we are about to describe, it will not be out of place to take that description in this intermediate chapter.

The history of the two principal American Foreign Enlistment Acts of 1794 and 1818 begins, strictly speaking, with the trial of Gideon Henfield on the 22nd of May, 1793; but the narrative of that event may fitly be preceded by a notice of two letters from Washington to Alexander Hamilton[1]. In the first, dated April the 12th, 1793, speaking of the war then commenced between Great Britain and France, the President said: "It behoves

[1] See Hamilton's *Works*, Vol. IV. pp. 357 and 359.

the government of this country to use every means in its power to prevent the citizens thereof from embroiling us with either of those powers by endeavouring to maintain a strict neutrality. I therefore require that you will give the subject mature consideration that such measures as shall be deemed most likely to effect this purpose may be adopted without delay, for I have understood that vessels are already designated as privateers, and are preparing accordingly." In the second, dated the 18th of April, he alludes to a meeting to be held the next day to discuss the measures necessary for preserving a strict neutrality, and specifies one question (among several others) as of paramount importance, viz. whether a proclamation should issue for the purpose of preventing interferences of the citizens of the United States in the war between France and Great Britain, and whether it should contain a declaration of neutrality. On the next day, the 19th, it was resolved that such a proclamation should issue, and by that proclamation the citizens were reminded of the neutral attitude of their government, of its intention strictly to preserve that attitude, and of the evil consequences to such of the citizens as should aid or abet hostilities in defiance of this proclamation. Within a month after its publication its effect and the neutral attitude of the United States were tested by the conduct of M. Genet, the minister plenipotentiary from the republic of France. The facts, as stated by Mr Hamilton[1], were, that M. Genet, on his arrival at Charleston, caused two privateers to be fitted out, to which he issued proclamations to cruise against the enemies of France. There also the privateers were manned partly with citizens of the United States, who were enlisted or engaged for the purpose, without the privity or permission of the American Government. One or both of these privateers made captures of British vessels in the neighbourhood of the United States coasts, and brought or sent their prizes

Case of M. Genet.

[1] Works of Alex. Hamilton, Vol. IV. p. 394.

into their ports. The British minister demanded restitution of these prizes. With that demand, Mr Hamilton thought there should be a compliance; but this view was opposed both by Mr Jefferson, and the then Attorney General. It is not necessary to dwell at any further length upon these facts, or upon the language and conduct of M. Genet[1]. What we have just stated is for the purpose of showing the point in which the neutral attitude of the United States was imperilled, and the reasons and necessity for the prosecution of Gideon Henfield. From the brief statement of the evidence against him, as set out in Wharton's *State Trials of the United States*[2], it appears that Gideon Henfield was a citizen of the United States, and that his family resided in Salem, Massachusetts. Being a sea-faring man, he had been absent from them some time; and, about the 1st of May, 1793, whilst at Charleston, South Carolina, and desirous of coming to Philadelphia, he applied to the master of a packet, who asked him more for his passage than he could afford to pay, whereupon he entered on board the *Citizen Genet,* a French privateer, commissioned by the French republic, and commanded by a Frenchman; by him Henfield, having been promised the post of prize-master on board the first prize captured, was put on board a ship belonging to, and captured from, British subjects, and in that capacity arrived at Philadelphia. Upon these facts he was indicted for a breach of the neutrality laws of the United States, by unlawfully and maliciously sailing and cruising on board a ship of war, called the *Citizen Genet,* and seizing and taking as prize a ship belonging to certain subjects of the king of Great Britain. After a long and anxious trial, and after a careful and impartial charge, and a still more careful and impartial summing up, Henfield was acquitted. In his life of Washington[3], Chief Justice Marshall says: "By the acquittal of Gideon Henfield, the ad-

Gideon Henfield's trial.

1 As to that see *American State Papers,* Vol. I. pp. 77—82.

2 Wharton's *State Trials,* p. 49.

3 Vol. II. p. 273, 4.

ministration received additional evidence of the difficulty that would attend an adherence to the system commenced by them. As the trial approached a great degree of sensibility was displayed, and the verdict was celebrated with extravagant marks of joy and sensibility. It bereaved the executive of the strength to be derived from an opinion, that punishment might be legally inflicted on those who should openly violate the rules prescribed for the preservation of neutrality, and exposed that department to the obloquy of having attempted a measure which the laws would not justify." So grave was the crisis in Washington's opinion that, on the 3rd of August, 1793, he wrote to the heads of departments and the Attorney General to ask their advice whether it were proper or not to convene the legislature at an earlier day than that on which it was to meet by law[1]. On the 5th of June, 1794, an Act of Congress was passed to meet the difficulty into which the government was cast, and to protect its neutrality obligations and duties by municipal regulations[2]. It was not long before this Act, like the proclamation of neutrality above recorded, was tested.

Guinet's trial.

Etienne Guinet, a citizen of Philadelphia, and J. B. Le Maitre, of the same place, were indicted[3] May 11, 1795, for being knowingly and unlawfully concerned in furnishing and fitting out and arming a ship called *Les Jumeaux* with intent that she should be employed in the service of the French Republic, then at peace with the United States, to cruise and commit hostilities upon the subjects and property of the king of Great Britain; and the facts proved were that *Les Jumeaux* entered at the port of Philadelphia laden with merchandise from Port au Prince, and mounting four guns and two swivels, it being necessary to repair her (she being then owned by Le Maitre and others); the repairs were commenced and

[1] Washington's *Writings*, by Sparks, Vol. X. p. 362. The correspondence on this subject will be found in the Appendix to that volume.

[2] *United States Statutes at Large*, Vol. I. p. 311.

[3] On the 3rd and 4th Sections of the Statute.

being prosecuted when the master warden by order of the government instituted an inquiry, and on his report the government directed that all the equipment of a warlike nature should be dismantled and the vessel restored to the state in which she was on her arrival. In spite however of these efforts, the vessel managed to make her way out of Philadelphia, and was brought up at Wilmington. There, it was deposed in evidence, she took on board by night muskets, lanterns, cans, &c. and thirty or forty additional men, intending to have received six more guns for which a pilot boat had been despatched to Philadelphia; but that was prevented by the marshal seizing the boat and the guns and apprehending the persons on board her. In his summing up the learned judge, Patterson, after shortly specifying the nature of the charge, thus interpreted the language of the statute. "Much has been said upon the construction of the 3rd and 4th sections of the Act of Congress; but the Court is clearly of opinion that the 3rd section was meant to include all cases of vessels armed within our ports by one of the belligerent powers, to act as cruisers against another belligerent power in peace with the United States, converting a ship from her original destination with intent to commit hostilities, or in other words, converting a merchant ship into a vessel of war, must be deemed an original outfit; for the act would otherwise become nugatory and inoperative. It is the conversion from the peaceable to the warlike purpose that constitutes the offence[1]." He then told the jury that if it was intended so to convert this ship every man knowingly concerned in so doing was guilty in the eye of the law, and with reference to the defendant's knowledge, his defence being that he had acted only as an interpreter in a fair mercantile business, the learned judge reminded the jury of the secret nature of the transaction. The prisoner was found guilty[1]. In this trial then we have the first judicial

[1] Trial of Guinet and others, Wharton's *State Trials*, p. 94.

exposition of the legal meaning of those clauses which in later days have in an English statute caused so much difficulty and provoked so much discussion.

American decisions upon the Act of 1794.

But besides this case, valuable as it is for Justice Patterson's direction, there are several important decisions upon the American act of 1794, some of which we shall now briefly state. Thus, in a case where a vessel had been built in the United States for the purpose of being employed in a war with England, supposing such war had broken out, and was afterwards sold to a French citizen who used her as a privateer, the Supreme Court refused to hear counsel against the allegation that this was an original construction or outfit of the vessel for the purposes of war[1]. Again, where a French privateer had taken out her guns, masts and sails, which remained on shore until the general repairs were completed and were again put on board, after which she sailed on a cruise and captured a British vessel which she sent into Charleston; on a claim of restitution preferred by the British consul, on the ground that the vessel had been originally fitted out in the United States in a neutral port, the court decided that the mere replacement of her force could not be considered as an augmentation, even if an augmentation of force should be considered a cause for restoration[2]. On the other hand, it was laid down that, though a neutral nation may, if so disposed, without a breach of her neutrality, allow both belligerents to equip their vessels of war within her territories, if such permission be not given, the subjects of such belligerents have no right to equip vessels of war or to augment their force either with arms or men within the neutral territory. Not only do such unauthorized acts violate her sovereignty and her rights as a neutral and render all captures illegal in relation to such nation, but are directly at variance with the act of June 1794, which gave the courts of the United States power to punish the offender, and in the 7th section provided for

[1] Moodie *v.* The Alfred, 3 Dallas, 307.

[2] Moodie *v.* Ship Phœbe Anne, 3 Dallas, 319.

all vessels fitted out in contravention of the act. So that as Mr J. Washington said, "If there were any doubt as to the rule of the law of nations upon this subject, the illegality of equipping a foreign vessel of war within the territory of the United States is declared by the above law, and the power and duty of the courts of the United States to restore prizes made in violation of the law are clearly recognised[1]. So too it was held to be a violation of the Act to concert an expedition from the United States to commit hostilities against a power at peace with the United States, and it was declared to be unimportant that such expedition originated beyond seas if carried on from the United States, and equally unimportant whether the persons engaged in such a purpose took the whole vessel or departed as passengers[2].

In several of these early cases too, the questions what constituted an illegal outfit in American ports, and what equipments therein amounted to a breach of the neutrality laws, were fully discussed. Thus in Jansen v. *Vrow Christina Magdalena*[3], where an American vessel was equipped within the jurisdiction of the United States with eight guns, one hundred-weight of powder, and some shot, &c., taken to a French port and there sold to an American born but a naturalized French citizen of three days' standing, the American registry cancelled; and the vessel commissioned as a French privateer, commanded by a quasi-French citizen, commenced preying on the high seas on the commerce of enemies of the French republic, but allies of the United States; it was decided that this was an arming and equipment within the Act. So too where a privateer belonging to one of two powers hostile to each other, but at peace with the United States, came unarmed into an American port, received there

[1] The Alerta *v.* Blas Moran, 9 Cranch, 359.

[2] Ex parte Needham, 1 Peters, *C. C. R.* 487. See also Williams *v.* The Betsy, Bee's *Admiralty Decisions*, 67.

[3] Bee, 11, same case on appeal, 3 Dallas, 159. See also the same question discussed in U S. *v.* Guinet, 2 Dall. 321.

some alterations (it does not appear what), applied for permission to arm, which was refused, and departed having trebled her crew there, and when at one hundred leagues from shore, on the third day of the voyage, was proved to have had both cannons and swivels mounted. All this it was said created the most violent presumptions that the guns were taken in in the United States, and the court held that there was such an augmentation of force as amounted to a breach of the Act of 1794[1]. Again, where a French privateer arrived at Philadelphia with only twelve guns mounted, and while in the river below the city opened new ports and mounted fourteen or sixteen more, every person concerned in such increasing of its armament or in procuring the same was held to be an offender[2]. In a later case an attempt was made to escape the consequences of the statute by contending that the arms and ammunition were cleared out as cargo, and the men hired for a common mercantile voyage, but the court held that of these facts the former did not vary the case and the latter was not material. The vessel being constructed for war and not for commerce, the whole of the cargo adapted for war, and the crew being too numerous for a merchant ship and sufficient for a privateer, were circumstances that demonstrated the intent with which the vessel sailed out of the American port[3].

The Act of 1794 with its amending statute of 1797 remained in full force and unaltered for several years[4].

Necessity for a new Act.

In 1816, however, in consequence of complications arising out of the revolt and contest for independence

[1] British Consul *v.* Nancy, Bee, 76. See also on the same point U.S. *v.* Grassin, 3 Washington's *Reports*, 66.

[2] Moodie *v.* Betty Cathcart, Bee, 298. See on the other hand in Moodie *v.* Ship *Brothers*, Bee 77, what does not amount to such equipment.

[3] The *Gran Para*, 7 Wheaton, 486. N.B. The Statute was held not to extend to vessels owned and repaired abroad though they might have been originally American bottoms. Williams *v.* The Betsy, Bee, 67.

[4] In the 2nd Volume of the *American State Papers*, p. 114, the reader will see a very interesting discussion of the matters contained in these Statutes, and a defence of the neutrality of the United States government against the reclamations of the French government.

carried on by the Spanish Colonies of South America, it became necessary to apply to Congress for a revision of the neutrality municipal regulations of the United States. Accordingly, on the 26th Dec. 1816, President Maddison addressed a message to Congress stating that the existing laws had not their proper efficacy, and that it would be expedient for Congress to devise further legislative provisions for detaining vessels actually equipped, or in the course of equipment, or for obtaining adequate securities against the abuse of armaments[1]. In introducing the desired bill to Congress Mr Forsyth stated that the Act of 1794 applied to certain things committed within the waters of the United States, and that of 1797 (a supplementary Act) to acts of the same character within the limits of the United States; but that there was no provision in either to forbid a citizen from arming and equipping a vessel within the United States, and then selling it to a foreigner to be taken out of the United States and used contrary to law: "In other words," said Mr Forsyth, "the citizen and foreigner might do that conjointly which neither of them could do separately under the former laws." The first section of the bill therefore was aimed at this defect, whilst the second section remedied another equally important, viz. that of not authorizing the interference of the executive to prevent the commission of the offence, or where there was not sufficient evidence to justify punishment for its commission. The remedy applied was that of calling on the owners to give security that they would not violate the neutral obligations of the United States.

Deliberations in Congress thereon.

The bill encountered strong opposition in its passage through Congress, Mr Clay denouncing it as an act for the benefit of his Majesty the King of Spain, as a measure calculated to affect the struggle going on in the South, and therefore as a partial unneutral piece of legislation; whilst Mr Robertson protested against it as going beyond

[1] Statesman's *Manual*, Vol. III. p. 431—434.

the Act of 1794 in two points, first, in giving a collector power to stop a vessel for any cause justifying suspicion; and, secondly, in enabling the authorities to exact a bond from the owners of vessels manifestly built for war, though intended to be sold (as well as of armed vessels) ere they could be cleared out of American ports[1]. In spite of opposition the bill became law on the 20th April, 1817, and remains in the statute book as the existing Foreign Enlistment Act of the United States.

Provisions of the American Act of 1817.

The Act contains thirteen clauses. By the 1st, punishment of fine and imprisonment is imposed for the offence of accepting a commission from a foreign belligerent against a prince or people at peace with the United States. By the 2nd, punishment of the same nature for enlisting or procuring another to enlist in the service of a foreign power. The 3rd, with the 5th, the 10th, and the 11th, relate specially to the offence of fitting out vessels within the limits of the United States to aid one foreign belligerent against another who is at amity with the United States, and will be noticed at a little more length further on. The 4th enacts the penalty of fine and imprisonment for fitting out privateers to cruise against the commerce of the United States. The 6th makes provision for the offence of setting on foot an expedition against a foreign power in amity with the United States[2]. And the 8th and 9th give power to the President to employ the forces of the United States to suppress such expeditions, and to compel, if necessary, foreign vessels to depart the United States.

The consideration of the 3rd, the 5th, the 10th, and the 11th sections, has been reserved in order that in the first place some of the leading American cases, and comments of writers, upon these important sections may

[1] *Abridgement of Debates in Congress*, Vol. VI. p. 123.

[2] As to this section, see Ex parte Needham, Peters' *Circuit Cases*, 487, and more especially the comments on it in two charges to the Grand Juries of Indiana and Ohio, 5 Maclean's *Reports*, pp. 250 and 307, and in the Preface to 2 Wheeler's *Criminal Cases*, p. xlviii.

be noticed, and next, that its distinctive features may be contrasted with those of the corresponding sections of the English act.

The 3rd section is as follows:—If any person shall within the limits of the United States fit out and arm, or attempt to fit out and arm, or procure to be fitted out and armed, or shall knowingly be concerned in the furnishing, fitting out, or arming of any ship or vessel, with intent that such ship or vessel shall be employed in the service of any foreign prince or state, or of any colony, district, or people, to cruise or commit hostilities against the subjects, citizens, or property, of any foreign prince or state, or of any colony, district, or people, with whom the United States are at peace; or shall issue or deliver a commission within the jurisdiction of the United States for any ship or vessel to the intent that she may be employed as aforesaid, every person so offending shall be deemed guilty of a high misdemeanour, and shall be fined not more than ten thousand dollars, and be imprisoned not more than three years, and every such ship or vessel, with her ammunition and stores, which may have been procured for the building and equipment thereof shall be forfeited; one-half to the use of the informer, and the other half to the United States. The 5th section is directed in the same way against the offence of increasing or augmenting, or procuring to be increased or augmented, or being knowingly concerned in the increasing or augmenting, in the manner specified in this section, the force of any ship of war, cruiser, or other armed vessel, to be employed in the service of any foreign prince or state, &c., at war with another prince or state, &c., with whom the United States are at peace. Whilst in the 10th, it is provided that owners, &c., of armed vessels sailing out of the United States are to give a bond, &c., not to commit hostilities against the subjects, citizens, or property of any friendly power. And in the 11th it is enacted that collectors of the customs shall detain vessels built for warlike purposes, and about to depart the United States, when circumstances render it probable that they are intended to commit hostilities against a friendly power.

Case of the *Santissima Trinidada.*

Two cases upon the construction of this 3rd section of the Act of 1818, and its correspondent clause in the old Act of 1794, deserve to be set out and noticed at a little length. The first case is that of the *Santissima Trinidada*[1], which was a libel filed by the Consul of Spain in the District Court of Virginia, in April, 1817, against part of the cargoes of two Spanish ships, the *Santissima Trinidada,* and the *St Ander,* alleged to have been unlawfully and piratically taken out of those vessels on the high seas, by a squadron consisting of two armed vessels, the *Independencia del Sud,* and the *Altravida,* manned and commanded by persons assuming themselves to be citizens of the United Provinces of Rio de la Plata; and three reasons were assigned for the restitution, two of them being that the capturing vessels were owned in the United States, and were originally equipped, fitted out, armed and manned in the United States, contrary to law, and that their force and armament had been illegally augmented within the United States. The evidence, as briefly stated by Mr J. Story in his judgment, was as follows: "The *Independencia* was originally built and equipped at Baltimore as a privateer during the war with Great Britain, rigged as a schooner, and called the *Mammoth,* and cruised against the enemy. After the peace she was rigged as a brig and sold by her original owners. In January, 1816, she was loaded with a cargo of munitions of war by her new owners, inhabitants of Baltimore, and being armed with 12 guns, part of her original armament, she was despatched from that port under the command of the claimant, on a voyage ostensibly to the North-west Coast, but in reality to Buenos Ayres. By the written instructions to the supercargo he was authorized to sell the vessel to the government of Buenos Ayres if he could obtain a suitable price. She duly arrived at Buenos Ayres, having exercised

[1] 7 Wheaton, 284.

no act of hostility, but sailed under the protection of the American flag during the voyage. At Buenos Ayres the vessel was sold to Captain Chaytor and two other persons, and soon afterwards she assumed the flag and character of a public ship, and was understood by the crew to have been sold to the government of Buenos Ayres. Captain Chaytor made known these facts to the crew, and asserted that he had become a citizen of Buenos Ayres, having received a commission to command the vessel as a national ship; and having invited the crew to enlist in the service, the greater part of whom did enlist."

Upon these facts the first question was, whether the *Independencia* was a public ship. And as to that it was held that, independent of corroborative testimony adduced, the commission of the captain to command the ship afforded satisfactory evidence of her public character. The commission of a public ship, signed by the proper authorities of the nation to which she belongs, being, in general, complete proof of her national character. But the next and most important question was, whether the property in controversy was captured in violation of the neutrality of the United States, so that restitution should be decreed, and that upon the two reasons above set out. The judgment of the court, it was said, might be made apart from the testimony of the witnesses, for the case did not stand alone upon that evidence. "The question as to the original illegal armament and outfit may be dismissed in a few words. It is apparent that though equipped as a vessel of war, she was sent to Buenos Ayres on a *commercial adventure*, contraband, indeed, but in no shape violating our laws or our national neutrality. If captured by a Spanish ship of war during the voyage, she would have been justly condemned as good prize for being engaged in a traffic prohibited by the law of nations. But there is nothing in our laws, or in the law of nations, that forbids our citizens from sending armed vessels, as well as munitions of war, to foreign ports for sale. It is a commercial adventure which no nation is bound to prohibit, and which only exposes the persons engaged in it to the penalty of confiscation. Supposing, therefore, the voyage to have been for commercial purposes, and the sale at Buenos Ayres to have been a *bonâ fide* sale (and there is nothing in the evidence before us to contradict it), there is no pretence to say that the original outfit on the voyage was illegal, or that a capture made after the sale was for that cause alone invalid." So far for the point as to the illegal outfit: for that which concerned the augmentation of the force of the *Independencia*, the judgment of the court, that there was an illegal augmentation of her force in the United States ports by a substantial increase of her crew, was founded on regular evidence, as detailed by the learned Judge at pp. 341—344; the *onus probandi* being on the claimant, Chaytor, to show that the augmentation of force by enlistment was lawful; it was argued by the claimant that the augmentation complained of was not an infraction of the law of nations, or a violation of the neutrality of the United States, and that so far as it stood prohibited by their municipal laws the penalties were personal, and did not reach the case of restitution of captures made in the cruise during which such augmentation had taken place. To that the court replied that it had never been held that an augmentation of force or illegal outfit affected any captures made after the original cruise was terminated. By analogy to other cases of violation of public law the offence might well be deemed to be deposited at the termination of the voyage, and not to affect future transactions. But as to captures made during the same cruise, the doctrine of that court had long established that such illegal augmentation was a violation of the law of nations as well as of the municipal laws of the United States, and as a violation of their neutrality, by analogy to other cases, it infected the captures subsequently made with the character of torts, and justified and required a restitution to the parties who had been injured by such misconduct.

The case of the United States *v.* Quincey[1] arose out of an indictment found against the defendant in the Circuit Court for the district of Maryland in May, 1829, framed on the 3rd section of the Act of Congress April 20, 1818. The indictment contained fifteen counts, on the 12th and 13th of which evidence was given. The 12th charged the defendant with being knowingly concerned in the fitting out of a certain vessel called the *Bolivar*, &c. with intent to be employed in the service of a foreign people, &c. to commit hostilities against the subjects of a foreign prince, &c.; whilst the 13th varied the charge by alleging an intention to cruise, &c. against the subjects and property of a foreign prince. It was proved on the part of the United States that the work of repairing and fitting her out was done at the request of one Henry Armstrong, and of the defendant, who superintended it; that sails and masts larger than a merchant-vessel required were fitted, and that alterations were made in her to suit her carrying passengers, and with a port for a gun. It was also proved that she sailed from Baltimore to St Thomas, having on board besides provisions, thirty-two water casks, one gun-carriage and slide, a box of muskets, and thirteen kegs of gunpowder. At St Thomas she was fitted as a privateer and sailed to St Eustatia, having changed her name to *Las Damas Argentinas* the defendant being her captain during her subsequent cruise. From St Eustatia she proceeded under the Buenos Ayrean flag and captured several vessels, terminating her cruise on the 1st of March, 1828.

Case of United States *v.* Quincey.

In delivering judgment, Mr Justice Thompson after shortly stating the case and noticing the section of the Act on which the indictment was founded, proceeded to examine in detail the instructions to the jury that were prayed for; they were as follows:—In the first place the

[1] 6 Peters, 447. As to this see Baron Bramwell's criticisms in the case of Attorney General *v.* Sillem (the *Alexandra* case), *Exchequer Reports*, Vol. II. p. 541 (1864). The learned Baron thinks the case was wrongly decided.

court assented to the prayer on the part of the United States, that if the jury should find from the evidence that the defendant was, within the district of Maryland, knowingly concerned in fitting out the privateer with intent that she should be employed in the manner alleged in the indictment, then the defendant would be guilty of the offence charged, although the jury should find the equipments of the privateer were not complete within the United States, and that the cruise did not commence until men were recruited, and further equipments were made at St Thomas. To bring the defendant, said the court, within the words of the Act, it is not necessary to charge him with being concerned in fitting out *and* arming, either will do—it is sufficient if the indictment charges the offence in the words of the Act—an attempt to fit out and arm is made an offence, which is certainly doing something short of a complete fitting out and arming. The second and third instructions, which were given in favour of the defendant, were as follows:—That if the jury believed that when the *Bolivar* was fitted and equipped at Baltimore, the owner and equipper intended to go to the West Indies in search of funds with which to arm and equip the said vessel, and had no *present intention* of using and employing her as a privateer, but intended when he equipped her to go to the West Indies to endeavour to raise funds to prepare her for a cruise, then the defendant could not be guilty. Or if the jury believed that when the *Bolivar* was equipped at Baltimore, and when she left the United States the equipper *had no fixed intention to employ* her as a privateer, but had a wish so to employ her, the fulfilment of which wish depended on his ability to obtain funds in the West Indies for the purpose of arming and preparing her for war, then the defendant is not guilty. In assenting to this view the court pointed out that whilst the offence consisted principally in the intention with which the preparations were made, those preparations must be made within the limits of the United States; it being equally necessary that the intention with respect to the employment of the vessel should be formed before she left the United States, and should be fixed, not conditional or contingent on future arrangements. "The law," said the learned judge, "does not prohibit armed vessels of the United States from sailing out of our ports, it also requires the owners to give security that such vessels shall not be employed by them to commit hostilities against foreign powers at peace with the United States. The collectors are not authorized to detain vessels although manifestly built for warlike purposes, and about to depart from the United States, unless circumstances shall render it probable that they are intended to be employed by the owners to commit hostilities against some foreign power at peace with the United States."

U.S. Foreign Enlistment Act.

Such are some of the principal points in the judgments of these two cases, in which, as the present learned Attorney General of England (Sir R. Palmer) said, the American act received a construction by the highest tribunal of that country[1]; and from these and the other American cases already noticed, it is clear that as in this country so in the United States[2], "the act was a municipal statute, whose object was to give power to the neutral government for its own protection against the intrusive belligerent, not to create any obligation towards, or to supply the means of, affording protection to the injured belligerent;" and above all, that its aim and object is not to control or limit neutral commerce or interfere with it in any way, but to restrain private war and forbid warlike enterprises. "These acts are," as the writer just quoted tersely puts it, "directed not against the animus vendendi, but against the animus belligerandi, and are intended to prohibit a breach of allegiance by the subject against his sovereign, not to

[1] *Debate House of Commons*, March 27, 1863. Hansard's *Debates*, Vol. CLXX. p. 43.

[2] See Letter of Historicus on the *Foreign Enlistment Act*. Historicus on *International Law*, p. 171.

prevent transactions in contraband with the belligerent[1]."

British Foreign Enlistment Act.

From this sketch of the American acts and cases we proceed to examine the provisions of the British Foreign Enlistment Act of 1819. Between the statutes of the two countries will be found differences as well as resemblances of a close and striking nature both as regards their history and their detail. Like its American prototype of 1818 the British statute owed its birth to the revolutionary contest in the Spanish colonies, and whilst the effort of the United States government to maintain its neutrality in this way was denounced in the American congress as a measure calculated to affect that struggle and to benefit the King of Spain, no less vigorously was the same reproach fixed upon our own statute in the memorable debate[2], in which all its advantages and its drawbacks, the necessity for its admission into the Statute-book and the reasons for its rejection were so earnestly and so eloquently advocated. It is not our purpose here to record at any length the arguments that on that occasion were pressed by the supporters and the opponents of the bill. The small compass of a chapter does not of course permit any opportunity for extracting any part of the speeches of the great men who on both sides lent so much lustre to the birth of our English Foreign Enlistment Act, but to those who wish to dis-

[1] Letters of Historicus, p. 169. A writer of a paper read before the Juridical Society, 4th May, 1863, contests strongly the truth of this conclusion, arguing that however freely subjects of the Queen may trade in other contraband articles, they cannot by the 7th section of the 59 Geo. III. c. v. contract to equip or arm and deliver a ship of war; but as the language of the section shows, and as the writer goes on to state, the prohibition is not levelled against the contract to sell, but against the intention to commit hostilities against another State. *Juridical Society's Papers*, Vol. II. p. 674. No doubt, as the writer says, the liberty of manufacturing or selling in this case is restricted, but it is because of the intent to take part in the hostilities —because in fact the *animus vendendi* is converted into the *animus belligerandi.*

[2] See Sir Jas. Mackintosh's Speech, *Parliamentary Debates* (1819), Vol. XL. p. 366.

cover the real motives that induced the government of the day with Canning and Lord Castlereagh in the van to enrol such a measure in the Statute-book, and to those who may not be of opinion that a Foreign Enlistment Act is a necessary or a useful addition thereto, the perusal of the speeches of Brougham, Denman, Scarlett, Wilson, and above all Mackintosh, is recommended[1].

Debates on the Bill.

From those debates it will be seen that the bill was introduced to prevent two distinct acts, enlistments of troops and equipments of vessels for foreign service, part of its object being to amend two statutes that had been passed in the reign of George II. The first of these, the 9th of George II. c. 30, was passed in the year 1736; a period of time when, as Sir James Mackintosh said, the unremitting efforts of the Jacobite party to carry out their schemes and plots induced them to enter into various foreign services, with the view of availing themselves of that spirit of discontent which they were perpetually fancying they observed at home. Whether the two houses of parliament were satisfied that the danger from such a cause was real and imminent, or whether the great minister, Sir Robert Walpole, who then ruled supreme, was enabled to carry the measure unchallenged, we cannot say. From the absence of debate or notice of any kind respecting it, the probability is that the fears of the houses, or their knowledge of threatening danger, induced them to pass at once and without question an act by which the enlisting or procuring his Majesty's servants to enlist in foreign service was declared to be a felony punishable with death without benefit of clergy[2]. Twenty years later a danger similar in kind attracted the notice

[1] See the *Parliamentary Debates* (1819), Vol. XL. pp. 362, 867, 1094, 1235. (Sir James Mackintosh, says the report, sat down amidst the loudest cheers from both sides of the House, which continued for several minutes, p. 1102.)

[2] There were two statutes of an older date punishing as felons those who entered into the service of another State. (3 Jac. I. c. 4 and Wm. and M. st. 1, c. 8.)

of the legislature, and accordingly an act was passed in the year 1756[1], the preamble of which states that whereas divers of his Majesty's subjects had been induced to serve as officers under the French king, which practice was highly to the dishonour and greatly prejudicial to the safety and welfare of the kingdom; as a remedy it should be enacted that the accepting of any military commission from, or otherwise entering the military service of that king without leave or license of his Majesty, the King of Great Britain, should be a felony punishable with death, without benefit of clergy. It was also provided by way of amendment upon the previous stat. (9 Geo. II. c. 30) that British subjects contracting or agreeing or engaging to enlist into foreign service, and persons engaging them without license from his Majesty, should be guilty of felony, and be punished with death as above mentioned. In the same statute provision was made for the case of British subjects accepting commissions in the Scotch Brigade in the service of the states general, who were required to take the oaths of allegiance and abjuration, and transmit a certificate thereof with the date of their commissions to the Secretary of State for War, and it was further declared that no attainder for any offence made felony by the statute should work a corruption of blood, loss of dower or disherison of heir. Such then was the second of these Foreign Enlistment Acts of Great Britain "passed in the war of 1756 after France had seized a number of British ships, when the government were in possession of information that an invasion was intended either here or in Ireland, and when there was a Pretender to the throne residing near Paris with some thousand adherents to his person, or employed in the French service[2]."

One glance at their contents coupled with but a slight knowledge of the history of the time, shows how little

[1] 29 Geo. II. c. 17.

[2] *Parliamentary Debates*, June 3, 1819, Vol. XL. p. 875. (Sir Robert Wilson.)

these statutes owed, for their introduction, to any feeling of delicacy towards friendly powers at war with other states, or to any wish on the part of the government to preserve its neutrality, how much to the fear of a Pretender, and the succours he might obtain from foreign princes. At the end of upwards of half a century the legislature again thought fit to recast in a different mould, and for another set of reasons, the regulations on the subject of Foreign Enlistment[1].

In introducing the bill of 1819 it was argued by the government, that if a neutrality was to be preserved it should be preserved between states that claimed to themselves the right to act as states, as well as between those that were acknowledged to be states; that for this special reason, as well as with the view of reducing the quality of the crime and diminishing the punishment, the Stat. 29 Geo. III. c. 17, required alteration; and that as by the common law of the land it was a high misdemeanor to enter into the service of a foreign prince without the leave of the king, so it was important that that law should be made applicable to all powers acknowledged as well as unacknowledged. Besides it was advisable that this country should have the right, possessed by every legitimate country, of breaking the neutrality existing between it and all other states. And as it was found that the mere prohibition of enlisting in foreign service was not sufficient—for assistance might be rendered to foreign states by fitting out ships for purposes of war or by supplying vessels with warlike stores—a supplement to the enactments of former times was required. Accordingly that addition aimed at two objects; first, to prevent the fitting out of armed vessels, and secondly, to prevent the fitting out or supplying other ships with warlike stores in any of the king's ports. To the arguments in favour of the measure it was answered that such

59 Geo. III. c. 69.

[1] On the 16th of April, 1823, Lord Althorp moved for the repeal of the Foreign Enlistment Act, but the motion was rejected by a majority of 106, Mr Canning making a strong speech against the motion.

a change as was contemplated was unnecessary, because whilst every government could always protect its neutrality by preventing its subjects from engaging in the wars of other states, and by ordering them to abstain from any acts by which the relations with other states might be disturbed, those who engaged in the service of insurgent states might be treated as rebels; whilst the bill itself it was urged, so far from being an impartial enactment in favour of neutrality, was nothing but a law of preference in favour of one of two contending parties. In spite, however, of the fierce denunciations of its opponents, and after prolonged debates, the bill was finally carried by a majority of 61 in the Lower, and 53 in the Upper House, and is known as the Foreign Enlistment Act of 1819[1].

Analysis of the Act.

After reciting that the laws in force against enlistment or engagement in foreign service without his Majesty's license are not effectual, the act proceeds to repeal the two statutes above mentioned passed in the reign of George the IInd, and the corresponding Irish Acts (11 Geo. II. and 19 Geo. II.). It then declares that all subjects enlisting or engaging to enlist or serve in foreign service military or naval, accepting commissions, engaging to go or going into foreign countries with intent to enlist, and retaining or procuring others to enlist, shall be guilty of a misdemeanor, and punishable with fine and imprisonment, or either at the discretion of the court, after conviction upon any information or indictment[2].

Power is also given to justices of the peace to issue warrants for the apprehension of offenders under the act, the offences being triable in his Majesty's court of King's Bench at Westminster, or at the assizes or sessions of Oyer and Terminer, or at any quarter and general sessions of the peace in and for the county where the offence was committed[3].

[1] 59 Geo. III. c. 69.
[2] *Ib.* s. 2.
[3] *Ib.* s. 4.

By the fifth section it is enacted that vessels with persons on board engaged in foreign service may be detained in any port of his Majesty's dominions by the officers of the customs; and by the sixth section a penalty of fifty pounds for every person found on board is given against any master or person in command of a vessel, who shall take on board persons enlisted contrary to the act. The seventh section makes it a misdemeanor punishable by fine and imprisonment, or either at the discretion of the court, for persons to fit out armed vessels in order to aid in military operations with any foreign powers without the leave and license of the crown, or to issue commissions for vessels to be employed as above mentioned. It also declares that every ship or vessel with the tackle, arms, ammunition, and stores then on board, shall be forfeited, and that the officers of customs and excise may seize such ship or vessel. And by the eighth section the aiding the warlike equipment of vessels of foreign states, &c. is made a misdemeanor punishable by fine and imprisonment, or either.

Such is a brief summary of an act of parliament that after becoming law, in spite of earnest and eloquent opposition, slumbered for nearly fifty years in the Statute-book undisturbed and unthought of; and certainly it is a remarkable fact that whereas in the law reports of the United States a large number of judicial decisions will be found wherein their Foreign Enlistment Acts have received constructions on various points, in England not one legal argument was heard, nor one judgment passed upon the British act before the well-known case of the Alexandra. A sketch of the statute would therefore be incomplete without some notice of that important and, it must be confessed, unsatisfactory trial.

The first breach however of the Foreign Enlistment Act occurred in the escape to sea of a vessel built, as it was alleged, to the order and as it turned out for the service of the so-called confederate government, and known afterwards as the notorious Alabama. It is not proposed here to dwell upon the facts of that case, for though as the correspondence shews it was one of a very grave nature, seriously affecting our position as a neutral nation, yet inasmuch as by the escape of the vessel no opportunity was given for testing the value, or construing the language of the Foreign Enlistment Act, we pass it by in order to consider the case of the Alexandra.

The United States' Act and that of Great Britain compared.

But ere we give that notice, it will not be out of place here to draw attention to two or three features by which the American is distinguished from the British act. The first is that by the American Statute the owners or consigners of armed vessels sailing out of the United States are to give a bond to the United States with sufficient sureties prior to clearing out in double the amount of the value of the vessel and cargo on board not to employ them to cruise or commit hostilities against the subjects, citizens, or property, of any friendly power. The second is, that the collectors of customs are authorized and required to detain any vessel manifestly built for war purposes and about to depart from the United States when circumstances render it probable her owner intends to cruise or commit hostilities, until the President's decision thereon be had, or until a bond be taken[1]. Whilst the third is, that by the British act, the enlistment of troops and the armament of ships within the British dominions are not as in the American act of Congress, prohibited absolutely, but only if they take place without the leave and license of the Crown, signified by an order in Council, or by a Proclamation[2]. We now proceed to the case of the *Alexandra*[3].

The Alexandra case.

This was an information by the Attorney General that, on the 5th of April, 1863, an officer of the customs at Liverpool, by law empowered to do so, did seize and arrest

[1] As to these two clauses, see a paper read before the Juridical Society, 9th Feb. 1863, by W. W. Kerr. *Juridical Society's Papers*, Vol. II. p. 648.

[2] See as to this the *Times Newspaper*, Sept. 6, 1863.

[3] Attorney General *v.* Sillem. *Exchequer Reports*, Vol. II. p. 431 (1864).

as forfeited, a certain ship or vessel called the *Alexandra*, together with the furniture, tackle, and apparel, belonging to, and on board, the said ship or vessel. There were 98 counts in it, setting out in various ways that the defendants did equip and furnish and attempt and endeavour to equip and furnish the said vessel with intent to cruise and commit hostilities contrary to the form of the Statute, and the defendants pleaded that the said ship or vessel, furniture, tackle, &c. was not, nor any nor either of them, forfeited, for the several causes mentioned in the information. The trial took place in the Middlesex sitting, at Westminster, some time in June, 1863, the facts being that the ship was seized at Liverpool for a contravention of the 59 Geo. III. c. 69[1]; that she was built in the yard of Messrs. Miller and Sons of Liverpool, who stated that she was built for Messrs. Frasers, Trenholm, and Co., Merchants of Liverpool, and agents of the Confederate States of America; was launched in March, and taken to Toxteth dock for completion, being strongly built of teak wood, with beams and hatches stronger and wider apart than those in merchant vessels; that at the time of her seizure workmen were engaged in fitting her with stanchions for hammock nettings; that she had besides iron stanchions in the hold, cooking apparatus for 150 or 200 people, with complete accommodation for men and officers, but only stowage room sufficient for her crew, supposing them to be 32 men; and that she was apparently built for a gun boat with low bulwarks, over which pivot guns could play. The Commander of Her Majesty's ship *Majestic*, stationed at Liverpool, stated that she certainly was not intended for mercantile purposes, that she might be used for a yacht, and was easily convertible into a man of war. In his direction to the Jury, the learned Judge told them, the question he should submit was, whether the

[1] The claimants carried on business as Engineers at Liverpool, under the firm of Fawcett, Preston, and Co., and were allowed to defend on their attorney making the affidavit prescribed by the Customs Consolidation Act, 16 and 17 Vict. c. 107, s. 309.

*Alexandra* was merely in the course of building, in order to be delivered in pursuance of a contract, an act which was perfectly lawful; or whether there was any intention that, in the port of Liverpool or any other English port, the vessel should be equipped, fitted out, and furnished or armed for the purpose of aggression. His Lordship, after stating that the object of the Statute was not the protection of belligerents, but the prevention of equipments for war, finally left the question thus to the Jury: "Was there any intention of equipping, furnishing, &c. in the port of Liverpool, or in any other port, in order to take part in the contest? If you think the object was to equip, furnish, fit out, or arm, the vessel at Liverpool, that is a sufficient matter; but if you think the object really was to build a ship in obedience to an order and in compliance with a contract, leaving to those who bought it to make what use they thought fit of it, then it appears to me that the Foreign Enlistment Act has not been broken." The Jury found a verdict for the Defendants, and a rule *nisi* for a new trial was obtained by the Attorney General on seven grounds, amounting practically to two; first, that the Lord Chief Baron had misdirected the Jury, or had insufficiently directed them in point of law; and secondly, that the verdict was against the weight of evidence. The rule was argued in the Michaelmas Term 1863; and, after a very long hearing, the Court being equally divided in opinion as to whether the rule ought to be made absolute, on Baron Pigott withdrawing his judgment, it was discharged. It would of course be impossible here to do more than notice very briefly some of the positions that were laid down by the judges; and utterly impossible to do justice to the arguments of counsel, in a case of nearly 150 pages in length. What was actually decided was as follows. That the building, in pursuance of a contract with intention to sell and deliver to a belligerent power, the hull of a vessel suitable for war, but manned and not equipped, furnished or fitted out with anything which enables her to cruise or commit hostilities, or do any warlike

Direction of the Lord Chief Baron to the Jury.

Decision of the Barons of the Exchequer.

act whatever, is not a violation of the Foreign Enlistment Act. The Lord Chief Baron Pollock and Baron Bramwell holding, that what is forbidden is an equipment of such a warlike nature as shall enable the ship on leaving a port in this kingdom to cruise or commit hostilities, Baron Channell maintaining, that if the equipment be such as renders the ship capable of being used for war, though at the time she leaves the port she may not be in a condition at once to commit hostilities, when the intent is clear that she is to be used for war, then that case is within the Statute; whilst Baron Pigott held, that any act of equipping, furnishing or fitting out, done to the hull or vessel, if done with the prohibited intent, is within the language and spirit of the Act. We have said that in consequence of Baron Pigott withdrawing his judgment, the rule was discharged. Upon that result, the Crown appealed to the Exchequer Chamber; but as it appeared that, before the Common Law Procedure Act 1854, there could be no appeal; and that the power of appeal under that act applied only to personal actions commenced by writ of summons, the Court of Exchequer Chamber held that the 26th section of the Queen's Remembrancer's Act[1] did not confer a power by rule or order, to extend, apply or adapt, to the revenue side of the Court of Exchequer, the provisions of the Common Law Procedure Act 1856 as to appeal[2]. Such was the termination of the only case in which the British Act of Parliament received anything like an interpretation or construction[3]; a termination to be regretted because of its incomplete nature. Yet from this case, and

Appeal to the Exchequer Chamber.

[1] 22 and 23 Vict. c. 21.

[2] *Exchequer Reports*, Vol. II. (1864), p. 581.

[3] As to the meaning of the word equip, see Gibbs' *Foreign Enlistment Act*, London, 1863, "a pamphlet well worth perusing, as collecting all the authorities in a convenient form" (see the Chief Baron's judgment in 'Attorney General *v.* Sillem'). As to the meaning of the words, equip, furnish, fit out, &c. see the judgments of the Lord Chief Baron and Baron Channell in the case above discussed at pages 526 and 555; and as to the construction of the statute looked upon as a penal statute, see the able remarks of Baron Bramwell at page 531.

the American decisions above noticed, thus much is clear, that the main point of an enquiry, under the Statute apart from the question, as to whether there has been an equipping or fitting out will be, what was the owner's intent at the time of such equipping, whether a fixed and present intention to commit a hostile act, or simply to prosecute a mercantile operation? And of all Foreign Enlistment Acts such as we have been engaged in examining, it may be said, that by making municipal regulations of this kind, a nation changes its whole mode of proceeding, points out a specific and technical method of punishing its citizens for this class of breaches of neutrality, and is bound by all the niceties and difficulties of such a technical remedy.

It only remains to add a few words upon a question of no little gravity and moment connected with this subject —Whether a nation is liable to make compensation for injuries committed by cruisers fitted out in violation of a Foreign Enlistment Act.

Liability of State to make compensation.

This question, it will be seen, from the correspondence between Earl Russell and Mr Adams, commencing April 7, and ending Sept. 18, 1865[1], gave rise to a very complete examination of the whole law and practice of the two countries upon this subject. In that important correspondence two matters were pressed upon the attention of the British authorities, (1) that the recognition of the Confederate States by according to them belligerent rights was precipitate and partial, (2) that compensation was due by the British Government for the injuries inflicted upon the mercantile marine of the United States by vessels built in British Ports, and afterwards equipped with an armament from the British Coast. As regards the first question, there is no necessity to notice it here. It has been already discussed in a previous Chapter, and is so thoroughly examined in the correspondence, that it is sufficient to refer to that correspondence, as well as to the letter of Historicus, and the pamphlet published by Mr Bemis, at Boston, who does battle with that writer. But

[1] Supplement to the *London Gazette* of Oct. 13, 1865.

to the second will be devoted the remainder of this chapter. Now there can be no doubt that if a nation professing neutrality, and either by Proclamation or by municipal regulations, prohibiting its subjects from enlisting in the service of one or other of the belligerents, or aiding either of them by equipments of armed vessels, does knowingly and wilfully allow what it professes to prohibit, "if it does not act with due diligence or show good faith and honesty in the maintenance of the neutrality it proclaims," it is guilty of partial and unneutral conduct, which will render it liable to be treated by the offended belligerents as an enemy, and for which in honour it is bound, where it escapes the direct consequences of that hostile attitude, to make compensation for the injuries it has thus caused. But the case is different where such a nation has faithfully and conscientiously performed its obligations as a neutral. It may, and frequently will be, that in spite of Proclamation, in spite of Statute, its subjects, for the sake of the great gains thereby resulting, will use every artifice to evade the provisions thus published. It is as impossible for a government entirely to defeat their efforts, as for the legislature to prevent its most carefully drawn enactment from being evaded. If, therefore, when the government "has done all in its power to prevent and to punish[1]," its honest efforts to maintain neutrality are set at nought, to hold it liable for the deceits and frauds of its subjects would be most burdensome and dangerous, would render a maritime nation (to use Earl Russell's words), whose people occupy themselves in constructing ships and cannon and arms, responsible for the whole damages of a war in which that nation had no part, and would, as the well considered and approved language of the United States, both diplomatic and judicial, shows, be introducing a doctrine new to politics, and new to International Jurisprudence. All that a neutral nation possessed of a Foreign Enlistment Act has to do is to draw the public attention of its subjects to its

[1] Earl Russell's *Letter* to Mr Adams, May 4, 1865.

provisions, to warn them of the consequences of a breach thereof, itself to put the law in force on sufficient proof of its intended infraction, either by detaining and seizing the vessels, whose owners are obnoxious to the provisions of the statute, or by exacting a bond, or adopting whatever other kind of precaution may be established, and to give every facility for prosecuting and punishing offenders against the Statute. If this has been the course of proceedings on the part of the neutral state, if its attitude and conduct have in this way been irreproachable, then in the diplomatic and judicial language of the United States, so aptly cited in the correspondence above referred to, and so ably expressed, the neutral state may thus reply to demands for compensation. "This government having used all the means in its power to prevent the fitting out and arming of vessels in their ports to cruise against any nation with whom they are at peace, and having faithfully carried into execution the laws enacted to preserve inviolate its neutral and pacific obligations, cannot consider itself bound to indemnify individual foreigners for losses by captures over which it has neither control nor jurisdiction. For such events no nation can in principle, nor does in practice, hold itself responsible. A decisive reason for this, if there were no other, is the inability to provide a tribunal before which the facts can be proved[1], as in the case of two steam rams in the Mersey, and of another called the *Pampero*, in the Clyde[2]."

[1] *Despatch* from Mr Adams to the Portuguese minister at Washington, March 14, 1818. For the practice of the United States Courts see Mr Justice Story's judgment in the case of the *Aimstad de Rues*, 5 Wheaton, 388, to the effect that a neutral state is not bound to do more than restore property captured by cruisers in fraud of the Foreign Enlistment if found within its ports. See also the *Alerta*, 3 Curtis's *Rep.* p. 382.

[2] In the Supplement to the *London Gazette* of Friday, Nov. 10th, 1865, appeared a correspondence between Mr Adams and Earl Russell, in the last letter of which his lordship enumerates all the cases in which the British Government had by detention of vessels and prosecutions of individuals endeavoured to maintain its neutrality; according to that document proceedings were taken against five vessels and eight persons were prosecuted under the Foreign Enlistment Act, six of whom were convicted.

On the 30th Nov. 1865, Captain Corbett was indicted and tried for an alleged infringement of the Foreign Enlistment Act, by engaging men at Blackwall for a vessel called the *Sea King*, in which he sailed to Madeira, where he was joined by another vessel called the *Laurel*. The two went in company to a desert island, and there a large quantity of guns was loaded on board the *Sea King*, which soon afterwards hoisted the Confederate flag, was called the *Shenandoah*, and became a cruiser in the Confederate service, commanded by an American officer; Captain Waddell. The main question at the trial being, whether the defendant really did attempt in any place to induce the men to enlist, or whether, as was contended by his counsel, the real attempts were made by the American officers who joined the *Shenandoah* at the desert island above-mentioned; and there being considerable doubt as to the language used by Captain Corbett in his address to the crew at the time of the transfer, and as to the fact of its being uttered not by him, but by Captain Waddell. The Jury gave him the benefit of the doubt, and returned a verdict of Not Guilty, several points of law being reserved for the consideration of the Court above[1].]

[1] See *Times Newspaper*, Nov. 30th, Dec. 1st and 2nd, where the case is reported at full length.

## CHAPTER VIII.

### OF THE GENERAL RIGHTS AND DUTIES OF NEUTRAL NATIONS[1].

---

THE rights and duties which belong to a state of neutrality form a very interesting title in the code of international law. In the United States they ought beyond all doubt to be objects of particular study, because whilst it is the true policy of that country to cherish a spirit of peace, so it has ever been the avowed aim of its government to keep itself free from those political connexions which would tend to draw it into the vortex of European contests[2]. [Nor should they be less regarded with attention and respect in Europe where, if on the one hand owing to the complications arising out of family compacts, political confederations or alliances for mutual aid and defence many of the powers find no little difficulty in keeping out of hostilities when war breaks out; on the other, in case they do succeed in standing aloof therefrom and maintaining a neutral attitude, they experience a fact which war soon makes patent, that their neutrality is by the belligerents con-

[1] On the general principles connected with neutrality and neutrals see Heffter, Liv. II. ch. iii. §§ 144—154, where most of the leading continental authorities are cited. Ortolan, *Règles Internationales et Diss. de la Mer*, Liv. III. ch. iv. Wheaton, Vol. II. Part IV. ch. iii. §§ 1—5. Halleck *On International Law*, ch. xxvi. §§ 1—4. Phillimore, Vol. III. Twiss *On the Law of Nations*, Vol. II. ch. xi.

[2] Heffter, Liv. II. ch. iii. § 145.

sidered as a stumblingblock in their paths, and that these watch with the most jealous suspicion the conduct of all who profess neutrality, contest with energy the rights they claim, and insist upon the strictest attention to the obligations by which as neutrals they are bound. A correct appreciation therefore of the rights and duties attaching to a state of neutrality is a matter of primary importance, in the upholding of which both neutrals and belligerents are equally concerned.] For whilst every nation that maintains a firm and scrupulously impartial neutrality, and commands the respect of all other nations by its prudence, justice, and good faith, has the best chance to preserve unimpaired the blessings of its commerce, the freedom of its institutions, and the prosperity of its resources; so belligerents are interested in the support of the just rights of neutrals, for the intercourse which is kept up by means of their commerce contributes greatly to mitigate the evils of war. The public law of Europe has established the principle, that, in time of war, countries not parties to the war, nor interposing in it, shall not be materially affected by its action; but shall be permitted to carry on their accustomed trade, under the few necessary restrictions which we shall hereafter consider[1].

Neutrals must be impartial.

It belongs not to a common friend to judge between the belligerent parties, or to determine the question of right between them[2]. The neutral is not to favour one of them to the detriment of the other; and it is an essential character of neutrality, to furnish no aids to one party, which the neutral is not equally ready to furnish to the other[3]. A nation which would be admitted to the privileges of neutrality, must perform the duties it enjoins.

[1] Vattel, Bk. III. ch. vii. § 104. Wheaton's *Elements*, Vol. II. Pt. IV. ch. iii. § 1. De Cussy, *Droit Maritime*, Liv. I. tit. iii. § 9, and *Opinions of Attorneys-General* (American), Vol. II. p. 87.

[2] Bynk. *Q. J. P.* Lib. I. ch. ix. Burlamaqui, Vol. II. Pt. IV. c. v. §§ 16, 17.

[3] Manning's *Law of Nations*, p. 180.

A loan of money to one of the belligerent parties, is considered to be a violation of neutrality[1], [if contracted by the act, consent, advice of, or even collusion on the part of the neutral state. But so far as this country, at all events, is concerned, as the judgment in Chavasse *v.* Grazebroch shews[2], the acts of individuals independent of, and unknown to, their government, cannot in the matters of loans any more than sales of munition of war be considered violations of neutrality[3].] A fraudulent neutrality is no neutrality. But the neutral duty does not extend so far as to prohibit the fulfilment of antecedent engagements, which may be kept consistently with an exact neutrality, unless they go so far as to require the neutral nation to become an associate in the war[4]. If a nation be under a previous stipulation, made in time of peace, to furnish

[1] Mr Pickering's *Despatch to Messrs Pinckney, Marshall, and Gerry,* Envoys and Ministers Plenipotentiary to the French Republic, March 2nd, 1798. *American State Papers,* Vol. IV. p. 142. [This document however shews that what was prohibited was an advance of money by loan or otherwise from *the representatives of a neutral state* to one of the belligerent parties. "In no event," says Mr Pickering, "is a treaty to be purchased with money by loan or otherwise."]

[2] 34 *Law Journal,* Bankruptcy Cases, p. 17.

[[3] The following cases have been cited by Mr Chancellor Kent and other writers, in support of the doctrine of the learned Chancellor's, as to the illegality of a loan of money; but as to the first (De Wutz *v.* Hendricks) it is sufficient to say that the statement in it to the effect that it is contrary to the law of nations, for persons residing in England, to enter into engagements to raise money by way of loan, for the purpose of supporting subjects of a foreign state in arms against a government in friendship with England, was but an *obiter dictum* of the learned Judge who delivered the judgment of the Court of Common Pleas, and that the case itself did not turn upon that point at all. As to the others, on reference to them, it will be found that whilst they have little or no bearing upon the subject referred to in the text, they certainly do not support the learned author's statement in its broad and unlimited sense—these cases are: De Wutz *v.* Hendricks, 9 Moore's (*B. Reports,* 586. Yrisarri *v.* Clement, 11 Moore, *C. B.*) *Reports,* 308. Thompson *v.* Powles, 2 Simon, 194. Jones *v.* Garcia Del Rio, 1. Turner and Russell, 297.]

[4] Vattel, Bk. III. ch. vi. § 101; ch. vii. §§ 104, 105. Mr Jefferson's *Letter to Mr Pinckney,* Sept. 7, 1793, Jefferson's *Works,* Vol. IV. p. 61; and see also Wheaton's *Elements,* Vol. II. Pt. IV. ch. iii. § 5, and Twiss *On the Law of Nations,* Vol. II. ch. xi. § 212.

a given number of ships or troops to one of the parties at war, the contract may be complied with, and the state of peace preserved. In 1788, Denmark furnished ships and troops to Russia, in her war with Sweden, in consequence of a previous treaty prescribing the amount, and this was declared by Denmark to be an act consistent with a spirit of amity and commercial intercourse with Sweden. It was answered by the latter in her counter declaration, that though she could not reconcile the practice with the law of nations, yet she embraced the Danish declaration, and confined her hostility, so far as Denmark was concerned, to the Danish auxiliaries furnished to Russia[1]. But if a neutral power be under contract to furnish succours to one party, he is said not to be bound if his ally was the aggressor; and in this solitary instance the neutral may examine into the merits of the war, so far as to see whether the *casus fœderis* exists[2]. An inquiry of this kind, instituted by the party to the contract, for the purpose of determining on its binding obligation, holds out strong temptations to abuse; and, in the language of Mr Jenkinson[3], "when the execution of guaranties depends on questions like these, it will never be difficult for an ally who hath a mind to break his engagements, to find an evasion to escape."

Neutral territory inviolable.

A neutral has a right to pursue his ordinary commerce[4], and he may become the carrier of the enemy's goods, without being subject to any confiscation of the ship, or of the neutral articles on board; though not without the risk of having the voyage interrupted by the seizure of the hostile property. As the neutral has a right to carry the property

[1] *New A. Reg.* for 1788, tit. Public Papers, p. 99.

[2] This subject has already been discussed in a preceding chapter (III). Bynk. *Q. J. P.* Lib. I. ch. ix. Vattel, Bk. II. ch. xii. § 168. Twiss's *Law of Nations*, Vol. II. ch. xii. § 129.

[3] *Discourse on the Conduct of the Government of Great Britain in respect to Neutral Nations*, 1757, see Jenkinson's *Treaties*, Vol. I. p. 36.

[4] See Jefferson's *Letter to Pinckney*, above cited. Twiss's *Law of Nations*, Vol. II. ch. xi. § 215, and the case of the Ionian ships, Spink's *Prize Cases*, p. 203.

of enemies in his own vessel, so, on the other hand, his own property is inviolable, though it be found in the vessels of enemies.

But the general inviolability of the neutral character goes further than merely the protection of neutral property. It protects the property of the belligerents when within the neutral jurisdiction. It is not lawful to make neutral territory the scene of hostility, or to attack an enemy while within it; and if the enemy be attacked, or any capture made, under neutral protection the neutral is bound to redress the injury, and effect restitution[1]. [But beyond this, as Mr Justice Story in the case of La Amistad de Rues said[2], it is not obliged to interpose, for were it otherwise there would be no end of the difficulties and embarrassments of neutral tribunals.] The books are full of cases recognising this principle of neutrality. In the year 1793, the British ship Grange was captured in Delaware Bay by a French frigate, and, upon due complaint, the American government caused the British ship to be promptly restored[3]. So, in the case of the *Anna*[4], the sanctity of neutral territory was fully asserted and vindicated, and restoration made of property captured by a British cruiser near the mouth of the Mississippi, and within the jurisdiction of the United States.

It is a violation of neutral territory, for a belligerent ship to take her station within it, in order to carry on hostile expeditions from thence, or to send her boats to capture vessels being beyond it. No use of neutral territory, for

[1] Grotius, Bk. III. ch. iv. § 8, n. 2. Bynk. Lib. I. ch. viii. Vattel, Bk. III. ch. vii. § 132. Burlamaqui, Vol. II. Pt. IV. ch. v. § 19. [The case of the General Armstrong (noticed in Chap. III.) may be referred to in connection with the subject discussed in the text above. The principle to be extracted from it would seem to be that if, in the event of a capture in a neutral vessel the commander of the captured vessel chooses to resort at once to force instead of demanding the protection of the neutral state, by his act the neutral state is released from all responsibility.]

[2] 5 Wheaton's *Reports* (Amn.), p. 385.

[3] Mr Jefferson's *Letter to M. Ternant* of 15th May, 1793. *American State Papers*, Vol. I. p. 77.

[4] 5 Rob. 373, and Soult *v.* L'Africaine, Bee's *Reports* (American), p. 204.

the purposes of war, can be permitted. This is the doctrine of the government of the United States[1]. It was declared judicially in England, in the case of the *Twee Gebrœders*[2]; and though it was not understood that the prohibition extended to remote objects and uses, such as procuring provisions and other innocent articles, which the law of nations tolerated, yet it was explicitly declared, that no proximate acts of war were in any manner to be allowed to originate on neutral ground; and for a ship to station herself within the neutral line, and send out her boats on hostile enterprises, was an act of hostility much too immediate to be permitted. No act of hostility is to be commenced on neutral ground. No measure is to be taken that will lead to immediate violence. The neutral is to carry himself with perfect equality between both belligerents, giving neither the one nor the other any advantage[3]; and if the respect due to neutral territory be violated by one party, without being promptly punished by just animadversion, it would soon provoke a similar treatment from the other party, and the neutral ground would become the theatre of war[4].

[1] Mr Randolph's *Circular to the Governors of the Several States*, April 16, 1795. The American Commissioners to the Court of France (Messrs Benjamin Franklin, Silas Deane, and Arthur Lee), in their Circular Letter, in 1777, to the Commanders of American armed vessels, carried very far the extension of neutral protection, when they applied it indiscriminately to all captures "within sight of a neutral coast." *Diplomatic Correspondence*, by J. Sparks, Vol. II. 110. *Vide supra*, Chap. II.

[2] 3 Rob. 162. See this case commented on in Tudor's *Leading Cases in Mercantile Law*, pp. 622—642.

[3] Ortolan, *Règles Internationales*, &c., pp. 62 and 64.

[4] When Don Miguel, in 1828, ascended the throne of Portugal by a voto of the Portuguese Cortes, in violation of the title by succession of his niece Donna Maria, England declared herself neutral as between those claimants in their domestic quarrel for the crown. Having declared her neutrality, England maintained it with fidelity and vigour. She would not allow any warlike equipments by either party in her ports, and when an armament had been fitted out in disguise, and sailed from Plymouth, in support of the claims of Donna Maria, England sent a naval force, and actually intercepted the Portuguese armament in its destination to the island Terceira. [Alison's *History of Europe from the Fall of Napoleon*,

Passage of ships over neutral waters.

If a belligerent cruiser inoffensively passes over a portion of water lying within neutral jurisdiction, that fact is not usually considered such a violation of the territory as to affect and invalidate an ulterior capture made beyond it. The passage of ships over territorial portions of the sea, is a thing less guarded than the passage of armies on land, because less inconvenient, and permission to pass over them is not usually required or asked. To vitiate a subsequent capture, the passage must at least have been expressly refused, or the permission to pass obtained under false pretences[1].

Refusal of passage of troops over neutral territory.

The right of a refusal of a pass over neutral territory to the troops of a belligerent power, depends more upon the inconvenience falling on the neutral state, than on any injustice committed to the third party, who is to be affected by the permission or refusal. It is no ground of complaint against the intermediate neutral state, if it grants a passage to belligerent troops, though inconvenience may thereby ensue to the adverse belligerent. It is a matter resting in the sound discretion of the neutral power, who may grant or withhold the permission, without any breach of neutrality[2].

Bynkershoek's exception.

Bynkershoek[3] makes one exception to the general inviolability of neutral territory, and supposes that if an enemy be attacked on hostile ground, or in the open sea, and flee within the jurisdiction of a neutral state, the victor may pursue him *dum fervet opus,* and seize his prize within the neutral state. He rests his opinion entirely on the authority and practice of the Dutch, admitting that he had never seen the distinction taken by the publicists, or in the practice of nations. It appears, however, that

Vol. IV. ch. xxii. § 13, and *Annual Register* for 1829, Vol. LXXI. p. 189. Cf. Phillimore, Vol. III. ch. ix. §§ 159, 160, where will be found a short abstract of the discussions upon this case in the British Houses of Parliament.]

[1] The *Twee Gebrœders,* 3 Rob. 336.

[2] Grotius, Bk. II. ch. ii. § 13. Vattel, Bk. III. ch. vii. § 119, 123, 127. Sir William Scott, 3 Rob. 353.

[3] *Q. J. P.* Bk. I. ch. viii.

Casaregis, and several other foreign jurists mentioned by Azuni[1], held a similar doctrine. But d'Abreu, Valin, Emerigon, Vattel, Azuni, and others, maintain the sounder position, that when the flying enemy has entered neutral territory, he is placed immediately under the protection of the neutral power. The same broad principle that would tolerate a forcible entrance upon neutral ground or waters, in pursuit of the foe, would lead the pursuer into the heart of a commercial port. There is no exception to the rule, that every voluntary entrance into neutral territory, with hostile purposes, is absolutely unlawful[2]. The neutral border must not be used as a shelter for making preparations to renew the attack; and though the neutral is not obliged to refuse a passage and safety to the pursued party, he ought to cause him to depart as soon as possible, and not to lie by and watch his opportunity for further contest. This would be making the neutral country directly auxiliary to the war, and to the comfort and support of one party. In the case of the *Anna*[3], Sir William Scott was inclined to agree with Bynkershoek to this extent: that if a vessel refused to submit to visitation and search, and fled within neutral territory, to places which were uninhabited, like the little mud islands before the mouth of the Mississippi, and the cruiser, without injury or annoyance to any person, should quietly take possession of his prey, he would not stretch the point so far, on that account only, as to hold the capture illegal. But, in this, as well as in every other case of the like kind, there is, *in stricto jure*, a violation of neutral jurisdiction, and the neutral power would have a right to insist on a restoration of the property. It was observed by the same high authority, in another case, depending on a

[1] *Droit Maritime*, Tit. II. ch. iv. art. 1, § 5, n. 1.

[2] Vattel, Bk. III. ch. vii. § 133. 1 Emerig. *Traité des Ass.* 449. Azuni, vol. ut supra, § 6. Valin, *Traité des Prises*, ch. iv. § 3, No. 4, art. 1. D'Abreu, Pt. 1. ch. iv. § 15, and see in support of this doctrine Jefferson's *Correspondence*, Vol. III. p. 243.

[3] 5 Rob. 365.

claim of territory, "that when the fact is established, it overrules every other consideration. The capture is done away; the property must be restored, notwithstanding that it may actually belong to the enemy[1]."

Prizes brought into neutral ports.

A neutral has no right to inquire into the validity of a capture, except in cases in which the rights of neutral jurisdiction were violated; and, in such cases, the neutral power will restore the property, if found in the hands of the offender, and within its jurisdiction, regardless of any sentence of condemnation by a court of a belligerent captor[2]. It belongs solely to the neutral government to raise the objection to a capture and title, founded on the violation of neutral rights. The adverse belligerent has no right to complain, when the prize is duly libelled before a competent court[3]. If any complaint is to be made on the part of the captured, it must be by his government to the neutral government, for a fraudulent, or unworthy, or unnecessary submission to a violation of its territory, and such submission will naturally provoke retaliation. In the case of prizes brought within a neutral port, the neutral sovereign exercises jurisdiction so far as to restore the property of its own subjects, illegally captured; and this is done, says Valin[4], by way of compensation for the asylum granted to the captor and his prize. It has been held, in the United States, that foreign ships offending against the laws of that country, within its jurisdiction, may be pursued and seized upon the ocean, and rightfully brought into its ports for adjudication, [but in such a case the party seizes at his peril.

[1] The *Vrow Catharina*, 5 Rob. 25. See also in confirmation of the above view Wheaton's *Elements*, Vol. II. Pt. IV. ch. iii. § 10. Manning's *Law of Nations*, p. 386. Phillimore, *Comm. on Internat. Law*, Vol. III. § 154. Heffter, *Le Droit Internat. Pub.* §§ 146, 147.

[2] *La Amistad de Rues*, 5 Wheaton, 390. The *Arrogante Barcelones*, 7 Wheaton, 496. The *Austrian Ordinance of Neutrality*, August 7, 1803, art. 18. Martens' *Treaties*, Vol. VIII. p. 111; and see as to this subject Twiss's *Law of Nations*, Vol. II. § 236, pp. 491—494.

[3] The *Eliza Ann*, 1 Dodson, 244. The *Diligentia*, 1 Dodson, 413.

[4] *Com.* Tom. II. p. 274.

If he establishes the forfeiture he is justified. If he fails he must make full compensation in damages[1]. There can be little doubt, however, that such a claim of authority as is here advanced would not only be vigorously resisted by foreign powers, but would in all probability be given up as tending to throw upon the nation that maintained it a grave and serious responsibility. Indeed within a very few years an attempt was made by one nation to insist upon its right to execute its authority upon the high seas over a ship belonging to another nation for an offence alleged to have been committed within its own jurisdiction. The case alluded to is that of the *Cagliari* which was a steam ship trading between Genoa and Tunis. On the 25th June, 1857, when on her regular voyage, the captain and crew were overpowered by some of the passengers on board, and diverted from their course to Ponza, an island belonging to the king of Naples and used as a state prison. There the prison was broken open by the insurgent passengers and the prisoners allowed to land at Sapri on the Italian coast. The *Cagliari* was then restored to the captain, who was making sail for Naples to report the affair, when at a considerable distance, more than six miles from the mainland, he was met by two Neapolitan frigates, who fired a gun across his bows, took him prisoner, seized and carried off to a Neapolitan dungeon two engineers (Englishmen) who were on board, and towed the ship into Naples in order to have her condemned as a prize. Strong remonstrances were made both by the British and the Sardinian authorities, and the restoration of the ship, captain and engineers was urgently demanded, the act being denounced as piracy, the legality of the whole proceedings being disputed and the pretended jurisdiction of the Neapolitan government being positively denied. On the 8th June, 1858, the Cagliari and her crew were delivered up to the English government and by them restored to the king of

Case of the Cagliari.

[1] *Marianna Flora*, 11 Wheaton's *Reports*, 42.

Sardinia. The two engineers, Messrs Parker and Watts, were set at liberty, and as a compensation for all they had suffered the sum of £3000 was paid by the Neapolitan government. Here then we have a case of seizure and detention of the ship of one state on the high seas for an offence against the laws of another state, followed by an immediate remonstrance against it as an act of violence illegal and unjustifiable, and an acknowledgment on the part of the offending power, "that it had neither argument to propound in favour of the act nor opposition to make to the demand of restitution." Mr Laurence in commenting upon the affair of the *Cagliari*, in connexion with the subject of the right of search[1], cites with approval the remarks of Dr Twiss and Sir R. Phillimore, and therefore it may be presumed is opposed to the doctrine laid down in the *Marianna Flora* being taken without reservation. And in truth a moment's reflection will shew that were a summary remedy of this kind to be permitted, and each nation allowed thus to execute its laws upon the high seas, the remedy would soon be worse than the original offences, and the ocean instead of being a peaceful highway open to the commerce of the world, would become a scene of strife and confusion where every nation that was sufficiently powerful to do so would execute its laws not for real grievances only, but for imaginary or even pretended ones. But the remedy thus preferred would be far less satisfactory than what International Law offers and international practice opposes; "for the privilege of the flag is the privilege of the state; and when there is *mala fides* in the wrong doers the state through courtesy waives its privileges, and either permits the nation which has been injured to avenge the breach of its laws, through its own tribunals, or will assist it to obtain redress against the wrong doers before the courts of their own country, if they have in any way made themselves amenable to punishment for a breach of their own laws[2],"

[1] Wheaton's *Elements*, Vol. I. Edition 1863, pp. 266—268 (note).

[2] Opinion of Dr Travers Twiss, the *Cagliari*, March 22, 1858.

or else it listens to the remonstrances and reclamations of the offended government, and gives redress for the wrongful acts committed.]

Arming in neutral ports.

The government of the United States was warranted by the law and practice of nations, in the declarations made in 1793, of the rules of neutrality, which are particularly recognised as necessary to be observed by the belligerent powers, in their intercourse with that country[1]. These rules were, that the original arming or equipping of vessels in American ports, by any of the powers at war, for military service, was unlawful; and no such vessel was entitled to an asylum in those ports. The equipment by them of government vessels of war, in matters which, if done to other vessels, would be applicable equally to commerce or war, was lawful. The equipment by them of vessels fitted for merchandise and war, and applicable to either, was lawful; but if it were of a nature solely applicable to war, it was unlawful. And if the armed vessel of one nation should depart from the jurisdiction of the United States, no armed vessel, being within the same, and belonging to an adverse belligerent power, should depart until twenty-four hours after the former, without being deemed to have violated the law of nations[2]. In the United States, as we have seen, Congress have repeatedly, by statute, made suitable provision for the support and

[1] Vattel, Bk. III. ch. vii. § 104. Wolfius, § 1174. *Austrian Ordinance of Neutrality,* August 7, 1803. Martens' *Treaties,* Vol. VIII. p. 111. *Cours de Droit Public,* par M. Pinheiro Ferreira, Tom. II. p. 44—47.

[2] *Instructions to the Collectors of Customs,* August 4, 1793. Mr Jefferson's *Letters to Mr Genet,* 5th and 7th June, 1793; his *Letter to Mr Morris,* 16th August, 1793. Mr Pickering's *Letter to Mr Pinckney,* Jan. 16, 1797. His *Letter to M. Adet,* Jan. 20, 1796. [The French doctrine identical with that contained in the text will be found in Ortolan, *Règles Internationales,* &c. Tome II. Liv. III. ch. viii. p. 255, and in Pistoye et Duverdy, *Des Prises Maritimes,* Tit. I. ch. i. § 3. In the recent war in the United States the delay of twenty-four hours above specified was insisted on by the British Government. See the *London Gazette,* 31st Jan. 1862, and *Parl. Papers,* 1862, *North America,* No. VI. pp. 19 and 29; see also Wheaton's *Elements of International Law,* Vol. II. Part IV. ch. iii. § 9, p. 716 (n. 216), ed. 1863, by W. B. Lawrence.]

due observance of similar rules of neutrality, and given sanction to the principle of them, as being founded in the universal law of nations. [These statutes have been already discussed at length in the preceding chapter. It is therefore unnecessary to do more in this place than to refer to those sections which provide against the setting on foot or preparing any military expedition against the territory of any foreign nation with whom the United States are at peace; or the hiring or enlisting troops or seamen for foreign military or naval service[1].

American cases upon the acts of 1794 and 1818.

[Upon these sections of the old statute of 1794 and the later one of 1818, there have been several state prosecutions, two or three of which are sufficiently important to deserve a short notice. In Smith and Ogden's case[2], which arose out of an attempt to assist the revolutionizing of the Spanish South American province of Caracas by Miranda and his party, the facts proved being held to be sufficient to constitute the offence contemplated by the act, the court intimated that provided the expedition was begun and the means were prepared to carry it on within the United States, it was not necessary it should be consummated without deviation of course. In the case of Workman and Kerr, jointly indicted[3], for unlawfully beginning and setting on foot a hostile expedition and military enterprise from the United States against the Spanish provinces of East and West Florida and those in Mexico, the court decided that the means for such an expedition might be prepared by enlisting men, or inducing others to enlist them. Whilst in the famous prosecution of two of the Cuban expeditionists, O'Sullivan and

[1] *Acts of Congress*, 5th June, 1794, and 20th April, 1818. *U. S. Statutes at Large*, Vol. I. p. 381 and Vol. III. p. 447. Another Act was passed March 10, 1838, to extend the provisions of that of 1818, but that Act expired by limitation at the end of two years.

[2] Tried in the U. S. C. C. for New York in July, 1806. See the case noticed at some length in Wharton's *American Criminal Law*, pp. 903—905.

[3] About the same time. See Wharton's *American Criminal Law*, p. 905.

Lewis, in "his able and elaborate charge" the learned judge who presided at the trial gave a most complete and exhaustive analysis of the Act of 1818 and its object and aim, a most eloquent denunciation of all attempts to fritter away the laws established by the United States for the maintenance of their neutrality, and a most luminous exposition of the words of the section on which the indictment was framed. As to the facts the jury were directed:

1st. To be satisfied beyond any reasonable doubt that persons were combined to begin, or set on foot a military expedition in the city of New York, to be carried on from thence against a territory with which the United States were at peace.

2ndly. That if from the evidence they found such a combination or agreement to have been made or understood by them, what any one of those persons might have said or done in relation to the expedition, became evidence against all.

3rdly. That the proof must establish that the expedition or enterprise was a military expedition; but that if the evidence shewed that the ends and objects were hostile or forcible against a nation at peace with the United States, then it would be to all intents and purposes a military expedition.

4thly. That the prosecution was bound to prove the act of beginning or setting on foot, or that the means were provided or procured within the Southern District of New York, and

Lastly. That the defendants had done the acts charged, or participated in their being done[1].]

Prizes in neutral ports.

Though a belligerent vessel may not enter within neutral jurisdiction, for hostile purposes, she may, consistently with a state of neutrality, until prohibited by the neutral power, bring her prize into a neutral port, and sell it[2].

[1] See the whole of Judge Judson's Charge set out at length in Wharton's *Criminal Law*, pp. 905—910. See also a very elaborate review of the subject of foreign enlistment within a neutral state by the United States Attorney-General Cushing, *Opinions of Attorneys-General*, Vol. VII. p. 367.

[2] Bynk. *Q. J. P.* Liv. I. ch. xv. Vattel, Bk. III. ch. vii. § 132. Ortolan,

["For in general," says Justice Story, in the case here cited, "neutral nations allow an asylum in their ports to the ships of belligerents. They may indeed prohibit their entry into their ports or the sale of their prizes there from motives of policy or public convenience (and if they do so, as Mr Chancellor Kent says in reference to this judgment and its purport, the refusal should be made as the privilege ought to be granted to both parties or to neither). Unless they do thus refuse, where is the principle of the law of nations which prohibits such a sale?.......If there be no prohibition, the right to sell arises silently from the general operations of commercial intercourse. A *bona fide* possessor of property may traffic with it in every country where the sovereign does not choose to establish a different rule, and this is the settled conclusion of jurists of high character[1]."]

The United States, while a neutral power, frequently asserted the right to prohibit, at discretion, the sale, within their ports, of prizes brought in by the belligerents, and the sale of French prizes was allowed as an indulgence merely, until it interfered with the treaty with England of 1794, in respect to prizes made by privateers[2]. In the opinion of some jurists, it is more consistent with a state of neutrality, and the dictates of true policy, to refuse this favour; for it must be very inconvenient to permit the privateers of contending nations to assemble, together with their prizes, in a neutral port. The edict of the States General of 1656 forbade foreign cruisers to sell their prizes in their neutral ports, or cause them to be unladen; and the French ordinance of the marine of 1681,

*Règles Internationales*, &c., Tom. II. Liv. III. ch. viii. p. 274. The reader may also refer to the *Times Newspaper*, June 16th, 1863, in order to see the use made of this passage by Captain Semmes of the *Alabama*. See also the letter of Historicus, *Times Newspaper*, January 11th, 1865.

[1] Bynk. *Q. J. P.* ch. xv. Dufonceau's ed. pp. 113, 120. Valin, T. II. *Des Prises*, ch. vii. § 24. Wheaton, *On Captures*, ch. ix. p. 260, § 6.

[2] *Instructions to the American Ministers to France*, July 15th, 1797. Mr Pickering's *Letters to Mr Adet*, May 24th, and November 15th, 1796; his *Letter to Mr Pinckney*, January 16, 1797.

contained the same prohibition, declaring that such vessels should not continue in port longer than twenty-four hours, unless detained by stress of weather[1]. The admission into neutral ports of the public ships of the belligerent parties, without prizes, is considered to be a favour, required on the principle of hospitality among friendly powers, and it has been uniformly conceded on the part of the United States[2].

[At the commencement of hostilities between the Northern and Southern portions of the United States, some of the Governments of Europe, in announcing their intention to observe a strict neutrality, insisted strongly upon their determination to prohibit the entry of the belligerent cruisers with their prizes into any of their ports. Thus, by an order dated 10th June, 1861, M. Thouvenel, on behalf of the French Imperial government, declared 1st. That no ship of war or privateer belonging to either of the belligerents should be allowed to enter any French port with its prize or prizes and remain for more than twenty-four hours, unless compelled by stress of weather. 2nd. That no sale of property whatever belonging to such prizes should take place in any French port. A similar order, and worded nearly in the same language, was published by Spain[3]; whilst Great Britain herself set the example, having a few days before either of the above orders, issued injunctions prohibiting armed ships and privateers belonging to the United Federal or the Confederate States of America, from carrying their prizes into British ports[4].

[1] Valin's *Com.* Tom. II. 272, and Ortolan, *Règles Internationales*, &c., Tom. II. Liv. viii. p. 279.

[2] Mr Jefferson's *Letter to Mr Hammond*, Sept. 9th, 1793. *Instructions to the American Commissioners to France*, July 15, 1797. *Cours de Droit Public*, par M. Pinheiro-Ferreira, Tom. II. p. 47. Such public vessels are exempt from the jurisdiction of the local authorities, but this exemption does not extend to private vessels. See *Opinions of Attorneys-General* (American), Vol. VII. pp. 130, 131, case of the *Sitka.*

[3] 17 June, 1861.

[4] *Letter of Lord John Russell to the Admiralty*, June 1st, 1861. See *Debates in the House of Commons*, 3rd June, 1861, Hansard, 3rd series, Vol. CLXIII. p. 471.

In the course of the war an attempt was made, and not unsuccessfully, to infringe the British order by Captain Semmes of the *Alabama*, who having captured a barque with a cargo of wool on board, sent her in with the cargo to Simon's Bay, under the pretence that she was not a prize but an armed tender to the *Alabama*, her armament consisting of two small rifled guns. Doubts however arose as to her real character, the United States Consul at the Cape of Good Hope protesting against her entry and that of the *Alabama* into port on the ground that she was a prize to the latter. A correspondence ensued between the Governor of the Cape, Sir P. Wodehouse, and the Duke of Newcastle. Two questions were raised, and answers to them thus given. The first question was whether the *Tuscaloosa*, for so the barque was named, was a prize or not[1]. Upon that question the British authorities held that the *Tuscaloosa* did not lose the character of a prize merely because at the time of her capture she was armed with two small rifled cannons, was under the charge of an officer and crew from the *Alabama*, and was used as a tender to that ship; they also held that Captain Semmes's contention that it was open to him to convert the *Tuscaloosa* into a vessel of war, and so render her admissible into a neutral port, was bad, in spite of the passages cited by him from Wheaton's *Elements*[2], which the British authorities contended had no bearing upon the case.

The second question was, whether the British interdiction, wherein prizes only were mentioned, and nothing was said of their cargoes, was intended to prevent the introduction of captured property picked up at sea and tendered for entry at the Custom House in the usual form from a neutral ship. In answer to that it was held that Her Majesty's orders applied as much to prize cargoes of every kind which might be brought by any armed

[1] The *Tuscaloosa* had never been condemned in a prize court.

[2] Wheaton's *Elements*, Vol. II. Part IV. ch. ii. § 11, pp. 629—633, and § 12, p. 663; "What constitutes a setting forth as a vessel of war," ed. 1863, by W. B. Lawrence.

ships or privateers of either belligerents into British waters as to the captured vessels themselves. They did not however apply to any articles which might have formed part of any such cargoes if brought within British jurisdiction not by armed ships or privateers of either belligerent, but by other persons who might have acquired or might claim property in them by reason of any dealing with the captors[1].]

[*Note.*—Unfortunately the following question put by Sir P. Wodehouse, and pressed as of grave importance, was not solved by the home authorities: "Whether the character of prize, within the meaning of her Majesty's orders, would or would not be merged in a national ship of war, in the case of a vessel duly commissioned as a ship of war after being made prize by a belligerent government without being first brought *infra præsidia*, or condemned by a Court of Prize." According to the passage in Wheaton, Vol. II. Pt. IV. ch. iii. pp. 663—664, it would seem that such a commission is a setting forth as a vessel of war within the meaning of the Prize Act: but if so, the whole effect of the interdictory orders above set out would be annulled, the territory of neutrals would cease to be under their jurisdiction, and a commander of a cruiser like the Alabama might defy neutral rules and neutral authority.]

Enemy's property on board neutral ships.

But neutral ships do not afford protection to enemy's property, and it may be seized if found on board a neutral vessel, beyond the limits of the neutral jurisdiction. This is a clear and well-settled principle of the law of nations[2]. It was formerly a question, whether the neutral ship conveying enemy's property was not liable to confiscation for that cause. This was the old law of France[3] in cases in which the master of the vessel knowingly took

[1] Duke of Newcastle to Sir P. Wodehouse, Nov. 4, 1863. *Parliamentary Papers, North America*, No. 6.

[2] Grotius, Lib. III. ch. vi. § 6. Heinec. *de Nav. ob. vect.* ch. ii. § 9. Bynk. *Q. J. P.* ch. 14. Loccenius, *De Jur. Mar. et Nav.* Lib. II. ch. ii. § 2. Molloy, *de Jure Maritimo*, Bk. I. ch. i. § 18. Lampredi, *Commerce des Neutres*, §§ 10, 11. Vattel, Bk. III. ch. vii. § 115. *Answer in* 1753 *to the Prussian Memorial. Consulat de la Mer*, par Boucher, Tom. II. ch. 273, 276, § 1004.

[3] *Ord. de la Marine*, Liv. III. Tit. IX. *des Prises*, art. 7.

on board enemy's property; but Bynkershoek truly observes, that the master's knowledge is immaterial in this case, and that the rule in the Roman law, making the vessel liable for the fraudulent act of the master, was a mere fiscal regulation, and did not apply; and for the neutral to carry enemy's goods is not unlawful, like smuggling, and does not affect the neutral ship[1]. If there be nothing unfair in the conduct of the neutral master, he will even be entitled to his reasonable demurrage, and his freight for the carriage of the goods, though he has not carried them to the place of destination. They are said to be seized and condemned, not *ex delicto*, but only *ex re*. The capture of them by the enemy is a delivery to the person, who, by the rights of war, was substituted for the owner[2]. Bynkershoek[3] thinks the master is not entitled to freight, because the goods were not carried to the port of destination, though he admits that the Dutch lawyers, and the *Consolato*, give freight. But the allowance of freight in that case has been the uniform practice of the English Admiralty for near two centuries past, except when there was some circumstance of *mala fides*, or a departure from a strictly proper neutral conduct[4]. The freight is paid, not *pro rata*, but *in toto*, because capture is considered as delivery; and the captor pays the whole freight because he represents his enemy, by possessing himself of the enemy's goods *jure belli*, and interrupts the actual delivery to the consignee[5].

Freight in such cases.

Discussion of the question.

The right to take enemy's property on board a neutral ship, has been much contested by particular nations,

[1] Bynk. *Q. J. P.* Lib. I. ch. xiv.

[2] Vattel, Bk. III. ch. vii. § 115.

[3] Lib. I. ch. 14.

[4] Jenkinson's *Discourse* in 1757, p. 13. The *Atlas*, 3 *Rob.* 304 (note). *Answer to the Russian Memorial*, 1713. See also Maud and Pollock's *Law of Merchant Shipping*, p. 246 n. (u).

[5] The *Copenhagen*, 1 *Rob.* 289. The cases, English and American, on this point are collected in the note above cited from Maud and Pollock's work on *Merchant Shipping*.

whose interests it strongly opposed. This was the case with the Dutch in the war of 1756, and Mr Jenkinson (afterwards Earl of Liverpool) published, in 1757, a discourse, very full and satisfactory, on the ground of authority and usage, in favour of the legality of the right, when no treaty intervened to control it. The rule has been steadily maintained by Great Britain. In France it has been fluctuating. The ordinance of the marine of 1681 asserted the ancient and severe rule that the neutral ship, having on board enemy's property, was subject to confiscation. The same rule was enforced by the arrêts of 1692 and 1704, and relaxed by those of 1744 and 1788[1]. In 1780, the Empress of Russia proclaimed the principles of the Baltic code of neutrality, and declared she would maintain them by force of arms. One of the articles of that code was, that "all effects belonging to the subjects of the belligerent powers should be looked upon as free on board of neutral ships, except only such goods as were contraband." The principal powers of Europe, as Sweden, Denmark, Prussia, Germany, Holland, France, Spain, Portugal and Naples, and also these United States, acceded to the Russian principles of neutrality[2]. But the want of the consent of a power of such decided maritime superiority as that of Great Britain, was an insuperable obstacle to the success of the Baltic conventional law of neutrality; and it was soon abandoned, as not being sanctioned by the existing law of nations, in every case in which the doctrines of that code did not rest upon positive compact. During the whole course of the wars growing out of the French revolution, the government of the United States admitted the English rule to be valid, as the true and settled doctrine of international law; and that enemy's

[1] Valin's *Com.* I. 3. Tit. IX. *des Prises*, art. 7.

[2] *N. A. Reg.* for 1780, tit. *Public Papers*, pp. 113—120. *Journals of Congress*, Vol. VII. pp. 68, 185. Heeren's *Manual of the Political Systems of Europe*, Bohn, 1846, p. 285. Schœll. *Hist. des Traités de Paix*, T. IV. p. 1, ed. 1817.

property was liable to seizure on board of neutral ships, and to be confiscated as prize of war[1]. It has, however, been very useful in commercial treaties, to stipulate, that free ships should make free goods, contraband of war always excepted; but such stipulations are to be considered as resting on conventional law merely, and as exceptions to the operation of the general rule, which every nation not a party to the stipulation is at perfect liberty to exact or surrender. The Ottoman Porte was the first power to abandon the ancient rule; she stipulated, in her treaty with France in 1604, that free ships should make free goods, and afterwards consented to the same provision in her treaty with Holland in 1612; according to Azuni[2], Turkey has, at all times, on international questions, given an example of moderation to the more civilized powers of Europe.

The effort made by the Baltic powers, in 1801, to recall and enforce the doctrines of the armed neutrality in 1780, was met, and promptly overpowered, and the confederacy dissolved, by the naval power of England. Russia gave up the point, and by her convention with England of the 17th June, 1801, expressly agreed, that enemy's property was not to be protected on board of neutral ships. The rule has for a long period been very generally acquiesced in; and was expressly recognised in the Austrian ordinance of neutrality, published at Vienna the 7th of August, 1803. Its reason and authority have been ably vindicated by English statesmen and jurists, particularly by Mr Ward, in his treatise *of the relative rights and duties of belligerent and neutral powers in maritime*

[1] Mr Jefferson's *Letter to M. Genet*, July 24th, 1793. Mr Pickering's *Letter to Mr Pinckney*, January 16th, 1797. *Letter of Messrs. Pinckney, Marshall, and Gerry, to the French Government*, January 27th, 1798.

[2] *Droit Maritime*, Tom. II. ch. iii. Art. 1, § 8. Flassan, in his *Hist. de la Diplomatie Française*, Tom. II. 226, says that it was not the object of the Ottoman Porte, in the instance mentioned in the text, to abandon the ancient rule, and that it was not a treaty, but a concession to France of privileges and exemption from pure liberality.

*affairs*, published in 1801, which exhausted all the law and learning applicable to the question[1].

Goods of neutrals on Enemy's vessels.

It is also a principle of the law of nations relative to neutral rights, that the effects of neutrals found on board of enemy's vessels shall be free; and it is a right as fully and firmly settled as the other, though, like that, it is often changed by positive agreement[2]. The principle is to be met with in the *Consolato del Mare*, and the property of the neutral is to be restored without any compensation for detention, and the other necessary inconveniences incident to the capture. The former ordinances of France of 1543, 1585, and 1681, declared such goods to be lawful prize: and Valin[3] justifies the ordinances, on the ground, that the neutral, by putting his property on board of an enemy's vessel, favours the enemy's commerce, and agrees to abide the fate of the vessel. But it is fully and satisfactorily shown, by the whole current of modern authority, that the neutral has a perfect right to avail himself of the vessel of his friend, to transport his property; and Bynkershoek has devoted an entire chapter to the vindication of the justice and equity of the right[4].

Enemy's goods on neutral ships and neutral goods on Enemy's ships distinct rules.

The two distinct propositions, that enemy's goods found on board a neutral ship may lawfully be seized as prize of war, and that the goods of a neutral found on board of an enemy's vessel were to be restored, have been explicitly incorporated into the jurisprudence of the United States,

[1] Mr Manning has discussed the question, whether free ships make free goods, quite at large and with great strength of reasoning, *Law of Nations*, pp. 203—244. He vindicates the belligerent right against the doctrine of the Baltic powers upon solid principle, and on the authority of the *Consolato del Mare*, and of the most eminent European jurists who have written on the law of nations.

[2] Grotius, Bk. III. ch. vi. and xvi. Bynk. ch. xiii. Vattel, Bk. III. ch. vii. § 116. *Answer to the Prussian Memorial*, 1753. Mr Jefferson's *Letter to M. Genet*, July 24th, 1793. Mr Pickering's *Letter to Mr Pinckney*, January 10, 1797.

[3] *Com.* Bk. III. tit. 9. *des Prises*, art. 7.

[4] *Consulat de la Mer*, par Boucher, Tom. II. ch. 276, §§ 1012, 1013 Heineccius, *de Nav. ob. vect.* ch. ii. § 9. Opera, Tom. II. Pt. I. pp. 349—355. Vattel, Bk. III. ch. vii. § 116. Bynk. ch. xiii

and declared by the Supreme Court[1] to be founded in the law of nations. The rule, as it was observed by the court, rested on the simple and intelligible principle, that war gave a full right to capture the goods of an enemy, but gave no right to capture the goods of a friend. The neutral flag constituted no protection to enemy's property, and the belligerent flag communicated no hostile character to neutral property. The character of the property depended upon the fact of ownership, and not upon the character of the vehicle in which it is found. After vindicating the simplicity and justice of the original rule of the law of nations, against the speculations of modern theorists, and the *ultima ratio* of the armed neutrality, which attempted to effect by force a revolution in the law of nations; the court stated, that nations have changed this simple and natural principle of public law, by conventions between themselves, in whole or in part, as they believed it to be for their interest, but that the one proposition, that free ships should make free goods, did not necessarily imply the converse proposition, that enemy's ships should make enemy's goods. If a treaty established the one proposition, and was silent as to the other, the other stood precisely as if there had been no stipulation, and upon the ancient rule. The stipulation that neutral bottoms should make neutral goods, was a concession made by the belligerent to the neutral, and it gave to the neutral flag a capacity not given to it by the law of nations. On the other hand, the stipulation subjecting neutral property found in the vessel of an enemy to condemnation as prize of war, was a concession made by the neutral to the belligerent, and took from the neutral a privilege he possessed under the law of nations; but neither reason nor practice rendered the two concessions so indissoluble, that the one could not exist without the other. It rested entirely in the discretion of the contracting parties, whether either or both should be granted. The two propositions are distinct and independent of each

[1] The *Nereide*, 9 Cranch, 388.

other, and they have frequently been kept distinct by treaties, which stipulated for the one, and not for the other[1]. Treaty regulations on the subject.

The government of the United States, in their negotiations with the republics in South America, pressed very earnestly for the introduction and establishment of the principle of the Baltic code of 1780, that the friendly flag should cover the cargo; and this principle is incorporated into the treaty between the United States and Colombia, in 1825, and into the treaty of navigation and commerce between the United States and the Republic of Chili in 1825[2]. The introduction of those new republics into the great community of civilized nations, was justly deemed a very favourable opportunity to inculcate and establish, under their sanction, more enlarged and liberal doctrines on the subject of national rights. It had been the desire of the United States' government to obtain the recognition of the fundamental principles, consecrated by the treaty with Prussia in 1785, relative to the perfect equality and reciprocity of commercial rights between nations; the abolition of private war upon the ocean; and the enlargement of the privileges of neutral commerce. The rule of public law, that the property of an enemy is liable to capture in the vessel of a friend, was declared, on the part of government, to have no foundation in natural right; for the usage rests entirely on force. Though the high seas are a general jurisdiction, common to all, yet each nation has a special jurisdiction over its

[1] The *Cygnet*, 2 Dodson's *Adm.* 299. S. P.

[2] It was stipulated in these treaties that as between the parties, free ships should make free goods—that the flag should cover the cargo even of enemies, contraband goods excepted, and should also cover the persons, though enemies, unless they were officers or soldiers in actual service, but the provision was only to apply to those persons who recognized the principle; and neutral property found on board enemy's vessels was under the above stipulation liable to capture. If, however, the neutral flag did not protect enemy's property then the goods of a neutral on board of an enemy's vessel were to be free. Treaty with Columbia, Art. 12, 13; with Chili, Art. 12, 17; with Venezuela, Art. 15; with the Peru Bolivian Confederation, Art. 11, 12; with Ecuador, in 1839, Art. 15. *United States Statutes at Large*, Vol. VIII. pp. 306, 424, 487, 534.

own vessels; and all the maritime nations of modern Europe have, at times, acceded to the principle, that the property of an enemy should be protected in the vessel of a friend. No neutral nation, it is said, is bound to submit to the usage; and the neutral may have yielded, at one time, to the usage, without sacrificing the right to vindicate, by force, the security of the neutral flag at another. The neutral right to cover enemy's property is conceded to be subject to this qualification: that a belligerent nation may justly refuse to neutrals the benefit of this principle, unless it be conceded also by the enemy of the belligerent to the same neutral flag[1].

But, whatever may be the utility or reasonableness of the neutral claim, under such a qualification, "I should apprehend," says the learned author, "that the belligerent right is no longer an open question; that the authority and usage on which that right rests in Europe, and the long, explicit, and authoritative admission of it by this country, have concluded us from making it a subject of controversy; and that we (Americans) are bound, in truth and justice, to submit to its regular exercise, in every case, and with every belligerent power who does not freely renounce it."

Change in the practice of nations since the Russian war.

[The subject just discussed has, like several other points of maritime law, been materially affected by the war between Russia and the two great European powers. Previous to that war, says Mr Tudor in his excellent work already quoted[2], it became necessary that the respective navies of England and France should act upon the same rules in matters of prize. This was effected by means of a compromise, for while by a legal declaration dated March 28th, 1854, followed by an order in council of the

[1] *Letter* of Mr. Adams, Secretary of State, to Mr. Anderson, 27th May, 1823. President's *Message* to the Senate of 6th December, 1825, and to the House of Representatives, March 15th, 1826. Statesman's *Manual*, pp. 678 and 728.

[2] Tudor's *Leading Cases in Mercantile Law*, Notes to the *Fortuna*, the *Bremen Fluge*, and the *Santa Cruz*, p. 805.

15th April, 1854, England announced her intention of waiving the right of seizing enemy's property on board a neutral vessel unless it were contraband of war[1]; France, on the other hand, by a declaration of the same date, acceded to the principle that neutral property on board enemy's ships should not be liable to confiscation. The same principle was adopted by the plenipotentiaries who signed the treaty of Paris; for in that treaty it was declared that the neutral flag covers enemy's goods with the exception of contraband of war (Art. 2), and that neutral goods with the exception of contraband of war are not liable to capture under the enemy's flag (Art. 3)[2].]

Summary of the doctrines as to Freight.

[The doctrine of the courts in both countries on the subject of freight may be summed up shortly as follows. First, as a general rule, in ordinary cases freight, or the price which is payable for the carriage of goods to their destination on a legal voyage[3], does not become due unless the voyage is completed and the goods are carried to their destination[4]. Secondly, freight *pro rata itineris* is due when the ship by inevitable necessity is unable to prosecute her voyage and is forced into a port short of her destination, where the owner of the goods voluntarily accepts them[5]. But thirdly, the shipowner will not necessarily lose his freight because there has been an interrup-

[1] Lesur, *Annuaire Historique*, 1854; Appendice, p. 51.

[2] On the subject of free ships, free goods, see American *State Papers*, Vol. II. p. 114; Jefferson's *Works*, Vol. IX. p. 443 Wheaton's *Elements*, Vol. II. Part IV. ch. iii. §§ 19—23, pp. 736—765, edn. 1863. And for a sketch of the armed neutrality and conventions since that period, see Manning's *Law of Nations*, ch. vi § 1; and see especially a very careful and well-drawn resumé of what has been written on the subject by the principal authors thereon, in Dr Travers Twiss's *Law of Nations*, Vol. II. ch. v. §§ 81—19. pp. 156—170.

[3] Freight denotes the price of *carriage*, not of receiving goods *to be carried*. N.B. Freight must be insured *eo nomine*, and is not covered by a policy on goods. Bailie *v.* Mondigliani, Park on *Insurance*, p. 116, 8th edn.; cf. Arnould on *Insurance*, Vol. I. ch. xi. sect. 1, Art. 1, §§ 99—101.

[4] Mashiter *v.* Bullar, 1 Campbell, 84. Crozier *v.* Smith, 1 M. and Gr. 407.

[5] Luke *v.* Lyde, 3 Burrows, 882. Mitchell *v.* Darthy, 2 Bingham, N. C. 555. The *Copenhagen*, 1 Robinson, 289.

tion (without any fault on his part) of the voyage which is afterwards completed[1]. Now as far as such interruption by means of capture and restoration are concerned, the principles to which the courts have adhered are these: As the captor succeeds to the right and some of the liabilities of the shipowner and the freighter immediately upon his becoming possessed of the prize, when (1) a ship is condemned as a prize, but not the cargo, in order to entitle himself to freight the captor must carry the cargo to its port of destination; (2), when however the cargo is condemned as prize, but not the ship, then the master's meritorious service is held to be complete, capture being in the eye of the law looked upon as equivalent to delivery, and so the captor is liable to the master for the full freight of the original voyage; (3) when there is no condemnation of either, and the ship and cargo are both restored, supposing there has been no authoritative separation of the one from the other, the original contract is not dissolved (the captor's rights until condemnation being but inchoate), and the parties to that contract are again at large, after a temporary inability, to fulfil their obligations and enforce their rights[2].]

**Freight in connexion with capture.** [Under the head of capture in connection with freight, there are two classes of cases which also deserve notice. One where, as frequently happens, enemies' goods are found on board neutral ships, the other where neutral goods are found on board an enemy's ship. In the first of these two classes, as a general rule, the captors take *cum onere*, and if the neutral's conduct has been entirely fair and impartial the prize courts in both countries allow him his full freight just as though the original voyage had been performed[3]; but the freight so allowed is only what is reasonable, not necessarily that which the parties have

[1] The *Race Horse*, 3 Robinson, 101. Beale v Thompson, 3 Bosan. and Puller, 405.

[2] Machlachlan, *Laws of Merchant Shipping*, p. 418.

[3] The *Hoop*, 1 Robinson, 196, 219. The *Antonia Johanna*, 1 Wheaton's *Reports*, 159.

agreed on if it be inflamed by extraordinary circumstances[1]. The fact of the enemies' goods thus carried by the neutral being carried to the other belligerent does not prevent the neutral carrier from claiming and obtaining his freight, for though so far as the subjects of the enemy are concerned the trade with the other is illegal, yet that is not so as regards neutrals, and therefore even if the voyage be from the port of one enemy to that of the other the neutral's trade is legal, and his claim for freight allowed[2]. But in order to entitle himself to freight the conduct of the neutral must be entirely free from fraud or unfairness; for fraud, or unfairness, or violation of belligerent rights will, under ordinary circumstances, work the forfeiture of his freight and expenses; in flagrant cases will even cause the confiscation of the ship itself and all on board her[3]. Therefore where he has used false papers, or carried contraband goods, or wilfully destroyed his ship's papers, he will be refused freight; and the same consequence follows where the cause of capture was the ship, not the cargo[4]. So far for the question of freight where the carrier is a neutral and the goods are those of a belligerent. In the next class of cases, where the position is reversed, the goods being neutral and the carrier a belligerent, it has been a matter of discussion, whether the captor of the enemy's vessel be entitled to freight from the owner of the neutral goods found on board and restored. As a general rule, he is not entitled to freight, unless he performs the voyage and carries the goods to the port of original destination, a rule that holds notwithstanding there may have been a sale of the goods beneficial to the owner]. Under certain circumstances, too, the captor has been considered to be entitled to freight

[1] The *Twilling Riget*, 5 Robinson, 82.

[2] The *Hoop*, 1 Robinson 196, 219. The *Wilhelmina*, 2 Rob. 101, note.

[3] Story on *Prize Law*, ed. 1854, by Dr. Pratt, p. 93.

[4] The *Atlas*, 3 Robinson, 299—304, note. The *Sarah Christian*, 1 Robinson, 237. The *Mercurius*, 1 Rob. 288. The *Commercen*, 1 Wheaton's *Reports*, 382. The *Rising Sun*, 2 Rob. 104. The *Fortuna*, Edwards, 56.

even though the goods were carried to the claimant's own country and restored[1]. [So also if the captors bring the cargo to the country where the claimants ultimately designed to send it, though compelled to take a circuitous route under existing circumstances, notwithstanding the ship was actually destined to another country there to land it. Or if the cargo be brought to the same country, but not to the port of actual destination, in both these cases the captors are entitled to freight[2].] But in no other case is freight due to the captor, and the doctrine of *pro rata* freight is entirely rejected, because it would involve a prize court in a labyrinth of minute inquiries and considerations, in the endeavour to ascertain, in every case, the balance of advantage or disadvantage which an interruption and loss of the original voyage, by capture, might have produced to the owner of the goods.

The *Nereide*. In the case of the *Nereide*[3], the Supreme Court of the United States carried the principle of immunity of neutral property on board an enemy's vessel, to the extent of allowing it to be laden on board an *armed* belligerent cruiser; and it was held that the goods did not lose their neutral character, not even in consequence of resistance made by the armed vessel, provided the neutral did not aid in such armament or resistance, notwithstanding he had chartered the whole vessel, and was on board at the time of the resistance. The act of arming was the act of the belligerent party, and the neutral goods did not contribute to the armament, further than the freight, which would be paid if the vessel was unarmed, and neither the goods nor the neutral owner were chargeable for the hostile acts of the belligerent vessel, if the neutral took no part in the resistance. A contemporary decision of an opposite character, on the same point, was made by the

[1] Bynk. *Q. J. P.* B. I. ch. xii. The *Fortuna*, 4 Robinson, 278. The *Diana*, 5 Rob. 67. The *Vrow Anna Catharina*, 6 Rob. 264.

[2] The *Diana*, *ut supra*. The *Vrow Henrietta*, in 5 Rob. 75, note. See also Story on *Prize Law*, pp. 94, 95.

[3] 9 Cranch's *Reports*, 398.

English High Court of Admiralty, in the case of the *Fanny*[1]; and it was there observed, that a neutral subject was at liberty to put his goods on board the merchant vessel of a belligerent; but if he placed them on board an armed belligerent ship, he showed an intention to resist visitation and search, by means of the association, and, so far as he does this, he was presumed to adhere to the enemy, and to withdraw himself from his protection of neutrality. If a neutral chooses to take the protection of a hostile force, instead of his own neutral character, he must take (it was observed) the inconvenience with the convenience, and his property would, upon just and sound principles, be liable to condemnation along with the belligerent vessel.

The *Fanny*.

The question decided in the case of the *Nereide* is a very important one in prize law, and of infinite importance in its practical results; and it is to be regretted that the decisions of two courts of the highest character, on such a point, should have been in direct contradiction to each other. The same point afterwards arose, and was again argued, and the former decision repeated, in the case of the *Atalanta*[2]. It was observed in this latter case, that the rule of the United States was correct in principle, and the most liberal and honourable to the jurisprudence of that country. The question may, therefore, be considered there as at rest, and as having received the most authoritative decision that can be rendered by any judicial tribunal in the United States.

Mr Duer's Criticism on the case of the *Nereide*.

[On these two cases Mr Duer's remarks deserve to be quoted: he says[3], "The authority of the decision in the *Nereide*, as a just exposition of the law of nations, is greatly impaired by the dissent of a learned judge (Mr J. Story), by whom the principles and doctrines of that law are known to have been profoundly studied, and whose decisions evince his masterly knowledge of the entire

[1] 1 Dodson, 443.

[2] 3 Wheaton's *Reports*, 409.

[3] Duer on *Insurance*, Vol. I. lect. viii. § 14. p. 731.

system to which they belong." In support of his opinion, which was in accordance with the view taken by Sir Wm. Scott in the case of the *Fanny* above mentioned, Mr. J. Story referred to the cases, then recent, of American ships captured, while under British convoy, by the Danes, and condemned by the highest prize tribunal in Denmark, and cited with approval the grounds of the decision in the case of the *Samson Barney*[1]. In spite therefore of the decision of the rest of the court in the *Nereide,* and in spite of Mr J. Johnson's elaborate vindication of that decision in his judgment in the *Atalanta,* Mr Duer doubts whether any change will be produced in the conviction that the arguments of Sir William Scott and Mr J. Story are fitted to impress[2]. It should, however, be noticed that the American government pressed their claims upon that of Denmark for the condemnation of the American ships above referred to. These claims, after a peremptory refusal in the first instance, and a long and elaborate argument in support of a renewal of them, were settled by a treaty between the two countries in 1830, by which the latter power agreed to indemnify the American claimants for the loss of their property by the payment of a fixed sum, to be apportioned by commissioners appointed by the American government[3].]

[1] Quoted in the *Maria,* 1 Robinson, 346.

[2] 1 Duer, p. 774.

[3] For a full account of the transaction, and the arguments involved in it, see Wheaton's *Elements,* Vol. II. Part 4. ch. iii. § 32. pp. 858—867. Laurence's ed. of 1863.

## CHAPTER IX.

### OF RESTRICTIONS UPON NEUTRAL TRADE.

---

THE principal restriction which the law of nations imposes on the trade of neutrals, is the prohibition to furnish the belligerent parties with warlike stores, and other articles which are directly auxiliary to warlike purposes[1]. Such goods are denominated contraband of war, but in the attempt to define them the authorities vary, or are deficient in precision, and the subject has long been a fruitful source of dispute between neutral and belligerent nations. For whilst, on the one hand, the list is an extensive one, and the catalogue has varied so much at times, as to make it very difficult to assign the reason for the variation[2], on the other, it is scarcely possible to lay down any general test that shall enable us at once to say what are, or are not, contraband articles. Contraband.

In the time of Grotius, some persons contended for the rigour of war, and others for the freedom of commerce. As neutral nations are willing to seize the opportunity which war presents, of becoming carriers for the belligerent powers, it is natural that they should desire to diminish the list of contraband as much as possible. Grotius distin- Ancient rules on the subject.

[1] Vattel, Bk. I. ch. viii. § 90. On this subject generally the reader may refer with advantage to Ortolan, *Règles Internationales*, &c. T. II. Liv. III. ch. vi. especially for an historical account of the French regulations on the subject to Cauchy, *Droit Marit. Intern.* T. II. ch. vi. § 3, and to Massé, *Droit Commercial*, T. I. Liv. II. ch. ii. § 11. Art. II.

[2] The *Jonge Margaretha*, 1 Robinson, 189.

guishes[1] between things which are useful only in war, as arms and ammunition, things which serve merely for pleasure, and things which are of a mixed nature, and useful both in peace and war. He agrees with other writers in prohibiting neutrals from carrying articles of the first kind to the enemy, as well as in permitting the second kind to be carried. As to articles of the third class, which are of indiscriminate use in peace and war, as money, provisions, ships and naval stores, he says that they are sometimes lawful articles of neutral commerce, and sometimes not; and the question will depend upon circumstances existing at the time. They would be contraband if carried to a besieged town, camp, or port. In a naval war, it is admitted, that ships, and materials for ships, become contraband, and horses and saddles may be included[2]. Vattel speaks with some want of precision, and only says, in general terms[3], that commodities particularly used in war are contraband, such as arms, military and naval stores, timber, horses, and even provisions, in certain junctures, when there are hopes of reducing the enemy by famine. Loccenius[4], and some other authorities referred to by Valin, consider provisions as generally contraband; but Valin and Pothier insist that they are not so, either by the law of France or the common law of nations, unless carried to besieged or blockaded places[5]. The marine ordinance of Louis XIV.[6] included horses, and their equipage, transported for military service, within the list of contraband, because they were necessary to war equipments, and this is, doubtless, the general rule. They are included in the restricted list of contraband articles mentioned in the treaty between the United States and Colombia in 1825. Valin says, that naval stores have been regarded as contraband from the beginning of the last century, and the Eng-

[1] Bk. III. ch. i. § 5.
[2] Rutherforth's *Inst.* Bk. II. ch. ix.
[3] Bk. III. ch. vii. § 112.
[4] *De Jure Maritimo*, Lib. I. c. iv. n. 9.
[5] Valin's *Com.* T. II. p. 264. Pothier, *de Propriété*, No. 104.
[6] *Des Prises*, Art. II.

lish prize law is very explicit on this point. Naval stores, and materials for ship building, and even corn, grain, and victuals of all sorts, going to the dominions of the enemy, were declared contraband by an ordinance of Charles I. in 1626[1]. Sailcloth is now held to be universally contraband, even on a destination to ports of mere mercantile naval equipment[2]; and in the case of the *Maria*[3], it was held, that tar, pitch, and hemp, and whatever other materials went to the construction and equipment of vessels of war, were contraband by the modern law of nations, though, formerly, when the hostilities of Europe were less naval than at the present day, they were of a disputable nature. The executive government of the United States has frequently conceded, that the materials for the building, equipment, and armament of ships of war, as timber and naval stores, were contraband[4]. But it does not seem that ship timber is, *in se*, in all cases, to be considered a contraband article, though destined to an enemy's port. In the case of the Austrian vessel *Il Volante*, captured by the French privateer *L'Etoile de Bonaparte*, and which was carrying ship timber to Messina, an enemy's port, it was held, by the Council of Prizes at Paris, in 1807, upon the opinion of the Advocate General, M. Collet Descotils, that the ship timber in that case was not contraband of war, it being ship timber of an ordinary character, and not exclusively applicable to the building of ships of war[5].

Questions of contraband were much discussed during the continuance of the neutral character maintained by the United States, in the furious war between England War of 1793.

1 Robinson's *Collec. Mar.* p. 63.

2 The *Neptunus*, 3 Rob. 108.

3 1 Rob. 287, Phil. ed.

4 Mr Randolph's *Letter to M. Adet*, July 6th, 1795, *American State Papers*, Vol. II. pp. 259—264. Mr Pickering's *Letter* to Mr Pinckney, January 16th, 1797, *American State Papers*, Vol. II. pp. 114—187. *Letter* of Messrs. Pinckney, Marshall, and Gerry, to the French Minister, January 27th, 1798, *American State Papers*, Vol. IV. pp. 27—81.

5 *Répertoire universel et raisonné de Jurisprudence*, par M. Merlin, Tom. IX. tit. *Prise Maritime*, § 3, Art. III. and *Traité des prises Maritimes*, par Pistoye et Duverdy, T. I. Tit. VI. ch. ii. § 3, p. 409.

and France, commencing in 1793, and the authorities in the United States professed to be governed by the modern usage of nations on this point[1]. The national convention of France, on the 9th of May, 1793, decreed, that neutral vessels, laden with provisions, destined to an enemy's port, should be arrested, and carried into France; and one of the earliest acts of England, in that war[2], was to detain all neutral vessels going to France, and laden with corn, Provisions. meal, or flour. It was insisted, on the part of England[3], that, by the law of nations, all provisions were to be considered as contraband, in the case where the depriving the enemy of those supplies was one of the means employed to reduce him to reasonable terms of peace; and that the actual situation of France was such, as to lead to that mode of distressing her, inasmuch as she had armed almost the whole labouring class of her people, for the purpose of commencing and supporting hostilities against all the governments of Europe. This claim on the part of England was promptly and perseveringly resisted by the United States; and they contended, that corn, flour, and meal, being the produce of the soil, and labour of the country, were not contraband of war, unless carried to a place actually invested[4]. The treaty of commerce with England, in 1794, in the list of contraband, stated, that whatever materials served directly to the building and equipment of vessels, with the exception of unwrought iron, and fir planks, should be considered contraband, and liable to confiscation; but the treaty left the question of provisions open and unsettled, and neither power was understood to

[1] President's *Proclamation of Neutrality*, April 22nd, 1793, *Statesman's Manual*, Vol. I. p. 123.

[2] *Instructions* of 8th June, 1793. Martens' *Récueil des Traités*, T. v. p. 596.

[3] Mr Hammond's *Letter* to Mr Jefferson, September 12th, 1793, and his *Letter* to Mr Randolph, 11th April, 1794, *American State Papers*, Vol. I. p. 398, and Vol. II. p. 16.

[4] Mr Jefferson's *Letter* to Mr Pinckney, September 7th, 1793, and Mr Randolph's *Letter* to Mr Hammond, May 1st, 1794, *American State Papers*, Vol. I. p. 392, and Vol. II. p. 19.

have relinquished the construction of the law of nations which it had assumed. The treaty admitted, that provisions were not generally contraband, but might become so, according to the existing law of nations, in certain cases, and those cases were not defined. It was only stipulated, by way of relaxation of the penalty of the law, that whenever provisions were contraband, the captors, or their government, should pay to the owner the full value of the articles, together with the freight, and a reasonable profit. The American government has repeatedly admitted, that, as far as that treaty enumerated contraband articles, it was declaratory of the law of nations, and that the treaty conceded nothing on the subject of contraband[1].

Doctrine of the English Admiralty as to Provisions.

The doctrine of the English admiralty, on the subject of provisions being considered contraband, was laid down very fully and clearly, in the case of the *Jonge Margaretha*[2]. It was there observed, that the catalogue of contraband had varied very much, and, sometimes, in such a manner as to make it difficult to assign the reasons of the variations, owing to particular circumstances, the history of which had not accompanied the history of the decisions. In 1673, certain articles of provision, as corn, wine, and oil, were deemed contraband, according to the judgment of a person of great knowledge and experience in the practice of the admiralty; and, in much later times, many other sorts of provisions have been condemned as contraband. In 1747 and 1748, butter, and salted fish, and rice, were condemned as contraband; and those cases show that articles of human food have been considered as contraband, when it was probable they were intended for naval or military use. The modern established rule is, that provisions are not generally contraband, but may become so, under circumstances arising out of the particular

[1] Mr Pickering's *Letter* to Mr Monroe, September 12th, 1795. His *Letter* to Mr Pinckney, January 16th, 1797. *Instructions* from the Secretary of State to the American Ministers to France, July 15th, 1797, *American State Papers*, Vol. II. p. 264, and Vol. III. pp. 457—473.

[2] 1 Rob. 190.

situation of the war, or the condition of the parties engaged in it. Among the circumstances which tend to preserve provisions from being liable to be treated as contraband, one is, that they are of the growth of the country which produces them. Another circumstance to which some indulgence is shown by the practice of nations, is when the articles are in their native and unmanufactured state. Thus, iron is treated with indulgence, though anchors and other instruments fabricated out of it, are directly contraband. Hemp is more favourably considered than cordage; and wheat is not considered as so noxious a commodity, when going to an enemy's country, as any of the final preparations of it for human use. The most important distinction is, whether the articles were intended for the ordinary use of life, or even for mercantile ships' use, or whether they were going with a highly probable destination to military use. The nature and quality of the port to which the articles are going, is not an irrational test. If the port be a general commercial one, it is presumed the articles are going for civil use, though occasionally a ship of war may be constructed in that port. But if the great predominant character of that port, like Brest in France, or Portsmouth in England, be that of a port of naval military equipment, it will be presumed that the articles were going for military use, although it is possible that the articles might have been applied to civil consumption. As it is impossible to ascertain the final use of an article *ancipitis usus,* it is not an injurious rule, which deduces the final use from the immediate destination; and the presumption of a hostile use, founded on its destination to a military port, is very much inflamed, if at the time when the articles were going, a considerable armament was notoriously preparing, to which a supply of those articles would be eminently useful.

These doctrines of the English prize law were essentially the same with that adopted by the American Congress in 1775, for they declared, that all vessels, to whomsoever belonging, carrying provisions, or other necessaries, to the British army or navy, within the colonies, should be liable to seizure and confiscation[1]. They were likewise fully adopted by the Supreme Court of the United States, when that country came to know and feel the value of belligerent rights, by becoming a party to a maritime war. In the case of the *Commercen*[2], a neutral vessel, captured by a United States cruiser, in the act of carrying provisions for the use of the British armies in Spain, the court held, that provisions, being neutral property, but the growth of the enemy's country, and destined for the supply of the enemy's military or naval force, were contraband. The court observed, that, by the modern law of nations, provisions were not generally contraband, but that they might become so on account of the particular situation of the war, or on account of their destination. If destined for the ordinary use of life, in the enemy's country, they were not contraband; but it was otherwise if destined for the army or navy of the enemy, or for his ports of military or naval equipment. And if the provisions were the growth of the enemy's country, and destined for the enemy's use, they were to be treated as contraband, and liable to forfeiture, even though the army or navy were in a neutral port, for it would be a direct interposition in the war.

This case followed the decisions of Sir William Scott, and carried the doctrine of contraband, as applied to provisions, to as great an extent. It held the voyage of the Swedish neutral so illegal, as to deserve the infliction of the penalty of loss of freight.

It is the *usus bellici* which determine an article to be contraband, and as articles come into use as implements of war, which were before innocent, there is truth in the remark, that as the means of war vary and shift from time to time, the law shifts with them; not, indeed, by the change of principles, but by a change in the application of them to new cases, and in order to meet the varying uses of war. [Such being the doctrines laid down

The usus bellicus the test.

[1] *Journals of Congress*, Vol. I. 241. [2] 1 Wheaton, 382.

in both countries on this subject, and the rational test of the contraband quality of certain articles being the nature and quality of the port of destination, it may happen that articles which in themselves are innocent may from peculiar circumstances change their nature. Now of some things there can be no doubt, their very name and appearance proclaim them contraband quality, such as warlike instruments or materials by their own nature fit to be used in war. There are however others which may be used for ordinary civil purposes as well as for war, and if it be impossible to give an exhaustive catalogue of them, the doubtful nature of articles not hitherto called contraband will be best settled by Lord Stowell's test, what is the port of destination.

Contraband quality of various articles.

The following articles have been held in several cases to be undoubtedly contraband. Pitch and tar, unless protected by treaty, or the produce of the country whence they are exported, in which case they may be purchased by the government of the captor for its own use and not confiscated. Sailcloth, hemp, not the produce of the importing country (in which case the same privilege of pre-emption is conceded), unless unfit for naval purposes. Ships constructed so as to be convertible into privateers. Anchors and other instruments converted out of iron, and masts for ships.

The quality of the following articles depends upon the port of destination. Rosin and tallow, ship timber, iron in its unmanufactured state, and in all probability coal[1]. As to provisions, their contraband quality, as we have seen, will depend not only on the test of the port of destination, but also on the circumstances arising out of the particular

[[1] See all the cases collected in Tudor's *Leading Cases on Merc. Law*, pp. 188 and 739. As to coal, in answer to an enquiry whether the Queen's Proclamation of the 13th May, 1859, contemplated coal as contraband, it was said "The Prize Court of the captor is the competent tribunal to decide whether coal is or is not contraband of war and it is obviously impossible for her Majesty's government as a neutral sovereign to anticipate the result of such decision. It appears however to Her Majesty's government that having regard to the present state of naval armaments coal may in

situation of the war, or the conditions of the parties engaged in that war; it is therefore useless to attempt to catalogue them.]

Confiscation the consequence of carrying contraband.

When goods are once clearly shown to be contraband, confiscation to the captor is the natural consequence. This is the practice in all cases, as to the article itself. excepting provisions; and as to them, when they become contraband, the ancient and strict right of forfeiture is softened down to a right of pre-emption, on reasonable terms[1]. But, generally, to stop contraband goods, would, as Vattel observes[2], prove an ineffectual relief, especially at sea. The penalty of confiscation is applied, in order that the fear of loss might operate as a check on the avidity for gain, and deter the neutral merchant from supplying the enemy with contraband articles. The ancient practice was, to seize the contraband goods, and keep them, on paying the value. But the modern practice of confiscation is far more agreeable to the mutual duties of nations, and more adapted to the preservation of their rights. It is a general understanding, grounded on true principles, that the powers at war may seize and confiscate all contraband goods, without any complaint on the part of the neutral merchant, and without any imputation of a breach of neutrality in the neutral sovereign himself[3]. It was contended, on the part of the French nation, in 1796, that neutral governments were bound to restrain their subjects from selling or exporting articles, contraband of war, to the belligerent powers. But it was successfully shown, on the part of the United States, that neutrals may lawfully sell, at home, to a belligerent purchaser, or

many cases be rightly held to be contraband of war, and therefore that all who engage in the traffic must do so at a risk from which her Majesty's Government cannot relieve them (*The Jurist*, 1859, Vol. v. Part II. p. 203), see also *Parliamentary Debates*, House of Lords, May 26, 1861, and *Edinburgh Review*, Vol. C. p. 203.]

[1] Case of the *Haabet*, 2 Rob. 182, and see De Cussy, *Droit Maritime*, Liv. I. Tit. III. § 18.

[2] Bk. III. ch. vii. § 113.

[3] Vattel, Bk. III. ch. vii. § 113.

carry, themselves, to the belligerent powers, contraband articles, subject to the right of seizure, *in transitu*[1]. This right has since been explicitly declared by the judicial authority of that country[2]. The right of the neutral to transport, and of the hostile power to seize, are conflicting rights, and neither party can charge the other with a criminal act[3].

Contraband articles infectious.

Contraband articles are said to be of an infectious nature, and they contaminate the whole cargo belonging to the same owners. The innocence of any particular article is not usually admitted, to exempt it from the general confiscation. By the ancient law of Europe, the ship, also, was liable to condemnation; and such a penalty was deemed just, and supported by the general analogies of law, for the owner of the ship had engaged it in an unlawful commerce, and contraband goods are seized and condemned *ex delicto*. But the modern practice of the courts of admiralty, since the age of Grotius, is milder; and the act of carrying contraband articles is attended only with the loss of freight and expenses, unless the ship belongs to the owner of the contraband articles or the carrying of them has been connected with malignant and aggravating circumstances; and among those circumstances, a false destination and false papers are considered as the most heinous. In those cases, and in all cases of fraud in the owner of the ship, or of his agent, the

[1] M. Adet's *Letter* to Mr Pickering, March 11th, 1796, *American State Papers*, Vol. II. pp. 438—451. Mr Pickering's *Letter* to M. Adet, January 20th, and May 25th, 1796, *American State Papers*, Vol. II. pp. 446—461, and 460—467. *Circular Letter* of the Secretary of the Navy to the Collectors August 4th, 1793, query 1798; see *Statesman's Man.* Vol. I. p. 221, and *American State Papers*, Vol. IV. p. 152. [In confirmation of this statement, the reader is referred to the arguments on behalf of the claimants in the case of the *Peterhoff*, heard and decided in the United States Prize Court at New York, July 1863. See Report of that case (published by L. H. Biglow, New York), p. 225.]

[2] Richardson *v.* Marine Ins. Company, 6 *Mass. Rep.* 113. The *Santissima Trinidad*, 7 Wheaton, 283, and see President Pierce's message, Dec. 31st, 1855, *Statesman's Manual*, Vol. III. pp. 2111, 2112.

[3] See the remarks of Historicus on the whole of this passage, and in condemnation of Monsieur Hautefeuille's absurd doctrine on this subject. *Letters* of Historicus (1863) p. 129.

penalty is carried beyond the refusal of freight and expenses, and is extended to the confiscation of the ship, and the innocent parts of the cargo[1]. [Both ship and cargo too are liable to confiscation on the homeward as well as the outward voyage, notwithstanding she may have discharged and loaded again several times in the intermediate ports, and is at the time of capture clear of contraband on board[2].] This is now the established doctrine; but it is sometimes varied by treaty, in like manner as all the settled principles and usages of nations are subject to conventional modification[3].

Law of blockades.

A neutral may also forfeit the immunities of his national character by violations of blockade; and, among the rights of belligerents, there is none more clear and incontrovertible, or more just and necessary in the application, than that which gives rise to the law of blockade. Bynkershoeck[4] says it is founded on the principles of natural reason, as well as on the usage of nations; and Grotius[5] considers the carrying of supplies to a besieged town, or a blockaded port, as an offence exceedingly aggravated and injurious. They both agree that the neutral may be dealt

[1] Bynk. *Q. J. Pub.* Bk. I. ch. xii. and xiv. Heinec. *de Nav. ob. Vect. Merc. vetit. Com.* ch. ii. § 6. *Opera*, T. II. 348. The *Staadt Embden*, 1 Rob. 23. The *Jonge Tobias*, 1 Rob. 277. The *Franklin*, 3 Rob. 217. The *Neutralitat*, 3 Rob. 295. The *Edward*, 4 Rob. 68. The *Ranger*, 6 Rob. 125. The *Ernst Merek*, Spinks's *Prize Cases*, p. 103. The *Mercurius*, 1 Rob. 288. The *Ringende Jacob*, 1 Rob. 89 [See all these cases most carefully examined and ably commented on in the American case of the *Stephen Hart*, decided in the United States District Court of Admiralty, and reported in the year 1863, *Reports of Maritime Law Cases*, Vol. II. Part II. p. 89. (See Part III. p. 88.) London 1864. The reader will find all the law on the subject of contraband so carefully and ably arranged in Mr Tudor's excellent work already cited, *Leading Cases in Mercantile Law* in the note to the case of the *Jonge Margaretha*, pp. 737—748, that it is quite sufficient here to refer to those pages.]

[2] The *Margaret*, 1 Acton, 333. *Santissima Coraçao de Maria*, 2 Acton, 91. The *Nancy*, 3 Rob. 122. The *Charlotte*, 6 Rob. 386 note.

[3] In the treaty between the United States and the Republic of Colombia, it is provided, that contraband articles shall not affect the rest of the cargo, or the vessel, for it is declared that they shall be left free to the owner.

[4] *Q. J. P.* Bk. I. ch. iv. § 11.

[5] Bk. III. ch. i. § 5.

with severely; and Vattel says, he may be treated as an enemy[1]. The law of blockade is, however, so harsh and severe in its operation, that, in order to apply it, the fact of the actual blockade must be established by clear and unequivocal evidence; the neutral must have had due previous notice of its existence; the squadron allotted for the purposes of its execution, must be fully competent to cut off all communication with the interdicted place or port; and the neutral must have been guilty of some act of violation, either by going in, or attempting to enter, or by coming out with a cargo laden after the commencement of the blockade. The failure of either of the points requisite to establish the existence of a legal blockade, amounts to an entire defeasance of the measure, even though the notification of the blockade had issued from the authority of the government itself[2].

Blockade defined.

A blockade must be existing in point of fact, and, in order to constitute that existence, there must be a power present to enforce it. All decrees and orders, declaring extensive coasts, and whole countries, in a state of blockade, without the presence of an adequate naval force to support it, are manifestly illegal and void, and have no sanction in public law. The ancient authorities all referred to a strict and actual siege or blockade. The language of Grotius[3] is *oppidum obsessum vel Portus clausus,* the investing power therefore must be able to apply its force to every point of the blockaded place, so as to render it dangerous to attempt to enter, nor is there any blockade of that part where its power cannot be brought to bear[4].

[1] Bk. III. ch. vii. § 117.

[2] The *Betsey,* 1 Rob. 93. 1 Chitty *on Commercial Law,* 450. *Letter* from Mr Clay the Secretary of State to Mr Tudor, dated October 23rd 1827.

[3] Bk. III. ch. i. § 5.

[4] The *Mercurius,* 1 Rob. 82. The *Betsey,* 1 Rob. 78. An important English case not reported but referred to in the *Mercurius,* is that of the West Indian Blockade of 1794, decided by the Lords of Appeal and particularly commented on in the *Edinburgh Review,* Vol. XIX. p. 299. The *Stert,* 4 Rob. 65. The *Arthur,* 1 Dodson, 425. *Letter* of the Secretary of the Navy to Commodore Preble, February 4th, 1804.

The definition of a blockade given by the convention of the Baltic powers in 1780, and again in 1801, and by the ordinance of Congress in 1781, required that there should be actually a number of vessels stationed near enough to the port to make the entry apparently dangerous. The government of the United States have uniformly insisted, that the blockade should be effective by the presence of a competent force, stationed, and present, at or near the entrance of the port, having protested with great energy against the application of the right of seizure and confiscation to ineffectual or fictitious blockades[1]. [Whilst by the 4th article of the declaration attached to the Treaty of Paris, bearing date 15th April, 1856, the neutrality Powers stipulated that blockades, in order to be binding, must be effective; that is to say, maintained by a force sufficient really to prevent access to the coast of the enemy.]

Accidental absence of blockading squadron.

The occasional absence of the blockading squadron, produced by accident, as in the case of a storm, and when the station is resumed with due diligence, does not suspend the blockade, provided the suspension, and the reason of it, be known; and the law considers an attempt to take advantage of such an accidental removal, as an attempt to break the blockade, and as a mere fraud[2]. The American government seemed disposed to admit the continuance of the blockade in such a case[3]; and the language of the judicial authorities in New York, has been in favour of the solidity and justness of the English doctrine of blockade on this point[4]. But if the blockade be raised by

[1] Mr King's *Letter* to Lord Grenville, May 23rd, 1799, *American State Papers*, Vol. VII. p. 391. Mr Marshall's *Letter* to Mr King, September 20th, 1800, *American State Papers*, Vol. VII. p. 391. Mr Madison's *Letter* to Mr Pinckney, October 25th, 1801. *Letter* of the Secretary of the Navy to Commodore Preble, February 4th, 1804. Mr Pinckney's *Letter* to Lord Wellesley, Jan. 14th, 1811, *American State Papers*, Vol. VIII. pp. 139—147.

[2] The *Frederick Molke*, 1 Rob. 72. The *Columbia*, 1 Rob. 130. The *Juffrow Maria Schroeder*, 3 Rob. 155. The *Hoffnung*, 6 Rob. 116, 7.

[3] Mr Marshall's *Letter* to Mr King, September 20th, 1800.

[4] Radcliff, J. 2 Johnson's *Cases in the Supreme Court*, 187. Radcliff *v.* U. Ins. Co. 7 Johnson's *Rep.* 38, and 53.

the enemy, or by applying the naval force, or part of it, though only for a time, to other objects, or by the mere remissness of the cruisers, the commerce of neutrals to the place ought to be free. The presence of a sufficient force is the natural criterion by which the neutral is enabled to ascertain the existence of the blockade. He looks only to the matter of fact, and if the blockading squadron is removed when he arrives before the port, and he is ignorant of the cause of the removal, or if he be not ignorant, and the cause be not an accidental one, but voluntary, or produced by an enemy, he may enter, without being answerable for a breach of the blockade. When a blockade is raised voluntarily, or by a superior force, it puts an end to it absolutely; and if it be resumed, neutrals must be charged with notice *de novo*, and without reference to the former state of things, before they can be involved in the guilt of a violation of the blockade[1].

Egress as well as ingress forbidden.

The object of a blockade is not merely to prevent the importation of supplies, but to prevent export as well as import, and to cut off all communication of commerce with the blockaded port. The act of egress is as culpable as that of ingress, if it be done fraudulently, [though if there be merely a maritime blockade of a place, it will not be violated by any egress or communication by means of inland navigation to which the blockade is not applied[2].] A ship therefore coming out of a blockaded port is, in the first instance, liable to seizure, and, in order to obtain a release, the party must give satisfactory proof of the innocency of his intention. But, according to modern usage, a blockade does not rightfully extend to a neutral vessel found in port when the blockade was instituted, nor prevent her coming out with the cargo, *bona fide* purchased,

[1] Williams *v.* Smith, 2 Caines, 1. *Letter* of the Secretary of State to Mr King, September 20th, 1800, *American State Papers*, Vol. VII. p. 391. The *Hoffnung*, 6 Rob. 112. The *Tisketeir*, 6 Rob. 65.

[2] Bynk. *Q. J. P.* Bk. I. ch. iv. The *Frederick Molke*, 1 Rob. 72. The *Neptunus*, 1 Rob. 144. The *Vrow Judith*, 1 Rob. 126. The *Stert*, 4 Rob. 65.

and laden on board before the commencement of the blockade. [If she afterwards takes on board a cargo, it is a fraudulent act, and a violation of the blockade[1].] The modern practice does not require that the place should be invested by land as well as by sea, in order to constitute a legal blockade; and, as we have seen, if a place be blockaded by sea only, it is no violation of belligerent rights for the neutral to carry on commerce with it by inland communications[2].

Notice of blockade necessary.

It is absolutely necessary that the neutral should have had due notice of the blockade, in order to affect him with the penal consequences of a violation of it. This information may be communicated to him in two ways: either actually, by a formal notice from the blockading power; or constructively, by notice to his government, or by the notoriety of the fact. It is immaterial in what way the neutral comes to the knowledge of the blockade. If the blockade actually exists, and he has knowledge of it, he is bound not to violate it. A notice to a foreign government, is a notice to all the individuals of that nation, and they are not permitted to aver ignorance of it, because it is the duty of the neutral government to communicate the notice to their people. [Therefore a neutral master cannot be allowed to aver against a notification of blockade that he is ignorant of it. If he really be so, it may be a subject of representation to his own government, and may raise a claim of compensation from them, but it can be no plea in the court of the belligerent[3].] In the case of a blockade without regular notice, notice in fact is generally requisite; and there is this difference between a blockade regularly

[1] The *Betsey*, 1 Rob. 78. The *Vrow Judith*, 1 Rob. 151. The *Comet*, 1 Edw. 32. The *Neptunus*, 1 Rob. 170. The *Johanna Maria*, Spinks, 307, Cremidi *v.* Powell, 11 Moore, *P. C. C.* 116. Oliera *v.* Union Ins. Com. 3 Wheaton's *Reports*, 183.

[2] The *Ocean*, 3 Rob. 297. The *Stert*, *ibid.* 299, note. *Letter* of the Secretary of State to Mr King, Sept. 20th, 1800, *American State Papers*, Vol. VII. p. 391.

[3] The *Neptunus*, 2 Rob. 111. The *Adelaide*, 2 Rob. 111, n. The *Spes and Irene*, 5 Rob. 76. The *Welvaart van Pillaw*, 2 Rob. 131.

notified, and one without such notice: that, in the former case, the act of sailing for the blockaded place, with an intent to evade it, or to enter contingently, amounts, from the very commencement of the voyage, to a breach of the blockade, for the port is to be considered as closed up, until the blockade be formally revoked, or actually raised; whereas, in the latter case, of a blockade *de facto*, the ignorance of the party as to its continuance, may be received as an excuse for sailing to the blockaded place, on a doubtful and provisional destination[1]. The question of notice is a question of evidence, to be determined by the facts applicable to the case. The notoriety of a blockade is of itself sufficient notice of it to vessels lying within the blockaded port. In the case of the *Adelaide*[2], it was the doctrine of the English admiralty, that a notification given to one state, must be presumed, after a reasonable time, to have reached the subjects of neighbouring states, and it affects them with the knowledge of the fact, on just grounds of evidence. And after the blockade is once established, and due notice received, either actually or constructively, the neutral is not permitted to go to the very station of the blockading force, under pretence of inquiring whether the blockade had terminated, because this would lead to fraudulent attempts to evade it, and would amount, in practice, to a universal license to attempt to enter, and, on being prevented, to claim the liberty of going elsewhere. Some relaxation was very reasonably given to this rule, in its application to distant voyages from America; and ships sailing for Europe before knowledge of the blockade reached them, were entitled to notice, even at the blockaded port. If they sailed after notice, they might sail on a contingent destination for the blockaded port, with the purpose of calling for information at some European port, and be allowed the benefit of such a contingent destination, to be rendered definite by the information. But in no case is the information, as to the existence of the

Question of notice, one of evidence.

[1] The *Columbia*, 1 Rob. 130. The *Neptunus*, 2 Rob. 110.
[2] 2 Rob. 113, *in notis*.

blockade, to be sought at the mouth of the port[1]. [It is scarcely necessary to say that the notice of the blockade must not be more extensive than the blockade itself. If therefore a belligerent has proclaimed a blockade of several ports, when he has in truth only blockaded one, a neutral is at liberty to disregard such a notice, and is not liable to the penalties attending a breach of blockade for afterwards attempting to enter the port which really is blockaded[2].]

A neutral cannot be permitted to place himself in the vicinity of the blockaded port, if his situation be so near that he may, with impunity, break the blockade whenever he pleases, and slip in without obstruction. If that were to be permitted, it would be impossible that any blockade could be maintained. It is a presumption, almost *de jure*, that the neutral, if found on the interdicted waters, goes there with an intention to break the blockade; and it would require very clear and satisfactory evidence to repel the presumption of a criminal intent[3].

The judicial decisions in England, and in the United States, have given great precision to the law of blockade, by the application of it to particular cases, and by the extent, and clearness, and equity of their illustrations. They are distinguished, likewise, for general coincidence and harmony in their principles. [Of those principles none is clearer than that which decides upon the offender's guilt or innocence, according to his knowledge of the existence of the blockade. It is therefore a matter of primary importance, first, to ascertain by whose authority a blockade is established. Now a declaration of blockade being a high act of sovereign authority, it cannot in general be either

By whose authority is a blockade established?

[1] The *Spes* and *Irene*, 5 Rob. 76.

[2] The *Henrick* and *Maria*, 1 Rob. 148. Northcote *v.* Douglas, 10 Moore, *P. C. C.* 59.

[3] The *Neutralitat*, 6 Rob. 30. The *Charlotte Christine*, ibid. 101. The *Gute Erwartung*, ibid. 182. Bynk. *Q. J. Pub.* Bk. I. ch. xi. The *Arthur*, 1 Edw. *Rep.* 202. Radcliff *v.* U. Ins. Co. 7 Johnson's *Rep.* 47. Fitzsimmons *v.* Newport Ins. Co. 4 Cranch, 185.

imposed or extended by a commander without special authority[1], but as it may happen that hostilities are carried on in such distant parts of the world, that the sovereign power cannot be at hand to superintend and direct the course of operations; then, under such circumstances, a commander may reasonably be supposed to carry with him a portion of delegated sovereign authority, sufficient to provide for the exigencies of the service in which he is employed. Hence a blockade, imposed by him as a necessary means of more effectually reducing the enemy, would be to all intents and purposes effective, and must be observed[2].] That being so, another doctrine of equal weight follows upon it. For all the cases admit, that the neutral must be chargeable with knowledge, either actual or constructive, of the existence of the blockade, and with an intent, and with some attempt, to break it, before he is to suffer the penalty of a violation of it. The evidence of that intent, and of the overt act, will greatly vary, according to circumstances; and the conclusion to be drawn from those circumstances will depend, in some degree, upon the character and judgment of the prize courts; but the true principles which ought to govern have rarely been a matter of dispute. The fact of clearing out or sailing for a blockaded port, is, in itself, innocent, unless it be accompanied with knowledge of the blockade. Such a vessel, not possessed of such previous knowledge, is to be first warned of the fact, and a subsequent attempt to enter constitutes the breach. This was the provision in the treaty with England in 1794, and it has been declared in other cases, and is considered to be a correct exposition of the law of nations[3].

Intent as well as an attempt to break blockade necessary.

Is sailing for a blockaded port an attempt?

It has been a question in the courts of the United States, whether they ought to admit the law of the En-

[1] The *Henrick and Maria*, 1 Rob. 148, and 6 Rob. 138, n. (*a*).

[2] The *Rolla*, 6 Rob. 364, 366.

[3] Fitzsimmons *v*. Newport Ins. Co. 4 Cranch, 185. British Instructions to their fleets on the West India station, 5th of January, 1804. *Letter* of the Secretary of the Navy to Commodore Preble, February 4th, 1804. Philips *on Insurance*, 459, Art. 832.

glish prize courts, that sailing for a blockaded port, knowing it to be blockaded, was, in itself, an attempt, and an act sufficient to charge the party with a breach of the blockade, without reference to the distance between the port of departure and the port invested, or to the extent of the voyage performed when the vessel was arrested[1]. But in *Yeaton* v. *Fry*[2], the Supreme Court of the United States coincided essentially with the doctrine of the English prize courts; for they held, that sailing from Tobago for Curraçoa, knowing the latter to be blockaded, was a breach of the blockade; and, according to the opinion of Mr Justice Story, in the case of the *Nereide*[3], the act of sailing with an intent to break a blockade, is a sufficient breach to authorize confiscation. The offence continues, although, at the moment of capture, the vessel be by stress of weather driven in a direction from the port, for the hostile intention still remains unchanged. The distance, or proximity of the two ports, would certainly have an effect upon the equity of the application of the rule. A Dutch ordinance, in 1630, declared, that vessels bound to the blockaded ports of Flanders, were liable to confiscation, though found at a distance from them, unless they had voluntarily altered the voyage before coming in sight of the port; and Bynkershoek contends for the reasonableness of the order[4]. What that distance must be is not defined; and if the ports be not very wide apart, the act of sailing for the blockaded port may reasonably be deemed evidence of a breach of it, and an overt act of fraud upon the belligerent rights. [The case of the *Stephen Hart*[5], very recently decided in the prize courts of the United States, is not only pertinent to this part of our subject, but bears upon the

Case of the *Stephen Hart.*

[1] Fitzsimmons *v.* Newport Ins. Co. 4 Cranch, 185. Voss and Graves *v.* U. Ins. Co. 2 Johnson's *Cases*, 180. 469.

[2] 5 Cranch, 335.

[3] 9 Cranch, 440. 446.

[4] *Q. J. P.* Bk. I. ch. xi. 5 Rob. 326. *in notis.*

[5] See the case reported at full length in Vol. II. of *Maritime Cases*, pp. 73—89, London, October, 1864; and see also the case of the *Peterhoff* above mentioned, which vessel was condemned (*inter alia*), for that though ostensibly on a voyage between the neutral ports of London and Matamoras

rule which lays down the *usus bellicus* as the test of the contraband nature of goods. The *Stephen Hart*, it appears, was captured as lawful prize of war by the United States vessel of war *Supply*, off the northern coast of Florida, when about 25 miles from key west. Her cargo was a large and valuable one of a contraband quality, viz. arms and munitions of war, uniforms, cloth, boots, &c. This cargo she had loaded in England, her destination being Cardenas. And the main question for the court to decide was, whether she was attempting to introduce contraband goods into the enemy's territory by breach of blockade. It was urged, among other points, by the claimants against the libellants, that if a neutral vessel with a cargo belonging to neutrals be in fact on a voyage from one neutral port to another, as was the case here, she cannot be seized and condemned as lawful prize, though laden with contraband of war, unless it be determined that she was actually destined to a port of the enemy upon the voyage in which she was seized, or unless taken in the act of violating a blockade. To that the libellants replied, that if the facts should turn out to be, as they maintained they were, that the cargo was entirely contraband, and was destined, when the ship left London, to be delivered to the enemy, either directly by being carried into an enemy's port, or indirectly by being transshipped at Cardenas to another vessel; and that the papers were simulated and fraudulent in respect to destination and cargo, then the vessel would be properly subject to condemnation. The court, in a very long and elaborate judgment in decreeing condemnation, having based its decision upon the instructions delivered to the United States Naval Commanders of the 18th August, 1862, noticed, with approval, and, as by way of confirmation, the following documents: 1st, Earl Russell's statement in the House of Lords, 1863, as to the profitable nature of block-

Judgment of the court.

she was laden with a cargo composed largely of contraband goods destined to be delivered either directly or indirectly by transshipment to the enemy's port and market and for the enemy's use.

ade running, and the use made of Nassau for that purpose; 2ndly, Sir R. Palmer's statement in the House of Commons, 29th June, 1863, respecting the cases of the *Dolphin* and the *Pearl*, captured while sailing from Liverpool to Nassau; and 3rdly, to the letter from the Foreign Office, addressed by Earl Russell to the owners of the *Peterhoff*, and bearing date the 3rd April, 1863; and then laid down the following principles as the rules by which the prize courts of the United States would be guided. First, with reference to the broad issue, whether the adventure of the *Stephen Hart* was the honest voyage of a neutral vessel with neutral goods from one neutral port to another, or a simulated voyage with a contraband cargo for the enemy's use; the court said, the commerce in such a case is in the destination and intended use of the property, not in the incidental ancillary and temporary voyage; and the question must turn, not on whether the vessel is documented for and sailing upon a voyage from one neutral port to another, nor whether the immediate destination of the goods is to a port of the enemy[1], but the true test is this, "Are the contraband goods destined for sale or consumption in the neutral market, or is the direct and intended object of their transportation to supply the enemy with them[2]?" In the second place, the court held that the division of a continuous transportation of contraband goods into several intermediate voyages cannot make any of the parts of the entire transportation a lawful transport.

Thirdly, it was ruled that if the guilty intention existed when the goods left their own port, such guilty intention cannot be obliterated by the innocent intention of shipping at a neutral port in the way[3].

And, lastly, the court ruled that such voyages were

[1] Halleck on *International Law*, ch. vi. § 11. p. 576.

[2] Duer on *Insurance*, 630. The *Commercen*, 1 Wheaton's *Report*, 388, 389.

[3] Halleck, p. 504. 2 Wildman on *International Law*, p. 20. *Jonge Pieter*, 4 Rob. 79. The *Maria*, 5 Rob. 325.

not separate and distinct but part of one unit, forming one entire transaction[1].]

A relaxation of the rule has been required and granted in the case of distant voyages, such as those across the Atlantic, and the vessel is allowed to sail on a contingent destination for a blockaded port, subject to the duty of subsequent enquiry at suitable places[2]. The ordinance of Congress of 1781, seems to have conceded this point to the extent of the English rule, for it made it lawful to take and condemn all vessels, of all nations, "destined to any such port," without saying any thing of notice or proximity[3].

Consequence of breach of blockade.

The consequence of a breach of blockade is the confiscation of the ship; and the cargo is always, *prima facie*, implicated in the guilt of the owner, or master of the ship; with whom it lies to remove the presumption, that the vessel was going in for the benefit of the cargo, and with the direction of the owner[4]. Where, therefore, as in the case of the *Mercurius*, it may appear that the shippers at the time of shipment could not have known of the blockade, though the ship be condemned the cargo will

1 The *Nancy*, 3 Rob. 122. The *United States*, Stewart's *Admiralty Reports*, 116.

2 5 Rob. 76. 6 Cranch, 29. Sperry *v.* The Delaware Ins. Co. 2 *Wash. Cir. R.* 243. Naylor *v.* Taylor, 9 B. & Cress. 718.

3 *Journals of Congress*, Vol. VII. p. 186. The mere act of sailing to a blockaded port is not an offence if there was no premeditated design of breaking the blockade, though it should be found to continue when the vessel arrives off the port. See the opinion of Sir W. Scott in the case of the *Shepherdess*, 5 Rob. 264, and of Lord Tenterden in Naylor *v.* Taylor, 9 Bk. C. 718, and of Tyndal, *L. C. J.* in Medeiros *v.* Hill, 8 Bingham, 231. [Mr Maclachlan has pointed out with considerable acumen, and very forcibly, that the doctrine here stated as drawn from Chief Justice Tindal's doctrine, is neither consonant with the received doctrines of international law, nor warranted by Sir W. Scott's language in the *Shepherdess*, for in truth the test is, not whether there was no premeditated design of breaking the blockade, but whether there was a knowledge of the existence of the blockade at the time of sailing. According to Mr Maclachlan it is a matter for strong doubt whether the decision in Medeiros *v.* Hill can hereafter be followed, and certainly there is very much in favour of his view.]

4 The *Mercurius*, 1 Rob. 67. The *Columbia*, Ibid. 130. The *Neptunus*, 3 Rob. 173. The *Alexander*, 4 Rob. 93. The *Exchange*, 1 Edw. 39.

be restored, but when at the time of shipment the blockade either is or might be known to the owners of the cargo, who may therefore possibly be aware of an intention of violating the blockade, they will be considered as concluded by the illegal act of the master, although done without their privity, or perhaps contrary to their wishes[1]. The old doctrine was much more severe, and often inflicted, not merely a forfeiture of the property taken, but imprisonment, and other personal punishment[2]; but the modern, and milder usage, has confined the penalty to the confiscation of the ship and goods. If a ship has contracted guilt by a breach of blockade, the offence is not discharged until the end of the voyage. The penalty never travels on with the vessel further than to the end of the return voyage; and if she is taken in any part of that voyage, she is taken *in delicto*. This is deemed reasonable, because no other opportunity is afforded to the belligerent force to vindicate the law[3]. The penalty for a breach of blockade is also held to be remitted, if the blockade has been raised before the capture; "for when that is raised a veil is thrown over every thing that has been done, the vessel is no longer taken *in delicto*, that *delictum* is completely done away when the blockade ceases[4]."

Conveyance of hostile despatches.

There are other acts of illegal assistance afforded to a

[1] Baltazzi *v.* Ryder, 12 Moore, *P. C. C.* 168.

[2] Bynk. *Q. J. P.* Bk. I. ch. xi.

[3] The *Welvaart Van Pillaw*, 2 Rob. 128. The *Jeffrow Maria Schroeder*, 3 Rob. 147. In cases of contraband, the return voyage has not usually been deemed connected with the outward, and the offence was deposited with the offending subject; but in distant voyages, with contraband and false papers, the rule is different, the fraud contaminates the return cargo, and subjects it to condemnation, as being one entire transaction. The *Rosalie* and *Betty*, 2 Rob, 343. The *Nancy*, 3 ibid. 122.

[4] The *Lisette*, 6 Rob. 387. [The reader is referred to the more recent English cases of the *Franciska* (Northcote *v.* Douglas) 10 Moore, *P. C. C.* 59; the *Chrysis*, Spinks, 343; Cremidi *v.* Powell, 11 Moore, *P. C. C.* 116; and to the American prize cases reported in 2 Black's *Supreme Court Cases*, p. 635, for the latest application of the principles enunciated in the older authorities. A good *resumé* of the law of blockade will be found in Mr Tudor's note to the *Frederick Moltke*, see *Leading Cases on Mercantile Law*, pp. 757—775.]

belligerent, besides supplying him with contraband goods, and relieving his distress, under a blockade. Among these acts, the conveyance of hostile despatches is the most injurious, and deemed to be of the most hostile and noxious character. The carrying of two or three cargoes of stores is necessarily an assistance of a limited nature; but in the transmission of despatches may be conveyed the entire plan of a campaign, and it may lead to a defeat of all the projects of the other belligerent in that theatre of the war. The appropriate remedy for this offence is the confiscation of the ship; and, in doing so, the courts make no innovation on the ancient law, but they only apply established principles to new combinations of circumstances. There would be no penalty in the mere confiscation of the despatches. The proper and efficient remedy is the confiscation of the vehicle employed to carry them; and if any privity subsists between the owners of the cargo and the master, they are involved by implication in his delinquency. If the cargo be the property of the proprietor of the ship, then, by the general rule, *ob continentiam delicti*, the cargo shares the same fate, and especially if there was an active interposition in the service of the enemy, concerted and continued in fraud[1].

A distinction has been made between carrying despatches of the enemy between different parts of his dominions, and carrying despatches of an ambassador from a neutral country to his own sovereign. The effect of the former despatches is presumed to be hostile; but the neutral country has a right to preserve its relations with the enemy, and it does not necessarily follow that the communications are of a hostile nature. Ambassadors resident in a neutral country are favourite objects of the protection of the law of nations, and their object is to preserve the relations of amity between the governments; and the presumption is, that the neutral state preserves its integrity, and is not concerned in any hostile design[2].

[1] The *Atalanta*, 6 Rob. 440.

[2] The *Caroline*, 6 Rob. 461.

[The rules on the subject of the carriage of despatches by neutrals, whether generally or specially, as from an ambassador resident in a neutral country to his sovereign, are here stated too briefly to be dismissed, the more so as the well-known case of the *Trent* has invested this part of our subject-matter with a particular interest. It is therefore proposed now to add some few remarks to the foregoing:

Examination of the rules on this subject.

The transportation of despatches in the service of the enemy, says Mr Wheaton, is of the same nature as the carrying of contraband goods, and the fraudulently carrying these articles will subject the neutral vessel to capture and confiscation[1].

Ambassador's despatches.

On the general principle thus laid down several exceptions have been grafted, some by way of explanation, some by way of limitation. And the first that may be noticed is the exception laid down in the *Caroline*, to the effect that the carrying the despatches of an ambassador, or other public minister of the enemy, resident in a neutral country, does not produce the same consequences stated in the former case; "they are the despatches of some persons who are in a peculiar manner the favourite object of the protection of the Law of Nations; and as a neutral nation has a right to preserve its relations with the enemy, the one is not at liberty to conclude that any communication between them can partake of the nature of hostility;" and then follows that important passage with regard to ambassadors, which Mr Seward has emphasized so strongly in his reply to the British Government, and which will be referred to by and bye. But, secondly, all papers found on board a neutral vessel, although of a public nature and relating to public affairs, will not necessarily, and at all events, be despatches of a contraband quality; for if the person to whom they are committed is a neutral, and not invested with a public character[2],

Neutral papers.

[1] *Elements of International Law,* Vol. II. p. 563, edition 1863, by W. B. Lawrence.

[2] The *Rapid,* Edw. 228.

they are not despatches, nor is the carriage of them an offence. Again, it has been decided that where despatches are conveyed on board a neutral vessel, going from a hostile port to a consul of the enemy, resident in a neutral country[1], or to a port of destination which ceased to be a colony of the enemy before the vessel reached it, neither of these is an illegal act from which any penal consequences would ensue[2]. Of course there is nothing criminal in transporting despatches of a purely commercial character[3], or where the master, having exercised due caution to prevent their being carried, has been deceived[4].

Despatches from enemy's country to enemy's consul in neutral country.

Ortolan referred to.

Ortolan, while citing with approval the rule as laid down by Wheaton, and extracted from Lord Stowell's judgment in the *Atalanta*[5], at the same time draws attention especially to the exception to that rule in the case of despatches of an ambassador or other public minister, resident in a neutral country, an exception so clearly and forcibly put by Lord Stowell in the case of the *Caroline*[6], as to be adopted by Wheaton, and approved of by his editor, Mr Lawrence[7]. It need hardly be said that the exception is viewed with favour by De Hautefeuille, for his ardour in the cause of Neutral Rights would lead him to cut the rule itself down to the lowest proportions[8]. At all events, he maintains the carriage of despatches by a regular postal packet in the ordinary course of business is not a criminal act. But as the whole law on these important topics is set out in the cases just cited, it may be as well to run briefly through them, and note the remarks of Mr Lawrence upon the doctrine laid down in that of the *Caroline*. It is unnecessary to repeat Sir W. Scott's invective against the heinousness of the offence arising from the important bearing of despatches upon the fate of the war, because every court administering Prize Law has adopted his view, and every Interna-

De Hautefeuille.

Sir Wm. Scott in the *Atalanta*.

[1] The *Madride*, Edw. 224.
[2] The *Trende Sostre*, 6 Rob. 457.
[3] The *Hope*, 6 Rob. 390, n. (*a*).
[4] The *Lisette*, 6 Rob. 457.
[5] 6 Rob. 440.
[6] 6 Rob. 461.
[7] Wheaton, p. 566, note (*a*).
[8] Hautef. Vol. II. 184.

tional Jurist of distinction echoes his words; but there are one or two expressions in the judgment of the *Atalanta* worth dwelling on. In the first place, Lord Stowell uses the term *fraudulent;* it is the *fraudulently* carrying despatches that is one element in the offence. In the next place, he says, such carrying must be in the *service of the enemy;* and why he insists upon this qualification is visible in another part of the judgment, where, whilst enlarging upon the offence as being greater than that of carrying contraband under ordinary circumstances, he points out that the usual penalty of confiscation of the noxious article alone would be ridiculous when applied to despatches. It seems clear then that the mere proof of carrying despatches of this kind, of being possessed of them, is not sufficient to establish a charge of contraband carriage, that besides the transportation, a *fraudulent intention* must be made out against the master, not simply presumed to exist because ambassadors or agents with despatches are found on board, and that to this proof of fraud must be added full and satisfactory proof that the carrying was in the service of the enemy, not accidental or in the ordinary way of business, but with the intention and design of assisting the enemy, an intention and design to be substantiated either by the direct evidence of correspondence with, request from, and offers to the enemy, or in the absence of direct proof, by circumstances that leave no doubt upon the mind as to what the neutral master's intention was[1].

[1] In the cases of the *Atalanta*, the *Constantia*, 6 Rob. 461, and the *Susan*, 6 Rob. 462, the voyage was either from a belligerent port or to a belligerent port, or from the colony to the mother-country of the enemy. The conveying despatches from the colony to the mother-country of the enemy has always subjected the party to confiscation, and the fact that the voyage was to a neutral port does not seem to change the transaction. The *Commercen*, 1 Wheaton, 391. But if the commencement of the voyage is in a neutral country, and is to terminate at a neutral port, or at one to which an open trade is allowed, in such case there is less to excite the neutral master's vigilance, and therefore in such case it may be proper to make allowance. The *Maddison*, Edw. 226. The *Rapid*, Edw. 229. We doubt, however, whether Mons. Hautefeuille's view is a correct one, that a voyage from one

What are despatches?

The fraudulent carriage of despatches therefore in the service of the enemy being so serious an offence, and so penal in its consequences, as to cause the forfeiture of ship and cargo, of course an important question is, what are despatches? This is answered by Lord Stowell[1]. They are all official communications of official persons on the public affairs of the government[2]. They are all papers relating to public concerns, great or small, civil or military; whether they are of any importance or not is not for the court to enquire into, it is sufficient that they relate to the public business of the enemy; the true criterion being this, "are they on the public business of the state? do they, pass between public persons in the public service?"

Mr Lawrence's views examined.

But in addition to the exceptions just stated, as laid down by Lord Stowell, and apparently accepted by American jurists, another has been strongly urged by a writer above mentioned; and as his proposition has some bearing on the very case in which he has expressed a strong adverse opinion to the claim of the British Government for redress, and as this proposition, oddly enough, is inspired by the same dislike to, and jealousy of, England, so visible in his *Treatise on the Law of Search*, it is worth noticing here. Mr Lawrence, in a note to Wheaton's *Elements*[3], after noticing that part of the English Order in Council published at the breaking out of hostilities with Russia, and bearing date April 15th, 1854, which declares enemy's despatches to be contraband, and therefore not free, adds these words, "It is conceived that the carrying of despatches can only invest a neutral vessel with a hostile character, in the case of its being employed for that purpose by the belligerent, and *that it cannot affect with criminality either a regular postal packet, or a merchant ship, which takes despatches in the ordinary course of conveying letters,* and with the contents of which the master

neutral port to another is so far innocent as to exempt the neutral vessel from visitation and search.

[1] The *Caroline*, 6 Rob. 465.

[2] The *Susan*, 6 Rob. 461, n.

[3] Vol. I. p. 567.

must necessarily be ignorant." This view is not inconsistent with the text (Wheaton's), which refers to a fraudulent carrying "of the despatches of an enemy;" and then he notices the great change since former European wars, produced by regular postal packets carrying not only the despatches of the government, but all letters sent to it from the post office[1].

Now, whilst admitting that the exception thus proposed by Mr Lawrence is not on all fours with the *Trent* affair, for that was a case where persons in a public official capacity were themselves alleged to be carrying supposed despatches, it might not be out of place to enquire whether in the event of the *Trent* being an American postal packet carrying passengers as well as letters, and England then at war with Mexico say, and seizing two of her Mexican passengers with letters of this kind in their possession, Mr Lawrence would not have felt inclined to urge the importance of exempting postal packets from search, when it was part of their duty to carry passengers as well as letters; at all events, we cannot help thinking that he would have hesitated to maintain to a New York mob, or even to a knot of quiet friends, that the seizure by a British cruiser under such circumstances was not only justifiable but perfectly legal.

The *Trent* affair.

Such then being the principal rules relative to the right of search in connection with the carriage of despatches by a neutral, it will be a fitting conclusion to these remarks to add a short narrative of the *Trent* affair; and, in order to avoid the slightest appearance of partiality, the account of the transaction will be taken from Mr

[1] Hautefeuille, *Droits des nationes neutres*, II. 463. Postal Treaty of December, 1848. *U. S. Statutes at Large*, Vol. IX. p. 965.

N.B. In the case of the *Peterhoff* an important preliminary decision of Judge Betts deserves notice, in which, in answer to the application of the Attorney of the United States, he ruled that though it may be that a mail-bag on board a captured vessel may be opened and searched, yet in this case, for reasons given, the mail-bag carried by the *Peterhoff* should be delivered to the Attorney-General (by whom it was handed to the British Consul). See *Report*, pp. 28—34.

Seward's own words[1]. The royal mail-contract steamer, the *Trent*, in her passage from Havannah to England, with her Majesty's mail-bags and numerous passengers on board, on the 8th of Nov. 1861, observed a war-steamer ahead not showing colours (the *San Jacinto*, Captain Wilkes, American). The *Trent* "was moving under a full head of steam," when, at about 1.15 p. m., the *San Jacinto* fired a *round shot* from her pivot gun, "in a direction obviously divergent from the course of the *Trent*," and shortly afterwards *discharged a shell* across the bows of the *Trent*, which exploded at half a cable's length from her. An officer, Lieutenant Fairfax, with a large armed guard of marines, put off in a boat, "and leaving the marines in the boat," boarded the *Trent* alone. Lieutenant Fairfax, "in a respectful and courteous, though decided manner," stated that his instructions from Captain Wilkes were to search for four persons, whom he named. He then asked for the passenger list, which was refused; and after some parley, one of the four persons named stepped forward and pointed out the individuals. "Lieutenant Fairfax, on that, without employing absolute force in transferring the passengers, used just so much as was necessary to satisfy the parties concerned, that refusal or resistance would be unavailing against this act." The Captain of the *Trent* and Commander Williams both protested, on the ground that the four passengers were under the protection of the British Flag. "The Commander of the *Trent* was not requested to go on board the *San Jacinto*." These are the

[1] See *Parly. Papers*, Session 1862, North America, No. 5, p. 19. But at the same time it is fair, nay, it is absolutely due to the British Government to notice one or two features in Mr Seward's document. In the first place, it is *assumed* that Commander Williams and the Captain of the *Trent* have exaggerated the conduct of the *San Jacinto*, and that Mr Fairfax her Lieutenant's version is a more trustworthy one than theirs; and, secondly, that the owner, agent and all the officers of the *Trent* were aware of the character and position of the individuals on board who were seized; but, thirdly, the American Government were apprized so long back as Nov. 30th, 1861, that one of their officers had, without any instructions or authority, boarded a British colonial steamer and taken two (not ambassadors but) *insurgents* from her deck. *Letter* dated Nov. 30th, 1861.

facts of the case as given by Mr Seward, but differing from the version of the English captain. The British Government demanded the restoration of the persons thus seized, and a suitable apology. That restoration was made, and accompanied by a long state paper, in which Mr Seward discusses the question, whether the proceeding was authorized by, and conducted according to, the Law of Nations. In that despatch Mr Seward having raised one or two points of an important nature in their bearing upon the subject of contraband, they are worth a brief notice. Now, without stopping to enquire whether Captain Wilkes might not lawfully stop and search the *Trent*, there are two questions that it is impossible to overlook, and in which it is very difficult to agree with the American minister in his reasons. One is, whether the persons named, and their supposed despatches, are contraband of war. The other, whether such persons may be captured in a neutral vessel. As to the first, Mr Seward urges that the persons are contraband on four grounds. First, because contraband, means contrary to proclamation, prohibited, illegal, unlawful. Secondly, because naval and military persons are contraband. Thirdly, because Vattel and Sir W. Scott say, you may cut off your enemy's resources, and may stop your enemy's ambassador on his voyage; and fourthly, because of Sir W. Scott's reasoning, that if the service of the enemy requires the sending out public persons, at the public expense, then the forfeiture of the vessel that may be let out for such a hostile purpose is just. Let us take each of these reasons in turn. And first, are these persons without their despatches (pub lic officers or ambassadors) contraband simply on the ground of the definition of contraband above given. We venture to think not, because nowhere is it laid down that ambassadors, or public ministers, are articles contrary to proclamation, prohibited, or illegal. Nowhere is it laid down that the sending them to neutral countries is denounced by International Law. Indeed, ambassadors are looked upon with so much favour as to be specially pro-

Mr Seward's despatch examined.

tected by that law; and though it is true one belligerent may hinder the safe passage of the other's ambassador, neutral nations are so far from being forbidden to receive them in their territory, that the presumption of law is, that the neutral state where they are resident preserves its integrity, and is not concerned in any hostile design; and a clear distinction has been made between carrying despatches of the enemy to and from different parts of his dominion[1], and carrying despatches of an ambassador from a neutral country to his own sovereign. We therefore assert, that though despatches are classed as contraband articles, and their carriage is illegal because of their peculiar character, ambassadors are neither contraband articles, nor denounced by International Law. But if the question is to be decided by definitions alone, then it is clear they are not contraband; for contraband relates to goods or articles—not to persons, except by way of special rule. Ammunition, stores, provisions, horses, and other goods, according to circumstances, become contraband, and are things prohibited, illegal, unlawful; but military and naval persons are stated by name to be contraband, and are included in the list of contraband for special causes in a special manner, not as coming under the general definition of the term, *expressio unius est exclusio alterius.* If naval and military persons who are as much employed in a public capacity by and as serviceable to the enemy are specified by name as contraband, what are we to infer from the omission of ambassadors and public ministers? Surely not, in the absence of a single instance or case in support thereof, that they are prohibited and denounced by International Law. Moreover, despatches we know are declared to be contraband; then why not ambassadors? probably because International Law or custom, instead of considering them illegal and unlawful, throws its ægis over them as far as is consistent with certain rules of war. But then, secondly, Mr Seward says,

[1] 1 Kent, 153. The *Caroline*, 6 Rob. 461.

ambassadors are contraband, because naval and military persons are so. To that, it may be replied, that what Mr Seward should have said is, That if one is, the other ought to be; not 'one is, because the other is:' to point out defects in a law or in the law, and have them solemnly decided and formally altered, is one thing; to make the alteration yourself, in order to suit particular circumstances, is another altogether. Granted that naval and military persons are contraband, what single instance from Admiralty decisions, what single expression from International jurists, can be cited to show that ambassadors or public officers are so too? The rule about naval and military persons has been in existence a long time; questions of contraband of all kinds have been argued; the list of contraband has been varied and extended; the right of search and capture has been exercised over and over again; and yet we defy any one to say that ambassadors have been put on the same footing as naval and military persons, or that the tendency of the courts has not been to relax their rules in favour of ambassadors, rather than to make them more stringent. In the third place, Mr Seward, resting on expressions of Vattel and Sir W. Scott, that you may stop your enemy's resources, and therefore stop his ambassador, argues that they are contraband. Now if that part of Vattel is examined, in which the position of ambassadors is discussed, it will be found that Vattel is a strong supporter of the privileged position of public ministers; and he nowhere attempts to make out that they are things denounced as contraband or illegal: it is true he says, Stop your enemy's resources, hinder him from sending ministers to ask for assistance, if you can; but that is widely different from saying that they are contraband, infectious articles, and that neutrals carrying them are liable to capture and condemnation. We reply, therefore, that nowhere in Vattel will be found any passage to bear out Mr Seward's view, that such persons are contraband. But Sir W. Scott says you may stop ambassadors: yes, but in a very different

Vattel's dictum as to stopping ambassadors.

Sir Wm. Scott's dictum as to stopping ambassadors.

spirit to what Mr Seward is contending for. For if the case is looked at[1] in which this dictum appears, it will be seen how strongly his Lordship leans to the sacred character of ambassadors, and to the advisability of affording them every opportunity for a residence in neutral countries; and though he over and over again describes despatches as contraband articles, he nowhere, either in the very case we are now considering, or in any other, applies the term to ambassadors; nay, he argues that the mere presence of an ambassador on board a neutral ship does not lead to the presumption that the neutral is acting contrary to his neutral character; and although he does say the belligerent may stop the ambassador of his enemy on his passage, he says, he may act in that way by virtue of his rights of war against the enemy: he does not say that he may stop him anywhere and everywhere, in a neutral ship for instance; he does not say he may seize him in that ship; and he carefully abstains from saying the ambassador is contraband: if he is not contraband, how can he be stopped in a neutral ship? Now it happens that Vattel, in laying down the rule that one enemy may stop the ambassador of another on his passage, cites a case in illustration of what he means. The French ambassador, on his way to Berlin, a neutral state, was rash enough to stop in Hanover, which then was a part of the dominions of the British King, and of course belligerent territory: he was captured there by England, and neither France nor Prussia remonstrated: why? because the capture was effected not on neutral territory, but on the enemy's soil; and the person of the ambassador was not sacred enough to prevent the capture there. We therefore repeat, that neither in Vattel, nor Sir W. Scott, will any expression be found which shall class ambassadors as contraband articles. Nor is the fourth reason one whit stronger. In Lord Stowell's test, if it is of sufficient importance to the enemy that civil magistrates should be sent out on the public service, at the public expense, it is a ground of

[1] The *Caroline.*

forfeiture against the vessel that *may be let out* for so hostile a purpose. The test, even if correctly stated, does not apply to the present case; for, in the first place, what proof had Captain Wilkes, or the American Government, that these men were in the public service, sent out at the public expense? They never asked for their documents, they never saw the ship's papers; they only asked for four suspected persons; whilst, as far as the Captain of the *Trent* was concerned, what did he know of them, save as passengers paying their fare, and treated like any other passengers. Whatever position they occupied was officially unknown to him, and officially unknown to Captain Wilkes. They had a perfect right to be in Havannah, a neutral port, where they had been residing for some weeks. The captain was perfectly justified in taking them as passengers in the absence of any public notification to him of their character; and inasmuch as they were embarking at one neutral port and going to another, there was no just cause for suspicion on his part; but if there was no evidence, beyond mere hearsay, to justify Captain Wilkes's suspicion, what proof was there that the vessel was let out to the enemy for the particular purpose of carrying public ministers? not only none, but everything in favour of the master's innocence—a mail-packet, making regular periodical voyages, calling at Havannah in the usual course of business, taking in all passengers that came, and neither stopping nor hurrying in the passage. How can it be said that this test of Lord Stowell's can apply? How can it be said, on any of the four grounds just discussed, that Messrs Mason and Slidell were contraband of war? Then, if such is the case—if they were not contraband of war—it is scarcely necessary to say that they could not be captured in a neutral vessel. Mr Seward further says, that Captain Wilkes acted from combined sentiments of prudence and generosity; but his own version of the story shows that he acted on a foregone conclusion; and that rather than not make prisoners of certain persons on board a neutral vessel who could not have been taken on neutral territory, he was prepared to make the law-books suit his purpose, by calling them the embodiment of contraband. Every one will grant that, in case of fair suspicion, the right of search may be executed even between one neutral port and another. Every one will grant that the presence of despatches on board is a good cause for suspicion, so as to warrant a belligerent cruiser to detain the neutral cruiser. Every one will grant that if, on the proper hearing, it is proved that there was a fraudulent carriage by the neutral master, and in the enemy's service, that is a good cause for condemnation. But who can admit that ambassadors are contraband? Who can admit that the PRESUMED possession of despatches gives a right even to stop the vessel; that ambassadors can be seized in a neutral vessel; that the right of a belligerent cruiser is to do anything but take the ship into port and have her condemned; or that the captain of a belligerent cruiser is entitled to act as judge in doubtful cases, and settle the law in the way that best suits his purpose?]

[NOTE. The above remarks on the affair of the *Trent* were penned and read to an audience at Gresham College some few weeks before Earl Russell's despatch to Lord Lyons appeared, dated Foreign Office, January 23rd, 1862. It will be seen on reference to that document that the editor's views above given are in the main supported by Earl Russell's language. His Lordship, after showing that as by Mr Seward's own acknowledgment the nature of the question really concerned the respective rights of belligerents and neutrals, the allegation that the captured persons were rebels, might be entirely discarded, argues at great length and seriatim, against the propositions laid down by the United States Minister, and then finishes with this important passage: "Mr Seward asserts that if the safety of the Union required the detention of the captured persons it would be the right and the duty of the government to detain them, but the waxing proportions of the insurrection, &c. forbid him from resorting to that defence. Mr Seward does not here assert any right founded on international law; however inconvenient or irritating to neutral nations, he entirely loses sight of the vast difference which exists between the exercise of an extreme right and the commission of an unquestioned wrong. His frankness compels me to be equally open, and to inform him that Great Britain could not have submitted to the perpetration of that wrong, however flourishing might have been the insurrection in the South, and however important the persons captured." *Parly. Papers*, 1862, Vol. LXII. p. 647.]

Visitation and Search.

In order to enforce the rights of belligerent nations against the delinquencies of neutrals, and to ascertain the real as well as assumed character of all vessels on the high seas, the law of nations arms them with the practical power of visitation and search. The duty of self-preservation gives to belligerent nations this right. It is founded upon necessity, and is strictly and exclusively a war right, and does not rightfully exist in time of peace, unless conceded by treaty[1].

Discussion between Great Britain and the United States as to the right of search.

[The British Parliament, by statute, in August 1839, in order more effectually to suppress the slave-trade, especially against Portugal, a country that had grossly violated her treaty with England on that subject, authorized the power of visitation and search in time of peace. The British Government at one time drew a distinction between the right of visit and the right of search, and though disavowing any claim to exercise the latter in time of peace, insisted on the former in order to know whether a vessel hoisting a flag really was entitled to the protection of that flag[2]. On the other hand, the Government of the United States through its organ Mr Webster, urging that the right to visit to be effectual must come in the end to include search, and so introduce in time of peace a practice that was confined to times of war, refused to be bound by any such distinction as that set up by Great Britain[3]. The discussion thus briefly noticed arose out of the claim of British cruisers on the coast of Africa to visit American vessels suspected of being engaged in the slave-trade. Neither country was willing to withdraw from the view maintained by each, though the matter itself was settled for a time by an arrangement that each government should maintain a specified naval force on the coast of Africa to prevent the fraudulent use of their respective

[1] *Le Louis*, 2 Dodson, 245. The *Antelope*, 10 Wheaton's *Report*, 119.

[2] Lord Aberdeen's *Despatch*, Dec. 1841, to the American Minister, Mr Stevenson. *British and Foreign State Papers*, Vol. XXX. p. 1165. Webster's *Works*, Vol. VI. p. 332.

[3] Mr Webster's *Despatch* to Mr Everett, March 28, 1843.

flags. In 1858, however, the question was again brought into a prominent position in consequence of the activity of the British cruisers in the Gulf of Mexico, in their endeavours to suppress the slave-trade. A long correspondence ensued upon the reclamations of the United States Government, who, while admitting the abuses to which the fraudulent assumption of the flag of one power by the citizens or subjects of another might give rise, still adhered to their determined opposition to the claim of a right by the cruiser of one nation to search or visit upon the ocean the merchant-vessels of another in time of peace. In the course of that correspondence the views of the French as well as the American Governments were elicited, and eventually a set of instructions were agreed upon, to be issued to the commanding officers of ships and vessels employed by each country. In reference to the instructions to the officers of British cruisers[1], General Cass, in a

[1] [*Instructions about to be issued to the Commanders of British Cruisers.*

Sir, *Admiralty,*

Instructions to the commanders of British cruisers.

1. THE Treaty with France for the suppression of the Slave Trade having been abrogated, I am commanded by my Lords Commissioners of the Admiralty to acquaint you that, under an arrangement which has been adopted provisionally between the British and French Governments, their Lordships desire that all commanding officers of Her Majesty's ships will strictly attend to the following Regulations with regard to visiting merchant-vessels suspected of fraudulently assuming the French flag.

2. In virtue of the immunity of national flags, no merchant-vessel navigating the high seas is subject to any foreign jurisdiction. A vessel of war cannot therefore visit, detain, arrest, or seize (except under Treaty) any merchant-vessel not recognized as belonging to her own nation.

3. The colours of a vessel being *primâ facie* the distinctive mark of her nationality, and, consequently, of the jurisdiction to which she is subject, it is natural that a merchant-vessel on the high seas, on finding herself in presence of a ship of war, should hoist her national flag in declaration of her nationality. So soon as the ship of war has made herself known by the display of her own colours, the merchant-vessel should, accordingly, hoist her proper national flag.

4. Should the merchant-vessel refuse to do so, it is admitted by both Governments that a warning may be given to her; first, by firing a blank gun, and should that be without effect, it may be enforced by a second gun, shotted, but pointed in such a manner as to ensure that she is not struck by the shot.

despatch to Lord Lyons, dated May 12th, 1859, made the

5. Immediately that the colours are hoisted, and that the merchant-vessel has in this manner announced her nationality, the foreign vessel of war can no longer pretend to exercise a control over her. At most, in certain cases, she may claim the right to speak with her, and demand answers to questions addressed to her by a speaking-trumpet or otherwise, but without obliging her to alter her course. When, however, the presumption of nationality resulting from the colours which may have been shown by a merchant-vessel, may be seriously thrown in doubt, or be questionable from positive information, or from indications of a nature to create a belief that the vessel does not belong to the nation whose colours she has assumed, the foreign vessel of war may have recourse to the verification of her assumed nationality.

6. A boat may be detached for this purpose towards the suspected vessel, after having first hailed her to give notice of the intention. The verification will consist in an examination of the papers establishing the nationality of the vessel—nothing can be claimed beyond the exhibition of these documents.

7. To inquire into the nature of the cargo, or the commercial operations of the vessel, or any other fact, in short, than that of the nationality of the vessel, is prohibited. Every other search, and every inspection whatever, is absolutely forbidden.

8. The officer in charge of the verification should proceed with the greatest discretion, and with every possible consideration and care, and should quit the vessel immediately that the verification has been effected, and should offer to note on the ship's papers the circumstances of the verification, and the reasons which may have led to it.

9. Except in the case of legitimate suspicion of fraud, it should never otherwise be necessary for the commander of a foreign ship of war to go on board, or to send on board a merchant-vessel. Apart from the colours shown, the indications are numerous which should be sufficient to satisfy seamen of the nationality of a vessel.

10. In every case it is to be clearly understood, that the captain of a ship of war who determines to board a merchant-vessel, must do so at his own risk and peril, and must remain responsible for all the consequences which may result from his own act.

11. The commander of a ship of war who may have recourse to such a proceeding should, in all cases, report the fact to his own Government, and should explain the reason of his having so acted. A communication of this report, and of the reasons which may have led to the verification, will be given officially to the Government to which the vessel may belong which shall have been subjected to inquiry as to her flag.

In all cases in which this inquiry shall not be justified by obvious reasons, or shall not have been made in a proper manner, a claim may arise for indemnity.

You will clearly understand that the foregoing instructions have reference only to vessels navigating under the French flag, and are intended following remarks: He stated first, that there was no longer any doubt that the three governments were entirely agreed upon the principles held by them respectively upon the mode in which the nationality of merchant-vessels is to be verified by ships of war meeting them at sea; he then further went on to say that the United States Government concurred with those of Great Britain and France as to the propriety of an exhibition of her flag by every merchantman on the ocean, whenever she meets a ship of war, either of her own or any foreign nation; that in reference to the friendly approach of a suspected vessel for the purpose of observation, no objection could exist to such course where practicable, and where the suspicions were of such a nature as to justify an observation; and as in accordance with the doctrine laid down in the *Marianna Flora*[1], the right of approach by ships of war, sailing under authority, to arrest pirates and other public offenders, would seem to be indispensable for the fair and discreet exercise of their authority, so its use could not be justly deemed indicative of any intention to insult, injure, or impede, those who are approached, who on the other hand would not be bound to lie by or await the approach[2]].

mutually to prevent misunderstanding between the British and French Governments, but cannot affect the vessels of other nations with whom Great Britain has Treaties for the suppression of the Slave Trade, or deprive Her Majesty of the right to seize and detain vessels engaged in the Slave Trade, when not entitled to the protection of any national flag.]

1 11 Wheaton's *Reports*, 43.

2 See the *Correspondence* with the United States Government on the question of the Right of Visit, presented to both houses of Parliament, 1859. See also the *Debates* in the House of Lords, and notably, Lord Lyndhurst's *Speech*, 26th July, 1858. Hansard's *Debates*, Vol. CLI. p. 2078. It is presumed that the subject of the Right of Visit and Search in time of peace is so clearly examined and defined in that Correspondence, that it is unnecessary to add anything further thereto, save that it is impossible to accept the views of Sir Robert Phillimore, propounded in the 3rd Vol. of his *International Law*, §§ 322—326. N.B. The matter is now provided for by Treaty between the United States and Great Britain, ratified April 1, 1863; see 26 and 27 Vict. c. 34.

All writers upon International law, and the highest authorities, acknowledge the right of search as resting on sound principles of public jurisprudence, and upon the institutes and practice of all great maritime powers[1]. And if, upon making the search, the vessel be found employed in contraband trade, or in carrying enemy's property, or troops, or despatches, she is liable to be taken and brought in for adjudication before a prize court.

Neutral nations have frequently been disposed to question and resist the exercise of this right. This was particularly the case with the Baltic confederacy, during the American war, and with the convention of the Baltic powers in 1801. The right of search was denied, and the flag of the state was declared to be a substitute for all documentary and other proof, and to exclude all right of search. Those powers armed for the purpose of defending their neutral pretensions; and England did not hesitate to consider their determination as an attempt to introduce, by force, a new code of maritime law, inconsistent with her belligerent rights, hostile to her interests, and one which would go to extinguish the right of maritime capture. The attempt was speedily frustrated and abandoned, and the right of search has, since that time, been considered incontrovertible[2].

The whole doctrine was very ably discussed in the English High Court of Admiralty, in the case of the *Maria*[3], in which it was adjudged, that the right was incontestable, and that a neutral sovereign could not, by the interposition of force, vary that right. Two powers may agree among themselves, it was said, that the presence of one of their armed ships along with their mer- The *Maria*.

[1] Vattel, Bk. III. ch. vii. § 114. The *Maria*, 1 Rob. 340; The *Le Louis*, 2 Dodson's *Adm. Rep.* 245; The *Marianna Flora*, 11 Wheaton, 42.

[2] In the convention between England and Russia on the 17th June, 1801, Russia admitted the belligerent right of search even of merchant-vessels navigating under convoy of a ship of war, provided it was examined by a ship of war belonging to Government.

[3] 1 Rob. 340. See the notes to and comments on this case in Tudor's *Leading Cases in Mercantile Law*, § 43—672.

chant-ships shall be mutually understood to imply that nothing is to be found, in that convoy of merchant-ships, inconsistent with amity or neutrality[1]. But no belligerent power can legally be compelled, by mere force, to accept of such a pledge; and every belligerent power who is no party to the agreement has a right to insist on the only security known to the law of nations on this subject, independent of any special covenant, and that is the right of personal visitation and search, to be exercised by those who have an interest in making it. The penalty for the violent contravention of this right is the confiscation of the property so withheld from visitation; and the infliction of this penalty is conformable to the settled practice of nations, as well as to the principles of the municipal jurisprudence of most countries in Europe. There may be cases in which the master of a neutral ship may be authorized, by the natural right of self-preservation, to defend himself against extreme violence threatened by a cruiser grossly abusing his commission; but, except in extreme cases, a merchant-vessel has no right to say for itself, and an armed vessel has no right to say for it, that it will not submit to visitation or search, or to be carried into a proximate port for judicial inquiry. Upon these principles, a fleet of Swedish merchant-ships, sailing under convoy of a Swedish ship of war, and under instructions from the Swedish Government to resist, by force, the right of search claimed by British lawfully commissioned cruisers, was condemned. The resistance of the convoying ship was a resistance of the whole convoy, and justly subjected the whole to confiscation[2].

English doctrine recognized in the United States.

The doctrine of the English Admiralty on the right of visitation and search, and on the limitation of the right,

[1] In the treaty of commerce between the United States and the Republic of Chili in 1832, it was agreed that the right of visitation and search should not apply to vessels sailing under convoy. See too the convention between the United States and the Peru-Bolivian Confederacy, Art. XIX.

[2] The *Maria*, 1 Rob. 377. The *Elsabe*, 4 Rob. 408.

has been recognised in its fullest extent by the courts of justice in the United States[1]. That Government too admits the right of visitation and search by belligerent government vessels of their private merchant-ships for enemy's property, articles contraband of war, or men in the land or naval service of the enemy. But it does not understand the rules of international law to authorize, nor does it admit the right of search for subjects or seamen. The very fact of sailing under the protection of a belligerent, or neutral convoy, for the purpose of resisting search, is a violation of neutrality. The Danish Government asserted the same principle in its correspondence with the Government of the United States, and in the royal instructions of the 28th of March, 1810[2]; and none of the powers of Europe have called in question the justice of the doctrine[3]. Confiscation is applied by way of penalty for resistance of search to all vessels, without any discrimination as to the national character of the vessel or cargo, and without separating the fate of the cargo from that of the ship.

**Resistance to search.**

This right of search is confined to private merchant-vessels, and does not apply to public ships of war. Their immunity from the exercise of any jurisdiction but that of the sovereign power to which they belong, is uniformly asserted, claimed, and conceded. A contrary doctrine is not to be found in any jurist or writer on the law of nations, or admitted in any treaty; and every act to the contrary has been promptly met and condemned[4]. In

**The right confined to Merchant-ships.**

[1] The *Nereide*, 9 Cranch, 427. 438. 113. 115. 453. The *Marianna Flora*, 11 Wheaton, 42.

[2] 4 Hall's *L. Journal*, 263. *Letters* of Count Rosenkrantz to Mr Erving, 28th and 30th of June, and 9th of July, 1811. *American State Papers*, Vol. VIII. pp. 221.

[3] The *Austrian* ordinance of neutrality of August 7th, 1803, enjoined it upon all their vessels to submit to visitation on the high seas, and not to make any difficulty as to the production of the documentary proofs of property. See Art. VI. Martens' *Recueil des Traités*, Tom. VIII. p. 106.

[4] Thurloe's *State Papers*, Vol. II. p. 503. Mr Canning's *Letter* to Mr Monroe, August 3rd, 1807; *American State Papers*, Vol. VI. p. 89; *Edinburgh Review* for October, 1807, Art. I.

Public ships in foreign port.

the English case of the *Prins Frederik*[1], the question was raised, and learnedly discussed, whether a public armed ship, belonging to the King of the Netherlands, was liable to civil or criminal process in a British port. She was brought in, by assistance, in distress, and salvage was claimed, and the ship was arrested upon that claim, and a plea to the jurisdiction interposed. The question went off by arrangement, and was not decided, though the immunity of such vessels from all private claims was forcibly urged, on grounds of general policy and the usage of nations. "In the United States it was decided[2], after great discussion, that a public vessel of war of a foreign sovereign, at peace with the United States, coming into their ports, and demeaning herself in a friendly manner, was exempt from the jurisdiction of the country." In that interesting case, the schooner *Exchange*, it was shown that the exemption of a public ship in port from the local jurisdiction was not founded on the absolute right of another sovereign to such an exemption, but upon principles of public comity and convenience, and arose from the presumed consent of nations; that that consent might be withdrawn, upon notice, without just offence; that if a foreign ship, after such notice, comes into the port, she becomes amenable to the local laws in the same manner as other vessels; and that though a public ship and her armament might be excepted, the prize property which she brings into port is subject to the local jurisdiction, for the purpose of examination and inquiry, and, in a proper case, for restitution.

American Law.

Serving process on foreign ships.

It has also been asserted, on the part of the executive authority of the United States, that a writ of *habeas corpus* may be lawfully awarded, to bring up a subject illegally detained on board a foreign ship of war in their waters. So, also, it was the official opinion of the Attorney-General of the United States, in 1799, that it was lawful to serve civil or criminal process upon a person on board a foreign ship

[1] 2 Dodson, 451.

[2] The schooner *Exchange* v. *McFaddon*, 7 Cranch, 116.

of war lying within a harbour of the United States[1]. But these opinions, of course, do not apply to any process against the ship itself.

French Law. as to merchant ships.

The French rules on the subject of crimes and offences committed on board foreign merchant-vessels in French ports are thus stated by Mons. Ortolan. In the case of acts of mere interior discipline of a vessel, or of crimes and offences committed by a person forming a part of its officers and crew, against another person belonging to the same, where the peace of the port is not disturbed, the French courts hold that the rights of the power to which the vessel belongs should be respected, that the local authority ought not to interfere unless its aid is demanded, and that consequently these acts remain under the police and jurisdiction of the State to which the vessel belongs. But where crimes and offences are committed on board the vessel against persons not forming part of its officers and crew, or by any other individual than those who belong to the vessel, or where they are committed by the officers and crew upon each other, if the peace of the port is thereby disturbed, then the local authority is entitled to interfere; for a vessel admitted into a port of the State is of right subjected to the police regulations of the place, and its crew are amenable to the tribunals of the country for offences committed on board against persons not belonging to the ship, as well as in actions for civil contracts entered into with them[2].

The exercise of the right of visitation and search must be conducted with due care, and regard to the rights and

[1] See *Opinions of Attorneys-General of the United States*, Vol. I. pp. 47, Vol. VII. p. 131 (case of the *Sitka*), and Vol. VIII. pp. 79, 80 (case of the *Atalanta*).

[2] Ortolan's *Règles Internationales de la Mer*, Tom. I. pp. 293—298, and the two cases of the *Sally* and the *Newton* cited by him in the *Appendice Annexe* H, p. 441. See also the case of the *Carlo Alberto*, Sirey, *Recueil Général de Jurisprudence*, Tom. XXXII. Partie I. p. 578, and Cussy, *Droit Maritime*, Liv. II. ch. xii. § 11, where will be found M. Dupin's eloquent and learned argument. Wheaton's *Elements*, Part II. ch. ii. § 9, pp. 201—208, Edn. 1863, by W. B. Lawrence.

safety of the vessel[1]. If the neutral has acted with candour and good faith, and the inquiry has been wrongfully pursued, the belligerent cruiser is responsible to the neutral in costs and damages, to be assessed by the prize court which sustains the judicial examination. The mere exercise of the right of search involves the cruiser in no trespass, for it is strictly lawful. But if he proceeds to capture the vessel as prize, and sends her in for adjudication, and there was no probable cause, he is responsible. It is not the search, but the subsequent capture, which is treated in such a case as a tortious act[2]. If the capture be justifiable, the subsequent detention for adjudication is never punished with damages; and in all cases of marine torts, courts of admiralty exercise a large discretion in giving or withholding damages[3].

Rescue. A rescue effected by the crew, after capture, and when the captors are in actual possession, is unlawful, and considered to be a resistance within the application of the penalty of confiscation, for it is a delivery by force from force[4]. And where the penalty attaches at all, it attaches as completely to the cargo as to the ship, for the master acted as agent of the owner of the cargo, and his resistance was a fraudulent attempt to withdraw it from the rights of war[5].

[The doctrine just stated requires a little explanation, at least with reference to the position of the state to which the rescued ship belongs, and its obligations towards that of the captor.

The rule itself is thus stated, and correctly, by Mr J. Story :—"The rights of capture are completely devested

[1] The *Anna Maria*, 2 Wheaton, 327. The right of visitation and search is sometimes laid under special restrictions by convention between maritime states; see, for instance, Art. XVII. of the convention of navigation and commerce between the United States and the Peru-Bolivian Confederacy, May, 1838.

[2] 2 Mason, 439.

[3] 11 Wheaton, 54—56. Story, J.

[4] The *Despatch*, 3 Rob. 295. Brown *v.* Union Ins. Co. 5 Day's *Rep.* 1. Brig *Short Staple v.* U. S. 9 Cranch, 63.

[5] The *Catharina Elizabeth*, 5 Rob. 232.

by a hostile recapture, escape, or a voluntary discharge of the captured vessel. And the same principle seems applicable to a hostile rescue; but if the rescue be made by a *neutral* crew of a neutral ship it may be doubtful how far such an illegal act, which invites the penalty of confiscation, would be held in the courts of the captor's country to devest his original right in case of a subsequent recapture." The consequences of such an act attach to the ship and cargo, and through the misconduct of the master or crew the owners will be affected, but beyond that there is no further responsibility; for, as Earl Russell very truly stated the law in a case already referred to in another part of this work, "Acts of forcible resistance to the rights of belligerents, such as rescue from capture, &c., however cognizable or punishable as offences against International Law in the prize-courts of the captors administering such law, are not cognizable by the municipal law of a country, and cannot by that law be punished either by the confiscation of the ship or by any other penalty[1]."

At the same time the warning uttered by Sir W. Scott should never be lost sight of by neutral masters disposed to attempt the unlawful act of recapture; for if such acts are persisted in the conduct of belligerents must be proportionately severe and harsh.]

Documents requisite to support neutral character.

A neutral is bound not only to submit to search, but to have his vessel duly furnished with the genuine documents requisite to support her neutral character[2]. The most material of these documents are, the register, passport, sea-letter, muster roll, log-book, charterparty, invoice, and bill of lading[3]. The want of some of these

[1] The *Emily St. Pierre*, *Parly. Papers*, North America, 186. No. XI. p. 5.

[2] *Answer to the Prussian Memorial*, 1753.

[[3] The register or certificate of registry is the paper that specifies the name, occupation, and residence of every owner, the ship's name, place to which she belongs, tonnage, master's name, time and place of build or of condemnation, her rig and the description of her stern, and on the back is endorsed, with the owners' names, the number of 64th shares held by each. (See the forms in the Appendix to the Merchant Shipping Act, 17 & 18 Vict. c. 94, and in the Appendix to Pratt's edition of Story *On Prize Courts*, 1854).

papers is strong presumptive evidence against the ship's neutrality; yet the want of any one of them is not absolutely conclusive[1]. *Si aliquid ex solemnibus deficiat, cum equitas poscit, subveniendum est.* And therefore with regard to what among other things may constitute probable cause for captors, it may be observed that if the ship pretend to be neutral and has not the usual documents of a neutral ship on board, the captors are justified in bringing in the ship and cargo for adjudication[2]. The

The passport or sea-letter is a permission from the neutral state to the master of the vessel to proceed on the intended voyage, and usually contains his name and residence, the name, description and destination of the vessel, with such other matter as the local law and practice require.

The muster-roll, or rôle d'equipage, contains the names, ages, quality and national character of every person of the ship's company.

The log-book or ship's journal contains an accurate account of the ship's course, with a short history of the occurrences during the voyage.

The charterparty is the written statement of the contract by which an entire ship, or at least the principal part of it, is let for a determined voyage.

Invoices contain the particulars and prices of each parcel of goods, with a statement of the charge thereon, which are usually transmitted from the shipper to the consignee.

And the bill of lading is the instrument by which the master acknowledges the receipt of the goods specified therein, and promises to deliver them to the consignee or his order. There are usually several duplicates, of which one is delivered to the master, one retained by the shipper, and one sent to the consignees.]

[1] *Danish Instructions*, 28th March, 1810. Martens, *Nouveau Recueil*, Gottingen, 1817, T. v. p. 495. The register of a vessel is the only document which need be on board a vessel, in time of universal peace, to prove national character. Catlette *v.* Pacific Ins. Co. 1 Paine, 594. [By the 17 and 18 Vict. ch. 104, § 102, It is enacted that no officer of customs shall grant a clearance or transire for any ship until the master of such ship has declared to such officer the name of the nation to which he claims that she belongs, and such officer shall thereupon inscribe such name on the clearance or transire, and if any ship attempts to proceed to sea without such clearance or transire, any such officer may detain her until such declaration is made. With us in England the certificate of registry of a ship is, it seems, the authentic evidence to such of her Majesty's officers as are entitled to interfere in these matters of her national character and compliance with the law. See 17 & 18 Vict. ch. 104, §§ 19, 40, 45, 50, and Maclachlan's *Law of Merchant Shipping*, p. 80.]

[2] The *Anna*, 5 Rob. 382. Story *On Prize Law*, by F. T. Pratt, D.C.L. 1854, p. 36.

concealment of papers material for the preservation of the neutral character, justifies a capture, and carrying into port for adjudication, though it does not absolutely require a condemnation. It is good ground to refuse costs and damages on restitution, or to refuse further proof to relieve the obscurity of the case, where the cause laboured under heavy doubts, and there was *prima facie* ground for condemnation independent of the concealment[1]. The spoliation of papers is a still more aggravated and inflamed circumstance of suspicion. That fact may exclude further proof, and be sufficient to infer guilt; but it does not in England, as it does by the maritime law of other countries, create an absolute presumption *juris et de jure;* and yet, a case that escapes with such a brand upon it is saved so as by fire[2]. The Supreme Court of the United States has followed the less rigorous English rule, and held that the spoliation of papers was not, of itself, sufficient ground for condemnation, and that it was a circumstance open for explanation; for it may have arisen from accident, necessity, or superior force[3]. If the explanation be not prompt and frank, or be weak and futile; if the cause labours under heavy suspicions, or there be a vehement presumption of bad faith, or gross prevarication, it is good cause for the denial of further proof; and the condemnation ensues from defects in the evidence, which the party is not permitted to supply. The observation of Lord Mansfield in *Bernardi* v. *Motteaux*[4] was to the same effect. By the maritime law of all countries, he said, throwing papers overboard was considered as a strong presumption of enemy's property; but, in all his experience, he had never known a condemnation on that circumstance only. [Whenever the captors, says Mr Justice Story (and the rule holds in both countries, as the cases shew), are justified in the capture, they are con-

[1] Livingston and Gilchrist *v.* Mar. Ins. Co. 7 Cranch, 544.

[2] The *Hunter*, 1 Dodson, 480.

[3] The *Pizarro*, 2 Wheaton, 227.

[4] 2 Doug. 581.

sidered as having a *bonâ fide* possession, and are not responsible for any subsequent losses or injuries arising to the property from mere accident or casualty, as from stress of weather, recapture by the enemy, shipwreck, &c. They are however, in all cases, bound for fair and safe custody, and if the property be lost from the want of proper care they are responsible to the amount of the damage: for subsequent misconduct may forfeit the fair title of a *bonâ fide* possessor, and make him a trespasser from the beginning[1]. If however the capture is made without probable cause the captors are liable for damages, costs and expenses to the claimants. If the captors unjustifiably neglect to proceed to adjudication, the court will, in cases of restitution, decree demurrage against them, or if they agree to restitution but unreasonably delay it. And although a spoliation of papers be made, yet if it be produced by the misconduct of captors, as by firing under false colours, it will not protect them from damages and costs[2].]

Captors bound for fair and safe custody.

[1] See the cases collected in Story *On Prize Law*, pp. 36, 38.

[2] Story *On Prize Law*, p. 40.

# CHAPTER X.

## OF TRUCES, PASSPORTS, AND TREATIES OF PEACE.

---

HAVING considered the rights and duties appertaining to a state of war, we proceed to examine the law of nations relative to negotiations, conventions and treaties, which either partially interrupt the war, or terminate in peace.

(1.) A truce, or suspension of arms, does not terminate the war, but it is one of the *commercia belli* which suspends its operations. These conventions rest upon the obligation of good faith, and as they lead to pacific negotiations, and are necessary to control hostilities, and promote the cause of humanity, they are sacredly observed by civilised nations[1]. Truces.

A particular truce is only a partial cessation of hostilities, as between a town and an army besieging it. But a general truce applies to the operations of the war; and if it be for a long or indefinite period of time, it amounts to a temporary peace, which leaves the state of the contending parties, and the questions between them, remaining in the same situation as it found them. A partial truce may be made by a subordinate commander, and it is a power necessarily implied in the nature of his trust; but it is requisite to a general truce, or suspension of hostilities throughout the nation, or for a great length of time, that it may be made by the sovereign of the country,

[1] Klüber, *Droit des Gens*, 2de Partie, Tit. II. § ii. ch. i. §§ 277, 278. Wheaton's *Elements of International Law*, Vol. II. Pt. IV. ch. ii. §§ 19—22.

26—2

or by his special authority[1]. The general principle on the subject is, that if a commander makes a compact with the enemy, and it be of such a nature that the power to make it could be reasonably implied from the nature of the trust, it would be valid and binding, though he abused his trust. The obligation he is under not to abuse his trust, regards his own state, and not the enemy[2].

A truce binds the contracting parties from the time it is concluded, but it does not bind the individuals of the nation so as to render them personally responsible for a breach of it, until they have had actual or constructive notice of it. Though an individual may not be held to make pecuniary compensation for a capture made, or destruction of property, after the suspension of hostilities, and before notice of it had reached him, yet the sovereign of the country is bound to cause restoration to be made of all prizes made after the date of a general truce. To prevent the danger and damage that might arise from acts committed in ignorance of the truce, it is common and proper to fix a prospective period for the cessation of hostilities, with a due reference to the distance and situation of places[3].

A truce only temporarily stays hostilities; and each party to it may, within his own territories, do whatever he would have a right to do in time of peace. He may continue active preparations for war, by repairing fortifications, levying and disciplining troops, and collecting provisions, and articles of war. He may do whatever, under all the circumstances, would be deemed compatible with good faith, and the spirit of the agreement; but he is justly restrained from doing what would be directly injurious to the enemy, and could not safely be done in the midst of hostilities. Thus, in the case of a truce between the governor of a fortified town and the army besieging

[1] Vattel, Bk. III. ch. xvi. §§ 233—238. Grotius, Bk. III. ch. xxi.

[2] Rutherforth, Bk. II. ch. ix. Vattel, Bk. III. ch. xvi. § 261. Grotius, Bk. III. ch. xxii. § 4.

[3] Vattel, Bk. III. ch. xv. §§ 239, 244.

it, neither party is at liberty to continue works, constructed either for attack or defence, and which could not safely be done if hostilities had continued; for this would be to make a mischievous and fraudulent use of the cessation of arms. So, it would be a fraud upon the rights of the besieging army, and an abuse of the armistice, for the garrison to avail themselves of the truce to introduce provision and succours into the town, in a way, or through passages, which the besieging army would have been competent to prevent[1]. The meaning of every such compact is, that all things should remain as they were in the places contested, and of which the possession was disputed at the moment of the conclusion of the truce[2].

At the expiration of the truce hostilities may recommence without any fresh declaration of war; but if it be for an indefinite time, justice and good faith would require due notice of an intention to terminate it[3].

Grotius and Vattel[4], as well as other writers on national law, have agitated the question, whether a truce for a given period, as, for instance, from the first of January to the first of February, will include or exclude the first day of each of these months. Grotius says, that the day from whence a truce is to be computed, is not one of the days of the truce, but that it will include the whole of the first day of February, as being the day of its termination. Vattel, on the other hand, is of opinion, that the day of the commencement of the truce would be included, and as the time ought to be taken largely and liberally, for the sake of humanity, the last day mentioned would also be included. Every ambiguity of this kind ought always to be prevented by positive and precise stipulations, as from such a day to such a day, both inclusive[5].

1 Vattel, Bk. III. ch. xvi. §§ 247, 248.

2 Ibid. § 250.

3 Ibid. Bk. III. ch. xvi. § 260.

4 Grotius, Bk. III. ch. xxi. § 4. Vattel, Bk. III. ch. xvi. § 244.

5 The rule proposed by the English Commissioners, in their report on the practice of the English Courts, in July, 1831, is recommended by its simplicity and certainty. They proposed to compute the first day exclu-

Safe conducts or passports.

(2.) A passport, or safe conduct, is a privilege granted in war, exempting the party from the effects of its operation, during the time, and to the extent prescribed in the permission. It flows from the sovereign authority; but the power of granting a passport may be delegated by the sovereign to persons in subordinate command, who are invested with that power, either by an express commission, or by the nature of that trust[1]. The general of an army, from the very nature of his power, can grant safe conducts; but the permission is not transferable by the person named in the passport; for it may be that the government had special reasons for granting the privilege to the very individual named, and it is presumed to be personal. If the safe conduct be granted, not for persons, but for effects, those effects may be removed by others besides the owner, provided no person be selected as the agent against whom there may exist a personal objection sufficient to render him an object of suspicion or danger within the territories of the power granting the permission.

He who promises security, by a passport, is morally bound to afford it against any of his subjects or forces, and to make good any damage the party might sustain by a violation of the passport. The privilege being so far a dispensation from the legal effects of war, it is always to be taken strictly, and must be confined to the purpose, and place, and time, for which it was granted. A safe conduct generally includes the necessary baggage and servants of the person to whom it is granted; and, to save doubt and difficulty, it is usual to enumerate, with precision, every particular branch and extent of the indulgence. If a safe conduct be given for a stated term of

sively and the last day inclusively in *all cases*. 3rd *Report of Commissioners on Courts of Common Law*, p. 44. See Archbold's *Practice* as to this, Vol. I. pp. 159—160 (11th edition).

[1] Vattel, Bk. III. ch. xvii. [Wheaton's *Elements of International Law*, Vol. II. Pt. IV. ch. ii. § 25. Heffter, *Droit des Gens*, Liv. 2, § 142. Klüber, *Droit des Gens*, 2de Partie, Tit. II. sect. ii. ch. i. § 274.]

time, the person in whose favour it was granted must leave the enemy's country before the time expires, unless detained by sickness, or some unavoidable circumstance, and then he remains under the same protection. The case is different with an enemy who comes into the country of his adversary during a truce. He, at his own peril, takes advantage of a general liberty, allowed by the suspension of hostilities, and, at the expiration of the truce, the war may freely take its course, without being impeded by any claims of such a party for protection[1].

It is stated that a safe conduct may even be revoked by him who granted it, for some good reason; for it is a general principle in the law of nations, that every privilege may be revoked, when it becomes detrimental to the state. If it be a gratuitous privilege, it may be revoked, purely and simply; but if it be a purchased privilege the party interested in it is entitled to indemnity against all injurious consequences, and every party affected by the revocation is to be allowed time and liberty to depart in safety[2].

Licenses.

The effect of a license given by the enemy to the subjects of the adverse party, to carry on a specified trade, has already been considered[3], in respect to the light in which it is viewed by the government of the citizens accepting it. A very different effect is given to these licenses by the government which grants them, and they are regarded and respected as lawful relaxations or suspensions of the rules of war. It is the assumption of a state of peace to the extent of the license, and the act rests in the discretion of the sovereign authority of the state, which alone is competent to decide how far considerations of commercial and political expediency may, in particular cases, control the ordinary consequences of war. In the country which grants them, licenses to carry on a pacific commerce are *stricti juris*, as being exceptions to a general rule; though

[1] Vattel, Bk. III. ch. xvii. §§ 273, 274.

[2] Ibid. Bk. III. ch. xvii. § 276.

[3] Supra, Chap. IV. pp. 204, 206.

they are not to be construed with pedantic accuracy, nor will every small deviation be held to vitiate the fair effect of them[1]. An excess in the quantity of goods permitted to be imported might not be considered as noxious to any extent, but a variation in the quality or substance of the goods might be more significant. Whenever any part of the trade assumed under the license is denuded of any authority under it, such part is subject to condemnation.

Another material circumstance in all licenses, is the limitation of time in which they are to be carried into effect; for what is proper at one time, may be very unfit and mischievous at another time. Where a license was limited to be in force until the 29th of September, and the ship did not sail from the foreign port until the 4th of October, yet, as the goods were laden on board by the 12th of September, and there was an entire *bona fides* on the part of the person holding the license, this was held to be legal[2]. But where a license was to bring away a cargo from Bordeaux, and the party thought proper to change the license, and accommodate it to another port in France, it was held, by the English Admiralty, in the case of the *Twee Gebroeders*[3], that the license was vitiated, and the vessel and cargo were condemned. It has also been held, that the license must be limited to the use of the precise persons for whose benefit it was obtained. The great principle in these cases is, that subjects are not to trade with the enemy without the special permission of the government; and a material object of the control which the government exercises over such a trade, is that

[1] The *Cosmopolite*, 4 Rob. 8. Grotius, Bk. III. ch. 21, § 14, lays down the general rule, that a safe conduct, of which these licenses are a species, is to be liberally construed; *laxa magis quam stricta interpretatio admittenda est.* And licenses were eventually construed with great liberality in the British Courts of Admiralty. Judge Croke, in the case of the *Abigail*, Stewart's *Vice-Adm. Rep.* 360. [Duer *On Insurance*, Vol. I. 595—619. The English Admiralty and Common law decisions on this subject of license are collected and examined by Mr Duer with his usual diligence and sagacity.]

[2] Schroeder *v.* Vaux, 15 East, 52. 3 *Campb. N. P.* 83.

[3] 1 Edw. *Adm. Rep.* 95.

it may judge of the particular persons who are fit to be intrusted with an exemption from the ordinary restrictions of a state of war[1].

Conventions and treaties.

(3.) The object of war is peace; and it is the duty of every belligerent power to make war fulfil its end with the least possible mischief, and to accelerate, by all fair and reasonable means, a just and honourable peace. The same power which has the right to declare and carry on war, would seem naturally to be the proper power to make and conclude a treaty of peace; but the disposition of this power will depend upon the local constitution of every nation; and it sometimes happens that the power of making peace is committed to a body of men who have not the power to make war. In Sweden, after the death of Charles XII., the king could declare war without the consent of the national Diet, but he made peace in conjunction with the Senate[2]. So, by the constitution of the United States, the President, by and with the advice and consent of two thirds of the Senate, may make peace, but it is reserved to Congress to declare war. This provision in their constitution is well adapted to unite, in the negotiation and conclusion of treaties, the advantage of talents, experience, stability, and a comprehensive knowledge of national interests, with the requisite secrecy and despatch. In England, as the sole prerogative of making war or peace is vested in the Crown, so also is it the Crown's prerogative to make treaties, leagues and alliances with foreign states and princes; and though this power has in theory no limits, yet practically it is controlled by the authority of Parliament, and the contingency of its abuse is checked by means of parliamentary impeachment for the punishment of such ministers as

[1] The *Jonge Johannes*, 4 Rob. 263. See the law as to licences collected in 1 Holt's *N. P. Rep.* 129, note. Mr Holt says, that Sir William Scott was, in fact, the author of the whole learning of the law relating to the system of licences. [But the reader will see a much more complete and useful exposition of the law on this subject in Mr Tudor's *Leading Cases on Mercantile Law;* see the notes to the *Hoop*, pp. 693—696.]

[2] Vattel, Bk. IV. ch. ii. § 10.

from criminal motives advise or conclude any treaty derogatory to the honour and interest of the nation[1].

Treaties of peace.

Treaties of peace, when made by the competent power, are obligatory upon the whole nation. If the treaty requires the payment of money to carry it into effect, and the money cannot be raised but by an act of the legislature, the treaty is morally obligatory upon the legislature to pass the law, and to refuse it would be a breach of public faith. The department of the government that is intrusted by the constitution with the treaty-making power, is competent to bind the national faith in its discretion; for the power to make treaties of peace must be coextensive with all the exigencies of the nation, and necessarily involves in it that portion of the national sovereignty which has the exclusive direction of diplomatic negotiations and contracts with foreign powers. All treaties made by that power become of absolute efficacy, because they are the supreme law of the land.

Alienation of public property.

There can be no doubt that the power competent to bind the nation by treaty may alienate the public domain and property by treaty. If a nation has conferred upon its executive department, without reserve, the right of treating and contracting with other states, it is considered as having invested it with all the power necessary to make a valid contract. That department is the organ of the nation, and the alienations by it are valid, because they are done by the reputed will of the nation. The fundamental laws of a state may withhold from the executive department the power of transferring what belongs to the state; but if there be no express provision of that kind, the inference is, that it has confided to the department charged with the power of making treaties, a discretion commensurate with all the great interests, and wants, and necessities of the nation. A power to make treaties of peace necessarily implies a power to decide

[1] Blackstone's *Commentaries*, Vol. I. p. 250, edition by R. M. Kerr. As to the extent of the treaty-making power in confederated governments, see Wheaton's *Elements*, Pt. IV. ch. iv. § 2, pp. 875, 876.

the terms on which they shall be made; and foreign states could not deal safely with the government upon any other presumption. The power that is entrusted generally and largely with authority to make valid treaties of peace, can, of course, bind the nation by alienation of part of its territory; and this is equally the case whether that territory be already in the occupation of the enemy, or remains in the possession of the nation, and whether the property be public or private[1]. In the case of the schooner *Peggy*[2], the Supreme Court of the United States admitted, that individual rights acquired by war, and vested rights of citizens, might be sacrificed by treaty for national purposes. So in the case of *Ware* v. *Hylton*[3], it was said to be a clear principle of national law, that private rights might be sacrificed by treaty to secure the public safety, though the government would be bound to make compensation and indemnity to the individuals whose rights had thus been surrendered. The power to alienate, and the duty to make compensation, are both laid down by Grotius[4] in equally explicit terms.

Treaty of peace; its binding effect.

A treaty of peace is valid and binding on the nation, if made with the present ruling power of the nation, or the government *de facto*. Other nations have no right to interfere with the domestic affairs of any particular nation, or to examine and judge of the title of the party in possession of the supreme authority. They are to look only to the fact of possession[5]. And it is an acknowledged

[1] Vattel, Bk. I. ch. xx. § 244. Ibid. ch. xxi. § 262; Bk. IV. ch. ii. § 11, 12. Vattel admits that the fundamental laws of a nation may withhold the power of alienation by treaty, and it would seem by necessary inference to be a violation of a fundamental law for the treaty-making power, acting under such an instrument as the Constitution of the United States, to agree by treaty for the abolition or alteration of any part of the constitution. The stipulation would go to destroy the very authority for making the treaty. See Wheaton's *Elements*, Pt. IV. ch. iv. § 2, p. 874, edit. 1863, and especially Heffter, *Droit des Gens*, § 182, p. 352.

[2] 1 Cranch, 103.

[3] 3 Dallas, 199, 245, by Chase, J.

[4] Bk. III. ch. 20, § 7.

[5] Vattel, Bk. IV. ch. ii. § 14.

rule of international law, that the principal party in whose name the war is made cannot justly make peace without including those defensive allies in the pacification who have afforded assistance, though they may not have acted as principals; for it would be faithless and cruel for the principal in the war to leave his weaker ally to the full force of the enemy's resentment. The ally is, however, not to be bound by the stipulations and obligations of the treaty beyond what he has been willing to accede to. All that the principal can require is, that his ally be considered as restored to a state of peace. Every alliance in which all the parties are principals in the war, obliges the allies to treat in concert, though each one makes a separate treaty of peace for himself[1].

The effect of a treaty of peace is to put an end to the war, and to abolish the subject of it. Peace relates to the war which it terminates. It is an agreement to waive all discussion concerning the respective rights of the parties, and to bury in oblivion all the original causes of the war[2]. It forbids the revival of the same war, by taking arms for the cause which at first kindled it, though it is no objection to any subsequent pretensions to the same thing, on other foundations[3]. After peace, the revival of grievances arising before the war is not to be encouraged, for treaties of peace are intended to put an end to such complaints; and if grievances then existing are not brought forward at the time when peace is concluded, it is to be presumed that it is not intended to bring them forward at any future time[4]. Peace leaves the contracting parties without any right of committing hostility for the very cause which kindled the war, or for what has passed in the course of it. It is, therefore, no longer permitted to take up arms again

[1] Ibid. Bk. IV. ch. ii. §§ 15 and 16.

[2] Sir William Scott, *The Eliza Ann*, 1 Dodson, 249. Though private rights existing before the war may not be remitted by peace, the presumption is otherwise as to the rights of kings and nations. Grotius, Bk. III. ch. xx. § 19.

[3] Vattel, Bk. IV. ch. ii. § 19.

[4] Sir William Scott, *The Molly*, 1 Dodson's *Adm. Rep.* 396.

for the same cause[1]. But this will not preclude the right to complain and resist, if the same grievances which kindled the war be renewed and repeated, for that would furnish a new injury and a new cause of war equally just with the former war. If an abstract right be in question between the parties, the right, for instance, to impress at sea one's own subjects from the merchant-vessels of the other, and the parties make peace without taking any notice of the question, it follows of course that all past grievances, damages, and injury, arising under such claim, are thrown into oblivion, by the amnesty which every treaty implies: but the claim itself is not thereby settled, either one way or the other. It remains open for future discussion, because the treaty wanted an express concession or renunciation of the claim itself[2].

A treaty of peace leaves every thing in the state in which it finds it, if there be no express stipulation on the subject. If nothing be said in the treaty of peace about the conquered country or places, they remain with the possessor, and his title cannot afterwards be called in question. During war the conqueror has only a usufructuary right to the territory he has subdued, and the latent right and title of the former sovereign continues, until a treaty of peace, by its silence, or by its express stipulation, shall have extinguished his title for ever[3].

**Treaty does not affect private right.**

The peace does not affect private rights which had no relation to the war. Debts existing prior to the war, and injuries committed prior to the war, but which made no part of the reasons for undertaking it, remain entire, and the remedies are revived[4]. There are certain cases in which even debts contracted, or injuries committed, be-

[1] Vattel, Bk. IV. ch. ii. § 19.

[2] Vattel, Bk. IV. ch. ii. § 19, 20. Heffter, *Droit des Gens*, §§ 179, 180, pp. 347—350.

[3] Sir William Scott, 1 Dodson, 452. Vattel, Bk. III. ch. xiii. § 197, 198. Ibid. Bk. IV. ch. ii. § 1. Grotius, Bk. III. ch. vi. §§ 4, 5. Mably's *Droit de l'Europe*, Tom. I. ch. ii. p. 144. Heffter, *Droit des Gens*, §§ 181, 182.

[4] Grotius, Bk. III. ch. xx. §§ 16, 18. Heffter, § 181.

tween two subjects of the belligerent powers, during the war, are the ground of a valid claim, as in the case of ransom bills, and of contracts made by prisoners of war for subsistence, or in a trade carried on under a license[1]. This would be the case if the debt between them was contracted, or the injury was committed, in a neutral country[2].

Time from which treaties bind.

A treaty of peace binds the contracting parties from the moment of its conclusion, and that is understood to be from the day it is signed[3]. A treaty made by the minister abroad when ratified by his sovereign relates back to the time of signing it[4]; but, like a truce, it cannot affect the subjects of the nation with guilt, by reason of acts of hostility subsequent to the date of the treaty, provided they were committed before the treaty was known. All that can be required in such cases is, that the Government make immediate restitution of things captured after the cessation of hostilities; and to guard against inconvenience from the want of due knowledge of the treaty, it is usual to fix the period at which hostilities are to cease at different places, and for the restitution of property taken afterwards[5].

Civil responsibility of individuals.

But though individuals are not deemed criminal for continuing hostilities after the date of the peace, so long as they are ignorant of it, a more difficult question to determine is, whether they are responsible, *civiliter*, in such cases. Grotius[6] says, they are not liable to answer in damages, but it is the duty of the Government to restore what has been captured and not destroyed. In the case

[1] Crawford *v.* *The William Penn*, 3 Wash. *Cir. R.* 484. 1 Peters' *Cir. Rep.* 106. S. C.

[2] Vattel, Bk. IV. ch. ii. § 22.

[3] Vattel, Bk. IV. ch. iii. § 24. In re Metzger, 5 Howard's *Reports*, 182. United States *v.* Reynes, 9 How. *R.* 127.

[4] Lessee of Hylton *v.* Brown, 1 Wash. *Cir. Rep.* 312.

[5] Vattel, Bk. IV. ch. iii. §§ 24, 25. Ibid. Bk. II. ch. xii. §§ 156, 157. Ibid. Bk. III. ch. xvi. 2 Dallas, 40. Azuni, *Droit Marit.* T. II. ch. iv. Art. I. § 11. Lessee of Hylton *v.* Brown, 1 Wash. *Cir. Rep.* 311. 312. 342. 351.

[6] Bk. III. ch. xxi. § 5.

of the American ship *Mentor*[1], which was taken and destroyed off Delaware Bay, by British ships of war, in 1783, after the cessation of hostilities, but before that fact had come to the knowledge of either of the parties, the point was much discussed; and it was held, that the injured party could not pass over the person from whom the alleged injury had been received, and fix it on the commander of the English squadron on that station, who was totally ignorant of the whole transaction, and at the distance of thirty leagues from the place where it passed. There was no instance in the annals of the prize courts of such a remote and consequential responsibility in such a case. The actual wrong-doer is the person to answer in judgment, and to him the responsibility (if any) is attached. He may have other persons responsible over to him, but the injured party could look only to him. The better opinion was, that though such an act be done through ignorance of the cessation of hostilities, yet mere ignorance of that fact would not protect the officer from civil responsibility in a prize court; and that, if he acted through ignorance, his own Government must protect him and save him harmless. When a place or country is exempted from hostility by articles of peace, it is the duty of the Government to use due diligence to give its subjects notice of the fact; and the Government ought, in justice, to indemnify its subjects, who act in ignorance of the peace. And yet it would seem, from that case, that the American owner was denied redress in the British Admiralty, not only against the Admiral of the fleet on that station, but against the immediate author of the injury. Sir William Scott denied the relief against the admiral; and ten years before that time relief had equally been denied by his predecessor against the person who did the injury. If that decision was erroneous, an appeal ought to have been prosecuted. We have then the decision of the English High Court of Admiralty, denying any

Case of the *Mentor*.

[1] 1 Rob. 179.

relief in such a case, and an opinion of Sir William Scott, many years afterwards, that the original wrong-doer was liable. The opinions cannot otherwise be reconciled, than upon the ground, that the prize courts have a large and equitable discretion, in allowing or withholding relief, according to the special circumstances of the individual case, and that there is no fixed or inflexible general rule on the subject[1].

Effect of treaty on prior captures.

If a time be fixed by the treaty for hostilities to cease in a given place, and a capture be previously made, but with knowledge of the peace, it has been a question among the writers on public law, whether the captured property should be restored. The better, and the more reasonable opinion, is, that the capture would be null, though made before the day limited, provided the captor was previously informed of the peace; for, as Emerigon[2] observes, since constructive knowledge of the peace, after the time limited in the different parts of the world, renders the capture void, much more ought actual knowledge of the peace to produce that effect[3].

[[1] What really was decided in the case was, that the actual wrongdoer is the only person responsible in a Court of Admiralty for injuries of seizure; and if the Admiral of the station is not privy to the fact, a suit will not be entertained against him. It must be admitted that the case, as it thus stands, is one of hardship, but the claimant might have appealed from the first decision.]

[2] Valin, *Traité des Prises*, ch. iv. §§ 4, 5. Emerigon, *Traité des Ass.* ch. xii. § 19. Azuni, *Droit Maritime*, T. II. ch. iv. Art. I. §§ 9—12.

[3] This point was very extensively discussed in the French prize courts, in the case of the capture of the British ship *Swineherd* by the French privateer *Bellona*, and what was sufficient knowledge of the fact of the peace to annul the capture, was the great question. It appeared that the *Bellona* sailed from the Isle of France the 27th of November, 1801, before news had arrived at the island of the signing of the preliminaries of peace between France and England, and which had been signed on the 1st of October preceding. The capture was made on the 24th of February, 1802, within the period of five months from the date of the treaty; and, by the 11th article of the treaty, it was provided, that captures made in any part of the world, after five months from the ratification of the treaty, should be null and void. The capture was made in a place where a shorter period than five months did not apply. The proclamation of the King of Great Britain, of the 12th of October, 1801, announced the fact of the signature of the preliminary arti-

Another question arose subsequent to the treaty of Ghent of 1814, in one of the British vice-admiralty courts, on the validity of a recapture by a British ship of war, of a British vessel captured by an American privateer. The capture made by the American cruiser was valid, being made before the period fixed for the cessation of hostilities, and in ignorance of the fact; but the prize had not been carried into port and condemned, and while at sea she was recaptured by the British cruiser after the period fixed for the cessation of hostilities, but without knowledge of the peace. It was decided, that the possession of the vessel Case of the *Legal Tender*

cles of peace; and it stated the substance of the 11th article, and ordered all hostilities to cease in the different places, from and after the respective periods mentioned in that article; and this proclamation was published in the *Calcutta Gazette*, and made known by the production of that paper, to the French cruiser, at several times, by distinct vessels, some days previous to the capture. This evidence of the peace was also communicated to the captain of the French vessel as soon as the capture took place, and yet, notwithstanding this notice, the English ship was taken possession of, and carried into the Isle of France, and libelled, and condemned, as lawful prize of war. The sentence of condemnation was affirmed in 1803, on appeal to the Council of Prizes at Paris, and M. Merlin has reported at large the elaborate argument and opinion of M. Collet Descotils, the Imperial Advocate General in the Council of Prizes, in favour of the captors. The ground he took, and upon which the Council of Prizes proceeded, was, that the king's proclamation, unaccompanied by any French attestation, was not that sufficient and indubitable evidence to the French cruiser, of the fact of the peace, upon which he ought to have acted, and that the period of the five months had not elapsed, within which it was lawful, in the Indian seas, to continue hostilities. The learned and venerable author of that immense work, the *Repertory of Jurisprudence*, says, on introducing the case, that he shall be silent on the question, and contents himself with giving the discussions, and particularly the opinion of the Advocate General, and the reasons of the Council of Prizes. See *Repertoire Universel et Raisonné de Jurisprudence*, par M. le Comte Merlin, Tom. IX. tit. *Prise Maritime*, § 5. [In the Baron de Cussy's work, *Droit Maritime*, the reader will find the case of the *Swineherd* (which the Baron calls '*Le Porcher*') reported at full length, and the decision justified on the ground of the absence of documents on board the captured ship showing the fact of the existence of peace. The Baron also reports the case of the *Nymph*, captured by the French privateer, *La petite Renommée*, off Guadaloupe, 23 November, 1801, and restored on the ground of fraud and perfidy in the seizure on the part of the captain of the *Renommée*. Cussy, *Droit Maritime*, Tom. II. Liv. II. ch. XIX. §§ 2, 3, pp. 158—164.]

by the American privateer was a lawful possession, and that the British cruiser could not, after the peace, lawfully use force to divest this lawful possession. The restoration of peace put an end, from the time limited, to all force, and then the general principle applied, that things acquired in war remain, as to title and possession, precisely as they stood when the peace took place. The *uti possidetis* is the basis of every treaty of peace, unless it be otherwise agreed. Peace gives a final and perfect title to captures without condemnation, and, as it forbids all force, it destroys all hopes of recovery as much as if the vessel was carried *infra præsidia*, and condemned[1]. A similar doctrine was held in the case of the schooner *Sophia*[2], and the treaty of peace had the effect of quieting all titles of possession arising from the war, and of putting an end to the claim of all former proprietors to things of which possession was acquired by right of war.

Obligation to restore.

If nothing be said to the contrary, things stipulated to be restored are to be returned in the condition they were taken; but this does not relate to alterations which have been the natural consequence of time, and of the operations of war. A fortress or a town is to be restored in the condition it was when taken, as far as it shall still be in that condition when the peace is made[3]. There is no obligation to repair, as well as restore, a dismantled fortress, or a ravaged territory. The peace extinguishes all claim for damages done in war, or arising from the operations of war. Things are to be restored in the condition the peace found them; and to dismantle a fortification, or to waste a country, after the conclusion of the peace, and previous to the surrender, would be an act of perfidy[4].

Treaties of every kind, when made by the competent authority, are as obligatory upon nations, as private con-

[1] Case of the *Legal Tender*, Halifax, April, 1815, cited Wheaton's *Digest of the Law of Maritime Captures*, p. 302.

[2] 6 Rob. 138.

[3] Vattel, Bk. IV. ch. iii. §§ 31. 34.

[4] Ibid. Bk. IV. ch. iii. § 32.

tracts are binding upon individuals; and they are to receive a fair and liberal interpretation, and to be kept with the most scrupulous good faith. Their meaning is to be ascertained by the same rules of construction and course of reasoning which we apply to the interpretation of private contracts[1]. If a treaty should in fact be violated by one of the contracting parties, either by proceedings incompatible with the particular nature of the treaty, or by an intentional breach of any of its articles, it rests alone with the injured party to pronounce it broken. The treaty, in such a case, is not absolutely void, but voidable, at the election of the injured party[2]. If he chooses not to come to a rupture, the treaty remains obligatory. He may waive or remit the infraction committed, or he may demand a just satisfaction.

Distinction between new war and breach of treaty.

There is a very material and important distinction made by the writers on public law, between a new war for some new cause, and a breach of a treaty of peace. In the former case, the rights acquired by the treaty subsist, notwithstanding the new war; but, in the latter case, they are annulled by the breach of the treaty of peace, on which they are founded. A new war may interrupt the exercise of the rights acquired by the former treaty, and, like other rights, they may be wrested from the party by the force

[1] Ibid. Bk. II. ch. xvii. §§ 263—298. Eyre, Ch. J. in Marryatt *v.* Wilson 1 Bos. and Pull. 438, 439. Opinion of Sir James Marriot, cited in 1 Chitty *On Commercial Law*, 44. But, if the legislative and executive branches of the government have given and asserted a construction to a treaty with a foreign power, under which it claims dominion over a territory in its possession, the courts of justice will not set up or sustain a different construction. Foster *v.* Neilson, 2 Peter's *U. S. Rep.* 253. If a treaty be ambiguous in any part of it the party who had the power, and on whom it was peculiarly incumbent to speak clearly and plainly, ought to submit to the construction most unfavourable to him, upon the reasonable maxim of the Roman law that 'Pactionem obscuram iis nocere in quorum fuit potestate legem apertius conscribere.' Vattel, Bk. II. ch. xvii. § 264. See as to the interpretation of treaties, Rutherforth's *Inst.* Bk. II. ch. vii. § 1. Heffter, *Droit des Gens*, § 94, p. 393, and the excellent remarks of Halleck, *International Law*, ch. xxxvi. § 15.

[2] Grotius, Bk. II. ch. xv. § 15; Bk. III. ch. xx. §§ 35—38. Burlamaqui, Pt. IV. ch. xiv. § 8, p. 335. Vattel, Bk. IV. ch. iv. § 54.

of arms. But then they become newly acquired rights, and partake of the operation and result of the new war. To recommence a war, by breach of the articles of a treaty of peace, is deemed much more odious than to provoke a a war by some new demand and aggression; for the latter is simply injustice, but, in the former case, the party is guilty both of perfidy and injustice[1]. The violation of any one article of a treaty, is a violation of the whole treaty; for all the articles are dependent on each other, and one is to be deemed a condition of the other; and a violation of any single article overthrows the whole treaty, if the injured party elects so to consider it. This may, however, be prevented by an express provision, that if one article be broken, the others shall, nevertheless, continue in full force[2]. There is a strong instance in the history of the United States of the annihilation of treaties by the act of the injured party. In 1798, the Congress of that country[3] declared that the treaties with France were no longer obligatory on the United States, as they had been repeatedly violated on the part of the French Government, and all just claims for reparation refused.

**Obligations of treaties dissipated by hostility.**

As a general rule, the obligations of treaties are dissipated by hostility. But if a treaty contains any stipulations which contemplate a state of future war, and make provision for such an exigency, they preserve their force and obligation when the rupture takes place. All those duties of which the exercise is not necessarily suspended by the war, subsist in their full force. The obligation of keeping faith is so far from ceasing in time of war, that its efficacy becomes increased, from the increased necessity of it. What would become of prisoners of war, and the terms of capitulation of garrisons and towns, if the word of an enemy was not to be relied on? The faith of promises and treaties which have reference to a state of war, is to be

[1] Grotius, Bk. III. ch. xx. §§ 27, 28. Vattel, Bk. IV. ch. iv. § 42.

[2] Grotius, Bk. III. ch. xix. § 14. Vattel, Bk. IV. ch. iv. §§ 47, 48; Bk. II. ch. xiii. § 202.

[3] Act of July 7th, 1798.

held as sacred in war as in peace, and among enemies as among friends. All the writers on public law admit this position, and they have never failed to recommend the duty and the observance of good faith, by the most powerful motives, and the most pathetic and eloquent appeals which could be addressed to the reason and to the moral sense of nations[1]. The tenth article of the treaty between the United States and Great Britain, in 1794, may be mentioned as an instance of a stipulation made for war. It provided, that debts due from individuals of the one nation to those of the other, and the shares or moneys which they might have in the public funds, or in public or private banks, should never, in any event of war, be sequestered or confiscated. There can be no doubt that the obligation of that article was not impaired by the war of 1812, but remained throughout that war, and continued binding upon the two nations, until they should mutually agree to rescind the article; for it is a principle of universal jurisprudence, that a compact cannot be rescinded by one party only, if the other party does not consent to rescind it, and does no act to destroy it. In the case of *The Society for Propagating the Gospel* v. *New-Haven*, the Supreme Court of the United States would not admit the doctrine that treaties became extinguished *ipso facto* by war, unless revived by an express or implied renewal on the return of peace. Such a doctrine is not universally true. Where treaties contemplate a permanent arrangement of national rights, or where, by their terms, they are meant to provide for the event of an intervening war, it would be against every principle of just interpretation to hold them extinguished by the event of war. They revive at peace, unless waived, or new and repugnant stipulations be made[2].

Cessions of territory.

With respect to the cession of places or territories by a treaty of peace, though the treaty operates from the making

[1] Vattel, Bk. III. ch. 10, § 174. Grotius, Bk. III. ch. xxv.

[2] Society for Propagating the Gospel *v.* New-Haven, 8 Wheaton, 494, and Sutton *v.* Sutton, 1 Russ. and Mylne, 663, where the same principle is maintained in an English Court of Chancery.

of it, it is a principle of public law, that the national character of the place agreed to be surrendered by treaty, continues as it was under the character of the ceding country, until it be actually transferred. Full sovereignty cannot be held to have passed by the mere words of the treaty, without actual delivery. To complete the right of property, the right to the thing, and the possession of the thing, must be united. This is a necessary principle in the law of property in all systems of jurisprudence. There must be both the *jus ad rem* and the *jus in re,* according to the distinction of the civilians, which Barbeyrac[1] (though without reason) says they borrowed from the canon law. This general law of property applies to the right of territory no less than to other rights. The practice of nations has been conformable to this principle, and the conventional law of nations is full of instances of this kind, several of them being stated by Sir Wm. Scott in the opinion which he gave in the case of the *Fama*[2].

No obligation on the government to indemnify after cession of territory by coercion.

The release of a territory from the dominion and sovereignty of the country, if that cession be the result of coercion or conquest, does not impose any obligation upon the government to indemnify those who may suffer a loss of property by the cession[3]. The annals of New-York furnish a strong illustration of this position. The territory composing the state of Vermont belonged to this state; and it separated from it, and erected itself into an independent state, without the consent, and against the will, of the government of New-York. The latter continued for many years to object to the separation, and to discover the strongest disposition to reclaim by force the allegiance of the inhabitants of that state. But they were unable to do it; and it was a case of a revolution effected by force, analogous to that which was then in action between this country and Great Britain. When New-York therefore found itself under the necessity of acknowledging the independence of Vermont, a question arose before the legis-

[1] Puff. par Barbeyrac, Liv. IV. ch. ix. § 8, note 2. [2] 5 Rob. 106.

[3] Vattel, Liv. I. ch. xx. § 244. Wheaton's *Elements,* Part IV. ch. iv. § 2.

lature, whether they were bound in duty to make compensation to individual citizens whose property would be sacrificed by the event, because their titles to land lying within the jurisdiction of Vermont, and derived from New-York, would be disregarded by the government of that state. The claimants were heard at the bar of the house of Assembly, by counsel, in 1787, and it was contended on their behalf, that the state was bound, upon the principles of the social compact, to protect and defend the rights and property of all its members, and that, whenever it became necessary, upon grounds of public expediency and policy, to withdraw the protection of Government from the property of any of its citizens, without actually making the utmost efforts to reclaim the jurisdiction of the country, the state was bound to make compensation for the loss. In answer to this argument, it was stated, that the independence of Vermont was an act of force beyond the power of this state to control, and equivalent to a conquest of that territory, and the state had not the competent ability to recover, by force of arms, their sovereignty over it, and it would have been folly and ruin to have attempted it. All pacific means had been tried without success; and as the state was compelled to yield to a case of necessity, it had discharged its duty; and it was not required, upon any of the doctrines of public law, or principles of political or moral obligation, to indemnify the sufferers. The cases in which compensation had been made for losses consequent upon revolutions in government, were peculiar and gratuitous, and rested entirely on benevolence, and were given from motives of policy, or as a reward for extraordinary acts of loyalty and exertion. No government can be supposed to be able, consistently with the welfare of the whole community, and it is, therefore, not required, to assume the burthen of losses produced by conquest, or the violent dismemberment of the state. It would be incompatible with the fundamental principles of the social compact[1].

[1] See Hamilton's *Works*, Vol. II. pp. 374—390.

This was the doctrine which prevailed; and when the act of July 14th, 1789, was passed, authorizing commissioners to declare the consent of the state to the independence of Vermont, it was expressly declared, that the act was not to be construed to give any person claiming lands in Vermont, under title from this state, any right to any compensation whatsoever from New-York[1].

[1] See on the whole of the subject above discussed, so far as Treaties of Peace, their incidents, and effect, are concerned, Klüber, *Droit des Gens*, 2de Partie, Tit. II. sect. II. ch. iii. §§ 317—329. De Cussy, *Droit Maritime*, Tom. I. Liv. I. tit. iii. § 1. p. 168—178. Heffter, *Droit des Gens*, §§ 179—184, pp. 347—355, edit. 1857, par Bergson. Wheaton's *Elements*, Pt. IV. ch. iv. pp. 872—888, edit. by W. B. Lawrence, 1863. Halleck's *International Law*, ch. xxxiv. and xxxvi.

## CHAPTER XI.

### OF OFFENCES AGAINST THE LAW OF NATIONS.

---

THE violation of a treaty of peace, or other national compact, is a violation of International Law, for it is a breach of public faith[1]. Nor is it to be understood that that law is a code of mere elementary speculation, without any efficient sanction. It has a real and propitious influence on the fortunes of the human race. It is a code of present, active, durable, and binding obligation. As its great fundamental principles are founded in the maxims of eternal truth, in the immutable law of moral obligation, and in the suggestions of an enlightened public interest, they maintain a steady influence, notwithstanding the occasional violence by which that influence may be disturbed. This law is placed under the protection of public opinion. It is enforced by the censures of the press, and by the moral influence of those great masters of public law, who are consulted by all nations as oracles of wisdom; and who have attained, by the mere force of written reason, the majestic character, and almost the authority, of universal lawgivers, controlling by their writings the conduct of rulers, and laying down precepts for the government of mankind. No nation can violate public law, without being subjected to the penal consequences of reproach and disgrace, and without incurring the hazard of punishment, to be inflicted in open and solemn war by the injured party.

[1] Vattel, Bk. 2. II. ch. xv. § 221. *Resolution of Congress* of November 23rd, 1781.

This law too is enforced by the sanctions of municipal law, and is adopted in its full extent by the law of England[1]. The offences which fall more immediately under its cognizance, and which are the most obvious, the most extensive, and most injurious in their effects, are the violations of safe conduct, infringements of the rights of ambassadors, and piracy. To these we may add the slave-trade, which may now be considered, not, indeed, as a piratical trade, absolutely unlawful by the law we are discussing, but as a trade condemned by the general principles of justice and humanity, openly professed and declared by the powers of Europe.

Passports or safe conducts.

(1.) A safe conduct or passport contains a pledge of the public faith, that it shall be duly respected, and the observance of this duty is essential to the character of the government which grants it. The statute law of the United States has provided, in furtherance of the general sanction of public law, that if any person shall violate any safe conduct or passport, granted under the authority of the United States, he shall, on conviction, be imprisoned for a term not exceeding three years, and fined at the discretion of the Court[2].

Ambassadors.

(2.) The same punishment is inflicted upon those persons who infringe the law of nations, by offering violence to the persons of ambassadors, and other public ministers, or by being concerned in prosecuting or arresting them[3]. This is an offence highly injurious to a free and liberal communication between different governments, and mischievous in its consequences to the dignity and well being of the nation. It tends to provoke the resentment of the sovereign whom the ambassador represents, and to bring upon the state the calamities of war. The English parliament, under an impression of the danger to the com-

[1] Blackstone, Vol. IV. ch. v. pp. 66—68.

[2] *Act of Congress*, April 30th, 1790, § 27. See further as to this topic, Wheaton's *Elements*, Part IV. ch. ii. § 25; and for the English law Blackstone's *Comm.* Vol. IV. ch. v. pp. 68—70.

[3] *Act of Congress*, supra, §§ 25, 26.

munity from violation of the rights of embassy, and urged by the spur of a particular occasion, carried the provisions of the Statute of 7 Ann, c. 12, to a dangerous extent. That statute prostrated all the safeguards to life, liberty, and property, which the wisdom of the English common law had established. It declared, that any person convicted of suing out or executing civil process, upon an ambassador, or his domestic servants, by the oath of the party, or of one witness, before the Lord Chancellor, and the two Chief Justices, or any two of them, might have such penalties and corporal punishment inflicted upon him, as the judges should think fit. The preamble to the statute contains a special and inflamed recital of the breach of the law of nations which produced it, by the arrest of the Russian minister in the streets of London[1].

The Congress of the United States, during the time of the American war, discovered great solicitude to maintain inviolate the obligations of the law of nations, and to have infractions of it punished in the only way that was then lawful, by the exercise of the authority of the legislatures of the several states. They recommended to the states to provide expeditious, exemplary, and adequate punishment for the violation of safe-conducts or passports, granted under the authority of Congress, to the subjects of a foreign power in time of war; for the commission of acts of hostility against persons in amity or league with the United States; for the infractions of treaties and conventions to which the United States were a party; and for infractions of the immunities of ambassadors, and other public ministers[2].

(3.) Piracy is robbery, or a forcible depredation on the high seas, without lawful authority, and done *animo* Piracy.

[[1] For a full account of the transaction here noticed see Blackstone's *Commentaries*, Vol. I. pp. 255, 256. With the criticism of the learned author upon the conduct of the British Parliament in passing this Act, which was certainly in accordance with recognized principles of Public International Law, we do not agree.]

[2] *Journals of Congress*, Vol. VII. 181.

*furandi*, and in the spirit and intention of universal hostility. It is the same offence at sea with robbery on land; and all the writers on the law of nations, and on the maritime law of Europe, agree in this definition of piracy[1]. Pirates have been regarded by all civilized nations as the enemies of the human race, and the most atrocious violators of the universal law of society[2]. They are everywhere pursued and punished with death; and the severity with which the law has animadverted upon this crime, arises from its enormity and danger, the cruelty that accompanies it, the necessity of checking it, the difficulty of detection, and the facility with which robberies may be committed upon pacific traders in the solitude of the ocean. Every nation has a right to attack and exterminate them without any declaration of war; for though pirates may form a loose and temporary association among themselves, and re-establish in some degree those laws of justice which they have violated with the rest of the world, yet they are not considered as a national body, or entitled to the laws of war as one of the community of nations. They acquire no rights by conquest, and both international law and the municipal law of every country authorize the true owner to reclaim his property taken by pirates, wherever it can be found; nor do they recognise any title to be derived from an act of piracy. The principle, that *a piratis et latronibus capta dominium non mutant*, is the received opinion of ancient civilians, and modern writers on general jurisprudence: and the same doctrine was maintained in the English courts of common

[1] The United States *v.* Smith, 5 *Wheaton*, 153, and note, ibid. 163. See Russell on Crimes, Vol. I. ch. viii. § 1. [Blackstone's *Commentaries*, Vol. IV. ch. v. p. 71. Bishop's *Comm. on the Criminal Law of America*, Vol. II. ch. xlvii., and Wharton's *Criminal Law* (of America), § 2825.

N.B. The note here referred to in which the doctrines of the civil, the maritime, and the common law, are collected, was written by Mr Justice Story, by whom the opinion of the court was delivered in the case here cited (Story's *Life of Story*, Vol. I. p. 285).]

[2] Cic. *in Verrem*, Lib. V. 3 *Inst.* 113.

law prior to the great modern improvements made in the science of international law[1].

By the Constitution of the United States, Congress were authorized to define and punish piracies and felonies committed on the high seas, and offences against the law of nations. In pursuance of this authority, it was declared, by the act of Congress of April 30th, 1790, sec. 8, that murder or robbery committed on the high seas, or in any river, haven, or bay, out of the jurisdiction of any particular state, or any other offence, which, if committed within the body of a county, would, by the laws of the United States, be punishable with death, should be adjudged to be piracy and felony, and punishable with death[2]. It was further declared, that if any captain or mariner should piratically and feloniously run away with any vessel, or any goods or merchandise to the value of fifty dollars; or should yield up any such vessel voluntarily to pirates; or if any seaman should forcibly endeavour to hinder his commander from defending the ship or goods committed to his trust, or should make a revolt in the ship; every such offender should be adjudged a pirate and felon, and be punishable with death. Accessaries to such piracies before the fact are punishable in like manner; but accessaries after the fact are only punishable by fine and imprisonment. By the act of March 3, 1819, sec. 5, (which act was made perpetual by that of 15th of May,

American Statutes.

[1] Bynk. *Q. J. Pub.* Bk. I. ch. xvii. Rutherforth, Bk. II. ch. ix. Azuni, T. II. ch. v. Art. III. Croke Eliz, 685. 2 Wooddeson's *Lect.* 429. Wheaton's *Elements*, Part II. ch. II. § 15 Heffter, *Droit des Gens*, Liv. I. ch. iii. § 104. Ortolan, *Règles Internationales*, T. I. ch. xi. And see, for the doctrines of the English law upon this subject of Piracy in the middle of the 17th century, an interesting chapter in Molloy, *De Jure Maritimo*, Vol. I. ch. iv. Property found on board a pirate ship goes to the crown of strict right as droits of the Admiralty, but the claim of the original owner is admitted upon equitable principles, on due application. The *Helen*, 1 Hagg. *Adm. Rep.* 142. The *Panda*, W. Rob. 423, 435.

[2] By the *Act of Congress*, of March 3rd, 1835, c. 313, the offence of making a revolt in a ship is no longer punishable as a capital offence, but only by fine or imprisonment, or hard labour.

1820, sec. 2), Congress declared, that if any person on the high seas should commit the crime of *piracy, as defined by the law of nations,* he should, on conviction, suffer death. It was again declared, by the act of Congress of 15th of May, 1820, sec. 3, that if any person upon the high seas, or in any open roadstead, or bay, or river, where the sea ebbs and flows, commits the crime of robbery in and upon any vessel, or the lading thereof, or the crew, he shall be adjudged a pirate. So, if any person concerned in any particular enterprize, or belonging to any particular crew, should land, and commit robbery on shore, such an offender shall also be adjudged a pirate. The statute, in this respect, seems to be only declaratory of the law of nations; for, upon the doctrine of the case of *Lindo* v. *Rodney*[1], such plunder and robbery ashore, by the crew, and with the aid of vessels, is a marine case, and of admiralty jurisdiction[2]. [On the 3rd of March, 1847, Congress passed another act on the subject of piracy, declaring that when any subject or citizen of any foreign state should be

[1] Doug. 613 (note).

[[2] The President of the United States having by proclamation, dated April 19, 1861, declared *inter alia* that any person acting under letters of marque issued by the authority of the so-called Confederate States would be held amenable to the laws of the Union for the prevention and punishment of piracy, an important debate ensued upon this proclamation in the British House of Lords, in the course of which strong opinions were expressed by several noble lords, both as to the impolicy and impropriety of this measure. Some trials of privateersmen acting under Confederate commission took place in New York and Philadelphia, under the 3rd section of the Act of 1820, but as not only no sentences were passed but retaliatory action took place on the part of the southern States, by an order dated 21st January, 1862, all the prisoners charged with piracy were transferred to a military prison as prisoners of war. Lord Russell in a despatch to Lord Lyons, dated January 24th, 1862, in noticing with satisfaction this change of feeling on the part of the Federal Government, takes the opportunity to express a strong opinion against the propriety and policy of the proclamation of April, 1861. See *Parliamentary Papers,* 1862, North America, No. I. p. 137. Hansard's *Debates,* Vol. CLXII. p. 1829, and Wheaton's *Elements,* Part II. ch. ii. pp. 250--254, notes by W. B. Lawrence.

It should be noticed that the Spanish Government have, it is asserted, by decree declared that all persons acting under letters of marque issued by the authorities of Chili will be treated as pirates.]

found and taken on the seas making war upon the United States, or cruising against the vessels or property thereof, contrary to the provisions of any treaty existing between the United States and the state to which the offenders belonged, such persons should be arraigned, tried, and, if convicted, punished as pirates. It further declared, that upon the capture and condemnation, in any port of the United States, of vessels guilty of piratical aggressions, the court might order a sale and distribution of them; and that the commander and crew of a merchant-vessel belonging to the United States might defend itself against the attack of any vessel not being the public armed ship of a nation in amity with the United States, and might retake the vessel in the event of capture. And by an act passed August 5th, 1861, it was enacted that vessels intended for piratical aggressions may be seized at sea or in port and condemned; and that not only are commanders of public ships or vessels acting under letters of marque to be instructed to seize, but collectors, surveyors, and marshals also are to seize.]

Case of U.S. v. Smith.

Under these legislative provisions, it has been made a question, whether it was sufficient to refer to international law for a definition of piracy, without giving the crime a precise definition in terms. The point was settled in the case of the *United States* v. *Smith*[1]; and it was there held that it was not necessary to give by statute a more logical enumeration in detail of all the facts constituting the offence, and that Congress might as well define it by using a term of a known and determinate meaning, as by expressly mentioning all the particulars included in that term. The crime of piracy was defined by that law with reasonable certainty, and it does not depend upon the particular provisions of any municipal code for its definition and punishment. Robbery on the high seas is, therefore, piracy by the act of Congress, as well as by the law of nations; [the term high seas being extended to the open roadsteads of a foreign country; for, as Mr Justice Johnson

[1] 5 Wheaton, 153.

says, in the case of the *United States* v. *Pirates*[1], "It is historically known that, in prosecuting trade with many places, vessels lie at anchor in open situations, and especially where the trade winds blow under the lee of the land. Such vessels are neither in a river, haven, basin, nor bay; and are no where, unless it be on the seas. Nor can it be objected that it is within the constitutional limits of a foreign state, for those limits, though neutral to war, are not neutral to crime."]

Piracy punishable everywhere.

There can be no doubt of the right of Congress to pass laws punishing pirates, though they may be foreigners, and may have committed no particular offence against the United States. It is of no importance, for the purpose of giving jurisdiction, on *whom* or *where* a piratical offence has been committed. A pirate, who is one by the law of nations, may be tried and punished in any country where he may be found, for he is reputed to be out of the protection of all laws and privileges[2]. The statute of any government may declare an offence committed on board its own vessels to be piracy, and such an offence will be punishable exclusively by the nation which passes the statute. But piracy, according to international law, is an offence against all nations, and punishable by all. In the case of the *United States* v. *Palmer*[3], it was held that the act of Congress of 1790 was intended to punish offences against the United States, and not offences against the human race; and that the crime of robbery, committed by a person who was not a citizen of the United States, on the high seas, on board of a ship belonging exclusively to subjects of a foreign state, was not piracy under the act, and was not punishable in the courts of the United States. The offence, in such a case, must, therefore, be left to be punished by the nation under whose flag the vessel sailed, and within whose particular jurisdiction all on board the vessel were. This decision was according to the law and

[1] 5 Wheaton, 200.
[2] Bynk. *Q. J. Pub.* ch. xvii.
[3] 3 Wheaton, 610.

practice of nations, for it is a clear and settled principle, that the jurisdiction of every nation extends to its own citizens, on board of its own public and private vessels at sea[1]. The case applied only to the fact of robbery committed at sea, on board of a foreign vessel, at the time belonging exclusively to subjects of a foreign state; nor was it intended to decide, that the same offence, committed on board of a vessel not belonging to the subject of any foreign power, was not piracy. The same court afterwards, in the case of the *United States* v. *Klintock*[2], admitted, that murder or robbery, committed on the high seas, by persons on board of a vessel not at the time belonging to the subjects of any foreign power, but in possession of a crew acting in defiance of all law, and acknowledging obedience to no government or flag whatsoever, fell within the purview of the act of Congress, and was punishable in the courts of the United States. Persons of that description were pirates, and proper objects for the penal code of all nations. The act of Congress did not apply to offences committed against the particular sovereignty of a foreign power; or to murder or robbery committed in a vessel belonging at the time, in fact as well as in right, to the subject of a foreign state, and, in virtue of such property, subject at the time to its control. But it applied to offences committed against all nations, by persons who, by common consent, were equally amenable to the laws of all nations.

It was further held, in the case of the *United States* v. *Pirates*[3], and in the case of the *United States* v. *Holmes*[4], in pursuance of the same principle, that the moment a vessel assumed a piratical character, and was taken from her officers, and proceeded on a piratical cruise, she lost all

[1] Rutherforth's *Inst.* Bk. II. ch. ix. Mr Jefferson's *Letter to M. Genet*, 17th June, 1793. *American State Papers*, Vol. I. pp. 89—94.

[2] 5 Wheaton, 144, and U. S. *v.* Pirates, 5 Wheaton, 184, and now see the Act, 3rd March, 1847, ch. li. § 1, which has provided for offences of this nature. See also a supplementary Act of August 5th, 1861. *U. S. Statutes at Large*, Vol. IX. p. 175 and Vol. XII. pp. 314, 315.

[3] 5 Wheaton, 184.

[4] Ibid. 412.

claim to national character, and the crew, whether citizens or foreigners, were equally punishable, under the act of Congress, for acts of piracy; and it would be immaterial what was the national character of the vessel before she assumed a piratical character. Piracy is an offence within the criminal jurisdiction of all nations. It is against all, and punished by all; and the plea of *autrefois acquit*, resting on a prosecution instituted in the courts of any civilized state, would be a good plea in any other civilized state. As the act of Congress of 1790 declares every offence committed at sea to be piracy, which would be punishable with death if committed on land, it may be considered as enlarging the definition of piracy, so as not only to include every offence which is piracy by the law of nations, and the act of Congress of 1819, but other offences which were not piracy until made so by statute. [The meaning of the act of 1819 was examined by the Supreme Court in the case of The claimants of the Brig *Malek Adhel* v. the United States. The vessel, in that case, was armed with a cannon and some ammunition, and there were also pistols and daggers on board, but nothing else beyond the usual equipment of a vessel of her class bound on an innocent commercial voyage from New York to a Pacific port. Whatever illegal acts were done after her departure were entirely without the knowledge or approbation of her owners; but it appeared conclusively that her commander had stopped by force several vessels on the seas, taking from them whatever he fancied. In deciding upon the question of adjudication, the Supreme Court held that the *Malek Adhel* was undoubtedly an armed vessel within the intent of the act of 1819, and that by the words "piratical aggression" is meant such offences as pirates are in the habit of perpetrating, whatever the motive, whether plunder, revenge, hatred, or wanton abuse of power; and consequently that actual plunder, or intent to plunder, need not appear in order to bring the case within the act[1].]

Explanation of the Act of 1819.

[1] Peter Harmony and others *v.* the United States, 2 Howard's *Reports*, 210. N.B. It was also laid down by the court that though the vessel may

Aliens acting under commissions.

An alien, under the sanction of a national commission, cannot commit piracy while he pursues his authority. His acts may be hostile, and his nation responsible for them. They may amount to a lawful cause of war, but they are never to be regarded as piracy[1]. The Barbary powers, notwithstanding some doubts which formerly existed, for a century and more prior to their extinction, were regarded as lawful powers, and not pirates. They were acknowledged to have all the insignia of regular independent governments, and to be competent to maintain the European relations of peace and war. Cicero, and, after him, Grotius, define a regular enemy to be a power which hath the elements or constituents of a nation, such as a government, a code of laws, a national treasury, the consent and agreement of the citizens, and which pays a regard to treaties of peace and alliance[2]; and all these things, says Bynkershoek[3], are to be found among the states of Barbary. In

The Barbary powers.

be condemned and sold, and its proceeds distributed, there is no authority for the condemnation of the cargo, whether the owners be innocent, or ignorant, or not; such confiscation, if permitted, can only be for serious and gross instances.

[1] Martens' *Essay on Privateers*, translated by Horne, p. 42. Manning's *Commentaries*, pp. 112, 113. States generally prohibit their subjects from taking letters of marque from a foreign power without the permission of their sovereign; and treaties are numerous in which the contracting parties stipulate that if the subjects of either party take letters of marque from the enemies of the other, they shall be treated as pirates. [In the war recently declared by Spain against the Chilian Republic the Minister of Marine in Spain has issued a circular, dated Madrid, Nov. 27th, ordering the commanders of Spanish ships to treat as pirates all vessels whose captains, officers, and majority of crews, are not Chilians, or who may not have received their commissions direct from the Chilian Government (see *Times* newspaper, Nov. 29th, 1865), a proceeding of a very high-handed and unusual nature, to say the least of it. See as to such a course the language of Mr Webster in the affair of Alexander Macleod, and his objection to the term pirates being applied to Americans aiding and joining in the Canadian disturbances. Webster's *Works*, Vol. v. p. 256.]

[2] Cic. *Philip.* IV. ch. vi. Grotius, Bk. III. ch. iii. § 1.

[3] *Q. J. Pub.* Bk. I. ch. xvii. A State, in the meaning of public law, is a complete or self-sufficient body of persons, united together in one community for the defence of their rights, and to do right to foreigners. A State has its affairs and interests; it deliberates, and becomes a moral

some respects their laws of war retained the barbarity of the middle ages, for they levied tribute or contributions on all such Christian powers as were not able to protect their commerce by force; and they also made slaves of their prisoners, requiring a heavy ransom for their redemption. But this, Bynkershoek insists, is conformable to the strict laws of war; and the nations of Europe who carried on war with the Barbary states, such as Spain, Naples, Holland, &c. did for a long time exercise the same rule of ancient warfare, upon the principle of retaliation.

Bombardment of Algiers.

When Lord Exmouth, in 1816, attacked Algiers, and compelled the Dey to terms of peace, he compelled him also to stipulate, that in the event of future wars with any European power, Christian prisoners of war should never more be consigned to slavery, but should be treated with all humanity as prisoners of war, until regularly exchanged according to the European practice; and that at the termination of hostilities, the prisoners should be restored without ransom. By that treaty of peace, upwards of 1000 prisoners belonging to Italy, Spain, Portugal, Holland, and Greece, were released from galling slavery, in which many of them had subsisted for thirty-five years. This stipulation in favour of general humanity, deserves some portion of that exalted eulogy bestowed by Montesquieu[1] on the treaty made by Gelon, king of Syracuse, with the Carthaginians. It would have been still more worthy of a comparison, if it had not left colour for the construction, that the renunciation of the practice of condemning Christian prisoners of war to slavery, was to be confined to the "event of future wars with any European power;" and if a great Christian power across the Atlantic, whose pre-

person, having an understanding and will, and is susceptible of obligations and laws. Grotius, Bk. I. ch. i. § 14. Ibid. Bk. III. ch. iii. § 2. Burlamaqui, Vol. II. Part I. ch. iv. § 9. Vattel, Bk. I. ch. i. *Respublica est cœtus multitudinis, Juris consensu et utilitatis communione sociatus.* Cic. *de Repub.* Lib. I. § 25. [But see for a definition and complete analysis of the term State, Austin's *Province of Jurisprudence determined*, Vol. I. p. 199 (note).]

[1] *Esprit des Loix*, Bk. X. ch. v.

sence and whose trade is constantly seen and felt in the Mediterranean, had not seemed to have been entirely forgotten[1].

But notwithstanding Bynkershoek had insisted, near a century ago, that captures by the Barbary powers worked a change of property by the laws of war, in like manner as captures made by regular powers, yet, in a case in the English admiralty so late as 1801, it was contended[2], that the capture and sale of an English ship by Algerines was an invalid and unlawful conversion of the property, on the ground of being a piratical seizure. It was, however, decided, that the African states had long acquired the character of established governments, and that though their notions of justice differ from those entertained by the Christian powers, their public acts could not be called in question; and a derivative title, founded on an Algerine capture, and matured by a confiscation in their way, was held to be good against the original owner. In the time of Richard I. when the laws of Oleron were compiled, all infidels were, by that code[3], regarded as pirates, and

[1] Declaration of the Dey of Algiers made with Lord Exmouth, August 25th, 1816. *Annual Register* for 1816. *App. to Chron.* p. 288, and Alison's *Hist. of Europe* (1815—1852), Vol. I. ch. ii. § 82.

[A short account of the Barbary pirates (of Morocco, Tunis, Algiers, and Tripoli) will be found in the 2nd Vol. of Baron Cussy's *Treatise*, well written and deserving praise in spite of a strong touch of anti-Anglican feeling running through it, not unnatural in a French writer recording the loss of French influence in the Mediterranean through the cession of Malta to England. After narrating the rise and progress of these scourges of ancient commerce and the efforts made to restrain them culminating in Lord Exmouth's crowning victory, the author with no little pride tells of their utter extinction through the conquest and seizure of Algeria by France in 1830, recounts the treaties of Bardo between France and Tunis in August, 1830, by which the Dey renounced for ever privateering, the imposition of slavery on Christians, and every attempt to hinder the spread of commerce, —and winds up with a short protest against the jealousy of England in the matter of the conquest of Algeria, and a slight sketch of the present empire of Morocco. De Cussy, *Droit Maritime*, T. II. Liv. II. ch. xxxii. § 2, pp. 417—431.]

[2] The *Helena*, 4 Rob. 3.

[3] Sec. 45. See Pardessus's *Collection de loix Maritimes*, T. I. p. 351, and Peter's *Admiralty decisions*, Vol. I. App. p. lxii.

their property liable to seizure wherever found. It was a notion, at that time, that such persons could not have any fellowship or communion with Christians.

In a case which occurred in 1675, Sir Leoline Jenkins held, that the commander of a privateer regularly commissioned, was liable to be treated as a pirate, if he exceeded the bounds of his commission[1]. Bynkershoek justly opposes this dangerous opinion[2]; and the true rule undoubtedly is, that the vessel must have lost its national and assumed a piratical character, before jurisdiction over it, to that extent, could be exercised.

Foreign commissions to cruise.

If a natural born subject was to take prizes belonging to his native country, in pursuance of a foreign commission, he would, on general principles, be protected by his commission from the charge of piracy. But to prevent the mischief of such conduct, the United States have followed the provisions of the English statute of 11 and 12 Wm. III. c. 7, and have, by the act of Congress of April 30th, 1790, sec. 9, declared, that if any citizen should commit any act of hostility against the United States, or any citizen thereof, upon the high seas, under colour of any commission from any foreign prince or state, or on pretence of authority from any person, such offender shall be adjudged to be a pirate, felon, and robber, and, on being thereof convicted, shall suffer death. The act of Congress not only authorizes a capture, but a condemnation in the courts of the United States, for all piratical aggressions by foreign vessels; and whatever may be the responsibility incurred by the nation to foreign powers, in executing such laws, there can be no doubt that courts of justice are bound to obey and administer them. All such hostile and criminal aggressions on the high seas, under the flag of any power, render property taken *in delicto* subject to confiscation by the law of nations[3].

1 *Life of Sir L. Jenkins*, Vol. II. p. 754.

2 *Quæst. J. P.* Bk. I. ch. xvii.

3 By Story J. in the *Marianna Flora*, 11 Wheaton, 39—41.

[In the two following treatises on American criminal law the reader will

English statute law.

[The subject of piracy, under the English law, is so thoroughly discussed from a legal point of view in such well known and accessible treatises as Blackstone's *Commentaries* and Russell *on Crimes*, that it is not at all necessary to dwell on it here. Suffice it to say, that whilst by the English common law it is not known as an offence *per se*, and was not even made felony by the earliest statute affecting it (the 28 Hen. VIII. c. 15), which declared it however to be a capital offence, several statutes have been passed since that date for the express purpose of supplying this deficiency. These statutes, running from the 28 Hen. VIII. c. 15 to the 1 Vict. c. 88[1], have dealt with the crime and made provision against it in various ways, but as they are all recorded and noticed at more or less length in the authorities specified below we pass them over without explanation. Nor will it be necessary to dwell upon the points of law arising out of the trials that have taken place. Important and interesting as many of them are, especially the latter ones[2], we must leave them unnoticed further than by reference to the first volume of Russell *on Crimes*, where in the eighth chapter they are recorded and examined at length. One very recent case however requires a short comment here—its importance rests on three grounds: first, its connection with the extradition

find all the statutes and the cases upon the subject of piracy. (1) Wharton's *Criminal Law*, Book VIII. chapter i. §§ 2816—2885. (2) Bishop's *Commentaries on Criminal Law*, Vol. II. chap. xlvii. where, in addition to the statutes, all the cases are collected and noticed under three heads:—1st. The Common Law doctrines. 2nd. English Statutes. 3rd. American Statutes and Treaties. The most recent American trial, as cited by Mr Bishop, is that of the officers and crew of the privateer Savannah. The learned author gives in note 5 to § 1017 of the above-named chapter a short abstract of Judge Nelson's elaborate definition of and comment on the offence of piracy, as delivered in that case.

The reader is also referred to an opinion of Attorney-General Wirt in the case of the schooner *Adonis*, Nov. 1825, for an exposition of the law as to statutory piracy. See opinions of Attorneys-General (American), Vol. II. p. 19, &c.]

[1] Extended by the 7 and 8 Vict. c. 2, and the 17 and 18 Vict. c. 114, § 267.

[2] Such as R. *v.* Lopez, R. *v.* Sutler, R. *v.* Sevra, and R. *v.* Zulueta.

treaty between Great Britain and the United States; secondly, the distinction between piracy *jure gentium* and municipal piracy on which the decision in the case turns; and thirdly, the dissentient view of the Lord Chief Justice of England. The case is that of 'In re Tirnan'[1], and it arose out of a writ of *habeas corpus* issued by the Court of Queen's Bench to bring up the bodies of Patrick Tirnan and others from the main bridewell of Liverpool. The return to that writ shewed that these persons had been detained under and by virtue of warrants upon a charge of piracy on the high seas within the jurisdiction of the United States, in consequence of a requisition made in conformity with the 6 and 7 Vict. c. 76, § 1 (the Extradition Treaty Act), by the United States minister at the Court of London; and from the information and examinations taken before the magistrates at Liverpool, upon which the different warrants had been granted, it appeared that the prisoners and others had risen upon the master and crew of the schooner *Joseph Gerrity*, of New York, and captured her for the purpose of making a Confederate cruiser of her, none of the captors having commission, letters of marque, or papers of any kind in their possession. Upon these facts and upon the return to the writ of *habeas corpus*, the Court of Queen's Bench were asked to discharge the prisoners on the ground mainly that the case did not fall within the treaty entered into between this country and the United States in 1842, nor within the provisions of the Act above cited. And it was argued for the prisoners that they were entitled to their discharge because they had been committed for piracy on the high seas and for piracy *jure gentium*, which was not a crime contemplated by the treaty or statute. The arguments are too long and the judgements, which were given *seriatim*, too long also to allow us to go into them. It is enough to state, that the majority of the Court holding that the enactments of the statute applied to crimes com-

Case of "In re Tirnan."

Decision of the Court.

[1] 5 Best and Smith, 645.

mitted within the jurisdiction of the United States, that the word piracy, which means, in its primary sense, piracy *jure gentium*, was cut down by the treaty and statute to piracy committed within the jurisdiction of either of the high contracting parties, that the words "within the jurisdiction" mean within the exclusive jurisdiction of the state requiring the extradition[1], and that as the offence was piracy *jure gentium*, which is punishable everywhere and within the jurisdiction of all civilized nations, it did not come within the jurisdiction of both countries, and therefore was not within the statute, decided that the prisoners ought not to be given up, and, having been detained under a warrant of a Justice in England, were entitled to be discharged. From the opinions of the majority of the court the Lord Chief Justice[2] dissented, laying down in a masterly judgement what he conceived to be, and what strikes us as being, the more correct interpretation of the statute. "What is there," said his Lordship, "to show that the term piracy is used in its restricted sense? If that had been the intention we should have had piracy by the municipal law distinguished from piracy *jure gentium*, and we should have found terms introduced into the Act, but the language contains no such limitation. Then why is it to be read as being used in the more limited sense?" His Lordship then proceeds to maintain that, whether looking at national dignity or character, or whether considering the general balance of convenience, if the treaty and Act were not capable of the construction put on them by him, they would have failed in the object they were intended to accomplish and ought to be amended, and adds this, "I think the true meaning of the word jurisdiction is that which was put upon it by Mr Lush when he argued that it meant the area over which the laws of the particular state prevail; and inasmuch as it is conceded that the

Judgement of the L. C. Justice.

[1] In accordance with the language of Mr Justice Nelson, "In re Kaine," 14 Howard's Report, U. S. Supreme Court.

[2] Sir Alexander Cockburn.

ship of a particular state is constructively part of its territory, or at all events a place where its laws prevail, this ship was within the jurisdiction of the United States."

Review of the case.

It seems to us, in reading these decisions, that if the opinion of the majority of the court does state the true construction of the Act, so far as the offence of piracy is concerned this extradition treaty is cut down to such narrow proportions as to be comparatively valueless; but we venture to think that the right construction is that which the Lord Chief Justice has laid down, and that whilst on the one hand it never was intended that the narrow limit which is now held to be law should be put upon the treaty, on the other the parties to the treaty had no other notion in their minds about piracy than the ordinary well known meaning attached to the term, and were thinking of providing as well against piracy *jure gentium* as against piracy by municipal law. The section no doubt is not very happily worded, all the offences enumerated in it being classed together and so placed as if the words "committed within the jurisdiction of either of the contracting parties" were to be applied to all; but when we consider how different in every respect the crime of piracy is from the rest of the crimes specified, and that in nine cases out of ten the offence of piracy is committed on the high seas and out of the exclusive jurisdiction of any particular nation, whereas the other offences are committed within that jurisdiction, there seems to be good reason "for not putting the narrower construction upon the term if there be evidence upon which the parties charged can be fairly convicted of piracy at all."]

The slave trade.

(4) The African slave trade is an offence against the municipal laws of most nations of Europe, and it is declared to be piracy by the statute laws of England and the United States. Whether it is to be considered as an offence against the law of nations, independent of compact, has been a grave question, much litigated in the courts charged with the administration of public law; and it will be useful to take a short view of the progress and

present state of the sense and practice of nations on this subject.

Personal slavery, arising out of forcible captivity, has existed in every age of the world, and among the most refined and civilized people. The possession of persons so acquired has been invested with the character of property. The slave trade was a regular branch of commerce among the ancients; and a great object of Athenian traffic with the Greek settlements on the Euxine was procuring slaves from the barbarians for the Greek market[1]. In modern times treaties have been framed and national monopolies sought to facilitate and extend commerce in this species of property[2]. It has been interwoven into the municipal institutions of all the European colonies in America, and with the approbation and sanction of the parent states. It forms to this day the foundation of large masses of property in the southern parts of these United States. But, for half a century past, the African slave trade began to awaken a spirit of remorse and sympathy in the breasts of men, and a conviction that the traffic was repugnant to the principles of Christian duty and the maxims of justice and humanity.

Montesquieu, who has disclosed so many admirable truths, and so much profound reflection, in his *Spirit of Laws*, not only condemned all slavery as useless and unjust, but he animadverted upon the African slave trade by the most pungent reproaches. It was impossible, he observed, that we could admit the negroes to be human beings, because, if we were once to admit them to be men, we should soon come to believe that we ourselves

1 Mitford's *Hist.* Vol. IV. 236. See Boeckh's *Public Economy of Athens*, ch. xiii. pp. 67—73. The Byzantines, says Polybius (*General History*, Bk. IV. ch. v), supplied from the Pontus the Greeks with honey, wax, salted meats, leather, and great numbers of very serviceable slaves.

2 Notably the Assiento treaty, made in the first instance between Spain and other powers in 1689, transferred by the treaty of Utrecht to England in 1713, and then vested in the South Sea Company, but afterwards given up to Spain at the peace in 1748. See A. Smith's *Wealth of Nations*, Bk. V. ch. i.

were not Christians. Why has it not, says he, entered into the heads of the European princes, who make so many useless conventions, to make one general stipulation in favour of humanity[1]? We shall see presently that this suggestion was, in some degree, carried into practice by a modern European congress.

Statutes of the U. S. against the slave trade.

The constitution of the United States laid the foundation of a series of provisions to put a final stop to the progress of this great moral pestilence, by admitting a power in Congress to prohibit the importation of slaves, *after* the expiration of the year 1807. The constitution evidently looked forward to the year 1808 as the commencement of an epoch in the history of human improvement. Prior to that time, Congress did all on this subject that it was within their oompetence to do[2]. By the Acts of March 22nd, 1794, and May 10th, 1800, the citizens of the United States, and residents within them, were prohibited from engaging in the transportation of slaves from the United States to any foreign place or country, or from one foreign country or place to another, for the purpose of traffic. These provisions prohibited American citizens from all concern in the slave trade, with the exception of direct importation into the United States; and the most prompt and early steps were taken, within the limits of the constitution, to interdict that part of the traffic also. By the Act of 2nd March, 1807, the importation of slaves into the United States was prohibited, under severe penalties, after the 1st of January, 1808; and, on the 20th of April, 1818, the penalties and punishments were increased,

[1] *L'Esprit des Loix*, Liv. XV. ch. V.

[2] The Continental Congress which assembled at Philadelphia in 1774, gave the first general and authoritative condemnation of the slave trade, by the resolution not to import, or purchase any slave imported after the first day of December in that year, and wholly to discontinue the trade. *Journals of Congress*, Vol. I. p. 32. The Convention of Delegates of the People of Virginia had anticipated this measure, for in August preceding they resolved to discontinue the importation of slaves. Pitkin's *History*, Vol. I. App. n. 16. Jones's *Defence of the Revolutionary History of North Carolina*, p. 145.

and the prohibition extended not only to importation, but generally against any citizen of the United States being concerned in the slave trade. It has been decided[1], that these statute prohibitions extend as well to the carrying slaves on freight as to cases where they were the property of American citizens, and to carrying them from one port to another of the same foreign empire as well as from one foreign country to another. The object was to prevent, on the part of American citizens, all concern whatever in such a trade.

The Act of March 3rd, 1819, went a step further, and authorized national armed vessels to be sent to the coast of Africa to stop the slave trade, so far as citizens or residents of the United States were engaged in that trade; and their vessels and effects were made liable to seizure and confiscation. The Act of 15th May, 1820[2], went still further, and declared, that if any citizen of the United States, being of the crew of any foreign vessel engaged in the slave trade, or any person whatever, being of the crew of any vessel armed in whole or in part, or navigated for or on behalf of any citizen of the United States, should land on any foreign shore and seize any negro or mulatto, with intent to make him a slave, or should decoy, or forcibly bring, or receive such negro on board such vessel, with like intent, such citizen or person should be adjudged a pirate, and, on conviction, should suffer death.

It is to be observed, that the statute operates only where the municipal jurisdiction might be applied, consistently with the general theory of public law, to the persons of American citizens, or to foreigners on board of American vessels. Declaring the crime piracy does not make it so, within the purview of international law, if it were not so without the statute; and the legislature

[1] The *Merino*, 9 Wheaton, 391. The declarations of the master, connected with his acts in furtherance of the voyage, have been held to be evidence on an indictment against the owner of the ship, under the Act of 20th April, 1818. United States *v.* Gooding, 12 Wheaton, 460.

[2] Ch. cxiii. §§ 4 and 5.

intended to legislate, only where they had a right to legislate, over their own citizens and vessels. The question, notwithstanding these expressions in the statute, still remained to be discussed and settled, whether the African slave trade could be adjudged piracy, or any other crime, within the contemplation of the code of international law. It had been attempted, by negotiation between the United States and Great Britain, to agree that both nations should consider the slave trade piratical; but the convention for that purpose between the two nations was not ratified[1], though the British nation carried their statute denunciation of the trade as far as the law of the United States.

Treaty of Washington, 1842.

[In August, 1842, the treaty of Washington[2] was signed between Great Britain and the United States, for the purpose of more effectually supporting the laws for the suppression of the slave trade; but though that trade had, as we have seen by statute[3], been made piracy, so far as citizens or vessels of the United States were concerned, the provision was not adopted in the treaty of 1842. We pass over the treaty and the discussions and debates[4] that ensued upon it in the houses of legislature in both countries,

Treaty of April 7, 1862.

and proceed to notice the treaty of the 7th of April, 1862, which was negotiated at Washington by Lord Lyons and Mr Seward. It stipulates for the reciprocal visitation and search in time of peace of the merchant-vessels of the two countries suspected of being engaged in the African slave trade; declares the mode in which the cruisers of the two navies are to conduct the search, the special instructions with which they are to be furnished, and the object and limits of that search; provides for the establishment of

[1] President Monroe's *Message*, 21st May, 1824, and *British and Foreign State Papers*, 1824—25, p. 850. See also Wheaton's *Elements*, Part II. ch. ii. § 15, pp. 260, 261 (note), ed. 1863, by W. B. Lawrence.

[2] *British and Foreign State Papers*, 1841—42, Vol. XXX. p. 360.

[3] *U. S. Statutes at Large*, Vol. III. p. 600.

[4] They are animadverted on at considerable length in Mr W. B. Lawrence's note, pp. 263—265, in Wheaton's *Elements*, Part II. ch. ii. ed. 1863 (and cited from his work on *Visitation and Search*). There is a strong anti-English feeling running through the whole note.

mixed tribunals for the purpose of bringing to adjudication the vessels detained by the cruisers employed by each of the powers; regulates the disposition of the matters, persons, and things, brought before these courts; and decrees the restoration to freedom of the negroes found on board the captured vessels. Such then are the international arrangements made by the United States for the purpose of putting an end to "the accursed traffic," and such the municipal regulations applied to the same object. "On these regulations or acts of Congress, the learned author, Mr Chancellor Kent, in a note appended to page 195 of the fourth edition[1], published in 1840, remarks, that they applied exclusively to *external* commerce in slaves, the *internal* commerce within the United States being left to the control and discretion of the state governments; and he further adds, that whilst in some of the slave holding states a traffic in slaves, as between citizens of different states, was permitted in the northern states, slavery was abolished, and the internal commerce in slaves was forbidden. Little more than twenty years have elapsed since that note was penned, and a change of a most sweeping and unexpected kind has taken place. A rebellion, remarkable for its extent and stubbornness has broken out, and a war has swept over a large portion of the United States, taxing severely the strength and endurance of the existing government, and bringing out, in striking outline, the energy, the military skill, and the gallantry of both sides engaged in it. Whether or not other questions than slavery were at the bottom of the strife, we leave to others to decide; but that the question of slavery was largely mixed up with the differences between the two contending parties, few can doubt who read attentively the history of the events immediately preceding the declaration of independence on the part of the seceding states. At all events this is clear, that slavery in every part of the United States has received its death-blow, and

Present state of the slave question in the United States.

[1] *Commentaries on American Law,* Vol. I. Lect. ix. p. 195, note a.

is doomed to extinction; and that the legislature has, in pursuance of the dictates of humanity which have inspired other portions of its anti-slavery enactments, deserved eternal praise for an act which will make the termination of the great contest memorable to all time. In Mr Bishop's treatise on Criminal Law, a work already referred to under the head of piracy, the learned author discusses in a note how the matter of the future of slavery stands, and with that view cites the following article[1] of the Act of Congress of 1865, which says, "That neither slavery, nor involuntary servitude, except as a punishment for crime, shall exist within the United States, and that Congress shall have the power to submit this to legislation." It is also provided that this Act be submitted to the legislatures of the several states for their ratification; and, as by a recent mail from the United States, it appears that three-fourths of the states have ratified the Act, it must now be taken to be the supreme law; "and so the great end for which the war was fought is practically accomplished[2]."]

British statutes.

The first British statute declaring the slave trade unlawful appeared in March, 1807[3]. This was a great triumph of British justice. It was called for by the sense of the nation, which had become deeply convinced of the impolicy and injustice of the slave trade; by the subsequent statute of 51 Geo. III. the trade was declared to be contrary to the principles of justice, humanity, and sound policy; and lastly, by the Act of Parliament of 31st March, 1824, the trade is declared to be piracy[4]. England is thus, equally with the United States, honestly and zealously engaged in promoting the universal abolition of the trade, and in holding out to the world her sense of its extreme criminality. Almost every maritime nation in

[1] Art. XIII. See Bishop's *Comment. on Criminal Law,* Vol. I. chapter xlix. note I.

[2] See the *Times* newspaper, Dec. 23rd, 1865, p. 10, where it is also stated that four Southern States, North Carolina, South Carolina, Georgia, and Alabama, have ratified the Act.

[3] Stat. 47 Geo. III.

[4] 5 Geo. IV. c. 17, and 5 Geo. IV. c. 113.

Europe has also deliberately and solemnly, either by legislative acts, or by treaties and other formal engagements, acknowledged the injustice and inhumanity of the trade, and pledged itself to promote its abolition. By the treaty of Paris of the 30th May, 1814, between Great Britain and France, Lewis XVIII. agreed that the traffic was repugnant to the principles of natural justice, and he engaged to unite his efforts at the ensuing congress to induce all the powers of christendom to decree the abolition of the trade, and to cause it to cease definitively, on the part of the French government, in the course of five years. The ministers of the principal European powers who met in congress at Vienna, on the 8th February, 1815, solemnly declared, in the face of Europe and the world, that the African slave trade had been regarded by just and enlightened men, in all ages, as repugnant to the principles of humanity and of universal morality, and that the public voice in all civilized countries demanded that it should be suppressed; and that the universal abolition of it was conformable to the spirit of the age and the generous principles of the allied powers[1]. In March, 1815, the emperor Napoleon decreed that the slave trade should be abolished; but this effort of ephemeral power was afterwards held to be null and void, as being the act of an usurper; and in July following, Lewis XVIII. gave directions that this odious and wicked traffic should from that present time cease. The first French decree, however, that was made public, abolishing the trade, was of the date of the 8th of January, 1817, and that was only a partial and modified decree. In December, 1817, the Spanish government prohibited the purchase of slaves on any part of the coast of Africa, after the 31st of May, 1820[2]; and in January, 1818, the Portuguese government made the like prohibition as

[1] A declaration that was renewed by the plenipotentiaries of the five great Powers assembled in Congress at Verona, in resolutions adopted in a conference held on the 28th Nov. 1822.

[2] By a decree, dated Oct. 27th, 1865, the slave trade in the Spanish colonies has been suppressed.

to the purchase of slaves on any part of the coast of Africa north of the equator. In 1821, there was not a flag of any European state which could legally cover this traffic to the north of the equator; and yet, in 1825, the importation of slaves covertly continued, if it was not openly countenanced, from the Rio de Plata to the Amazon, and through the whole American Archipelago[1].

Case of the *Amedie.*

The case of the *Amedie*[2] was the earliest decision in the English courts on the great question touching the legality of the slave trade, on general principles of international law. That was the case of an American vessel, employed in carrying slaves from the coast of Africa to a

[1] *Report of a Committee of the House of Representatives of the United States*, February 16th, 1825. See also the *Q. Review*, No. 68 and No. 89, pp. 243—246. Alison's *History of Europe*, 1815—52. Vol. VI. ch. xxxvii. § 118. It appears, from a reference to various documents, that the African slave trade was carried on to an enormous extent down to the year 1830. The trade was principally between Africa and Brazil and Cuba. In 1828, 45,000 African slaves were imported into the city of Rio Janeiro. But by a convention between England and Brazil, in 1826, it was made piratical for the subjects of Brazil to be engaged in the trade after the year 1830; and it is understood that the government of Brazil, in 1831, not only put a stop by law to the importation of slaves, but declared that all slaves thereafter imported should be free, and imposed a heavy assessment on the importers, and provided for the transportation of such negroes back to Africa. Further conventions have been made with Portugal in 1842, and with Brazil in 1845. These two countries having been notoriously the worst offenders in recent times. [Such are some out of the many treaties that have been made by and between the different European states, who at one time or other have been interested in this brutal and brutalizing traffic, for the purpose of putting a stop to it. They who may be desirous of inspecting these treaties and of examining at more length the history of the attempts to destroy the slave trade will find full information in the article on slavery and the slave trade in the *Family Cyclopædia*, and in that on the slave trade in the *Encyclopædia Britannica*. In the *Index to the British and Foreign State Papers* will be found all the treaties that have been made by this country with other powers. So far as British statutes and the judicial decisions of the British, the reader will find information in Russell *on Crimes*, Vol. I. ch. xviii. and in an American work published at Philadelphia in 1858 (Cobb's *History of Slavery*) he will see an elaborate and complete sketch of slavery from the earliest times, and a full examination into the law of the subject.]

[2] 1 Acton's *Rep.* 240.

Spanish colony. She was captured by an English cruiser, and the vessel and cargo were condemned to the captors in a vice-admiralty court in the West Indies, and, on appeal to the Court of Appeals in England, the judgment was affirmed. Sir Wm. Grant, who pronounced the opinion of the court, observed, that the slave trade being abolished by both England and the United States, the court was authorized to assert, that the trade, abstractedly speaking, could not have a legitimate existence, and was, *prima facie*, illegal, upon principles of universal law. The claimant, to entitle him to restitution, must show affirmatively a right of property under the municipal laws of his own country; for, if it be unprotected by his own municipal law, he can have no right of property in human beings carried as his slaves, for such a claim is contrary to the principles of justice and humanity. The *Fortuna*[1] was condemned on the authority of the *Amedie*, and the same opinion was again affirmed. But in the subsequent case of the *Diana*[2], the doctrine was not carried so far as to hold the trade itself to be piracy, or a crime against the law of nations. A Swedish vessel was taken by a British cruiser on the coast of Africa, engaged in carrying slaves from Africa to a Swedish island in the West Indies, and she was restored to the owner, on the ground that Sweden had not then prohibited the trade, and had tolerated it in practice. England had abolished the trade as unjust and criminal, but she claimed no right of enforcing that prohibition against the subjects of those states which had not adopted the same opinion; and England did not mean to set herself up as the legislator and *custos morum* for the whole world, or presume to interfere with the commercial regulations of other states. The principle of the case of the *Amedie* was, that where the principal law of the country to which the parties belonged had prohibited the trade, English tribunals would hold it to be illegal, upon general principles of justice and humanity,

Case of the *Fortuna.*

[1] 1 Dodson, 81. [2] 1 Dodson, 95.

but they would respect the property of persons engaged in it under the sanction of the laws of their own country.

The doctrine of these cases is, that the slave trade, abstractedly speaking, is immoral and unjust, and it is illegal, when declared so by treaty or municipal law; but that it is not piratical or illegal by the common law of nations, because, if it were so, every claim founded on the trade would at once be rejected everywhere, and in every court, on that ground alone.

Case of the *Le Louis.*

The whole subject underwent further, and a most full, elaborate, and profound discussion, in the case of the *Le Louis*[1]. A French vessel, owned and documented as a French vessel, was captured by a British armed force on the coast of Africa, after resistance made to a demand to visit and search. She was carried into Sierra Leone, and condemned by a court of vice-admiralty for being concerned in the slave trade contrary to the French law. On appeal to the British High Court of Admiralty, the question respecting the legality of the capture and condemnation was argued, and it was judicially decided, that the right of visitation and search on the high seas did not exist in time of peace. If it belonged to one nation, it equally belonged to all, and would lead to gigantic mischief and universal war. Other nations had refused to accede to the English proposal of a reciprocal right of search in the African seas, and it would require an express convention to give the right of search in time of peace. The slave trade, though unjust, and condemned by the statute law of England, was not piracy, nor was it a crime by the universal law of nations. To make it piracy, or such a crime, it must have been so considered and treated in practice by all civilized states, or made so by virtue of a general convention. On the contrary, it had been carried on by all nations, even by Great Britain herself, until within a few years, and was then carried on by Spain and Portugal, and not absolutely prohibited

[1] 2 Dodson, 210.

by France. It was, therefore, not a criminal traffic by the law of nations; and every nation, independent of treaty, retained a legal right to carry it on. No one nation had a right to force the way to the liberation of Africa by trampling on the independence of other states; or to procure an eminent good by means that were unlawful; or to press forward to a great principle, by breaking through other great principles that stood in the way. The condemnation of the French vessel at Sierra Leone was, therefore, reversed; and the penalties imposed by the French law (if any there were), were left to be enforced, not in an English, but in a French court.

Case of Madrazo *v.* Willes.

The same subject was brought into discussion in the King's Bench in 1820, in Madrazo *v.* Willes[1]. The court held, that the British statutes against the slave trade were only applicable to British subjects, and only rendered the slave trade unlawful when carried on by them. The British parliament could not prevent the subjects of other states from carrying on the trade out of the limits of the British dominions. If a ship be acting contrary to the general law of nations, she is thereby subject to condemnation; but it is impossible to say that the slave trade was contrary to the general law of nations. It was, until lately, carried on by all the nations of Europe; and a practice so sanctioned can only be rendered illegal, on the principles of international law, by the consent of all the powers. Many states had so consented, but others had not, and the cases had gone no further than to establish the rule, that ships belonging to countries that had prohibited the trade were liable to capture and condemnation if found engaged in it. ["Madrazo *v.* Willes," says Mr Justice Willes, in a very recent case (Santos *v.* Illidge[2]), first heard in the Common Pleas and then argued and decided in the Exchequer Chamber, "has been wondered at," but in Buron *v.* Denman[3], the Court of Exchequer

[1] 3 Barnwall and Alderson, 353.

[2] 6 C. B. N. S. 841 and in Error, and 29 L. J. C. P. 348.

[3] 2 Exch. 167.

seems to have adopted the principles laid down by Sir Wm. Scott in the *Le Louis*, whilst, as will presently be seen, the Court of Error, in the case of Santos *v.* Illidge, by a majority of six Judges to four, reversed the decision of the Court of Common Pleas, and adhered pretty closely to the doctrine laid down in Madrazo *v.* Willes. The facts in the case of Santos *v.* Illidge were, that the defendants, being British subjects, domiciled and resident in Great Britain, but members of a copartnership called the Imperial Brazilian Mining Association, were as such possessed of slaves in Brazil, where slavery was allowed; after the coming into operation of the 5 Geo. IV. c. 113, and before the 6 & 7 Vict. c. 98, they contracted to sell certain slaves purchased and possessed before the latter statute, with their offspring born subsequently to it, to the plaintiff, and having refused to deliver the slaves to the plaintiff, (the contract and all that was done being valid according to the law of Brazil,) the plaintiff brought his action for the breach of the contract. Upon the question thus raised, whether the contract of sale was or was not contrary to the law of England, the Court of Common Pleas unanimously decided in favour of the defendants, and held that as the purchase of slaves by British subjects within the Brazilian dominions after the passing of the Act of Geo. IV. was illegal before that of Victoria, a contract for the sale of such slaves and their offspring was illegal also[1]. The Exchequer Chamber, however, reversed this judgement; the majority of the court deciding that the contract was legal and might be enforced in this country, on the ground that the statute 6 & 7 Vic. c. 98, s. 5, permitted the sale of slaves, the holding of whom was not prohibited by any Act of Parliament, and that no statute prohibited the holding of the

Case of Santos *v.* Illidge.

[1] Mr Justice Willes delivered the judgement of the court and cited as authorities, R. *v.* Zulueta, 1 Carr. and Kirwan, 215, Pinner *v.* Arnold, Cro, Mee, and Roscoe, 613, and Esposito *v.* Bowden, 7 Ellis and Blacb. 763.

slaves in Brazil, even though the purchasing of them there might be a felony in a British subject[1].]

Cases of *La Jeune Eugenie* and the *Antelope.*

The final decision of the question in the United States has been the same as in the case of the *Le Louis.* In the case of the *La Jeune Eugenie*[2] it was decided in the Circuit Court of the United States, in Massachusetts, after a masterly discussion, that the slave trade was prohibited by universal law. But, subsequently, in the case of the *Antelope*[3], the Supreme Court of the United States declared that the slave trade had been sanctioned in modern times by the laws of all nations who possessed distant colonies; and a trade could not be considered as contrary to the law of nations which had been authorized and protected by the usages and laws of all commercial nations. It was not piracy, except so far as it was made so by the treaties or statutes of the nation to which the party belonged. It might still be lawfully carried on by the subjects of those nations who have not prohibited it by municipal acts or treaties.

[1] From this view the Lord Chief Baron (Pollock) and Mr Justice Wightman dissented, upholding the judgement above.

[2] 2 Mason, 409.

[3] 10 Wheaton, 66.

# APPENDIX.

## AN ACT FOR REGULATING NAVAL PRIZE OF WAR.

WHEREAS it is expedient to enact permanently, with amendments, such provisions concerning naval prize, and matters connected therewith, as have heretofore been usually passed at the beginning of a war;

Be it therefore enacted by the Queen's most Excellent Majesty, by and with the advice and consent of the Lords Spiritual and Temporal, and Commons, in this present Parliament assembled, and by the authority of the same as follows:

### *Preliminary.*

1. This Act may be cited as The Naval Prize Act, 1864. Short title.

2. In this Act— Interpretation of terms.

The term "the Lords of the Admiralty" means the Lord High Admiral of the United Kingdom, or the Commissioners for executing the office of Lord High Admiral:

The term "the High Court of Admiralty" means the High Court of Admiralty of *England:*

The term "any of Her Majesty's ships of war" includes any of Her Majesty's vessels of war, and any hired armed ship or vessel in Her Majesty's service:

The term "officers and crew" includes flag officers, Commanders and other officers, engineers, seamen, marines, soldiers, and others on board any of Her Majesty's ships of war:

The term "ship" includes vessel and boat, with the tackle, furniture, and apparel of the ship, vessel, or boat:

The term "ship papers" includes all books, passes, sea briefs, charter parties, bills of lading, cockets, letters, and other documents and writings delivered up or found on board a captured ship.

The term "goods" includes all such things as are by the course of Admiralty and law of nations the subject of Adjudication as prize (other than ships).

## I.—Prize Courts.

High Court of Admiralty and other Courts to be Prize Courts for purposes of Act.

3. The High Court of Admiralty, and every Court of Admiralty or of Vice-Admiralty, or other Court exercising Admiralty jurisdiction in Her Majesty's dominions, for the time being authorized to take cognizance of and judicially proceed in matters of prize, shall be a Prize Court within the meaning of this Act.

Every such Court, other than the High Court of Admiralty, is comprised in the term "Vice-Admiralty Prize Court," when hereafter used in this Act.

### *High Court of Admiralty.*

Jurisdiction of High Court of Admiralty.

4. The High Court of Admiralty shall have jurisdiction throughout Her Majesty's dominions as a Prize Court.

The High Court of Admiralty as a Prize Court shall have power to enforce any order or decree of a Vice-Admiralty Prize Court, and any order or decree of the Judicial Committee of the Privy Council in a prize appeal.

### *Appeal; Judicial Committee.*

Appeal to Queen in Council, in what cases.

5. An Appeal shall lie to Her Majesty in Council from any order or decree of a Prize Court, as of right in case of a final decree, and in other cases with the leave of the Court making the order or decree.

Every appeal shall be made in such manner and form and subject to such regulations (including regulations as to fees, costs, charges, and expenses) as may for the time being be directed by Order in Council, and in the absence of any such Order, or so far as any such Order does not extend, then in such manner and form and subject to such regulations as are for the time being prescribed or in force respecting maritime causes of appeal.

Jurisdiction of Judicial Committee in prize appeals.

6. The Judicial Committee of the Privy Council shall have jurisdiction to hear and report on any such appeal, and may therein exercise all such powers as for the time being appertain to them in respect of appeals from any Court of Admiralty jurisdiction, and all such powers as are under this Act vested in the High Court of

Admiralty, and all such powers as were wont to be exercised by the Commissioners of Appeal in prize causes.

Custody of processes, papers, &c.

7. All processes and documents required for the purposes of any such appeal shall be transmitted to and shall remain in the custody of the Registrar of Her Majesty in prize appeals.

Limit of time for appeal.

8. In every such appeal the usual inhibition shall be extracted from the registry of Her Majesty in prize appeals within three months after the date of the order or decree appealed from if the appeal be from the High Court of Admiralty, and within six months after that if it be from a Vice-Admiralty Prize Court.

The Judicial Committee may, nevertheless, on sufficient cause shown, allow the inhibition to be extracted and the appeal prosecuted after the expiration of the respective periods aforesaid.

### *Vice-Admiralty Prize Courts.*

Enforcement of orders of High Court, &c.

9. Every Vice-Admiralty Prize Court shall enforce within its jurisdiction all orders and decrees of the Judicial Committee in prize appeals and of the High Court of Admiralty in prize causes.

Salaries of Judges of Vice-Admiralty Prize Courts.

10. Her Majesty in Council may grant to the Judge of any Vice-Admiralty Prize Court a salary not exceeding five hundred pounds a year, payable out of money provided by Parliament, subject to such regulations as seem meet.

A Judge to whom a salary is so granted shall not be entitled to any further emolument, arising from fees or otherwise, in respect of prize business transacted in his court.

An account of all such fees shall be kept by the Registrar of the Court, and the amount thereof shall be carried to and form part of the Consolidated Fund of the United Kingdom.

Retiring pensions of Judges, as in 22 & 23 Vict. c. 26.

11. In accordance, as far as circumstances admit, with the principles and regulations laid down in The Superannuation Act, 1859, Her Majesty in Council may grant to the Judge of any Vice-Admiralty Prize Court an annual or other allowance, to take effect on the termination of his service, and to be payable out of money provided by Parliament.

Returns from Vice-Admiralty Prize Courts.

12. The Registrar of every Vice-Admiralty Prize Court shall, on the first day of *January* and first day of *July* in every year, make out a return (in such form as the Lords of the Admiralty from time to time direct) of all cases adjudged in the Court since the last half-yearly return, and shall with all convenient speed send the same to the Registrar of the High Court of Admiralty, who shall keep the same in the registry of that court, and who shall, as soon as conveniently may be, send a copy of the returns of each half-year to the

Lords of the Admiralty, who shall lay the same before both Houses of Parliament.

*General.*

General Orders for Prize Courts.

13. The Judicial Committee of the Privy Council, with the Judge of the High Court of Admiralty, may from time to time frame General Orders for regulating (subject to the provisions of this Act) the procedure and practice of Prize Courts, and the duties and conduct of the officers thereof and of the practitioners therein, and for regulating the fees to be taken by the officers of the Courts, and the costs, charges, and expenses to be allowed to the practitioners therein.

Any such General Order shall have full effect, if and when approved by Her Majesty in Council, but not sooner or otherwise.

Every Order in Council made under this section shall be laid before both Houses of Parliament.

Every such Order in Council shall be kept exhibited in a conspicuous place in each court to which it relates.

Prohibition of officer of Prize Court acting as Proctor, &c.

14. It shall not be lawful for any registrar, marshal, or other officer of any Prize Court, or for the Registrar of Her Majesty in prize appeals, directly or indirectly to act or be in any manner concerned as advocate, proctor, solicitor, or agent, or otherwise, in any prize cause or appeal, on pain of dismissal or suspension from office, by order of the Court or of the Judicial Committee (as the case may require).

Prohibition of Proctors being concerned for adverse parties in a cause.

15. It shall not be lawful for any proctor or solicitor, or person practising as a proctor or solicitor, being employed by a party in a prize cause or appeal, to be employed or concerned, by himself or his partner, or by any other Person, directly or indirectly, by or on behalf of any adverse party in that cause or appeal, on pain of exclusion or suspension from practice in prize matters, by order of the Court or of the Judicial Committee (as the case may require).

## II.—Procedure in Prize Causes.

*Proceedings by Captors.*

Custody of prize ship.

16. Every ship taken as prize, and brought into port within the jurisdiction of a Prize Court, shall forthwith, and without bulk broken, be delivered up to the marshal of the Court.

If there is no such marshal, then the ship shall be in like manner delivered up to the principal officer of Customs at the port.

The ship shall remain in the custody of the marshal, or of such officer, subject to the orders of the Court.

17. The captors shall, with all practicable speed after the ship is brought into port, bring the ship papers into the registry of the Court. Bringing in of ship papers.

The officer in command, or one of the chief officers of the capturing ship, or some other person who was present at the capture, and saw the ship papers delivered up or found on board, shall make oath that they are brought in as they were taken, without fraud, addition, subduction, or alteration, or else, shall account on oath to the satisfaction of the Court for the absence or altered condition of the ship papers or any of them.

Where no ship papers are delivered up or found on board the captured ship, the officer in command, or one of the chief officers of the capturing ship, or some other person who was present at the capture, shall make oath to that effect.

18. As soon as the affidavit as to ship papers is filed, a monition shall issue, returnable within twenty days from the service thereof, citing all persons in general to show cause why the captured ship should not be condemned. Issue of monition.

19. The captors shall, with all practicable speed after the captured ship is brought into port, bring three or four of the principal persons belonging to the captured ship before the Judge of the Court or some person authorized in this behalf, by whom they shall be examined on oath on the standing interrogatories. Examinations on standing interrogatories.

The preparatory examinations on the standing interrrogatories shall, if possible, be concluded within five days from the commencement thereof.

20. After the return of the monition, the Court shall, on production of the preparatory examinations and ship papers, proceed with all convenient speed either to condemn or to release the captured ship. Adjudication by Court.

21. Where, on production of the preparatory examinations and ship papers, it appears to the Court doubtful whether the captured ship is good prize or not, the Court may direct further proof to be adduced, either by affidavit or by examination of witnesses, with or without pleadings, or by production of further documents; and on such further proof being adduced the Court shall with all convenient speed proceed to adjudication. Further proof.

22. The foregoing Provisions, as far as they relate to the custody of the ship, and to examination on the standing interrogatories, shall not apply to ships of war taken as prize. Custody, &c. of ships of war.

### *Claim.*

Entry of claim; security for costs.

23. At any time before final decree made in the cause, any person claiming an interest in the ship may enter in the registry of the Court a claim, verified on oath.

Within five days after entering the claim, the claimant shall give security for costs in the sum of sixty pounds; but the Court shall have power to enlarge the time for giving security, or to direct security to be given in a larger sum, if the circumstances appear to require it.

### *Appraisement.*

Power to Court to direct appraisement.

24. The Court may, if it thinks fit, at any time direct that the captured ship be appraised.

Every appraisement shall be made by competent persons sworn to make the same according to the best of their skill and knowledge.

### *Delivery on Bail.*

Power to Court to direct delivery to claimant on bail.

25. After appraisement, the Court may, if it thinks fit, direct that the captured ship be delivered up to the claimant, on his giving security to the satisfaction of the Court to pay to the captors the appraised value thereof in case of condemnation.

### *Sale.*

Power to Court to order sale.

26. The Court may at any time, if it thinks fit, on account of the condition of the captured ship, or on the application of a claimant, order that the captured ship be appraised as aforesaid (if not already appraised), and be sold.

Sale on condemnation.

27. On or after condemnation the Court may, if it thinks fit, order that the ship be appraised as aforesaid (if not already appraised), and be sold.

How sales to be made.

28. Every sale shall be made by or under the superintendence of the marshal of the Court or of the officer having the custody of the captured ship.

Payment of proceeds to Paymaster General or official accountant.

29. The proceeds of any sale, made either before or after condemnation, and after condemnation the appraised value of the captured ship, in case she has been delivered up to a claimant on bail, shall be paid under an order of the Court either into the Bank of *England* to the credit of Her Majesty's Paymaster General or into the hands of an official accountant (belonging to the Commissariat or some other department) appointed for this purpose by the Commissioners of Her Majesty's Treasury or by the Lords of the Admiralty, subject in either case to such regulations as may from time to time be made, by Order in Council, as to the custody and disposal of money so paid.

*Small armed Ships.*

30. The captors may include in one adjudication any number, not exceeding six, of armed ships not exceeding one hundred tons each, taken within three months next before institution of proceedings. One adjudication as to several small ships.

*Goods.*

31. The foregoing provisions relating to ships shall extend and apply, *mutatis mutandis*, to goods taken as prize on board ship; and the Court may direct such goods to be unladen, inventoried and warehoused. Application of foregoing provisions to prize goods.

*Monition to Captors to proceed.*

32. If the captors fail to institute or to prosecute with effect proceedings for adjudication, a monition shall, on the application of a claimant, issue against the captors, returnable within six days from the service thereof, citing them to appear and proceed to adjudication; and on the return thereof the Court shall either forthwith proceed to adjudication; or direct further proof to be adduced as aforesaid, and then proceed to adjudication. Power to Court to call on captors to proceed to adjudication.

*Claim on Appeal.*

33. Where any person, not an original party in the cause, intervenes on appeal, he shall enter a claim, verified on oath, and shall give security for costs. Person intervening on appeal to enter claim.

## III.—Special Cases of Capture.

*Land Expeditions.*

34. Where, in an expedition of any of Her Majesty's naval or naval and military forces against a fortress or possession on land, goods belonging to the State of the enemy or to a public trading company of the enemy exercising powers of government are taken in the fortress or possession, or a ship is taken in waters defended by or belonging to the fortress or possession, a Prize Court shall have jurisdiction as to the goods or ship so taken, and any goods taken on board the ship, as in case of prize. Jurisdiction of Prize Court in case of capture in land expedition.

*Conjunct Capture with Ally.*

35. Where any ship or goods is or are taken by any of Her Majesty's naval or naval and military forces while acting in conjunction with any forces of any of Her Majesty's allies, a Prize Court Jurisdiction of Prize Court in case of expedition with ally.

shall have jurisdiction as to the same as in case of prize, and shall have power, after condemnation, to apportion the due share of the proceeds to Her Majesty's ally, the proportionate amount and the disposition of which share shall be such as may from time to time be agreed between Her Majesty and Her Majesty's ally.

*Joint Capture.*

Restriction on Petitions by asserted joint captors.

36. Before condemnation, a petition on behalf of asserted joint captors shall not (except by special leave of the Court) be admitted, unless and until they give security to the satisfaction of the Court, to contribute to the actual captors a just proportion of any costs, charges, or expenses or damages that may be incurred by or awarded against the actual captors on account of the capture and detention of the prize.

After condemnation, such a petition shall not (except by special leave of the Court) be admitted unless and until the asserted joint captors pay to the actual captors a just proportion of the costs, charges, and expenses incurred by the actual captors in the case, and give such security as aforesaid, and show sufficient cause to the Court why their petition was not presented before condemnation.

Provided, that nothing in the present section shall extend to the asserted interest of a flag officer claiming to share by virtue of his flag.

*Offences against Law of Prize.*

In case of offence by captors, prize to be reserved for Crown.

37. A Prize Court, on proof of any offence against the Law of Nations, or against this Act, or any Act relating to naval discipline, or against any Order in Council or Royal Proclamation, or of any breach of Her Majesty's instructions relating to prize, or of any act of disobedience to the orders of the Lords of the Admiralty, or to the command of a superior officer, committed by the captors in relation to any ship or goods taken as prize, or in relation to any person on board any such ship, may, on condemnation, reserve the prize to Her Majesty's disposal, notwithstanding any grant that may have been made by Her Majesty in favour of captors.

*Pre-emption.*

Purchase by Admiralty for public service of stores on board foreign ships.

38. Where a ship of a foreign nation passing the seas laden with naval or victualling stores intended to be carried to a port of any enemy of Her Majesty is taken and brought into a port of the United Kingdom, and the purchase for the service of Her Majesty of the stores on board the ship appears to the Lords of the Admiralty expedient without the condemnation thereof in a Prize Court, in that case the Lords of the Admiralty may purchase, on the account

or for the service of Her Majesty, all or any of the stores on board the ship; and the Commissioners of Customs may permit the stores purchased to be entered and landed within any port.

*Capture by Ship other than a Ship of War.*

39. Any ship or goods taken as a prize by any of the officers and crew of a ship other than a ship of war of Her Majesty shall, on condemnation, belong to Her Majesty in her office of Admiralty.

Prizes taken by ships other than ships of war to be droits of Admiralty.

## IV.—Prize Salvage.

40. Where any ship or goods belonging to any of Her Majesty's subjects, after being taken as prize by the enemy, is or are retaken from the enemy by any of Her Majesty's ships of war, the same shall be restored by decree of a Prize Court to the owner, on his paying as prize salvage one-eighth part of the value of the prize to be decreed and ascertained by the Court, or such sum not exceeding one-eighth part of the estimated value of the prize as may be agreed on between the owner and the re-captors, and approved by order of the Court: provided, that where the re-capture is made under circumstances of special difficulty or danger, the Prize Court may, if it thinks fit, award to the re-captors as prize salvage a larger part than one-eighth part, but not exceeding in any case one-fourth part, of the value of the prize.

Salvage to re-captors of British ship or goods from enemy.

Provided also, that where a ship after being so taken is set forth or used by any of Her Majesty's enemies as a ship of war, this provision for restitution shall not apply, and the ship shall be adjudicated on as in other cases of prize.

41. Where a ship belonging to any of Her Majesty's subjects, after being taken as prize by the enemy, is retaken from the enemy by any of Her Majesty's ships of war, she may, with the consent of the re-captors, prosecute her voyage, and it shall not be necessary for the re-captors to proceed to adjudication till her return to a port of the United Kingdom.

Permission to re-captured ship to proceed on voyage.

The master or owner, or his agent, may, with the consent of the re-captors, unload and dispose of the goods on board the ship before Adjudication.

In case the ship does not, within six months, return to a port of the United Kingdom, the re-captors may nevertheless institute proceedings against the ship or goods in the High Court of Admiralty, and the Court may thereupon award prize salvage as aforesaid to the recaptors, and may enforce payment thereof, either by warrant of arrest against the ship or goods, or by monition and attachment against the owner.

30

## V.—Prize Bounty.

Prize bounty to officers and crew present at engagement with an enemy.

42. If, in relation to any war, Her Majesty is pleased to declare, by proclamation or Order in Council, her intention to grant prize bounty to the officers and crews of her ships of war, then such of the officers and crew of any of Her Majesty's ships of war as are actually present at the taking or destroying of any armed ship of any of Her Majesty's enemies shall be entitled to have distributed among them as prize bounty a sum calculated at the rate of five pounds for each person on board the enemy's ship at the beginning of the engagement.

Ascertainment of amount of prize bounty by decree of Prize Court.

43. The number of the persons so on board the enemy's ship shall be proved in a Prize Court, either by the examinations on oath of the survivors of them, or of any three or more of the survivors, or if there is no survivor by the papers of the enemy's ship, or by the examinations on oath of three or more of the officers and crew of Her Majesty's ship, or by such other evidence as may seem to the Court sufficient in the circumstances.

The Court shall make a decree declaring the title of the officers and crew of Her Majesty's ship to the prize bounty, and stating the amount thereof.

The decree shall be subject to appeal as other decrees of the Court.

Payment of prize bounty awarded.

44. On production of an official copy of the decree the Commissioners of Her Majesty's Treasury shall, out of money provided by Parliament, pay the amount of prize bounty decreed, in such manner as any Order in Council may from time to time direct.

## VI.—Miscellaneous Provisions.

### *Ransom.*

Power for regulating ransom by Order in Council.

45. Her Majesty in Council may from time to time, in relation to any war, make such orders as may seem expedient, according to circumstances, for prohibiting or allowing, wholly or in certain cases, or subject to any conditions or regulations or otherwise, as may from time to time seem meet, the ransoming or the entering into any contract or agreement for the ransoming of any ship or goods belonging to any of Her Majesty's subjects, and taken as prize by any of Her Majesty's enemies.

Any contract or agreement entered into, and any bill, bond, or other security given for ransom of any ship or goods, shall be under the exclusive jurisdiction of the High Court of Admiralty as a Prize

Court (subject to appeal to the Judicial Committee of the Privy Council), and if entered into or given in contravention of any such Order in Council shall be deemed to have been entered into or given for an illegal consideration.

If any person ransoms or enters into any contract or agreement for ransoming any ship or goods, in contravention of any such Order in Council, he shall for every such offence be liable to be proceeded against in the High Court of Admiralty at the suit of Her Majesty in Her office of Admiralty, and on conviction to be fined, in the discretion of the Court, any sum not exceeding five hundred pounds.

*Convoy.*

Punishment of masters of merchant-vessels under convoy disobeying orders or deserting convoy.

46. If the master or other person having the command of any ship of any of Her Majesty's subjects, under the convoy of any of Her Majesty's ships of war, wilfully disobeys any lawful signal, instruction, or command of the commander of the convoy, or without leave deserts the convoy, he shall be liable to be proceeded against in the High Court of Admiralty at the suit of Her Majesty in Her office of Admiralty, and upon conviction to be fined, in the discretion of the Court, any sum not exceeding five hundred pounds, and to suffer imprisonment for such time, not exceeding one year, as the Court may adjudge.

*Custom Duties and Regulations.*

Prize ships and goods liable to duties and forfeiture.

47. All ships and goods taken as prize and brought into a port of the United Kingdom shall be liable to and be charged with the same rates and charges and duties of Customs as under any Act relating to the Customs may be chargeable on other ships and goods of the like description; and

All goods brought in as prize which would on the voluntary importation thereof be liable to forfeiture or subject to any restriction under the laws relating to the Customs, shall be deemed to be so liable and subject, unless the Commissioners of Customs see fit to authorize the sale or delivery thereof for home use or exportation, unconditionally or subject to such conditions and regulations as they may direct.

Regulations of Customs to be observed as to prize ships and goods.

48. Where any ship or goods taken as prize is or are brought into a port of the United Kingdom, the master or other person in charge or command of the ship which has been taken or in which the goods are brought shall, on arrival at such port, bring to at the proper place of discharge, and shall, when required by any officer of Customs, deliver an account in writing under his hand concerning such ship and goods, giving such particulars relating thereto as may be in his power, and shall truly answer all questions concerning such

ship or goods asked by any such officer, and in default shall forfeit a sum not exceeding one hundred pounds, such forfeiture to be enforced as forfeitures for offences against the laws relating to the Customs are enforced, and every such ship shall be liable to such searches as other ships are liable to, and the officers of the Customs may freely go on board such ship and bring to the Queen's warehouse any goods on board the same, subject, nevertheless, to such regulations in respect of ships of war belonging to Her Majesty as shall from time to time be issued by the Commissioners of Her Majesty's Treasury.

Power for Treasury to remit Customs duties in certain cases.

49. Goods taken as prize may be sold either for home consumption or for exportation; and if in the former case the proceeds thereof, after payment of duties of Customs, are insufficient to satisfy the just and reasonable claims thereon, the Commissioners of Her Majesty's Treasury may remit the whole or such part of the said duties as they see fit.

*Perjury.*

Punishment of persons guilty of perjury.

50. If any person wilfully and corruptly swears, declares or affirms falsely in any prize cause or appeal, or in any proceeding under this Act, or in respect of any matter required by this Act to be verified on oath, or suborns any other person to do so, he shall be deemed guilty of perjury, or of subornation of perjury (as the case may be), and shall be liable to be punished accordingly.

*Limitation of Actions, &c.*

Actions against persons executing Act not to be brought without notice, &c.

51. Any action or proceeding shall not lie in any part of Her Majesty's dominions against any person acting under the authority or in the execution or intended execution or in pursuance of this Act for any alleged irregularity or trespass, or other act or thing done or omitted by him under this Act, unless notice in writing (specifying the cause of the action or proceeding) is given by the intending plaintiff or prosecutor to the intended defendant one month at least before the commencement of the action or proceeding, nor unless the action or proceeding is commenced within six months next after the act or thing complained of is done or omitted, or, in case of a continuation or damage, within six months next after the doing of such damage has ceased.

In any such action the defendant may plead generally that the act or thing complained of was done or omitted by him when acting under the authority or in the execution or intended execution or in pursuance of this Act, and may give all special matter in evidence; and the plaintiff shall not succeed if tender of sufficient amends is made by the defendant before the commencement of the action; and in case no tender has been made, the defendant may, by leave of the Court in which the action is brought, at any time pay into Court such sum of money as he thinks fit, whereupon such proceeding and order shall be had and made in and by the Court as may be had and made on the payment of money into Court in an ordinary action; and if the plaintiff does not succeed in the action, the defendant shall receive such full and reasonable indemnity as to all costs, charges, and expenses incurred in and about the action as may be taxed and allowed by the proper officer, subject to review; and though a verdict is given for the plaintiff in the action he shall not have costs against the defendant, unless the Judge before whom the trial is had certifies his approval of the action.

Any such action or proceeding against any person in Her Majesty's naval service, or in the employment of the Lords of the Admiralty, shall not be brought or instituted elsewhere than in the United Kingdom.

*Petitions of Right.*

52. A petition of right, under the petitions of Right Act, 1860, may, if the suppliant thinks fit, be intituled in the High Court of Admiralty, in case the subject matter of the petition or any material part thereof arises out of the exercise of any belligerent right on behalf of the Crown, or would be cognizable in a Prize Court within Her Majesty's dominions if the same were a matter in dispute between private persons.

Jurisdiction of High Court of Admiralty on petitions of right in certain cases, as in 23 & 24 Vict. c. 34.

Any petition of right under the last-mentioned Act, whether intituled in the High Court of Admiralty or not, may be prosecuted in that Court if the Lord Chancellor thinks fit so to direct.

The provisions of this Act relative to appeal, and to the framing and approval of General Orders for regulating the procedure and practice of the High Court of Admiralty, shall extend to the case of any such petition of right intituled or directed to be prosecuted in that Court; and, subject thereto, all the provisions of the Petitions of Right Act, 1860, shall apply, *mutatis mutandis,* in the case of any such petition of right: and for the purposes of the present section the terms "Court" and "Judge" in that Act shall respectively be understood to include and to mean the High Court of Admiralty and the Judge thereof, and other terms shall have the respective meanings given to them in that Act.

*Orders in Council.*

53. Her Majesty in Council may from time to time make such Orders in Council as seem meet for the better execution of this Act.

Power to make Orders in Council.

Order in Council to be gazetted, &c.

54. Every Order in Council under this Act shall be published in the *London Gazette*, and shall be laid before both Houses of Parliament within thirty days after the making thereof, if Parliament is then sitting, and, if not, then within thirty days after the next meeting of Parliament.

*Savings.*

Not to affect rights of Crown; effect of Treaties, &c.

55. Nothing in this Act shall—

(1.) give to the officers and crew of any of Her Majesty's ships of war any right or claim in or to any ship or goods taken as prize or the proceeds thereof, it being the intent of this Act that such officers and crews shall continue to take only such interest (if any) in the proceeds of prizes as may be from time to time granted to them by the Crown; or

(2.) affect the operation of any existing treaty or convention with any foreign power; or

(3.) take away or abridge the power of the Crown to enter into any treaty or convention with any foreign power containing any stipulation that may seem meet concerning any matter to which this Act relates; or

(4.) take away, abridge, or control, further or otherwise than as expressly provided by this Act, any right, power, or prerogative of Her Majesty the Queen in right of her Crown, or in right of Her office of Admiralty, or any right or power of the Lord Admiral of the United Kingdom, or of the Commissioners for executing the Office of Lord High Admiral; or

(5.) take away, abridge, or control, further or otherwise than as expressly provided by this Act, the jurisdiction or authority of a Prize Court to take cognizance of and judicially proceed upon any capture, seizure, prize, or reprisal of any ship or goods, and to hear and determine the same, and, according to the course of Admiralty and the Law of Nations, to adjudge and condemn any ship or goods, or any other jurisdiction or authority of or exerciseable by a Prize Court.

THE following case[1] which was published while the last sheet of this work was going through the press is added to the Appendix, as being too important to pass by without notice.

It was an action for wages tried by the Judge of the High Court of Admiralty in England, Dr. Lushington, in which one Wardle the late master of the *Helen* was the plaintiff and the Albion Trading Company the owners of the ship were the defendants, and upon a motion to reject the fourth article of the defendants' answer which was to the effect, that the agreement between the parties was contrary to law, being entered into for the purpose of running the blockade of the Southern ports of the United States of America, the learned Judge in an elaborate judgment held that the carrying on trade with a blockaded port is not a breach of municipal law, nor illegal so as to prevent a Court of the loci contractûs from enforcing the contract of which the trade is the subject, and that a neutral state is not bound by the law of nations to impede or diminish its own trade by municipal regulations, and therefore directed that the fourth article should be struck out.

[1] The *Helen*, 35 Law Journal Admiralty, p. 2.

N.B. The case, it is said, will be carried to the Judicial Committee.

# INDEX.

---

B.



C.

D.

E.



F.

I.



J.



K.



L.



M.

S.



T.

U.



V.

THE END.

CAMBRIDGE: PRINTED AT THE UNIVERSITY PRESS.

## *ARITHMETIC AND ALGEBRA.*

### Pelicotetics, or the Science of Quantity. An
Elementary Treatise on Algebra and its groundwork Arithmetic. By ARCHIBALD SANDEMAN, M.A. 8vo. 20*s.*

### Arithmetic. For the Use of Schools and
Colleges. By A. WRIGLEY, M.A. 3*s.* 6*d.*

### Principles and Practice of Arithmetic. Com-
prising the Nature and Use of Logarithms, with the Computations employed by Artificers, Gagers, and Land Surveyors. Designed for the Use of Students By J. HIND, M.A., formerly Fellow and Tutor of Sidney Sussex College. *Ninth Edition,* with Questions. 4*s.* 6*d.*

A Second Appendix of Miscellaneous Questions, (many of which have been taken from the Examination Papers given in the University during the last few years,) has been added to the present edition of this work, which the Author considers will conduce greatly to its practical utility, especially for those who are intended for mercantile pursuits.

*** KEY, with Questions for Examination. *Second Edition.* 5*s.*

### A Progressive Course of Examples in Arithmetic.
With Answers. By JAMES WATSON, M.A., of Corpus Christi College, Cambridge, and formerly Senior Mathematical Master of the Ordnance School, Carshalton. *Second Edition, revised and corrected.* Fcp. 8vo. 2*s.* 6*d.*

### Principles and Practice of Arithmetical Algebra,
established upon strict methods of Mathematical Reasoning, and illustrated by Select Examples proposed during the last thirty years in the University of Cambridge. Designed for the Use of Students. By J. HIND, M.A. *Third Edition.* 12mo. 5*s.*

Designed as a sequel to the Arithmetic, and affording an easy transition from Arithmetic to Algebra—the process being fully exemplified from the Cambridge Examination Papers.

### Elements of Algebra. Designed for the Use of
Students in Schools and in the Universities. By J. HIND, M.A. *Sixth Edition, revised.* 540 pp. 8vo. 10*s.* 6*d.*

### Treatise on the Theory of Algebraical Equations.
By J. HYMERS, D.D. *Third Edition.* 8vo. 10*s.* 6*d.*

## *TRIGONOMETRY.*

**Trigonometry, required for the Additional Subjects** for Honours, according to the new scheme sanctioned by the Senate, June 1865. By J. McDOWELL, M.A., Pembroke College, Cambridge. Crn. 8vo. 3*s.* 6*d.*

**Elementary Trigonometry. With a Collection** of Examples. By T. P. HUDSON, M.A., Fellow and Assistant Tutor of Trinity College. 3*s.* 6*d.*

**Elements of Plane and Spherical Trigonometry.** With the Nature and Properties of Logarithms and Construction and Use of Mathematical Tables. Designed for the use of Students in the University. By J. HIND, M.A. *Fifth Edition.* 12mo. 6*s.*

**Syllabus of a Course of Lectures upon Trigonometry** and the Application of Algebra to Geometry. 8vo. 7*s.* 6*d.*

**Solutions of the Trigonometrical Problems proposed** at St. John's College, Cambridge, from 1829 to 1846. By T. GASKIN, M.A. 8vo. 9*s.*

## *MECHANICS AND HYDROSTATICS.*

**Mechanics for the Previous Examination and** the Ordinary B.A. Degree. By J. McDOWELL, M.A., Pembroke College, Cambridge. Crown 8vo. 3*s.* 6*d.*

**Elementary Hydrostatics. By W. H. Besant, M.A.** late Fellow of St. John's College. Fcap. 8vo. 4*s.*

**Elementary Hydrostatics for Junior University** Students. By R. POTTER, M.A., late Fellow of Queens' College, Cambridge, Professor of Natural Philosophy and Astronomy in University College, London. 7*s.* 6*d.*

Written to supply a Text-book for a Junior Mathematical Class, and to include the various Propositions that can be solved without the Differential Calculus.

The author has endeavoured to meet the wants of students who may look to hydraulic engineering as their profession, as well as those who learn the subject in the course of scientific education.

**A Treatise on Hydromechanics. By W. H.** BESANT, M.A. 8vo. *Second Edition, enlarged,* 10*s.* 6*d.*

**Problems in illustration of the Principles of** Theoretical Hydrostatics and Hydrodynamics. By W. WALTON, M.A. 8vo. 10*s.* 6*d.*

*MECHANICS AND HYDROSTATICS—continued.*

## Elementary Problems in Statics and Dynamics.
Designed for Candidates for Honours, first three days. By W. WALTON, M.A. 8vo. 10*s*. 6*d*.

## Elementary Statics. By H. Goodwin, D.D.,
Lord Bishop of Carlisle. Fcap. 8vo. 3*s*. cloth.

## Elementary Dynamics. By H. Goodwin, D.D.,
Lord Bishop of Carlisle. Fcap. 8vo. 3*s*. cloth.

## Treatise on Statics: containing the Theory
of the Equilibrium of Forces, and numerous Examples Illustrative of the General Principles of the Science. By S. EARNSHAW, M.A. *Fourth Edition.* 8vo. 10*s*.

## A Treatise on the Dynamics of a Rigid Body.
By W. N. GRIFFIN, M.A. 8vo. 6*s*. 6*d*.

*** SOLUTIONS OF THE EXAMPLES. 8vo. 6*s*.

## Problems in illustration of the Principles of
Theoretical Mechanics. By W. WALTON, M.A. *Second Edition.* 8vo. 18*s*.

## Treatise on the Motion of a Single Particle and
of Two Particles acting on one another. By A. SANDEMAN. 8vo. 8*s*. 6*d*.

## Of Motion. An Elementary Treatise. By J. R.
LUNN, M.A., Fellow and Lady Sadleir's Lecturer of St. John's College. 8vo. 7*s*. 6*d*.

*DIFFERENTIAL AND INTEGRAL CALCULUS.*

## Elementary Treatise on the Differential Calculus.
By W. H. MILLER, M.A. *Third Edition.* 8vo. 6*s*.

## Elementary Treatise on the Differential Calculus,
in which the method of Limits is exclusively made use of. By M. O'BRIEN, M.A. 8vo. 10*s*. 6*d*.

## Treatise on the Differential Calculus. By W.
WALTON, M.A. 8vo. 10*s*. 6*d*.

## Geometrical Illustrations of the Differential Calculus.
By M. B. PELL. 8vo. 2*s*. 6*d*.

## *CONIC SECTIONS AND ANALYTICAL GEOMETRY.*

### The Geometry of Conics for Beginners. By C.
TAYLOR, M.A., Fellow of St. John's College. Small 8vo. 3*s*. 6*d*.

### Text Book of Geometry. Part I. By T. S.
ALDIS, M.A., Trinity College, Cambridge, and Mathematical Master at Manchester Grammar School. Small 8vo. 2*s*. 6*d*.

CONTENTS :—Angles—Parallels—Triangles—Equivalent Figures—Circles.

The object of the work is to present the subject simply and concisely, leaving illustration and explanation to the Teacher, whose freedom text-books too often hamper. Without a Teacher however this work will possibly be found no harder to masters than others.

As far as practicable, exercises, largely numerical, are given on the different Theorems, that the pupil may learn at once the value and use of what he studies.

Hypothetical constructions are throughout employed. Important Theorems are proved in more than one way, lest the pupil rest in words rather than things. Problems are regarded chiefly as exercises on the Theorems.

Short Appendices are added on the Analysis of Reasoning and the Application of Arithmetic and Algebra to Geometry.

### Elementary Analytical Geometry for Schools and
Beginners. By T. G. VYVYAN, Fellow of Gonville and Caius College, and Mathematical Master of Charterhouse. *Second Edition, revised.* Crown 8vo. 7*s*. 6*d*.

### Trilinear Co-ordinates, and other methods of
*Modern Analytical Geometry* of Two Dimensions. An Elementary Treatise. By W. ALLEN WHITWORTH, M.A., Professor of Mathematics in Queen's College, Liverpool, and late Scholar of St. John's College, Cambridge. 8vo. 16*s*.

### Elementary Geometrical Conic Sections. By
W. H. BESANT, M.A. 4*s*. 6*d*.

### Conic Sections. Their principal Properties proved
Geometrically. By the late W. WHEWELL, D.D., late Master of Trinity. *Third Edition.* 8vo. 2*s*. 6*d*.

### Geometrical Construction of a Conic Section.
Subject to five Conditions of passing through given points and touching straight lines deduced from the properties of involution and anharmonic Ratio, with a variety of general properties of Curves of the Second Order. By T. GASKIN, M.A. 8vo. 3*s*.

### A Treatise on the Application of Analysis to
Solid Geometry. By D. F. GREGORY, M.A., and W. WALTON, M.A. *Second Edition.* 8vo. 12*s*.

### An Introduction to Analytical Plane Geometry.
By W. P. TURNBULL, M.A., Fellow of Trinity College. 8vo. 12*s*.

*CONIC SECTIONS AND ANALYTICAL GEOMETRY—continued.*

**An Elementary Treatise on Solid Geometry.** By W. S. ALDIS, M.A. 8vo. 8*s.*

**Problems in illustration of the Principles of** Plane Co-ordinate Geometry. By W. WALTON, M.A. 8vo. 16*s.*

**Elements of the Conic Sections.** With the Sections of the Conoids. By J. D. HUSTLER, B.D. *Fourth Edition.* 8vo. 4*s.* 6*d.*

**Treatise on Plane Co-ordinate Geometry.** Or the Application of the Method of Co-Ordinates to the Solutions of Problems in Plane Geometry. By M. O'BRIEN, M.A. 8vo. 9*s.*

**Solutions of the Geometrical Problems, consisting** chiefly of Examples, proposed at St. John's College, from 1830 to 1846. With an Appendix containing several General Properties of Curves of the Second Order, and the Determination of the Magnitude and Position of the axes of the Conic Section represented by the General Equation of the Second Degree. By T. GASKIN, M.A. 8vo. 12*s.*

## *ASTRONOMY, ETC.*

**An Introduction to Plain Astronomy.** For the use of Colleges and Schools. By P. T. MAIN, M.A., Fellow of St. John's College. Fcap. 8vo., cloth. 4*s.*

**Practical and Spherical Astronomy.** For the Use chiefly of Students in the Universities. By R. MAIN, M.A., Radcliffe Observer at Oxford. 8vo. 14*s.*

**Brunnow's Spherical Astronomy.** Part I. Including the Chapters on Parallax, Refraction, Aberration, Precession, and Nutation. Translated by R. MAIN, M.A., F.R.S., Radcliffe Observer at Oxford. 8vo. 8*s.* 6*d.*

**Elementary Chapters on Astronomy from the** "Astronomie Physique" of Biot. By HARVEY GOODWIN, D.D., Bishop of Carlisle. 8vo. 3*s.* 6*d.*

**A Chapter on Fresnel's Theory of Double Refraction.** By W. S. ALDIS, M.A. 8vo. 2*s.*

**Notes on the Principles of Pure and Applied** Calculation, and on the Mathematical Principles of Physical Theories. By J. CHALLIS, M.A., F.R.S., Plumian Professor of Astronomy and Experimental Philosophy in the University, and Fellow of Trinity College, Cambridge. 8vo. 15*s.*

**Choice and Chance. Two Chapters of Arithmetic.** By WM. A. WHITWORTH, M.A., Fellow of St. John's College, Cambridge. *Second Edition, enlarged.* Crown 8vo. 6*s.*

**Notes on Roulettes and Glissettes. By W. H.** BESANT, M.A. 8vo. 3*s.* 6*d.*

**Exercises on Euclid and in Modern Geometry,** containing Applications of the Principles and Processes of Modern Pure Geometry. By J. McDOWELL, B.A., Pembroke College. Crown 8vo. 8*s.* 6*d.*

**Elementary Course of Mathematics. Designed** principally for Students of the University of Cambridge. By HARVEY GOODWIN, D.D., Lord Bishop of Carlisle. *Sixth Edition,* revised and enlarged by P. T. MAIN, M.A., Fellow of St. John's College, Cambridge. 8vo. 16*s.*

**Problems and Examples, adapted to the** "Elementary Course of Mathematics." With an Appendix, containing the Questions proposed during the first three days of the Senate House Examination. By T. G. VYVYAN, M.A. *Third Edition.* 8vo. 5*s.*

**Solutions of Goodwin's Collection of Problems** and Examples. By W. W. HUTT, M.A., late Fellow of Gonville and Caius College. *Third Edition, revised and enlarged.* By T. G. VYVYAN, M.A. 8vo. 9*s.*

**Examples in Arithmetic, Algebra, Geometry,** Logarithms, Trigonometry, Conic Sections, Mechanics, &c., with Answers and Occasional Hints. By A. WRIGLEY, M.A., Professor of Mathematics in the late Royal Military College, Addiscombe. *Sixth Edition, corrected.* 8vo. 8*s.* 6*d.*

**A Companion to Wrigley's Collection of Examples** and Problems, being Illustrations of Mathematical Processes and Methods of Solution. By J. PLATTS, Esq., Head Master of the Government College, Benares, and A. WRIGLEY, M.A. 8vo. 12*s.*

**Figures illustrative of Geometrical Optics. From** SCHELLBACH. By W. B. HOPKINS, B.D. *Plates.* Folio. 10*s.* 6*d.*

**A Treatise on Crystallography. By W. H.** MILLER, M.A., Professor of Mineralogy in the University of Cambridge. 8vo. 7*s.* 6*d.*

**A Tract on Crystallography, designed for Students** in the University. By W. H. MILLER, M.A. 8vo. 5*s.*

**Physical Optics. Part II. The Corpuscular** Theory of Light discussed Mathematically. By RICHARD POTTER, M.A., late Fellow of Queens' College, Cambridge, Professor of Natural Philosophy and Astronomy in University College, London. 7*s.* 6*d.*

## *CLASSICAL.*

### Rome and the Campagna. An Historical and

Topographical Description of the Site, Buildings, and Neighbourhood of Ancient Rome. By ROBERT BURN, M.A., Fellow and Tutor of Trinity College, Cambridge. With Eighty-five fine Engravings by Jewitt, and Twenty-five Maps and Plans. Handsomely bound in cloth. 4to. £3. 3*s*.

### Ætna. Revised, emended, and explained, by

H. A. J. MUNRO, M.A., Fellow of Trinity College, Cambridge. 8vo., 3*s*. 6*d*.

### Æschylus. Translated into English Prose, by

F. A. PALEY, M.A., Editor of the Greek Text. *Second Edition, revised.* 8vo. 7*s*. 6*d*.

### Aristophanis Comoediae superstites cum deper-

ditarum fragmentis, additis argumentis adnotatione critica, metrorum descriptione, onomastico, et lexicon. By HUBERT A. HOLDEN, LL.D., Head-Master of Ipswich School, late Fellow and Assistant Tutor of Trinity College, Cambridge. 8vo.

Vol. I. containing the Text expurgated with Summaries and Critical Notes, 18*s*.
The Plays sold separately: Acharnenses, 2*s*. Equites, 1*s*. 6*d*. Nubes, 1*s*. 6*d*. Vespae, 2*s*. Pax, 1*s*. 6*d*. Aves, 2*s*. Lysistrata et Thesmophoriazusae, 3*s*. Ranae, 2*s*. Ecclesiazusae et Plutus, 3*s*.
Vol. II. Onomasticon Aristophanevm continens indicem geographicvm et historicvm. 5*s*. 6*d*.

### Six Lectures Introductory to the Philosophical

Writings of Cicero, with some Explanatory Notes on the subject matter of the ACADEMICA and DE FINIBUS. By T. W. LEVIN, M.A., St. Catharine's College, Inter-Collegiate Lecturer on Logic and Moral Philosophy. 8vo. 7*s*. 6*d*.

### Demosthenes. The Oration against the Law

of Leptines. With English Notes and a Translation of Wolf's Prolegomena. By W. B. BEATSON, M.A., Fellow of Pembroke College. Small 8vo. 6*s*.

### Demosthenes de Falsa Legatione. *Third Edition.*

*carefully revised.* By R. SHILLETO, M.A., Fellow of S. Peter's College, Cambridge. 8vo. 8*s*. 6*d*.

### Euripides. Fabulæ Quatuor. Scilicet, Hippo-

lytus Coronifer, Alcestis, Iphigenia in Aulide, Iphigenia in Tauris. Ad fidem Manuscriptorum ac veterum Editionum emendavit et Annotationibus instruxit J. H. MONK, S.T.P. *Editio Nova.* 8vo. 12*s*.

*Separately*—HIPPOLYTUS. 8vo. cloth, 5*s*. ALCESTIS. 8vo. sewed, 4*s*. 6*d*.

### Titi Lucreti Cari de Rerum Natura Libri Sex.

With a Translation and Notes. By H. A. J. MUNRO, M.A., Fellow of Trinity College, Cambridge. *Second Edition, revised throughout.* 2 vols. 8vo.

Vol. I. Text, 16*s*. Vol. II. Translation, 6*s*.
Sold separately.

### Mvsæ Etonenses sive Carminvm Etonæ Condi-

torvm Delectvs. Series Nova, Tomos Dvos, complectens. Edidit RICARDVS OKES, S.T.P., Coll. Regal. apvd Cantabrigienses Præpositvs. 8vo. 15*s*.

Vol. II., to complete Sets, may be had separately, price 5*s*.

**Plato. The Phaedo, with Notes, Critical and** Exegetical, and an Analysis, by WILHELM WAGNER, Ph. D. Small 8vo. 5*s*. 6*d*.

**Plato. The Apology of Socrates and Crito,** With Notes, Critical and Exegetical, by WILHELM WAGNER, Ph. D. Small 8vo. 4*s*. 6*d*.

**Platonis Protagoras. The Protagoras of Plato.** The Greek Text revised, with an Analysis and English Notes. By W. WAYTE, M.A., Fellow of King's College, Cambridge, and Assistant Master at Eton. 8vo. *Second Edition*. 4*s*. 6*d*.

**Plato's Gorgias, literally translated, with an** Introductory Essay containing a Summary of the Argument. By E. M. COPE, M.A., Fellow of Trinity College. 8vo. 7*s*.

**Plautus. Aulularia. With Notes, Critical and** Exegetical, and an Introduction on Plautian Prosody. By WILHELM WAGNER, Ph. D. 8vo. 9*s*.

**Plautus. Trinummus. With Notes, Critical and** Exegetical. By WILHELM WAGNER, Ph. D. Small 8vo. 4*s*. 6*d*.

**Verse-Translations from Propertius, Book V.** With a Revised Latin Text, and Brief English Notes. By F. A. PALEY, M.A., Editor of Propertius, Ovid's Fasti, &c. Fcp. 8vo. 3*s*.

**Terence, with Notes, Critical and Explanatory.** By WILHELM WAGNER, Ph. D. Post 8vo. 10*s*. 6*d*.

**Theocritus, with Short Critical and Explanatory** Latin Notes. By F. A. PALEY, M.A. *Second Edition*, corrected and enlarged, and containing the newly discovered Idyll. Crown 8vo. 4*s*. 6*d*.

**Theocritus. Translated into English Verse, by** C. S. CALVERLEY, M.A., late Fellow of Christ's College, Cambridge. Crown 8vo. 7*s*. 6*d*.

**Thucydides. The History of the Peloponnesian** War, by THUCYDIDES. With Notes and a careful Collation of the two Cambridge Manuscripts, and of Aldine and Juntine Editions. By RICHARD SHILLETO, M.A., Fellow of S. Peter's College, Cambridge. Book. I. 8vo. 6*s*. 6*d*.

**Translations into English and Latin, by C. S.** CALVERLEY, M.A., late Fellow of Christ's College, Cambridge. Post 8vo. 7*s*. 6*d*.

**Arundines Cami. Sive Musarum Cantabrigien-**sium Lusus Canori. Collegit atque edidit HENRICUS DRURY, A.M., Archidiaconus Wiltonensis Collegii Caiani in Græcis ac Latinis Literis quondam Prælector. Equitare in arundine longa. Editio Sexta. Curavit HENRICUS JOHANNES HODGSON, A.M., Collegii SS. Trinitatis quondam Socius. Crown 8vo. 7*s*. 6*d*.

## Sertum Carthusianum Floribus trium Seculorum

Contextum. Cura GULIELMI HAIG BROWN, Scholæ Carthusianæ Archididascali. 8vo. 14*s*.

## Foliorum Silvula. Part I. Being Passages for

Translation into Latin Elegiac and Heroic Verse, edited by HUBERT A. HOLDEN, LL.D., late Fellow of Trinity College, Head Master of Queen Elizabeth's School, Ipswich. *Sixth Edition.* Post 8vo. 7*s*. 6*d*.

## Foliorum Silvula. Part II. Being Select Passages

for Translation into Latin Lyric and Comic Iambic Verse. By HUBERT A. HOLDEN, LL.D. *Third Edition.* Post 8vo. 5*s*.

## Foliorum Silvula. Part III. Being Select

Passages for Translation into Greek Verse, edited with Notes by HUBERT A. HOLDEN, LL.D. *Third Edition.* Post 8vo. 8*s*.

## Folia Silvulæ, sive Eclogæ Poetarum Anglicorum

in Latinum et Græcum conversæ quas disposuit HUBERTUS A. HOLDEN LL.D. Volumen Prius continens Fasciculos I. II. 8vo. 10*s*. 6*d*.

Volumen Alterum continens Fasciculos III. IV. 8vo. 12*s*.

## Foliorum Centuriæ. Selections for Translation

into Latin and Greek Prose, chiefly from the University and College Examination Papers. By HUBERT A. HOLDEN, LL.D. *Fifth Edition.* Post 8vo. 8*s*.

## Greek Verse Composition, for the use of Public

Schools and Private Students. Being a revised edition of the Greek Verses of Shrewsbury School. By GEORGE PRESTON, M.A., Fellow of Magdalene College. Crown 8vo. 4*s*. 6*d*.

## A Complete Latin Grammar. *Third Edition.*

Very much enlarged, and adapted for the use of University Students. By J. W. DONALDSON, D.D., formerly Fellow of Trinity College, Cambridge. 8vo. 14*s*.

## A Complete Greek Grammar. *Third Edition.*

Very much enlarged, and adapted for the use of University Students. By J. W. DONALDSON, D.D. 8vo. 16*s*.

Index of Passages of Greek Authors quoted or referred to in Dr. Donaldson's Greek Grammar, price 6*d*.

## Varronianus. A Critical and Historical Intro-

duction to the Ethnography of Ancient Italy and to the Philological Study of the Latin Language. *Third Edition, revised and considerably enlarged.* By J. W. DONALDSON, D.D. 8vo. 16*s*.

## Classical Scholarship and Classical Learning con-

sidered with especial reference to Competitive Tests and University Teaching. A Practical Essay on Liberal Education. By J. W. DONALDSON, D.D. Crown 8vo. 5*s*.

## The Greek Testament: with a Critically revised

Text; a Digest of various Readings; Marginal References to Verbal and Idiomatic Usage; Prolegomena; and a Critical and Exegetical Commentary. For the Use of Theological Students and Ministers. By HENRY ALFORD. D.D., Dean of Canterbury. 4 vols. 8vo. Sold separately.

Vol. I. SIXTH EDITION, containing the Four Gospels. 1*l.* 8*s.*—Vol. II. SIXTH EDITION, containing the Acts of the Apostles, Epistles to the Romans and Corinthians. 1*l.* 4*s.* — Vol. III. FIFTH EDITION, containing the Epistles to the Galatians, Ephesians, Philippians, Colossians, Thessalonians,—to Timotheus, Titus, and Philemon. 18*s.*—Vol. IV. Part I. FOURTH EDITION. The Epistle to the Hebrews: The Catholic Epistles of St. James and St. Peter. 18*s.*—Vol. IV. Part II. FOURTH EDITION. The Epistles of St. John and St. Jude, and the Revelation. 14*s.*

## The Greek Testament. With English Notes,

intended for the Upper Forms of Schools and Pass-men at the Universities. By HENRY ALFORD, D.D. Abridged by BRADLEY H. ALFORD, M.A., late Scholar of Trinity College, Cambridge. One vol., crown 8vo. 10*s.* 6*d.*

## Annotations on the Acts of the Apostles. De-

signed principally for the use of Candidates for the Ordinary B.A. Degree, Students for Holy Orders, &c., with College and Senate-House Examination Papers. By T. R. MASKEW. *Second Edition, enlarged.* 12mo. 5*s.*

## Tertulliani Liber Apologeticus.

The Apology of Tertullian. With English Notes and a Preface, intended as an introduction to the Study of Patristical and Ecclesiastical Latinity. By H. A. WOODHAM, LL.D. *Second Edition.* 8vo. 8*s.* 6*d.*

## The Mathematical and other Writings of Robert

LESLIE ELLIS, M.A., late Fellow of Trinity College, Cambridge. Edited by WILLIAM WALTON, M.A., Trinity College, with a Biographical Memoir by HARVEY GOODWIN, D.D., Lord Bp. of Carlisle. 8vo. 16*s.*

## The Mathematical Writings of Duncan Farquhar-

SON GREGORY, M.A., late Fellow of Trinity College, Cambridge. Edited by WILLIAM WALTON, M.A., Trinity College, Cambridge. With a Biographical Memoir by ROBERT LESLIE ELLIS, M.A., late Fellow of Trinity College. 8vo. 12*s.*

## Lectures on the History of Moral Philosophy

in England. By W. WHEWELL, D.D., formerly Master of Trinity College, Cambridge. New and Improved Edition, with Additional Lectures. Crown 8vo. 8*s.*

## Elements of Morality, including Polity. By W.

WHEWELL, D.D. *New Edition,* in 8vo. 15*s.*

## Astronomy and General Physics considered with

reference to Natural Theology (Bridgewater Treatise). By W. WHEWELL. *New Edition,* uniform with the Aldine Editions. 5*s.*

## Kent's Commentary on International Law, re-

vised with Notes and Cases brought down to the present time. Edited by J. T. ABDY, LL.D., Barrister at Law, Regius Professor of Laws in the University of Cambridge, and Law Lecturer at Gresham College. 8vo. 16*s*.

## A Manual of the Roman Civil Law, arranged

according to the Syllabus of Dr. HALLIFAX. Designed for the use of Students in the Universities and Inns of Court. By G. LEAPINGWELL, LL.D. 8vo. 12*s*.

## A Syriac Grammar. By G. PHILLIPS, D.D.,

President of Queens' College. *Third Edition, revised and enlarged.* 8vo. 7*s*. 6*d*.

## A Concise Grammar of the Arabic Language.

By W. J. BEAMONT, M.A. Revised by SHEIKH ALI NADY EL BARRANY, one of the Sheikhs of the El Azhar Mosque in Cairo. 12mo. 7*s*.

## The Student's Guide to the University of Cambridge.

*Revised and corrected in accordance with the recent regulations.* Fcap. 8vo. 5*s*.

This volume is intended to give such preliminary information as may be useful to parents who are desirous of sending their sons to the University, to put them in possession of the leading facts, and to indicate the points to which their attention should be directed in seeking further information from the tutor.

Suggestions are also given to the younger members of the University on expenses and course of reading.

CONTENTS.

INTRODUCTION, by J. R. SEELEY, M.A., Fellow of Christ's College, Cambridge.

On University Expenses, by the Rev. H. LATHAM, M.A., Fellow and Tutor of Trinity Hall.

On the Choice of a College, by J. R. SEELEY, M.A.

On the Course of Reading for the Classical Tripos, by the Rev. R. BURN, Fellow and Tutor of Trinity College.

On the Course of Reading for the Mathematical Tripos, by the Rev. W. M. CAMPION, Fellow and Tutor of Queens' College.

On the Course of Reading for the Moral Sciences Tripos, by the Rev. J. B. MAYOR, Fellow and Tutor of St. John's College.

On the Course of Reading for the Natural Sciences Tripos, by J. D. LIVEING, M.A., Professor of Chemistry, late Fellow of St. John's College.

On Law Studies and Law Degrees, by J. T. ABDY, LL.D., Regius Professor of Laws.

Medical Study and Degrees, by G. M. HUMPHRY, M.D.

On Theological Examinations, by the Right Rev. the LORD BISHOP OF ELY.

The Ordinary (or Poll) Degree, by the Rev. J. R. LUMBY, M.A., late Fellow of Magdalene College.

Examinations for the Civil Service of India, by the Rev. H. LATHAM.

Local Examinations of the University, by H. J. ROBY, M.A., late Fellow of St. John's College.

Diplomatic Service.

Detailed Account of the several Colleges.

## Cambridge Examination Papers, 1859. Being

Supplement to the Cambridge University Calendar. 12mo. 2*s*. 6*d*.

Containing those set for the Tyrwhitt's Hebrew Scholarships.—Theological Examinations.—Carus Prize.—Crosse Scholarships.—Law Degree Examination.—Mathematical Tripos.—The Ordinary B.A. Degree.—Smith's Prize.—University Scholarships.—Classical Tripos.—Moral Sciences Tripos.—Chancellor's Legal Medals.—Chancellor's Medals.—Bell's Scholarships.—Natural Sciences Tripos.—Previous Examination.—Theological Examination. With Lists of Ordinary Degrees, and of those who have passed the Previous and Theological Examinations.

*The Examination Papers of* 1856, 1857 *and* 1858, *may still be had,* 2*s*. 6*d*. *each.*

www.ingramcontent.com/pod-product-compliance
Lightning Source LLC
LaVergne TN
LVHW021314110826
845150LV00003B/571

* 9 7 8 1 4 2 5 5 5 7 9 7 3 *